WE'LL FIND
THE PLACE

The Nauvoo Temple

WE'LL FIND THE PLACE

The Mormon Exodus
1846 - 1848

Richard E. Bennett

Deseret Book Company

Salt Lake City, Utah

Dedicated to the faith and sacrifice of the Mormon Pioneers—
and to modern pioneers everywhere

© 1997 Richard E. Bennett

All rights reserved. No part of this book may be reproduced in any form or by any means without permission in writing from the publisher, Deseret Book Company, P.O. Box 30178, Salt Lake City, Utah 84130. This work is not an official publication of The Church of Jesus Christ of Latter-day Saints. The views expressed herein are the responsibility of the author and do not necessarily represent the position of the Church or of Deseret Book Company.

Deseret Book is a registered trademark of Deseret Book Company.

Library of Congress Cataloging-in-Publication Data

Bennett, Richard Edmond, 1946–
    We'll find the place : the Mormon exodus, 1846–1848 / by Richard E. Bennett.
        p.   cm.
    Includes bibliographical references (p.   ) and index.
    ISBN 1-57345-286-6 (hardcover)
    1. Mormons—West (U.S.)—History. 2. Mormon Trail—History. 3. Frontier and pioneer life—West (U.S.) 4. West (U.S.)—History—To 1848. I. Title.
F592.B42   1997
978'.0088283—dc21   97-26740
                                                                            CIP

Printed in the United States of America   72082
10 9   8   7   6   5   4   3   2   1

"The 'Mormon' companies were all orderly, and were truly models by the side of those who followed in their trail who were not governed by the same strict rules and religious motives and principles that our people were. Our salvation, both temporal and spiritual, depended upon this course, and our history is a wonder and a marvel to those who have taken the trouble to hunt us and review it in all its ups and downs . . . and our experience, I think, comes nearest to that of the children of Israel after their departure out of the land of Egypt than any other people of whom we have any record, though I believe we were a more patient people. . . . God . . . has brought us deliverance every time; and it is our wish and purpose to trust Him still."

Helen Mar Kimball Whitney,
"Travels Beyond the Mississippi,"
Women's Exponent, 1 May 1884

CONTENTS

Illustrations   ix

Foreword, by Leonard J. Arrington   xi

Preface   xiii

Introduction   1

1. "It Would Take Years to Reach the Mountains":
   Across Iowa and the Enforced Winter Quarters   31

2. "The Word and Will of the Lord": Blueprint for Exodus   67

3. "A Great American Desert"   95

4. Wagons West: From the Elkhorn to Ash Hollow   116

5. "I Am about to Revolt": Mormon Thunder at Scottsbluff   147

6. "It's a Long Road That Never Turns":
   From Fort Laramie to Fort Bridger   171

7. "Hurra, Hurra, Hurra—There's My Home at Last":
   Fort Bridger to the Great Salt Lake   204

8. "It Is an Excellent Place to Serve the Lord"   225

9. "We Expect to See the Sun Rise Again":
   The Emigration Camp of 1847   251

10. "We Have Been in the Valley to Set the Big Wheel to Work"   279

11. "The Operations of the Church Are Paralysed with Poverty":
     The Salvation Missions of 1847–48   300

12. "We Have Now Laid the Foundation for Our Coming Day"   334

    Epilogue   359

    Appendix   367

    Historiographical Essay   381

    Selected Bibliography   385

    Index   419

ILLUSTRATIONS

The Nauvoo Temple	*frontispiece*
Brigham Young	2
James J. Strang	13
Defense of Nauvoo	24
Helen Mar Kimball Whitney	33
Slogging through Iowa	34
Camp at Keokuk, Iowa	38
Enlistment of the Mormon Battalion	41
Crossing the Missouri River	57
Orrin Porter Rockwell	75
Heber C. Kimball	76
Brigham Young speaking at Winter Quarters	78
Lucy Mack Smith	87
A New Map of Texas, Oregon and California	96–97
The Rocky Mountains	100–101
Wagons crossing the Platte	117
Mormon Train in Camp	123
Pioneers Crossing the North Platte River	148
Scottsbluff	157
Fort Laramie	172
Lilburn W. Boggs	177
Crossing the Platte	181
Independence Rock	187
Jim Bridger	192
Pioneers at Green River	193
Sam Brannan	195
Fort Bridger	205
Pathway to Zion	215
First Glimpse	219
Utah Indians in Utah Valley	232
Thomas Bullock journal entry	238

The Salt Lake Plat Map   239
Orson Pratt   244
Wagons moving out   257
Sunflowers and Buffalo Chips   260
Eliza R. Snow   264
Parley P. Pratt   271
Willard Richards   281
Log Tabernacle   291
Levee at St. Louis   303
City of St. Louis   307
Emma Smith   321
Oliver Cowdery   324
Defeat of the Settlers/Arrival of the Gulls   347

The artwork and photographs in this book were obtained from the following sources, and are used by permission:

Council Bluffs, Iowa, Public Library (art found on page 123)

Harper's New Monthly Magazine, Sept. 1862, used courtesy of Oregon Historical Society (art found on page 117)

Katie Gregory, Omaha, Nebraska (art found on page 291)

LDS Church Historical Department, Archives (art found on pages ii, 2, 13, 33, 41, 75, 87, 157, 181, 192, 195, 219, 232, 238, 244, 257, 264, 271, 281, 324, 347)

LDS Museum of Church History and Art (art found on pages 34, 38, 57, 172, 187, 193, 205, 215, 260, 321)

Mrs. Edith Joy Cannon and Gilbert Barton (art found on page 24)

Mrs. Lois G. Jensen (art found on page 148)

Picturesque America; or, The Land We Live In, ed. William Cullen Bryant, New York: D. Appleton & Co., 1872 (art found on pages 100–101, 303, 307)

Sons of the Utah Pioneers (art found on page 239)

Twentieth-Century Fox, *Brigham Young* (art found on page 78)

University of Utah, Special Collections (art found on pages 96–97)

FOREWORD

There is something about beginnings that never grows old. In this the 150th anniversary of the coming of the Mormon pioneers to the Salt Lake Valley, there is much to remember and to celebrate. The arrival of Brigham Young and his loyal followers in the summer of 1847 was a defining moment in the establishment of The Church of Jesus Christ of Latter-day Saints in the West. Likewise, it laid the foundation for the modern history of the state of Utah and left an indelible imprint on the larger history of the American West.

The essentials of the story are well known. Several important histories, musicals, pageants, and dramas have been written, composed, and produced through the years to mark this episode in American history. So much has been written, in fact, that one wonders if there is really anything more to say.

Now to add to this list, Richard E. Bennett has prepared a definitive new history that is refreshingly different from most earlier works on the topic. Author of the previous award-winning study on the history of Winter Quarters—*Mormons at the Missouri, 1846–1852: "And Should We Die"*—Dr. Bennett has written an essential sequel to his earlier work, an exciting, intimate study of the Mormon exodus.

Using an abundance of archival sources not seen before, Richard Bennett relies not only on the writings of the Mormons themselves but also on their many fellow overlanders on their way to California and Oregon. In the process, this modern historian of the trek tells a fascinating, well-documented, highly readable account of the internal workings, trials, and struggles of the early Latter-day Saints. From the moment of their departure from Nauvoo in February 1846 to their earliest Thanksgiving celebrations in the Salt Lake Valley in late 1848, this balanced account of the Exodus is well worth both the casual read and the careful study.

We'll Find the Place: The Mormon Exodus, 1846–1848 is certain to become a classic in Mormon and American history.

LEONARD J. ARRINGTON

PREFACE

In this, the 150th anniversary of the exodus of the Latter-day Saints from Nauvoo, Illinois, to the shores of the Great Salt Lake in the Great Basin of the Rocky Mountains, it is fitting that a new religious history be attempted of that unforgettable chapter in American history. The trails and details, the chronologies and genealogies of that trek have been told and retold so many times and by so many gifted writers that one might think there is nothing noteworthy left to say. Such worthy predecessors as Hubert H. Bancroft, Andrew Jenson, B. H. Roberts, Preston Nibley, Dale Morgan, and more recently Wallace Stegner, Leonard J. Arrington, and Stanley Kimball have each contributed to our appreciation of the history and meaning of the exodus, of the gathering to Zion, and of America's modern Moses—Brigham Young. The story has also been widely heralded in song and poetry, in art and drama. And well it should be, for the coming of Brigham Young and his band of faithful followers was a defining moment in the history of Mormonism, of the state of Utah, and of America.

Each new generation, however, must wend its own way across the landscape of history and see and feel for itself what previous generations of writers saw and interpreted for their own time and place. While so much has been written, the surprise is that so much of the story has never been told. New manuscript sources continue to come to light, demanding not only a retelling but also a reinterpretation.

This work, I submit, is not so much a study of the trail or of the trek but of a religious exodus of one of the 19th century's most persecuted and despised groups of religionists—the Latter-day Saints—who were bound neither for Oregon nor for California but either for survival or extinction. This was not just another march westward "across the wide Missouri" in fulfilment of America's Manifest Destiny; rather, it was a destiny in motion yet to be made manifest, for it was not at all certain that this enterprise of Joseph Smith Jr.—The Church of Jesus of Christ of Latter-day Saints— would ever survive to live a new day. The story of the Mormon exodus is that of a religion in torment desperately seeking to save itself from perse- cution, to rid itself of its own detractors and obstructionists, and to find itself in some unknown valley "far away in the West." It was Mormonism in the raw and on the move—forging a new identity while seeking a safe refuge in the tops of "the everlasting hills."

Missing in most earlier studies, for all their worth, is that peculiar yet essential combination of contemporary uncertainty amidst uncompromis- ing conviction, the immediate risk of the moment, the fears and doubts of a faithful people wondering where they were going and whether or not they would survive the getting there. These 12,000 sick and bedraggled believers would either make it to wherever their new and untested leader took them or they would perish by the thousands in the wilderness and abandon their faith in a misspent expenditure of religious conviction.

This work focuses on the original Pioneer Camp of 1847: on the lead- ership discussions and debates along the way, the march from Winter Quarters to the Great Basin, the earliest settlements in the valley, the Emigration Camp of the summer of 1847, and the return to Winter Quarters in late 1847. It ends in October 1848 with the first conference of the Church in the Salt Lake Valley. While some of my colleagues encour- aged me to cover the entire migration era from 1847 to 1896, I deliberately chose to focus on only the 1846 to 1848 period. I did not select so restrictive a study because the later years were any less important, but because this less-than-two-year period served as the foundation to all that came after. Furthermore, much of what happened in these first two years has never been fully told or amply analyzed. In one sense, the exodus was over in 1848, just as the migrations began.

One cannot help but ponder on the many "what ifs" of this movement. What would have happened, for instance, if a suitable resting place had not been found or if the crops had failed in advance of the tide of oncoming emigrants? Or if the U.S. Army, as rumored, had interrupted their leaving before it began? And if Brigham Young had lost the confidence of his people or died of the Rocky Mountain fever that laid him so low at the very moment of discovery, what then? Either Brigham Young and the Quorum of the Twelve Apostles would make it or Mormonism would likely go down. The ante was up. The Church was in flight, and in the absence of a certain tomorrow all that was left was the talent and inspiration of its leaders and the faith of its followers against the panorama of the great American desert.

It was, then, as Brigham Young put it, "for the salvation of the Church" that they moved west. It was an enforced risk of enormous consequence, while detractors and defectors sat back in scornful glee. For Mormonism was now moving out of the way, finally—out of the encroaching circles of persecution and misunderstanding and into the scorching sun of a sage-brush wilderness. The miracle of the exodus may be less the finding of a place and more the following of so many people to a new nowhere. The past thematic of a "This Is the Place" must include a wider vision, a view of "This Is the People" and "This Is Their Faith."

Hyppolite Taine, a French intellectual of the 1860s, gave tribute to their march in almost romantic terms:

> Since the exodus of the Israelites there is no example of so great a religious emigration executed across such great spaces in spite of such obstacles, by so great a number of men, with so much order, obedience, courage, patience, and devotion. . . . But the mainspring of this great will was faith. Without it men would not have done such things. These exiles thought that they were found-ing the city of God, the metropolis of mankind. They considered themselves the renovators of the world. Let us remember our youth, and with what force an idea . . . merely by the fact that it seems good and true to us hurls us forward despite natural egotism, daily weaknesses, habits that we have contracted, surrounding prej-udices, and accumulated obstacles! We don't know of what we are capable.[1]

And so, at this precipice in Mormon history, this story begins.

The writing of Mormon history is often a no-win situation, even for one who believes deeply, as I do, in the divine origin and purposes of this Church. Wallace Stegner once referred to it as a "swamp" where apologists are seldom gratified and antagonists rarely satisfied. For some, there is never enough promotion of faith; for others, there is far too little of fact. Well aware of these pitfalls, I am nonetheless certain of a growing body of readers, a questioning, searching audience, Mormon and otherwise, who is increasingly anxious to see Mormon history in the light of its own trials, mistakes, and successes and to draw their own conclusions. Rooted in primary manuscript and original documentation, this work aims at historical integrity and fairness, to let the participants speak for themselves, to tell a true story, and to provide a sound basis for my interpretations. Although some may argue with those interpretations, I trust that none will find occasion to doubt the sources or the accounts.

Some try to dismiss the relevancy of history in today's obsession with presentism. Certainly there are modern problems and challenges on all sides. Nevertheless, most readers understand that Mormonism has ever had a love affair with its past. It has ever been a priority for the Church to keep an accurate history and to learn of "things which have been, things which are, and things which must shortly come to pass."

On the very eve of their pioneer departure, Church leaders assured themselves and future historians of the central place of that history and of the archival record. "Dr. [Willard] Richards spoke of the bushels of papers now in his possession that are not now filed," wrote the Pioneer Camp clerk while paraphrasing a dialogue of Church leaders on the topic,

> and of the need of a place to gather them and arrange them for future history. A man must have his mind free who writes a history that is to last for time and through all eternity, and not bothered with other cares. W[ilford] Woodruff says this is a subject that will benefit the whole Church and Kingdom of God. When I heard Joseph [Smith] speak I could not rest until I had written it down in black and white. . . . The people ought to keep a strict eye upon the historian. I feel deeply interested in the books out of which I am to be judged. It is the duty of [the] High Council to let the Dr. have a box to put the papers in, to find wood, beef, etc. This is to be a book of books. I rejoice that we have a ready writer. Let the Dr. go to work and save the Church history. [2]

Having neither been assigned, cajoled, nor commissioned to write this work, nor discouraged or dissuaded from its undertaking, I sense keenly the responsibility of exploring a history so reverently held by so many descendants of the early pioneers and by so many Latter-day Saints. I do not argue that I am better qualified than some others for such an undertaking, but I have prepared myself.

As a child of 10, in company with family and relatives, I made my first trip across America on the Mormon Trail from Palmyra to Salt Lake City in 1956. It left an indelible impression on my mind. Later as a graduate student at Brigham Young University, I began researching and writing Mormon history. If Professor Marvin Hill taught me how to research Mormon history, it was Leonard J. Arrington, dean of modern Mormon historiography, who showed me how to love and appreciate it.

In 1987 I published the immediate predecessor of this work, *Mormons at the Missouri, 1846–1852: "And Should We Die"* (an outgrowth of my dissertation), with the University of Oklahoma Press. That award-winning work—a comprehensive study of the forced expulsion from Nauvoo, the march across Iowa in the spring of 1846, and the encampment in Winter Quarters on the banks of the Missouri River near present day Omaha—is the forerunner of this present work. Although chapters one and two rely on my earlier work, much new material has been added. Nevertheless, the serious reader will want to study that earlier work before embarking on this more recent and equally ambitious investigation.

For ease of reading, since there are so many quotations included in this study and since the original spellings are often phonetically based and distracting, I have taken the liberty of correcting the spelling in almost every case. I have, however, retained the original grammar, style, and sentence structure. Every reasonable effort has been made to give full, accurate citations and credit to depositories.

As a professional historian, archivist, and librarian, I am particularly sensitive to the invaluable assistance of my peers and colleagues at many sister institutions. First of all, I must credit my own institution—the University of Manitoba—for providing me with both the research study leave necessary and many of the secondary research materials required to provide context to the work. Of all the other agencies rich in manuscript material, first and foremost is the Historical Department of The Church of Jesus Christ of Latter-day Saints in Salt Lake City, Utah, with its vast archives of diaries, journals, and correspondence. Special thanks are in order to its staff, particularly Richard Turley, Steve Sorenson, Jim Kimball, Ron Watt, Randall Dixon, and Linda Haslem. Helpful in providing photographs were Bill Slaughter of the LDS Church Historical Department and Ron Read of the LDS Museum of Church History and Art.

I wish also to commend the staff at the following institutions: the Manuscript Division of the Library of Congress in Washington, D.C.; the Marriott Library at the University of Utah; the Harold B. Lee Library at Brigham Young University; the Missouri Historical Society and St. Louis Mercantile Association Library in St. Louis, Missouri; the Library and Archives of the Reorganized Church of Jesus Christ of Latter Day Saints in Independence, Missouri; the Oregon Historical Society in Portland, Oregon; the Bancroft Library at the Berkeley campus of the University of California; the Utah State Historical Society; Special Collections and Archives at Utah State University; the New York Public Library; the Free Public Library in Council Bluffs, Iowa; the Beinecke Rare Book and Manuscript Library at Yale University; and finally, and less importantly, the Huntington Library in San Marino, California.

I wish also to thank the following institutions for their significant financial assistance in the form of research grants: the University of Manitoba and the Canadian Social Sciences and Humanities Research Council; the Religious Studies Center at Brigham Young University; the Charles Redd Center at Brigham Young University; the American Philosophical Society of Philadelphia, Pennsylvania; and the Huntington Library, which granted me a Visiting Senior Fellowship.

Special thanks are in order to the publishers of this work, Deseret Book Company in Salt Lake City. Jay Parry, editor and project manager; Doreen McKnight, copy editor; Ron Stucki, designer; and Patricia Parkinson, typographer; and others on the Deseret Book staff provided invaluable assistance, suggestions, guidance, and support from the review right through to the delightful production of the book.

I have also enjoyed the valued help of good research assistants. Kevin Pinkney, Mark Ashurst-McGee, John Hartvigsen, and Harvard Heath have each made significant contributions to this work. My wife, Pat, has not only put up with me in this task, but has also been a valuable research assistant in her own right, at least as much as a family of five children has allowed her to be. Indeed, I owe enormous gratitude to her and every member of my family. I also owe a permanent debt to my mother and father, who had a profound influence for good on my life and thought, and to my brother, Gary, who nurtured within me an early love of Church history.

While so many have assisted me, I alone am responsible for the content and interpretations that characterize this work. I trust that it will be a lasting credit to them all.

NOTES

1. "Taine's Essay on the Mormons," trans. Austin E. Fife, in *Pacific Historical Review* 31, no. 1 (Feb. 1962): 60.

2. Journal of Willard Richards, 17 Dec. 1846, LDS Church Historical Department, The Church of Jesus Christ of Latter-day Saints, Church Office Building, 50 E. North Temple Street, Salt Lake City, Utah; cited hereafter as LDS Church Archives.

INTRODUCTION

L ate in the afternoon of 27 June 1844 in the obscure town of Carthage in southwest Illinois, Joseph Smith Jr., founding prophet and President of The Church of Jesus Christ of Latter-day Saints, and his loyal brother Hyrum were martyred by assassins' gunfire. Their road from Palmyra, New York, through Kirtland, Ohio, and Independence, Missouri, to Nauvoo, Illinois, had finally brought them to this inglorious end. Many concluded it was also the end of Mormonism.

So thought at least one Boston reader upon first learning of the Carthage carnage. "There is a report that Joe Smith, the Mormon Prophet, and his brother, have been murdered while in gaol under the protection of the Governor of the State, by a band of ruffians. . . . Gov. [Thomas S.] Ford, with his 60 men, has retired to Quincy, to give his orders to the surrounding counties to muster their forces. Warsaw, Carthage, Augusta and even Hannibal are in fear and commotion. So much for Mormonism!!!"[1]

Such sentiments were not, however, universally shared. Some other observers, such as the editor of the *New York Tribune*, though critical of the Latter-day Saint's beliefs and practices, predicted their survival and future progress. "What will become of Mormonism now?" he queried.

> Joseph Smith is dead—probably butchered in cold blood while a secure prisoner, and without the power, even if he had the will, to

Brigham Young

offer provocation for violence, but Mormonism has not died with him. Gross and monstrous as the delusions and perhaps abominations practiced in the name of that faith, yet it is a vital, living thing. Men and women, made of the same flesh and blood, and actuated by similar sensations and passions as Protestants, Catholics, Mahometans, or whatever creed or worship the sun shines upon, do actually believe in this Mormonism; are content to live and die by it; to yield up worldly wealth, domestic ties and the strong bonds of native land for it, and thus feeling and thus believing, to their dimmed and distorted spiritual vision, Joe Smith is as much the martyr hero as any whose shadow has ever fallen upon the world.[2]

Yet if Mormonism was to survive, it would have to pay an even heavier price than the loss of its founder—a toll measured in the suffering and death of hundreds of Latter-day Saints soon to be driven out of Nauvoo, their City of Joseph, in quest of some new home far away in the West.

Sixteen months passed between that forlorn afternoon in Carthage in 1844 and the fateful day in Nauvoo in early February 1846 when Brigham Young, the 44-year-old interim leader of the Church by right of his position as senior member of the Quorum of the Twelve Apostles, began leading his people on a perilous pilgrimage westward across the Mississippi River. Threatened, persecuted, and ultimately driven by armed and angry men, "Brother Brigham," as he was commonly called, knew that for the salvation of the Church the only way left was out: rather die in the wilderness than be slaughtered in the streets of their own city.

The musket balls that pierced the Prophet were really aimed at the heart of Mormonism, and Brigham Young knew it. For reasons still debated by historians, with Joseph Smith gone the Latter-day Saints themselves became the target. Nothing short of a mass exodus, unlike anything yet seen in American religious history, would answer the frenzied tenor of the time. Either they quit the state peacefully and go somewhere—anywhere—else, or vigilante groups would take the law into their own hands and drive these undesirables out. Fearful of mounting opposition and of increasing numbers of attempts on his own life, and worried about the rumored possibility of an advancing U.S. Army to hedge up their way, Brigham set his direction west, flintlike, no matter what the cost. He bent his energies toward preparing the people by establishing firm leadership over the Church, securing the allegiance of his followers, completing construction of the Nauvoo temple, and buying whatever time he could from their enemies in order to accommodate the safe and orderly departure of his people.

In addition to these external threats, the more subtle, disruptive, and potentially most damaging blows might well come from within. It was a time that tested the allegiance and faith of every Latter-day Saint in and out

3

of Nauvoo. With their prophet dead and their city and possessions soon to be abandoned for some unidentified new Zion a thousand miles or more away, and with new and emerging doctrines untested and unexplained, some were beginning to have second thoughts. To underestimate these concerns, particularly among the scattered membership outside of Nauvoo, is to misrepresent history.

The writing, then, was on the wall. The persecution was intense and the deadlines were firm. And defection was already happening at a faster rate than most wanted to admit. Clearly they had reached a crisis. And the solutions would not be easy. Consequently for the cause of Zion and "for the salvation of the Church," several things would now have to happen.

GET OUT!

It is a sad and deplorable fact of history that the Latter-day Saints had been a hounded and a harried people. From the inception of the Church in Palmyra, New York, in April 1830, its fate had been one of misunderstanding, overzealousness, persecution, and expulsion. Kirtland, Ohio, endured only slightly longer than Independence, Missouri, the location site revealed in Mormon scripture as their future and ultimate Zion and gathering place.[3] Driven out of Independence in 1834, the Latter-day Saints sought refuge in surrounding Missouri counties, ever hopeful of a final return to their "center stake of Zion." But Missouri would have none of it, with Governor Lilburn W. Boggs enacting his infamous "extermination order" in 1838, a proclamation that attempted to legitimize the pain and persecution, death and destruction of an entire religious community.[4] What followed was mob action that drove the Latter-day Saints back east to Illinois, imprisoned their leaders, and would surely have ended the life of Joseph Smith then had it not been for men like Alexander W. Doniphan, David R. Atchison, and other respectable Missouri citizens who stoutly resisted the current wave of lawlessness and ruthless disorder.

With nowhere else for these refugees to go, the residents of Quincy, Illinois, and surrounding towns graciously opened their homes and their hearts to a wounded and wearied people. Their tender kindness and hospitality opened the door to the resettlement of thousands of Latter-day Saints at Commerce, Illinois, a few miles north of Quincy on the banks of the Mississippi River. Here, at what became Nauvoo, they built a new home and resting place.

Nauvoo also provided opportunities for the Latter-day Saints to acquaint themselves with Joseph Smith and to learn more about his teachings on the nature of God, on mankind's filial relationship to Him, on the purpose of life, and on the mission of the Church. And it was in Nauvoo that they became acquainted with the temple covenants, ordinances, and worship characteristic of their newfound faith. The citizens of the city combined in sacrifice to build a temple so high and so grand that many flocked to this frontier town just to gaze on the spectacle: one of the largest, most beautiful buildings west of the Appalachians dominating the peaceful western Illinois landscape.[5]

The story of Nauvoo, "the City Beautiful," includes both triumph and tragedy. The city's very success determined its ultimate ruin. On a positive note, it provided a breathing space after the tragic persecutions in Missouri, a building time in which numerous recent American, British, and Canadian converts could come together, shoulder to shoulder, for the first time. Nauvoo became home, a place to build and a time to heal.

How such a once promising dream soured so suddenly and decidedly into a terrifying nightmare is the tragedy of the time. The city's spectacular surge in population, from a handful of outcasts in the spring of 1839 to almost 15,000 merely six years later, transformed the local social and economic landscape, giving the new move-ins political and economic influence—even dominance—undreamed of earlier by the local citizenry. Nauvoo grew so quickly and rose to such political power that the locals wondered if those they had once befriended would come to dominate their lives.

Many residents of Hancock County were as unprepared for Nauvoo's meteoric rise as were the newcomers themselves. The settlement that was once welcomed with a measure of relief became a large and rapidly growing city, bigger than any other north of St. Louis, Missouri. The once prevailing sense of sympathy gradually deteriorated into suspicion, economic jealousy, distrust, and fear, bordering on hysteria.

The expulsion of the Latter-day Saints also resulted from misunderstanding and miscommunication, and those frontier elements of lawlessness, religious bigotry, political instability, and economic jealousy that earlier incited so many Missourians to war against the Mormons. That unruly spirit of unchecked violence, bordering on mob rule, later spilled into

Illinois, further contaminating relationships and poisoning whatever prospects of peaceful coexistence may once have existed.

Neither were the Mormons without blame. Not all were "saints," and enough were of the baser sort to fan some of the rising tensions. The liberal provisions of the Nauvoo city charter gave the city wide-sweeping legal and even military powers. Evidence shows that some fugitives from justice may have been taking secret refuge in Nauvoo, clearly an irritant to surrounding communities.[6] These antagonisms, coupled with the intrigue of certain disaffected members and leaders who had become disillusioned with Joseph Smith, made serious trouble inevitable.

Furthermore, Brigham Young and his fellow leaders had come to understand the developing doctrines and teachings of their new religion well enough to know that it had become incompatible with frontier America. Theirs had become a theocratic state in a democratic republic. It saw itself as the restored Church of Jesus Christ and the only true and living church—within an evolving pluralistic society increasingly suspicious of such claims. And several of its new social practices, especially plural marriage, confronted the established order. No, if they were to survive and escape a pending catastrophe, the only way was out!

By October 1845, Hancock County residents were spelling out in one public resolution after another that either the Saints must leave the following spring or they would take the law into their own hands. The Quincy Convention of October passed several resolutions to that effect, demanding a complete withdrawal by the following May.[7] Just days later, the Carthage Convention, made up of concerned citizens from several surrounding counties and including many of the most bitter enemies of Joseph Smith and his followers, took an even more hostile stance. It called for the establishment of a local militia that would, in the expected case that the Mormons could not meet the Quincy Committee's deadline, force them out by bayonet and cannon.[8]

But if they were to go they would leave behind a curse on the land that had rejected them and a reiteration and prediction of divine retribution. From the beginning, Latter-day Saint scripture had told of coming calamities prior to the Second Coming of Christ and of pestilence on a sinful world. As early as March 1829, one of Joseph Smith's revelations had warned of "a desolating scourge [that] shall go forth among the inhabitants of the earth, and shall continue to be poured out from time to time, if they repent not, until the earth is empty, and the inhabitants thereof are consumed away and utterly destroyed by the brightness of my coming."[9]

Applying such dire divine warnings to their immediate conditions, the Latter-day Saints surely felt America must suffer the consequence of its inaction at the very moment of their severest trials. This theme of collective hurt, of almost Old Testament–style wrath on their enemies, was a carryover from their earlier Missouri persecutions, a negative corollary to the doctrine of establishing Zion, but came to the fore shortly after the martyrdom, reaching a crescendo by the time they left Nauvoo. Their diaries are replete with condemnation, warnings, and the expectation of almost imminent premillennial judgment and wrath.

Wrote Brigham before leaving Winter Quarters for the West:

> The whispering of the Spirit to us have invariably been of the same import, to depart, to go hence, to flee into the mountains, to retire to our strongholds that we may be secure in the visitation of the Judgments that must pass upon this land, that is crimsoned with the blood of Martyrs; and that we may be hid, as it were, in the clefts of the rocks, and in the hollows of the land of the Great Jehova, while the guilty land of our fathers is purifying by the overwhelming scourge.[10]

Writer after writer picked up on Brigham's point until it became almost a tenet of their faith. As Wilford Woodruff, another Apostle, wrote at the end of 1847: "[We] have made a journey more than one thousand miles to the Rocky Mountains, and sought out a place for a city, a stake of Zion, and a temple of the Lord that the Saints may have a place to flee to while the indignation of the Lord passeth over the nation that hath driven them out."[11]

FIND A NEW ZION

Fundamental to understanding the dynamics of Mormonism is the concept of place. As with the ancient Israelites (with whom their revelations compared themselves) and their exodus from Egypt to a promised land, the gathering again to a "New Jerusalem," a new Zion or a "new promised land" is intimate to the very soul of Latter-day Saint theology. As early as 1830, Joseph Smith's revelations had called for a gathering into one place, "even a land of promise, a land flowing with milk and honey, upon which there shall be no curse when the Lord cometh. And I will give it unto you for the land of your inheritance, if you seek it with all your hearts. And this shall be my covenant with you, ye shall have it for the land of your inheritance, and for the inheritance of your children forever."[12] In part this was to prepare for the premillennial return of Christ and in part to govern and prepare the people for the inevitable building up of the kingdom of God on the earth.

This fundamental belief in the establishment of a temporal and spiritual Zion, of a new Jerusalem and of a chosen and chastened people, explains their earlier compulsion and overriding expectation to settle at Independence, Missouri, "in the borders of the Lamanites" [Indians]—the revealed "center stake of Zion"—in the very teeth of opposition and persecution. So much of their earliest energies had been expended to reach that goal and to "be planted in the land of Zion."

The bitter fact that such a Zion was not "redeemed" or established in Missouri, with all the deep and lingering disappointments of having not achieved it, did not deter many Latter-day Saints from continuing the quest. After all, God would try His people and Missouri had been but the "beginning" of the gathering. (D&C 84:4.)

Yet the dilemma remained the place. If Kirtland had been prelude to the Missouri effort, Nauvoo was postlude to it and a temporary, if remarkable, substitute. To return to Missouri now was out of the question. And to retain the doctrine of Zion and to believe in a new transplanted location for it in a far away western wilderness once again "in the borders of the Lamanites" would require constant instruction and careful conviction. What would happen after Nauvoo—and, equally important, *where* it would happen—would inevitably call for a necessary postponement of the revealed ideal and center gathering place without surrendering the conviction that they were still moving in the right direction. If they could not now return to the original Zion, they would then carry the dream—and the doctrine— with them to a new interim gathering place.

And it would have to be found soon! Until such a new place was established and a new standard erected, the gathering impulse would invariably be postponed and the rate of defection would increase among its membership. Until and unless such a new Zion was located, the Church was in jeopardy.

They were seeking neither the congenial valleys of Oregon nor the sun-kissed coasts of California, but a place unsought and unclaimed by the advancing tide of overland emigrants, a place where neither the laws of the United States nor the sanctions of other religions could prevent them from freely living their religion. It must be a place of refuge that would insure protection, isolation, good health, and ample provision for a self-sustaining people, a rapidly growing young American religion desperately trying to find its way. In time it might take its place within a larger community and be part of a broader administration, but for now and for the foreseeable future, it needed time and place and freedom to develop on its own. As with the earlier Puritans who came to America in quest of religious freedom and preserving their ideals, the Latter-day Saints had to discover their own "city on a hill," a light and a nursery to their far-flung membership.

"Concerning the travels of the Saints westward," said Brigham to his followers at Mt. Pisgah, Iowa, in the winter of '47:

> This is a subject that has long attracted our attention and concerning which we have thought and felt deeply and well we might; for situated as the Church of Jesus Christ is, and has been, for a considerable length of time, the only human hope or prospect of her salvation, has appeared to rest on the removal of the Saints from a land of oppression and violence to some more congenial clime.[13]

Their Rocky Mountain plan probably owed much to Joseph Smith, a point Brigham knew full well. Remembered John Pulsipher: "Pres. Brigham Young said that Joseph Smith said in Nauvoo that the Devil had drove this people out of the pan—not into the fire but on the hearth. And if He ever give us another shove, we would go into the middle of the floor."[14] While some have argued otherwise, compelling evidence indicates that late in Joseph Smith's life, he had begun to look to the Rocky Mountains as the probable place of temporary refuge. Governor Ford, in an 1845 letter, indicated that he had been "informed by Gen. Joseph Smith last summer that he contemplated a removal west; and from what I learned from him and others at that time I think if he had lived he would have begun to move in the matter before this time."[15]

Neither was there ever any serious doubt as to where they were going. In fact their destination, at least in general terms, never was a question. "It must be somewhere in the Great Basin," noted one recorder after another in their diaries and letters. "With regard to our location," wrote Brigham from Shoal Creek in eastern Iowa Territory to Orson Hyde, a fellow Apostle stationed back in Nauvoo, "it will be over the mountains, but to define the exact spot we cannot at present. We shall fit out a company of Pioneers and start them from the Missouri River to put in crops and that the rest of the camps will follow as circumstances will allow."[16]

To assume that the Latter-day Saints had no idea where they were going, as some have concluded, leaves far too much to fate or disorganization. It is true that many of the rank and file were unaware of their precise destination. "All the material possessions we are transporting west," wrote Lorenzo Dow Young, "we are transporting . . . in two wagons . . . and our place of destination we know not." Others, like Clara Decker Young, spoke of it as an "uncertain pilgrimage." But what they lacked in precision they made up for in direction—it would have to be some valley in the Great Basin.[17]

The further west they traveled, the more precise their understanding of their intended location became, as more talks and discussions, advice and counsel inevitably focused on the topic. By the time they reached the Missouri River, leaders were already talking openly of the "Bear River valley, great basin, or salt lake."[18] In a proposed letter to the President of the United States, James K. Polk, Brigham declared unequivocally that their journey "shall end in a location west of the Rocky Mountains, and within the Basin of the Great Salt Lake or Bear River Valley, as soon as circumstances shall permit."[19] As Brigham indicated in a February 1847 letter, "It must be somewhere in the Great Basin, we have no doubt."[20]

Nevertheless, they had no intention of broadcasting their destination, and for good reasons. Prudence dictated that they speak about the subject in a general, even oblique, manner. There was awful fear that their Missouri enemies might disrupt their march. And there was concern that powerful senators, like Mormon-hating Thomas Benton, might influence Washington—then in the throes of settling the Oregon question with England and about to go to war with Mexico over California—to send in an army to obstruct their way. The government might wonder at the intentions of a wounded and persecuted people moving en masse amidst a troubled Indian population to some ill-defined homeland "beyond the states." By keeping them all guessing, the Latter-day Saints walked a fine line between intervention and invitation. Perhaps they could yet be allies of an American Manifest Destiny while fulfilling their own.

A NEW GOVERNMENT AND A NEW PROPHET

Ever since Carthage, the loss of a prophet-leader and, with him, the presiding quorum of the First Presidency had been a hindrance to the stability and growth of the Church. Confusion replaced confidence in the hearts of many as they waited to see whom to follow. They needed not only a new president, but more to the point, a prophet, as much as they had ever esteemed Joseph Smith as one.

The subtle corollary to this was the restoration of the conviction in the people generally that God had neither abandoned nor condemned His people since the martyrdom and that a legitimate and credible successor could still be called. The longer the time between prophet-leaders, just as with locations, the more exposed and weakened was the faith. Fully as important as finding a new home, then, was the need to call and ordain a new "Prophet, Seer, and Revelator" and organize a new First Presidency.

Although most members at Nauvoo and throughout the Church generally (which in 1846 totaled some 34,000 scattered throughout the East, the upper South, Canada, and England[21]) were leaning toward following Brigham Young and the Quorum of the Twelve, which man should eventually obtain the presidency was still unclear.[22]

The first to claim the mantle of leadership was Sidney Rigdon, Joseph Smith's longtime counselor in the First Presidency. Once a confidant of the prophet, a wonderful speaker and impressive scriptorian, Rigdon returned to Nauvoo in 1844 and declared a vision he had received concerning his role as "guardian" and "spokesman" over the leaderless flock. Rigdon explained that "he was the identical man that the ancient prophets had sung about, wrote and rejoiced over."[23]

In the minds of most, however, Rigdon had lost the confidence of the rank and file and had been away too long to be seriously considered.[24] Nonetheless, Sidney Rigdon might have been successful had it not been for the return of several of the Apostles from their recent campaigns in the East. In the famous meeting of 8 August 1844 in the temple grove, Brigham dismantled Rigdon's claims in a most compelling and convincing matter and called for public support of the Quorum of the Twelve. Rigdon never recovered from his failure, excommunication, and public humiliation and left Nauvoo for good on 10 September. Disheartened, if not disoriented, Rigdon's later halfhearted attempts at organizing a new church in Pennsylvania met with failure.[25]

Meanwhile, William Parker was using peepstones and impersonating leaders to induce acceptance of his claims.[26] Several others, including Lyman Wight, that "wild ram of the mountains" who in March 1845 had led a company of 150 souls to southern Texas on a mission to find a new settlement that he claimed had been authorized by Joseph, maintained—as did others—that the rightful heir to the presidency was Joseph Smith's oldest son, Joseph Smith III, who was then only thirteen years old.[27]

By early 1846, however, these claims paled to relative insignificance compared to that of James J. Strang. Born in Cayuga County, New York, in 1813, Strang possessed a strong desire for reading and at an unusually early age exhibited a keen ability as a writer and debater. Argumentative, if not combative, by nature, at the age of 21 he commenced the study of law and two years later, in 1836, entered into a law practice in Chatauqua County, New York. Though married later that same year, his restlessness led him to travel all over the eastern states, returning in 1838. Later he and his family moved west to Burlington, Wisconsin, where he again practiced law. While visiting in Ottawa, Illinois, early in 1844 he first heard the preaching of Joseph Smith and was almost immediately baptized. Soon after his ordination as an elder in early March, he abandoned the bar for the pulpit, giving his newfound religion virtually his entire attention.[28]

The colorfully charismatic Strang persuaded many that he was Joseph's legitimate successor. To prove it, he publicly proclaimed a letter dated 18 June in which Joseph Smith, just days before his death, supposedly had ordained him president with instructions to remove and reestablish the Church in Wisconsin. Expert with the pen and the press, Strang soon published revelations, claimed the discovery and translation of another book of ancient scripture ("The Book of the Law of the Lord"), laid claim to the powers of prophet and seer, and established a church in Spring Prairie, Wisconsin, which was soon renamed Voree (signifying "Garden of Peace"). Of no less significance, he organized a new First Presidency consisting of himself, John C. Bennett, and George J. Adams.[29]

Throughout 1846 and 1847 "Strangism" was a serious contender and, for many, a very real alternative to Brigham's efforts to reestablish the Church westward. Several other well-known Nauvoo personalities went over to Strang's side, including William Smith, Apostle and patriarch to the Church and brother to Joseph; Apostle John E. Page; William Marks, former Nauvoo stake president; and William McLellin. And with them came

James J. Strang

many of their followers. Wrote one admirer of John E. Page: "The only conclusion I can draw from the circumstances of your being at Voree and being an apostle there is that you have received that testimony you required. If so I wish you to write to me all the particulars."[30]

Why Strang made inroads is readily understandable. Contrasted dramatically with Brigham's pragmatic approach and rather stern bearing were Strang's charm and colorful personality, which reminded some of Joseph Smith. Others took comfort in his support of the Book of Mormon and other Latter-day Saint scripture. His particular genius, however, centered in his enormous self-confidence and unbridled ambition, his persuasive speaking and writing abilities, his opportunistic sense of timing, and his uncanny ability to capitalize on the fear and discontent among the people.

There can be little doubt that many felt confused, disillusioned, and adrift since Carthage. "I was a member of the Church for four years," wrote one Quincy resident, "and for the first two years I enjoyed religion . . . but alas, those blessings, those gifts and outpourings of the Spirit of God have taken, as it were, the wings of the morning and fled. Darkness seems to fill the minds of the people."[31] John E. Page put it this way: "In the absence of the first presidency I have looked on the Church as being like a clock without weights, or a watch without a main spring. All stops till they are restored."[32] One Asa Curtis, wondering why the Church was stalling so long to reorganize itself, spoke in behalf of seventeen other members of the Armada branch when he wrote: "We are all anxious to know the truth and would be glad of any information on the subject. Truth is what we want."[33]

That same sense of longing was even more aptly described in the following letter from a Swiss convert then living in Madison, Wisconsin:

At the death of the Prophet, I was completely at a loss who should be the true successor and leader of God's Church and

13

accordingly stood still to see and hear. Evident it was to me that twelve travelling apostles could never assume and constitute the first presidential triune. . . . So afterwards was I led to believe that Sidney Rigdon had a right to the claim, and acknowledged him as such, so far as he was the only surviving officer of that high tribunal. . . . I soon became convinced that some thing in the affair was not right. . . . So we were nearly all wandering in the dark.[34]

Strang sensed not merely the vacuum of leadership but also the intense longing for a new prophet-leader. Acting to fill the void almost simultaneously with Brigham's departure from Nauvoo, he formally claimed ownership of the church, established a new First Presidency, staked out his claim for divine appointment, and initiated a far-reaching missionary effort directly aimed at Mormon branches in the U.S. and England—and with almost immediate results, particularly in areas outside of Nauvoo.

This May 1846 letter from a longtime convert, a sister from Wisconsin, is indicative of the mind-set of some members outside of Nauvoo:

> I heard that the Prophet and all the Saints at Nauvoo and from all parts of the earth were going to California and my family were opposed being gathered with the saints or I should have been willing to go to the ends of the earth . . . but when I heard that the saints had all gone I felt completely discouraged and what to do I knew not. When to my astonishment, I received two numbers of the *Voree Herald* and found Bro. Joseph's letter in which I found God's choice of a Prophet through the mouth of a Prophet according to revelation. . . . I think a body travelling without a head will make poor steerage as a church without a prophet. I have always had implicit confidence in the Twelve in their respective calling but the arm cannot be the head.[35]

Strang's sudden appeal stemmed from his quick action in restoring a new church leadership and declaring himself Joseph Smith's true successor. "Now I have heard of no one claiming the appointment," wrote a new convert in Philadelphia,

> in accordance with the law of God, as written unto us, excepting yourself. But on the contrary, Brigham Young has told the people that there never would be another appointed to the Church in Joseph's stead, but that the Twelve were to preside over and dictate

the affairs of the Church in all the world. Thus we see the head is cut off, the eyes, the ears, and the mouth are gone! The body is left, but it can neither see, hear, nor speak neither can it receive nourishment, and according to the laws of nature it must die . . . suffice it to say "A Church without a Prophet, is not the Church for me; It has no head to lead it, in it I would not be."[36]

Strang's success also owed much to rising tensions, misunderstandings, and renunciations of the new and developing practice of plural marriage. Though practiced on a small scale by several leaders since 1843, polygamy had been publicly denied, mainly out of fear of inciting public hostility.[37] While some were opposed to it on theological and moral grounds, others found it hard to reconcile private performance with its public denial.[38] The following letter from one longtime Mormon missionary is illustrative of the attitude of many:

I have baptized scores and hundreds but I have never been to Nauvoo . . . and since Brother Joseph fell a martyr I have had some difficulty in reconciling myself to some of the movements of the Twelve and their authority to head the Church. They assumed a place and an office in the Church that never was conferred on them by revelation. In the second place the spiritual wife system. Third place—emigrating to California and in short not carrying out Joseph's measures. I have been waiting and looking for a prophet to come forth and set things in order in the Church. That time has arrived to the great joy of most all the Saints in this section . . . hundreds will flock to the great ensign that is lifted up in Zion.[39]

At best, plural marriage was misunderstood, but it was often also maligned and condemned, to the benefit of men like Strang. Brigham himself recognized that it was "like handling edge tools" in the garden—sharp, cutting, and potentially as divisive among the Latter-day Saints as it was misunderstood and condemned by their enemies. Such a practice required far better explanation, as well as sanction and careful control, by the leadership of the Church. And until such leadership was clarified, the practice could run unchecked and become a lightning rod of discontent besmirching the reputation of the Church and the faith of its members.

Meanwhile Strang's missionaries lost little time in spreading the word, in and around Nauvoo, back East, and, with less success, in England. "I was determined at all hazards to go to the wilderness with the Church," wrote one Benjamin Chapman,

> but having had a dream of the gathering of the Saints to your place three months before I heard of your claims. But I could not understand it until Bro. Moses Smith came to Nauvoo with the 1st no. of the Voree Herald. With some difficulty I borrowed one and read and to my utter astonishment I could not reject one word of it, for my heart was so rejoiced that the Great God had fulfilled his word in appointing a man through our beloved Joseph to fill his place when he was taken. So you see that I go for the man that has the tools (oracles, Urim and Thummim). For I know that the first President of the Church of Jesus Christ of Latter-day Saints must have those things or he cannot be a Seer and a Translator.[40]

Strang's use of the printed word in the form of pamphlets, broadsides, and issues of the *Voree Herald* beginning in December 1845 was well received among many troubled, information-starved listeners, especially in the absence of a Nauvoo paper. "I have understood that you published a periodical," wrote one would-be follower. "If such be the case, I would be glad if you would send me one of each number already published."[41] And from a woman in Wayne County, New York: "I feel very thankful to you for sending me the *Herald* although I have not sent the pay for them until now, as I have no other means of getting information from God's people."[42] And from Cincinnati came further evidence of Strang's successful use of the printed word. "On the reception of the first number of the *Voree Herald* the parties became united. And I think there is neither a man or woman in the place for [Sidney] Rigdon. The branch now meets together in union. And there are but one or two persons that I know of who are in favor of the California expedition."[43]

Though the *Herald* had only a handful of subscribers to its first issue, one thousand copies were printed and circulated vigorously by defenders and missionaries of Strang's nascent cause.[44]

According to the records, entire branches were moving over to Strang's banner. Consider these minutes of the Knoxville, Illinois, Branch of 17 May 1846:

> All for Strang as the first President of the Church. [The Twelve] had taken great advantage claiming their own measures to be mea-

sures of Joseph and Hyrum by which means thousands were made to believe a lie representing that Joseph and Hyrum had received all those abominations by way of revelations direct from the Lord by which means they were enabled to make the Saints believe some of the most unholy principles ever invented by man. . . . They declared the branch free and independent from all obligations exclusively belonging to the western expedition and declared a public renunciation to the Twelve and all their wicked and secret abominations.[45]

Jonas Putnam of Augusta, Iowa, wrote that "many of the church are wholly giving up the ship entirely and others are very restless not knowing the right way and want to find it. So it is with us. Strang has given some good revelations, if they were true, but time will soon tell the story."[46]

The Voree prophet also benefited for the most understandable of reasons. Many were simply too sick or infirm or too old to embark on a migration so grand as the one Brigham had in mind. Some wondered whether, if they did manage to go, they would ever see their families again. And for those in part-member families, how many could leave their husbands or wives and children not knowing when, or if, they might ever return? Moreover, the expense of such an enterprise was daunting and for many, totally out of the question. Besides, it was too dangerous and too fraught with uncertainty. No, a sizeable minority gave Strang the benefit of the doubt, at least temporarily, and considered following him to a more convenient gathering place.

Despite all of Strang's posturing, however, the overwhelming majority, certainly in Nauvoo and arguably elsewhere, were preparing to follow the Quorum of the Twelve into the American West, if not immediately then certainly later. Many could not accept Strang's choice of lieutenants, like John C. Bennett and George G. Adams, whom many in Nauvoo had come to detest and distrust. "There are some things that look very dark against you," complained one woman of Strang. "I cannot understand how a prophet of the Lord can take such a man as John C. Bennett for a bosom friend and counsellor when you so well know what his character has been in all times past. . . . How can you condemn others for what you approve in him?"[47]

Obviously most paid heed to the warnings and arguments of Brigham about Strang in a letter he wrote to outside communities just days before leaving for the West. "I feel it my duty as a watchman," he began,

> to apprize you of some circumstances relating to the matter. . . . I wish to show you that his pretended revelations or letter from Joseph Smith is a base and wicked forgery, and that the man who wrote it is a wicked liar. . . . Is it not surprisingly strange that Joseph Smith should appoint a man to succeed him in the presidency of the church some seven or ten days before his death and yet not tell it to the High Council, nor to any of the authorities of the church, neither to any man living on the earth? . . .
>
> Joseph Smith . . . would not act as president of the church in any general conference without first taking the vote of the people, and of the quorums separately. This is coming in by the door. . . . And he that climbed up any other way, the same is a thief and a robber. If Mr. Strang had received his appointment from Joseph, why did he not come here upon the death of Joseph and take charge of the Church and lead them to Voree? Because his own guilty heart would not let him come near the furnace of trial.

Brigham concluded his four-page letter by saying, "I say unto you beloved brethren, that Joseph Smith never wrote or caused to be written Strang's letter of appointment. It is a lie, a forgery, a snare. And let this testimony be had in remembrance before God."[48] Just days before leaving Nauvoo, Brigham listened to Moses Smith preach in Strang's favor at a meeting in the temple. After hearing Smith out, Brigham said "he would make no comment but simply asked the people if they heard the voice of the Good Shepherd in what had been advanced and when 'No' resounded all over the house it was proposed that Moses Smith be cut off from the Church which was carried unanimously."[49]

However, the many accounts and the fact that Strang's claims had to be refuted in letter and in public are evidence enough to show that for a brief moment, and for a minority of the Saints, the Voree Prophet had cast a long enough shadow over Brigham's plans to cause more than the occasional over-the-shoulder glance in times to come.

A TRIED AND A CHASTENED PEOPLE

A careful reading of Latter-day Saint scripture and doctrine, the kind Brigham obviously gave it, indicated that the root cause of their troubles was neither Methodist nor Missourian but had come from those within their own ranks. They believed, or at least their revelations so declared it, that the fundamental reason they had failed to establish Zion in Independence or a successful resettlement in Nauvoo was their own pride and disobedience to divine counsel. God would have a humble, a united, and a chastened people—"a righteous people, without spot and blameless."[50]

As early as 1833, when Joseph Smith was struggling to establish the Church in Independence, Missouri, their revelations had declared that Zion, the gathering of the "pure in heart," could only be established through good conduct and obedience.

> Behold, I say unto you, there were jarrings, and contentions, and envyings, and strifes, and lustful and covetous desires among them; therefore by these things they polluted their inheritances.
>
> They were slow to hearken unto the voice of the Lord their God; therefore, the Lord their God is slow to hearken unto their prayers, to answer them in the day of their trouble.[51]

Later, after the failure at Independence, their own scripture condemned them.

> Behold, I say unto you, were it not for the transgressions of my people, speaking concerning the church and not individuals, they might have been redeemed even now.
>
> But behold, they have not learned to be obedient to the things which I required at their hands, but are full of all manner of evil, and do not impart of their substance, as becometh saints, to the poor and afflicted among them;
>
> And are not united according to the union required by the law of the celestial kingdom. . . .
>
> And my people must needs be chastened until they learn obedience, if it must needs be, by the things which they suffer. . . .
>
> Therefore, in consequence of the transgressions of my people, it is expedient in me that mine elders should wait for a little season for the redemption of Zion.[52]

Brigham seemed never to tire of reminding his people that the Latter-day Saints, as trustees of the restored gospel, must be tried and purified. The 900-mile march of over 200 armed Latter-day Saints under the leadership of Joseph Smith from Kirtland, Ohio, to Jackson County, Missouri, in the spring of 1834—Zion's Camp in which Brigham and many other future Church leaders also participated—had failed in its ultimate purpose of lessening persecutions and reclaiming Independence. It fell short, however, not for military or political reasons but because of the criticisms, infighting, and disbelief of many within its ranks.[53]

This was no idle talk or mere theological platitude. It must be understood at the outset that Brigham would attribute their success, or failure, in the impending exodus to their collective unity and obedience, or lack thereof. His sermons, his counsels and exhortations, and those of his closest lieutenants all reveal this underlying conviction that came to permeate the thinking of so many leaders and pioneer followers. They would find their place if they would follow their God!

A COVENANT PEOPLE

Central to the plan of exodus was the place of the temple, that enduring religious symbol of a covenant-making people. From almost the beginning, temple-building was representative of the faith of the Latter-day Saints. In fact, they saw it as an obligation and divine appointment. "Therefore, I command you to build a house unto me, for the gathering together of my saints, that they may worship me."[54] Consequently they had marked off temple sites in Independence and, later, in Far West, Missouri. They had actually erected such a structure in Kirtland, Ohio. And in Nauvoo, they built again a "House of the Lord" in which to worship God and commit to living as a chosen people.

The final chapter in Nauvoo, in fact, was the completion of the temple. Had it been completed sooner, the exodus would have begun that much earlier. Wrote one young Nauvoo mother during that busy summer of 1845: "The temple progresses finely; the roof is nearly shingled; the frame work of the steeple is nearly as high from the roof up as the body of the Temple. . . . We hear the laborers sing and shout as they raise the timbers."[55] Brigham later admitted, "The main and only cause of our tarrying so long, was to give the brethren those blessings in the Temple, for which they have labored so diligently and faithfully to build, and as soon as it was prepared, we labored incessantly almost night and day to wait on them until a few days prior to our departure."[56]

Between 10 December and late January 1846, the Quorum of the Twelve oversaw three weeks of intensive temple ordinance work in which at least 5,500 and perhaps as many as 8,000 members received their endowments (a sacred ordinance of spiritual blessings based on personal covenants) and participated in such other temple ordinances as eternal marriage and baptism for the dead. The sacred nature and origin of the endowment is beyond the scope and purpose of this work, yet there can be no minimizing the importance the people placed on this temple ordinance. Since its introduction in 1842, the opportunity to receive their endowments became a compelling reason to finish the temple and explains, in part, why they stayed as long as they did in a condemned city.[57]

It was also in the temple that Brigham forged his famous "Nauvoo Covenant," by which the more wealthy and well-provisioned believers promised to do all they could to help in bringing the many hundreds, if not thousands, of poor and less advantaged—a covenant he would tenaciously hold his people to fulfil time and time again in the trying months ahead.[58] During most of the fall and winter of 1845 to 1846, Nauvoo witnessed the construction of 2,000 wagons, the gathering of supplies, and the organization of advance companies of wagon trains. Most everyone was anxious to save themselves and their belongings. Ironically, the city never was so alive as it was after the sentence of desertion had been passed on it.[59]

Thus, the Saints would go as a covenant people. And even if their wilderness circumstances prevented the erection of a new temple for a period of time, there would at least be a place and provision for it in their future home.

AFFORDABILITY

It was one thing to get out of Nauvoo and find a new Rocky Mountain home with all their faith and practices intact; it was quite another to pay the enormous costs of transporting so many people, in the poorest of conditions, such vast distances. For several families to make the overland trip to California and Oregon often required selling virtually every possession to pay for teams and wagons, supplies and provisions. To transplant an entire people, many of whom were facing personal bankruptcy in the collapse of Nauvoo real estate, would strain the imagination, creativity, and forethought of the best of leaders.

Where, indeed, would the money come from? Certainly there was little public sympathy for their cause. And Joseph Smith's personal estate, whatever was left in it, was soon tied up in claims and counterclaims.[60] Most of the immigrant converts from Europe, albeit skilled tradesmen, had found little work in and around Nauvoo except in building the temple. The Church, on the eve of its westward gamble, was in no position to underwrite or bankroll the costs of the pending enterprise.

Consequently, the solutions had to come from the personal sacrifices of the people, both in Nauvoo and elsewhere, in the payment of tithes and offerings; from the sale of Church properties, including the very temple they were still constructing; from begging missions to the American public; and from negotiating whatever contracts possible with governments near or far for services rendered as they moved west.

As for tithing income from the people, most in Nauvoo were either looking for work or underemployed. Many were in poverty. To further complicate matters, tithing receipts from England were in jeopardy of being lost to an immigration scheme that would require the closest attention of senior Church leaders at the precise moment they could ill afford to be away. And the few who had money could only be expected to sacrifice so much for the cause.

Meanwhile, property values in Nauvoo were already in steep decline as potential buyers chose to bide their time for a more favorable moment. The ability to realize funds from the sale of Church properties was damaged by the same downward spiral in real estate prices that affected private properties. And as for public support, could they really expect the United States government and the American public to come to their aid when it was their avowed purpose to quit the country and move west?

From the moment they made the decision to go west, they must have known that it was a daring and a costly proposition with absolutely no financial promise of resolution and fulfilment.

PROCLAIM THE WORD

There was one final requirement for the success of their exodus plan, and it had everything to do with proclaiming their desired achievement. The news had to be communicated to the scattered membership as quickly as possible by letter, by printed circular, by official proclamation, by missionary, by public celebration—by every means possible. Their ability to publish had been disrupted when Nauvoo's *Times and Seasons* press closed down. They did not print a paper at Winter Quarters until 1849 *(The Frontier Guardian)* and at Salt Lake City until 1852 *(The Deseret News)*. Only

the *Millennial Star*, the official organ of the Church in England, was opera-
tive throughout this period, and it had only limited distribution on the
American side of the Atlantic. Until the Church could publish its own story,
its detractors filled the void and used the power of the press to full advantage.

In review, the Latter-day Saints had little choice but to quit Nauvoo and
America and find a new safe place suitable for growth and sustenance, acces-
sible to all and affordable to as many who desired to go. No less important
was the matter of a new prophet-leader and a new First Presidency to send
a clear signal and set in order the teachings and developing practices of this
evolving new religion. Furthermore, they would find their place only to the
degree they were a humble and an obedient people, tried in the furnace of
their afflictions. Likewise they had to take their temples with them, at least
their covenants and expectations of a new temple-centered home. Finally,
they needed to communicate their achievement and spread the word near
and far.

Nauvoo, a city under siege, began its exodus in the darkness of a cold
February night, when portions of the vanguard companies began crossing
the Mississippi River westward. Those who could not go in the initial company of the Twelve followed in the weeks and months to come. Eventually
only scattered latecomers, sick, and wounded were left to follow as best they
could during the later months of 1846—many at the barrel of a cannon or
the point of a bayonet.

While many wept at the inexplicable tragedy of it all, others chose
deliberately to wear a happier face. "How can I go without you?" inquired
Irene Hascall of her non-supportive parents in New England.

> Or how can you stay behind? . . . Do not worry anything about it,
> there will be some way. I suppose father would not like to travel
> across the Rocky Mountains but I should think he might like it real
> well for he can hunt all the way. I think probably they will cross the
> Rocky Mountains to a healthier climate. What good times we will
> have journeying and pitching our tents like the Israelites.[61]

Within a relatively brief time, although none too short for those bent
on hounding out the last residents, Nauvoo, once the City Beautiful,
became a memory, a vacant expression of a departed faith, a victim of a

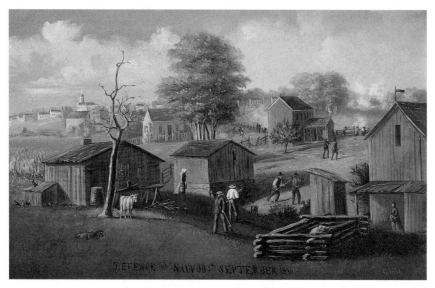

Defense of Nauvoo, *by C. C. A. Christensen*

clouded circumstance in Illinois history that still begs description and understanding.

Early in September 1846 the city was attacked, and for seven days a "Spartan Band" of about 100 Mormons and "new citizens" held off an attacking force of over 1,500 heavily armed men. Finally, recognizing the painfully obvious, the defenders signed an "article of accommodation, treaty and agreement" with the Quincy Committee. As Daniel H. Wells reminded them: "What interests have the Saints to expect from its defense? Our interests are not identified with it, but in getting away from it. Who could urge the propriety of exposing life to defend a place for the purpose of vacating it?"[62]

The invaders showed little respect for the treaty. Parties of armed men roamed the city, ordering families out in two hours or other such short notice. The sick were treated with cruelty in many instances, and families were molested while burying their dead. Many went from house to house tearing up floors, destroying property, and plundering cow yards, pig pens, hen roosts, and bee stands. On 18 September, an unidentified preacher ascended the temple tower and proclaimed with a loud voice: "Peace, Peace, Peace to the inhabitants of the Earth, now the Mormons are driven."[63] The temple stood for another two years until destroyed by an arsonist's torch and an angel's tornado, but not before reminding all who came that for one brief, shining moment, it had represented the hopes and dreams of these peculiar people.

The story of the exodus begins, then, with this farewell to a deserted Nauvoo, as well described in 1848 in the journal of a Nauvoo visitor:

> Next morning we went over to Nauvoo and spent 4 or 5 hours in surveying the Mormon city and the celebrated Mormon temple. The site of Nauvoo is one of the most beautiful in all the western country as well as in the country immediately surrounding. Before the Mormons left the city contained 12 to 15,000 inhabitants. . . . The temple of which so much has been said and written stands at the highest point of land in the city about 150 or 200' above the river . . . [and] at a distance it has the appearance of an immense church. . . . On ascending to the top one of the most grand and charming prospects meets the eye. The country on the east is an immense prairie and has once been peopled by the Mormons. But everything about the place is dull and stagnant. There are less than 2000 people now in the place.[64]

Three hundred miles and a thousand deaths to the west, Nauvoo residents in exile were struggling for a new home and a new life. "Here we are exiled from the United States," wrote Isaac Haight, "without a home, dwelling in tents and wagons exposed to the inclemency of the weather. We are even like the saints of old having no abiding city but we are wanderers and pilgrims on the earth but we count the present sufferings not worthy to be compared with the glory that is to be revealed to his Saints."[65]

NOTES

1. Journal of Thomas Edmonds, 11 and 13 July 1844, William Huntington Library, San Marino, California; cited hereafter as Huntington Library.

2. As quoted in G. W. Westbrook, *The Mormons in Illinois: with an Account of the Late Disturbances Which Resulted in the Assassination of Joseph and Hyrum Smith* (1844), 36, St. Louis Mercantile Association Library.

3. Doctrine and Covenants of The Church of Jesus Christ of Latter-day Saints, 57:3; cited hereafter as Doctrine and Covenants.

4. Repealed by executive order of Missouri Governor Christopher S. Bond in 1976.

5. For good accounts of the history of Nauvoo see the following works: Joseph Smith Jr., *History of The Church of Jesus Christ of Latter-day Saints*, ed. B. H. Roberts, 7

vols. (1973), especially vols. 3–5 [cited hereafter as *History of the Church*]; B. H. Roberts, *A Comprehensive History of The Church of Jesus Christ of Latter-day Saints*, 6 vols. (1930), esp. vols. 2–3 [cited hereafter as *Comprehensive History of the Church*]; Robert Bruce Flanders, *Nauvoo: Kingdom on the Mississippi* (1965); and David E. Miller and Della S. Miller, *Nauvoo: The City of Joseph* (1974).

6. See T. L. Barnes, "Recollections of the Mormons," in the Huntington Library, a relatively impartial unpublished recollection written by a nearby local Hancock County physician. See also Edward Bonney, *The Banditti of the Prairies* (1963), chapters 3 and 4, pp. 27–49.

7. *Comprehensive History of the Church*, 2:505. See also Dallin H. Oaks and Marvin S. Hill, *Carthage Conspiracy: The Trial of the Accused Assassins of Joseph Smith* (1979), 197–98.

8. The Carthage Convention assembled in Carthage, Illinois, 1 and 2 October at the Carthage Court House. I. N. Morris was president. Delegates came from nine surrounding counties. "Convinced that all the disturbances in the county have grown out of the continual and unceasing depredations of the Mormons," as the Preamble stated, the convention took a hard and militant line. Among its several resolutions was one "to adopt a military organization" to drive the Mormons out of the state. Furthermore "the whole body [of Latter-day Saints] should be held responsible for all lawless acts against the persons, or property of our citizens" (Josiah B. Convers, "A Brief History of the Hancock Mob in the Year 1846" [1846], 17–21, Beinecke Library, Yale University). See also Oaks and Hill, *Carthage Conspiracy*, 199.

9. Doctrine and Covenants 5:19.

10. Brigham Young to the Saints at Mt. Pisgah and Garden Grove, Iowa Territory, 25 Jan. 1847, Brigham Young Papers, LDS Church Archives.

11. Journal of Wilford Woodruff, 31 Dec. 1847.

12. Doctrine and Covenants 38:18–20. This revelation was given in early 1831, while the Church was still in New York.

13. Brigham Young to the Saints at Mt. Pisgah and Garden Grove, Iowa Territory, 25 Jan. 1847, Brigham Young Papers.

14. John Pulsipher Journal, 10 Dec. 1848, LDS Church Archives.

15. Thomas Ford to Brigham Young, 8 Apr. 1845, Brigham Young Papers. For more on this argument, see Ronald K. Esplin's definitive article "'A Place Prepared': Joseph, Brigham and the Quest for Promised Refuge in the West," *Journal of Mormon History* 9 (1982): 85–111. See also *Dale Morgan on Early Mormonism—Correspondence and a New History*, ed. by John P. Walker (Salt Lake City: Signature Books, 1986), 38–39.

16. Brigham Young to Orson Hyde, 2 Apr. 1846, Brigham Young Papers.

17. See Lewis Clark Christian's "A Study of Mormon Knowledge of the American Far West Prior to the Exodus (1830–February 1846)" (master's thesis, Brigham Young University, 1972). See also his dissertation, "A Study of the Mormon Westward Migration Between February 1846 and July 1847 . . ." (Brigham Young University, 1976).

18. Brigham Young to William Huntington, 28 June 1846, Brigham Young Papers.

19. Journal History of the Church, 9 Aug. 1846. This is a well-known and excellent resource available at the LDS Church Historical Department, consisting of scrap-

book-like entries from private journals, letters, various writings of all kinds, newspaper clippings, and so on, compiled by date by former Assistant Church Historian, Andrew Jenson; cited hereafter as Journal History.

20. Brigham Young to Thomas L. Kane, 15 Feb. 1847, Journal History.

21. *Deseret News 1993–1994 Church Almanac* (1992), 396.

22. It is clear the Apostles believed that they as a quorum had been authorized "to bear off the kingdom" since Joseph's death. See Leonard J. Arrington and Ronald K. Esplin, "The Role of the Council of the Twelve During Brigham Young's Presidency of the Church of Jesus Christ of Latter-day Saints," *Task Papers in LDS History* (1979), 31:11. See also D. Michael Quinn, "The Mormon Succession Crisis of 1844," *BYU Studies* 16, no. 2 (1976): 187–233 for a further study of alternative paths of succession.

23. *History of the Church*, 7:224.

24. One possible reason for Sidney's failure was the well-known fact that Joseph Smith himself had tried unsuccessfully in October 1843 to remove Rigdon from the First Presidency (*History of the Church*, 6:47–49).

25. Richard S. Van Wagoner, *Sidney Rigdon: A Portrait of Religious Excess* (1994), 352–63. For an earlier study of Sidney Rigdon, see Daryl Chase, "Sidney Rigdon: Early Mormon" (master's thesis, University of Chicago, 1931). The account of Brigham Young taking on the sound and visage of Joseph Smith while speaking at the grove that September afternoon is treated as myth in Richard S. Van Wagoner's "The Making of a Mormon Myth: The 1844 Transfiguration of Brigham Young," *Dialogue: A Journal of Mormon Thought* 28, no. 4 (Winter 1995): 1–24. There are, nonetheless, many contemporary writings and accounts that attest to the transformation of Brigham's voice and visage.

26. James Allen Scott Journal, 1 May 1846, LDS Church Archives.

27. Lyman Wight, a convert since 1830 and an Apostle since 1841, had gone south to teach the Indians, attract southern shareholders to the church, raise money, and generally hasten the return of the Church to Independence, Missouri. Wight was not disfellowshiped until 1849. After his death in 1856, remnants of his family and followers allied themselves either with the Utah Mormons or with the Reorganized Church of Jesus Christ of Latter Day Saints. See Davis Bitton, "Mormons in Texas: The Ill-Fated Lyman Wight Colony 1844–1858," *Arizona and the West* 2 (Spring 1969): 5–26. See also Richard E. Bennett, "Lamanism, Lymanism, and Cornfields," *Journal of Mormon History* 13 (1986–87): 45–59.

28. Elvira E. Strang and Charles J. Strang, "Biographical Sketch of J. J. Strang," James J. Strang Papers, Beinecke Library, Yale University, New Haven, Connecticut; cited hereafter as Strang Papers.

29. The best study of Strang still remains Milo Quaife, *The Kingdom of Saint James: A Narrative of the Mormons* (1930). The most recent reinterpretation is Roger Van Noord's *King of Beaver Island: The Life and Assassination of James Jesse Strang* (1988). See also Doyle C. Fitzpatrick, *The King Strang Story* (1970); Richard E. Bennett, *Mormons at the Missouri, 1846–1852: "And Should We Die . . ."* (1987), 18–20; *The Diary of James J. Strang*, ed. Mark A. Strang (1961); William D. Russell, "King James Strang: Joseph Smith's Successor," in *The Restoration Movement: Essays in Mormon History*, ed. F. Mark McKiernan, Alma R. Blair, and Paul M. Edwards (1973),

231–56. Strang later removed his followers to Beaver Island in northern Lake Michigan, where his settlement realized only modest success.

John C. Bennett, a former counselor in the First Presidency to Joseph Smith and former mayor of Nauvoo, was a clever opportunist with grandiose schemes. "Do you intend to have me in my original place in the First Presidency?" he wrote in March 1846 to Strang.

"I am willing to acknowledge you and sustain you as President, chief, first in all things, with Elder George J. Adams as an equal councilor, but I am not willing now, nor will I ever be, to yield supremacy to ignorant men simply because they are reputed pious. No one doubts your talent, and let me repeat again, have you chief men, vigorous, energetic and intellectual. Napoleon's councillors were great generals and statesmen, and they made him great—tho' he was, like yourself, great himself" (John C. Bennett to Strang, 24 Mar. 1846, Strang Papers).

Bennett, who disgraced himself in Nauvoo through immoral misconduct, saw in Strang's appointment a way to regain influence and reclaim his reputation while attacking his critics. Judge Adams, for similar reasons, had also lost favor among the Latter-day Saints.

30. William L. Hughey to John E. Page, 28 June 1846, Strang Papers.

31. William R. Dixon to James J. Strang, 15 June 1846, Strang Papers.

32. John E. Page to James J. Strang, 14 Feb. 1846, Strang Papers. Once known as "Son of Thunder" for his outspoken preaching abilities and missionary successes in Upper Canada (Ontario) in 1836 and 1837, during which time he baptized over a thousand people, Page later fell from grace within the Church. He failed to fulfil an assignment to go with Orson Hyde in 1842 to dedicate the Holy Land for missionary work. Married to a wife adamantly opposed to plural marriage, and continually plagued by financial setbacks and trials, Page turned bitter against the faith he had once so eloquently defended. He was especially resentful of the Quorum of the Twelve for not recognizing his "poor and destitute" condition and rendering financial aid. Late in 1845, encouraged by William Smith, Page made plans to join Strang. "I am fully persuaded by the word of the Lord and the spirit of truth, that you are the man to fill the place of Joseph Smith, as prophet, revelator, seer and translator to the Church" (John E. Page to James J. Strang, 12 Mar. 1846, Archives of the Reorganized Church of Jesus Christ of Latter Day Saints, Independence, Missouri). Soon afterward, Page was dropped from the Quorum of the Twelve before they left Nauvoo. Page was eventually excommunicated, on 27 June 1846, and was replaced by Ezra T. Benson. See also John Quist, "John E. Page: An Apostle of Uncertainty," *Journal of Mormon History* 12 (1985): 53–68.

33. Asa Curtis to James J. Strang, 20 Apr. 1846, Strang Papers.

34. Lewis van Buren to James J. Strang, 14 Mar. 1846, Strang Papers.

35. Esther Ormsby, Lake Mills, Wisconsin, to James J. Strang, 17 May 1846, Strang Papers.

36. Samuel M. Reese to James J. Strang, 12 July 1846, Strang Papers. Strang's new tribunals, while laying claim to the original name of the church, excommunicated Brigham Young, Heber C. Kimball, Orson Hyde, Parley P. Pratt, John Taylor, Willard Richards, and George A. Smith for conspiracy, tyranny, teaching false doctrines, assuming authority not given them, and blasphemy (*Voree Herald*, 1 Apr. 1846, 4).

37. James B. Allen and Glen M. Leonard, *The Story of the Latter-day Saints* (1992), 185–86.

38. James Blakeslee Journal, "My Reasons for Separating Myself from the Church at Nauvoo," typescript copy, James Blakeslee Papers, LDS Church Archives.

39. C. B. Childs to James J. Strang, 26 Apr. 1846, Strang Papers.

40. Benjamin Chapman, Pittsburgh, to James J. Strang, 24 Mar. 1846, Strang Papers. Moses Smith, a recent convert, preached his new religion in Nauvoo throughout February 1846, warning the people "to flock to Voree, Strang's new city in Wisconsin where he promised them peace and safety" (Journal of Norton Jacob, 1 Feb. 1846, LDS Church Archives).

41. William R. Dixon to James J. Strang, 15 June 1846, Strang Papers.

42. Lyse Seelye to James J. Strang, 6 Dec. 1846, Strang Papers.

43. James W. Pugh to James J. Strang, 23 Mar. 1846, Strang Papers.

44. Roger Van Noord, *King of Beaver Island: The Life and Assassination of James Jesse Strang* (1988): 38.

45. Minutes of the formation of the Knoxville, Illinois, branch, 17 May 1846, Strang Papers. Isaac Paden, clerk of the branch, had written an earlier letter to Brigham Young, prophetic of his defection: "I am convinced that Strang under the present situation of the Church will cause the greatest split that ever has been made" (Isaac Paden to Brigham Young, 26 Jan. 1846, Brigham Young Papers).

46. Jonas Putnam to Abel Putnam, 23 May 1847, LDS Church Archives.

47. Letter from "Louisa" to James J. Strang, no date, 1846, Strang Papers. For more on John C. Bennett's sordid but colorful career, see Andrew F. Smith, *The Saintly Scoundrel: The Life and Times of Dr. John Cook Bennett* (1997).

48. Brigham Young to "the branches of the church in the neighborhood of Ottawa, Illinois," 24 Jan. 1846, Strang Papers.

49. Journal of Norton Jacob, 1 Feb. 1846. Jacob admitted, however, that "many have been deluded by Strangism."

50. Doctrine and Covenants 38:31.

51. Doctrine and Covenants 101:6–7.

52. Doctrine and Covenants 105:2–4, 6, 9.

53. For more on Zion's Camp, see Peter Crawley and Richard L. Anderson, "The Political and Social Realities of Zion's Camp," *BYU Studies* 14, no. 4 (Summer 1974): 406–20. See also Roger D. Launius, *Zion's Camp: Expeditions to Missouri, 1834* (1984); and James L. Bradley, *Zion's Camp 1834: Prelude to the Civil War* (1990).

54. Doctrine and Covenants 115:8.

55. Irene Hascall to her parents, 6 and 26 July 1845, Hascall Papers, LDS Church Archives.

56. Brigham Young to James Emmett, 26 Mar. 1846, Brigham Young Papers.

57. For more on the historical development of temple work, see Andrew F. Ehat, "Joseph Smith's Introduction of Temple Ordinances and the 1844 Mormon Succession Question" (master's thesis, Brigham Young University, 1982).

58. The Nauvoo Covenant resembled very closely the earlier Missouri Covenant of 1839, when Brigham Young at Far West, Missouri, proposed "that we this day enter into a covenant to . . . never desert the poor who are worthy, till they shall be out of the reach of the exterminating order of General [John B.] Clark." Some 214 men

signed the covenant to assist others "to the utmost of our abilities." (*History of the Church*, 3:250–54).

59. Susan Easton Black, "Nauvoo on the Eve of the Exodus," in *The Iowa Mormon Trail: Legacy of Faith and Courage*, eds. Susan Easton Black and William G. Hartley (1997), 35–48. Black contends that nearly 1,500 wagons were ready for the trek by Thanksgiving of 1845, and another 2,000 were partially completed by midwinter (39).

60. Linda King Newell and Valeen Tippetts Avery, *Mormon Enigma: Emma Hale Smith* (1984), 231–67.

61. Irene Hascall to Mrs. Ursulia Hascall, North New Salem, Massachusetts, 31 Sept. 1845, Hascall Papers.

62. Journal History, 17 Sept. 1846. See also John E. Hallwas and Roger D. Launius, *Cultures in Conflict: A Documentary History of the Mormon War in Illinois* (1995). See also Richard E. Bennett, "'Dadda, I Wish We Were Out of This Country': The Nauvoo Poor Camps in Iowa, Fall 1846," in *The Iowa Mormon Trail*, 155–70.

63. Journal History, 18 Sept. 1846.

64. Journal of Charles Peabody, 2 June 1848, Journals and Diaries Collection, vol. 1, Missouri Historical Society, St. Louis, Missouri; cited hereafter as Missouri Historical Society.

65. Journal of Isaac Chauncey Haight, 16 Sept. 1846, LDS Church Archives. Isaac C. Haight, born in Windham, N. Y., in 1813, had converted to Mormonism in 1839 and came to Nauvoo in 1843.

I

"IT WOULD TAKE YEARS TO REACH THE MOUNTAINS"

Across Iowa and the Enforced Winter Quarters

> In a few days I start with my brethren, the Twelve, and as
> many more as can get ready as pioneers to find the place
> where a stake of Zion shall be located over the mountains,
> leaving all our families at this place [Winter Quarters],
> with the anticipation of returning here to winter and
> taking our families over one year hence.[1]

S o wrote Brigham Young in late March 1847, just days before setting
out from the Missouri River toward the Rocky Mountains. Simple
and direct though this statement was, it had taken months of deliberation, debate, and even divine revelation to make it so. The Latter-day
Saint's plan of exodus was late in arriving in its final form and was refined
only in the final few days leading up to their inevitable march. The purpose
of this chapter is to review those events that brought them to the Missouri
from their Nauvoo home on the Mississippi and postponed their march to
the mountains until the spring of 1847.

It all was to have happened in 1846. The fundamental reason Brigham
and his Company of the Twelve quit Nauvoo in the bitter cold of February
1846 was to allow sufficient time for an express company of "expert men"
and pioneers to reach the better climes of a safe Rocky Mountain Zion
later that summer, in time to put in crops both there and at selected way
stations along the trail. Once the decision to leave Nauvoo for good had

been made, it became their overriding imperative and Brigham's personal passion to find their new home as quickly as possible. The longer the membership lay stretched out tenuously from river to river and from bluff to bluff, the more exposed it would be to sickness, death, criticism, and defection. He seemed to never tire of saying that the one and only reason they would make such a perilous exodus was "for the salvation of the Church."[2]

With good late winter weather and cold solid ground they believed they could make it across Iowa Territory and reach the Missouri, only 300 miles away, in four to six weeks at even the moderate rate of seven and a half miles per day. After that they would establish one or two way stations or farm acreages at Council Bluffs or Grand Island and perhaps another near Fort Laramie. Meanwhile, that much-talked-about "express company of pioneers" of some 300 or more men, freed from the daily cares of camp life, would then make it "over the mountains" to some valley of the Great Basin in ample time to secure their new mountain home "far away in the West." This was their plan.

The rest of the Saints would come on as health and strength, provisions and teams would permit. Those who could not leave in February would do so at intervals during the late spring and early summer to reach any one of the proposed farming stations. Others might have to go to St. Louis and other Missouri River towns by steamboat. And finally a trio of hand-picked negotiators, the Nauvoo Trustees, would stay behind to sell off as many Church and private properties as possible, and at as fair a price as the deteriorating market would allow, to help meet the daunting costs of emigration.

Between 4 February and 1 March, 1,800 people crowded into makeshift quarters at their Sugar Creek staging ground across the river and just a few miles into Iowa Territory, almost in sight of their Nauvoo homes. These constituted the vanguard company, the Company of the Twelve or "Camp of Israel," who would pioneer the way across Iowa as quickly as possible before sending an express company over the Rocky Mountains later that summer.

Some, like George Whitaker, remembered their time of departure with fondness. "We could see grouped all around the camp fires, men, women and children" he wrote.

Helen Mar Kimball Whitney

Some were singing, some were dancing, some were playing music; everyone seemed full of life and joy. We felt as though we had been released from bondage and were free. . . . After singing we had prayers, every family in camp doing the same . . . that He would bless us with health and strength and that He would lead us and guide us to the place of our destination. . . . The men put down their beds in the tent on the wet ground. The women and children slept in the wagons. . . . At day break when we got up, the whole camp was astir in making fires and getting breakfast and preparing for our day's journey.[3]

Others were far less glowing in their wintry record-keeping. "The snow had to be cleaned away to pitch the tents, and our beds were made upon the frozen ground," remembered Helen Mar Kimball Whitney, young wife of Horace K. Whitney. "We were not blessed with a stove in our tent that night and it was impossible to get warm by the campfire; so that night I laid nothing off, not even my hood or josie." She admitted that

in that first exodus there was such a great desire among the people and such a determination to emigrate with the first company that there were hundreds started without the necessary outfit. They could neither procure sufficient teams nor provisions, which retarded our progress, and was the cause of a greater amount of suffering than there would otherwise have been. And my father [Heber C. Kimball], in speaking of it, said, under the circumstances it would take years to reach the mountains.[4]

The initial 1846 over-the-mountain plan died a very slow and frustrating death, and all because of heaven and earth or, rather, rain and mud. While normally it should have taken only five to six weeks to reach the Missouri River, instead it took over three and a half months. Delayed

Slogging through Iowa

several weeks, until early in March, in leaving their Sugar Creek encampment, the inadequately provisioned, overly populated companies soon sank to their wagon bottoms in one of the earliest, wettest springs in Iowa history. From the head forks of the Madison River, fifteen miles east of Grand River, Brigham wrote Orson Hyde: "It may not be uninteresting to you to hear a letter of our situation and calculations. You have heard of a great mud hole which reaches from Nauvoo nearly to this place. We have at length got through it and find ourselves once more on dry land."[5]

"WE WILL NOT CROSS THE MOUNTAINS"

Such good news, however, was premature, for the rains continued; within days the terrain had once again turned into a traveler's nightmare, a quagmire with creek levels eight, ten, even twelve feet higher than normal. Too wet for open fires and camp cooking and much too muddy for even a mile or two of travel, many must have wondered whose prayers were being answered.

Had it not ended in the suffering and death of hundreds of weakened, sickly followers later that year, their situation was almost comical. "But don't think for a moment brethren, that we are cast down or discouraged," Brigham said to Wilford Woodruff and Orson Hyde in his characteristic upbeat manner. "No! We are the happiest fellows you ever saw in the world. We have not the least desire to return back into Egypt."[6]

But as they suffered and slid across Iowa, time became the disquieting factor. The nonstop rainfall, sudden melting snows, and swollen creeks—all combined against them. And as bad as things were in March, they worsened in April. "We were strung along clear across Iowa," wrote one emigrant, "and such roads, from one rod to a mile in width on those bottomless prairies. When the turf would hold the wagons up, it was OK, but there might be a dozen or more all sunk in the mud at once, a short distance apart."[7]

The journal entries of William Huntington are instructive:

April 9: Never did as many of the Church spend so disagreeable and miserable a night together before—it was very cold with high wind and hard rain all night and no fire, mud knee deep around our tents, ground filled with and nearly covered with water—while our teams has little or nothing to eat—one cow chilled to death.

April 10: Same scenes of suffering continued high wind, cold and rain—teams sent back after the wagons left in the mud—wind blew down tents and turned over Bro. Farles [?] buggy—at 4 o'clock P.M. began to snow and froze hard during the night.

May 5: That night it rained in torrents all night, and the morning the streams were higher than we had seen them before and soon received intelligence from Grand River that roads were impassable for loaded teams and plowing had ceased. Everything is dubious for the Saints. In the afternoon came a great storm of wind, hail and rain which swelled the streams to a hitherto unknown degree and carried off our bridge.[8]

The rain affected more than the roads. "That portion between Nauvoo and Garden Grove [was] the darkest in my memory," Helen Mar Kimball Whitney later recalled.

During that time our sea biscuits, crackers, parched corn meal, etc. which were among the luxuries, molded, until finally they were fed out to our horses and cattle. At the beginning of the journey the crackers went very well to eat dry, but I'll never forget the first time I saw a meal made out of sea biscuit broken into milk. I had called at Uncle Brigham's tent . . . where he was just taking some for dinner and he invited me to have a bowl; but I declined, with thanks, and a feeling of wonder how he could relish it. When it came to sitting down daily to milk and water porridge and crackers in it, it became so nauseous that hunger could not tempt me to eat it.

She concluded: "Some of the strongest, who were more exposed, became prostrated with fever and ague, etc. before arriving at the Chariton River."[9]

Come the first water-logged day of spring, Helen's husband, Horace K. Whitney, could only say, "Oh, what dismal days those were!"[10]

Brigham's dream of securing a new resting place was drowning in the mudflats of Iowa. It may have been a church on the move, but in Iowa it mired in the mud, and the situation quickly became untenable. He was learning the hard way that he may have been able to flee his enemies but he could not get ahead of his people.

Little wonder he began to vent his rising frustrations at the bedeviling circumstances which enveloped them. "When we commenced to prepare for our exodus," he wrote,

> we were encouraged with the offer of teams, etc. for our benefit but when we left with some 1,800 souls . . . we also found that great company almost destitute of provision and after feeding and nourishing and nursing them as a mother does her infant till the last breast is sucked dry, we will give them a good farm, send their teams back to Nauvoo, bless them and leave them.[11]

By early April it became obvious that their original plan had to be revised. First, the summer way station once planned for Council Bluffs and Grand Island had to be moved eastward to hastily found clearings in south-central Iowa that they called Garden Grove and, further westward, Mt. Pisgah. Like it or not, the most poorly provisioned, as well as some of the better prepared, would have to remain at one of the farms to plant crops and prepare a refuge for the thousands yet to come. Then a much smaller, more mobile Company of the Twelve would be free to move ahead. Speaking at outdoor Sunday services at Garden Grove on 26 April, Brigham said:

> We have set out to find a land and a resting place where we can serve the Lord in peace. We will leave some here because they cannot go farther at present. They can stay here for a season and

36

recruit, and by and by pack up and come on, while we go a little farther and lengthen out the cords and build a few more stakes, and so continue on until we can gather all the saints, and plant them in a place where we can build the House of the Lord in the tops of the mountains.[12]

Hosea Stout, bodyguard and overall camp chief of police, noted in his diary of 29 April that at Garden Grove, not quite halfway across Iowa Territory, "it was determined now to send 100 men without any families across the mountains in time to put in as early a crop as possible and to this end Brother Orson Pratt made a report of the amount of things necessary for a fit out for one hundred."[13]

Brigham's tone turned more critical as their delay became longer. "When the removal westward was in contemplation at Nauvoo," he said, "had the brethren submitted to our counsel and brought their teams and means and authorized me to do as the spirit and wisdom of the Lord directed with them, then we could have outfitted a company of men that were not encumbered with large families and sent them over the mountains to put in crops and build houses." He continued:

> Instead of taking this course the Saints have crowded on us all the while, and have completely tied our hands by importuning and saying: 'Do not leave us behind. Wherever you go, we want to go and be with you,' and thus our hands and feet have been bound which has caused our delay to the present time, and now hundreds at Nauvoo are continually praying and importuning with the Lord that they may overtake us and be with us, and just so it is with the saints here. They are afraid to let us go on and leave them behind, forgetting that they had covenanted to help the poor away at the sacrifice of all their property.[14]

Mountain men, overlanders, and the Mormons themselves well knew that the latest safe date for leaving the Missouri River in time to cross the Rockies before the mountain snows was early- to mid-June and only then with adequate supplies and ample provisions. So it should come as no surprise to learn that three weeks after the above-mentioned Garden Grove outburst, with the lead companies only 37 miles further west at their next farm station at Mt. Pisgah, that their leader sounded even more critical. "If the brethren will continue to tie our hands so that we cannot find a resting

Camp at Keokuk, Iowa, *by Frederick Piercy*

place, our enemies will inquire 'Where is Zion?' Don't know. 'And where is your Gospel?' You have none."[15]

Meanwhile, James Strang was having a field day at Brigham's expense and continued to do so as long as the Saints lay scattered and exposed across an open prairie with no home in sight. "But did not Joseph contrive the California scheme a little before his death," he asked in a March 1846 article.

> No, nor at any other time. He contrived a scheme for 25 men with-out families to take a mission among the Indians and take measures for establishing a stake among them at which they could have the Gospel preached and be taught in the arts of civilization. Quite another thing from taking out thousands of women and children to perish by famine, flood and Indian war.[16]

"If they ever reach California," he later wrote in his *Voree Herald*,

> their dependence must be partly upon slow travel and partly upon miracle—but chiefly upon the latter. . . . Any person who may visit the 'Camp of Israel' and is in possession of the common necessities of life, will leave it better satisfied with his condition in life. If the

Mormons do not suffer some before they reach California we are not gifted with the spirit of prophecy.[17]

In the summer of 1846 Strang announced a new revelation concerning the future of his church and the westward traveling Latter-day Saints. "Trouble not yourselves any more concerning those who have been driven out of my city and gone into the wilderness," it began.

> For in the day that they fled to the wilderness where I had not told them to go and were cast out of my holy city, which they had polluted, and from their habitations round about; even in that very day were they rejected of me. For with much long suffering and patience had I waited on them and warned them and sent my servants unto them; and they would not return unto me . . . and therein have I judged them with grievous sickness and sore judgments; therefore are they utterly cast out.[18]

By early June, still several days east of Council Bluffs, although finally enjoying the dry warm weather that had eluded them since leaving Nauvoo, Brigham "told the Saints they were hedging up their own way by the course they were pursuing" and "he could safely prophesy that the Saints would not cross the mountains this season, and that is what many of the brethren wish—they would rather go to hell than be left behind."[19]

His final harangue on the topic came after it had become obvious that the 1846 exodus to the Rockies had been all but forfeited. "We will not cross the Mountains as soon as we anticipated," he admitted. "But I will not find fault. I will let God do that. . . . I can tell the brethren what they were doing . . . they have hedged up their own way by praying continually saying I am poor, I have done all I could for the church . . . and all the devils between this and the nethermost part of hell are acting in concert with their prayers."[20]

On 2 June 1846 the camp, now numbering over 500 wagons, having left several hundred behind at both Garden Grove and Mt. Pisgah, rolled out in the direction of Council Bluffs on dry land, determined to reach the Missouri. "I stopped my carriage on the top of a rolling prairie and I had [a] most splendid view," recorded Wilford Woodruff just west of Mt. Pisgah.

> I could stand and gaze to the east, west, north, and south and behold the Saints pouring out and gathering like clouds from the

hills and dales, grove and prairie with their teams, wagons, flocks, and herds by hundreds and thousands as it were until it looked like the movements of a great nation.[21]

They finally reached the Missouri River on 14 June. Their trek across Iowa had taken them sixteen weeks, three times as long as anyone had expected, and had cost them not merely provisions, time, and energy, but almost every hope of reaching the mountains that year.

In retrospect, some might wonder if Brigham may not have been as upset with himself as he was with his people. Surely he had many days to reconsider their hasty Nauvoo departure. Many more Saints should have been told to stay back until the wet part of spring had passed and to come on in May. No doubt their route plans might have been better formulated. Yet none could have foreseen the terrible weather that invariably wrecked their plans. And except for isolated instances, his people were still with him and their course still firmly set.

"BY THE RIVERS OF BABYLON
WE SAT DOWN AND WEPT"

In stark contrast to the estimated 2,700 other Oregon and California emigrants of 1846 that had long since started west along the Platte River trail, the Mormons presented a dazed and desperate spectacle. Exhausted, ill-provisioned, unwelcomed, and scattered across a wilderness of three hundred miles, 12,000 to 15,000 Latter-day Saints camped in peril. Some were still trying to get out of Nauvoo. Many without provisions were back at Sugar Creek and nearby eastern Iowa settlements. Hundreds more toiled to put in crops at Garden Grove and Mt. Pisgah. And the advance companies looked out on the Indian lands of the Missouri valley at Council Bluffs where there were no settlements, no crops to harvest, and little time to regroup. It was all but too late for even the most fully provisioned and rested to head west. And they still feared they would be barred from their westward exodus by their Missouri enemies, by Indian attacks, or by that rumored U.S. Army wary of Mormon intentions among Indian peoples already unhappy and distrustful of Washington.

Just hours before making contact with Captain James Allen of the U.S. Army—having heard rumors that Major R. B. Mitchell, Indian Agent at

Enlistment of the Mormon Battalion, *by C. B. Hancock*

Council Bluffs, had requested government troops to keep the peace and prevent the Mormons from allying with the Council Bluffs Indians—Brigham made one last chance at exodus. He instructed his newly-arrived pioneers to "report themselves and be enrolled in a company as one would be selected to go over the mountains and put in seed; for he was aware that all that men and hell could invent to hedge up the way of the camp would be hatched up."[22]

"It is for the salvation of the church," he once again reminded William Huntington, "that a pioneer company start immediately and we call upon all the saints at Mt. Pisgah and within call to listen to our delegates, learn the particulars from them and help them without delay."[23] The record then states:

> Pres. Young moved that we all go over the mountains, leaving our families, which was sustained by unanimous vote.
> Pres. Young asked who would volunteer to leave their families and go over the mountains; scores voted.
> Pres. Young said: If the church is blown to the four winds and never gathered again, remember—I have told you, how, when and

where to gather, and if you do not go now, remember and bear me witness in the day of judgment.

When God tells a man what to do, he admits of no argument, and I want no arguments, and if they will go, I will warrant them safety in so doing.[24]

Stephen W. Kearny's Army of the West was, in fact, in the region in full force, but instead of preventing the Mormons, it came petitioning them.

Although Washington had successfully enlisted sufficient numbers of cavalry regiments in such far western states as Illinois and Missouri, Kearny's critical need was for more infantry—foot soldiers from frontier regions who could step march into the intended areas of military action as quickly as possible. For all their expressions of wrath against Washington for its reluctance to mitigate their sufferings in Missouri and Illinois, the Mormons were in the right place: the direct line of fire in Washington's fight with Mexico. Better to have them as allies than as uncertain supporters in regions not yet part of the United States.[25]

Although many considered Kearny's invitation as a ploy, a government trick to deflect and deter the Mormon march westward, Brigham and those closest to him viewed it as divine assistance, if not intervention, a propitious culmination of secret negotiations in Washington by Jesse C. Little and other Mormon emissaries for any kind of government contracts—fort construction, mail delivery, map making, or trail development—to help finance their migration costs.

As early as 26 January, Little had received his appointment from Church leaders in Nauvoo to travel to Washington and "if our government shall offer any facilities for emigrating to the Western coast, embrace these facilities, if possible."[26] From there, he was to go on to Philadelphia and once again meet with Thomas L. Kane, their single most influential friend and advocate in government's inner circles. Son of Elisha Kane, a leading Pennsylvania judge and highly placed supporter of the Democratic party, Kane had the ear and the sympathy of administration officials, elected representatives and senators, and even of President Polk. Kane used his influence liberally to resist the anti-Mormon criticisms of Thomas Benton and other senators from the western states and to plead passionately their cause. More than any other man, Kane was responsible for the call of the Mormon Battalion.[27]

By 2 July, after no small amount of encouragement, promises, and assurances—in what really was a display of Brigham's spirited leadership—enough men had enlisted, albeit reluctantly, to make possible a new wilderness battalion. Distrustful of government intentions and fearful of leaving wives, families, and sweethearts in an unknown wilderness on an uncertain exodus, some 500 men agreed to go only on conditions that their leaders provide for and protect their loved ones, that their pay of $16 per month per enlistee be retrieved and brought back to help not only their own families but the covenant poor generally, and that they be led by their own officers as much as possible. Armed with these assurances and the long stock barreled rifles of the U.S. Army, the Mormon Battalion began its famous 2,000-mile march to the Pacific via the Santa Fe Trail, leaving the Mormon camps seriously weakened in numbers but significantly strengthened in influence.[28]

To celebrate the moment, a farewell ball was held with William Pitt's brass band furnishing the music. "A more merry dancing soul I have never seen, though the company went without refreshments," wrote Kane, who had come all the way from Washington to confer with the Mormon leaders.

> Dancing continued until the sun dipped below the Omaha hills. Silence was called, and a well cultivated mezzo-soprano voice, belonging to a young lady with fair face and dark eyes, gave with quartet accompaniment a little song . . . touching to all earthly wanderers.
>
> "By the rivers of Babylon we sat down and wept.
> We wept when we remembered Zion."[29]

In return for raising a battalion for the American cause, Brigham Young extracted written pledges from Captain Allen to allow the Latter-day Saints to settle not only in the Pottawattamie lands on the east bank of the Missouri River but, more surprisingly, also in Indian countries west of the Missouri.

President Young asked the captain if an officer enlisting men in Indian lands had not a right to say to their families, "You can stay till your husbands return." Allen replied that as a representative of the President of the United States he could act until "he notified the President, who might ratify his engagements, or indemnify for damage; the President might give permission to travel through the Indian country and stop whenever and wherever circumstances required."[30]

Wanting to settle as many as possible on the west bank of the Missouri and to get their vast cattle herds ahead of them to help ensure a speedier departure in the spring, when ferrying the swollen river would be more difficult, camp leaders accepted Allen's recommendation to settle at Grand Island, some sixty miles west on the Platte River. "There is a salt spring at the head of the island, where buffalo resort, and we can make our own salt. Thither we want to go without delay, with all the teams of the camp, unload from five hundred to one thousand of the wagons to return immediately to Nauvoo, Garden Grove, etc. and before spring carry to the Platte every poor but honest soul that has not the means to go."[31]

The Grand Island plan was short-lived, however. For one thing, just to ferry so many people, cattle, and other animals across the Missouri would take weeks, if not months. For another, scouts had located ideal pasture lands and rush bottoms up the Missouri River a few miles, which would do just as well, if not better, than Grand Island. Recent word out of the Platte country was that the Pawnee and Sioux were again at war and that Grand Island might turn into a battle zone between them.[32] Also, well-stocked Missouri merchants and farmsteads to the south could prove helpful through the coming winter. Finally, their plan to build a flour mill, complete with millstones and casting, would fare better closer to water transportation.

Some of their leading scouts—particularly the independent-minded George Miller and his assistant, James Emmett—were bent on exploring up the Platte or Niobrara Rivers as far west as Fort Laramie in order to identify the best route to the Rockies.[33] "The people was at liberty," wrote Heber C. Kimball, "to choose whether to go over the mountains with Br. [George] Miller, to go to Grand Island, or to go back on the other side [of] the river. The most of them was for going with Miller."[34]

Consequently, by early August the Council of the Twelve had taken into consideration the propriety of wintering on the Missouri and had concluded to settle on either side of the Missouri River in the Council Bluffs region.[35] "We are satisfied," wrote Brigham Young to George Miller, who was then taking settlement not among the Pawnees as instructed but among the Poncas on the Niobrara River some 60 miles northwest of the main camp, "that it will be impolitic for any company to attempt to cross the mountains this fall."[36]

There was also bad news coming from Nauvoo: hundreds were being driven out without time for adequate preparation and provision. The Carthage Convention had made good on its promise to expel, by mob force, the few Latter-day Saints still left in Nauvoo along with any new residents in town. The "Battle of Nauvoo" in mid-September included rifle and cannon fire; by 17 September, Nauvoo's defenders had no choice but to surrender to an overwhelming force of at least 1,500 armed men intent on expelling the population. The result was near pandemonium, with the citizens in their sick and weakened condition sheltering in hastily erected bivouacs across the river in Montrose, Iowa.

"In every part of the city," one impartial observer recorded,

> scenes of destitution, misery and woe met the eye. Families were hurrying away from their homes, without a shelter, without means of conveyance, without tents, money, or a day's provision, with as much of their household stuff as they could carry in their hands. Sick men and women were carried upon their beds, weary mothers with helpless babes dying in their arms hurried away—all fleeing they scarcely knew or cared whither, so it was from their enemies, whom they feared more than the waves of the Mississippi, or the heat and hunger and lingering life and dreaded death of the prairies in which they were about to be cast. The ferry boats were crowded, and the river bank was lined with anxious fugitives, sadly awaiting their turn to pass over and take up their solitary march to the wilderness.[37]

Such disturbing, though not entirely surprising, news could not have come at a more trying moment for the advance companies of pioneers, who were themselves struggling against time and nature to erect temporary settlements at Winter Quarters and across the Missouri River in the Council Bluffs regions of western Iowa. Nevertheless, in keeping with their promise to help bring on the poor and the less advantaged, and regardless of their own personal circumstances, many freed up their teams and wagons to send back to Montrose and other settlements where their relatives and friends languished behind.

On 21 July 1846, the Council of the Twelve Apostles had organized the "Pottawattamie High Council" among the settlers on the west side of the

Missouri River. Among its many responsibilities, this council was directed "to use all means in your power to have all the poor saints brought from Nauvoo and locate them here for the winter, or at either of the farms back as circumstances and your best judgement may dictate."[38]

On the very day the Battle of Nauvoo broke out, several volunteered to leave Winter Quarters and return to Nauvoo with teams "to bring up the poor Saints" as soon as their hay was cut, their lots surveyed, and cabins erected for their own immediate families. Orville M. Allen was appointed foreman of the first such relief company. Said Brigham Young in his call for help:

> I have felt sensibly there was a good deal of suffering among the saints in Nauvoo, as there has been amongst us, but the Lord God who has fed us all the day long, has his care still over us and when the saints are chastened enough, it will cease. I have never believed the Lord would suffer a general massacre of this people by a mob. If ten thousand men were to come against us, and no other way was open for our deliverance, the earth would swallow them up.[39]

In addition to Allen, James Murdock set out to travel the 327 miles back across Iowa with scores of spare teams of horses and mules; his instructions were to save as many as possible.

Their missions of mercy stand tall in the annals of Mormon and Iowa history. On 7 October, Allen reached the "misery camps" at Montrose, where he found over 300 men, women, and children huddled in makeshift shelters, subsisting on boiled and parched corn and river water. Some had died; others were falling victim to exposure and to typhus and other fevers. Allen soon gathered up a company of 157 souls in 28 wagons.

Such unhappy conditions set the stage for an incident that many saw as nothing less than miraculous. Thomas Bullock, official clerk to the Quorum of the Twelve and suffering with a sick family of his own at Montrose, recorded the following:

> This morning we had a direct manifestation of the mercy and goodness of God. A large, or rather several large flocks of quails, flew into camp. Some fell on the wagons, some under, some on the breakfast tables. The boys and the brethren ran about after them and caught them alive with their hands. Men who were not in the church marvelled at the sight. . . . The boys caught about twenty

alive. . . . Every man, woman and child had quails to eat for their dinner and after dinner the flocks increased in size. . . . The quails flew around the camp, many delighted in it. Then all the flock would rise, fly around our camp again a few rods off and then would alight again and close to the camp. This was repeated more than half a dozen times.[40]

Meanwhile, close behind, Murdock's rescue company finished what Allen had begun, bringing all that remained out of the poor camps of Nauvoo.[41]

Their plan to cross the mountains in 1846 was finally surrendered, a victim to nature's intransigence, their own undue haste and inadequate preparations, Hancock County's atrocities, and Washington's invitations. Yet if they could not reach their new mountain home that season, they had at least forged an opportunity to rest and regroup in the wilderness and to find the time and means to prosecute their relentless migration come spring. Zion would rest for a season.

"Our Object Is to Get Means to Assist Away" — Financing the Costs of Exodus

The costs of moving so many people so far would be enormous and would strain every budget, collectively and individually. Consequently, the Quorum of the Twelve decided on four critical strategies to raise the necessary income to make their journey possible. The first was to raise as much money as possible from the tithes and offerings of the membership everywhere.[42] The second was for the Church to advance to families, the poor especially, the necessary funds (almost always in the form of a wagon and teams), which were to be reimbursed later from the sale of their private Nauvoo properties and in future donations. The third was to petition governments near and far for as much assistance as possible. The fourth was to sell off valuable Church properties.[43]

The Carthage killings had wrought a complicated and devastating effect on Church finances. Joseph Smith had left no will and had seldom distinguished between his efforts to provide for his family and to help the new members flocking into the city. He had used his own personal credit to finance most of the original Church property purchases in Nauvoo and to fund various Nauvoo business dealings. At the time of his death, he was at least $70,000 in debt, mainly because of the slow rate of property repayments and other business challenges. His application for bankruptcy was denied and the question remained unresolved at the time of his death. The issue of ownership and obligation became a point of ceaseless irritation between his widow, Emma Smith, and Brigham Young. Each would claim the assets to pay their respective obligations. Neither won because property values soon declined to near zero, but the issue would sear for a century, unresolved and unforgiven.[44]

A full accounting of the financial state of the Church on the eve of the exodus is impossible to reconstruct, considering the scattered nature, scarcity, and confidentiality of extant records. But enough has survived to give more than a passing glance at such things. In Nauvoo members paid four kinds of tithing: cash, labor, in kind, and property. Those who made more contributed more. For instance, one member paid $500 cash in tithing toward the cost of outfitting the ship *Brooklyn*, in which Sam Brannan and hundreds of Saints sailed in the spring of 1846 from New York City to Yerba Buena, California. Another, one of Nauvoo's wealthier citizens, later contributed an amount double that above, also in tithing. On the other hand, one poor woman gave 10 knots of stocking yarn, value $.50, also one pair of stockings, and one pair of socks in tithing for value in kind donation of $1.37.[45]

Labor tithing—donating one day of work in ten—was contributed by those constructing the temple and was calculated at a differential rate depending on their particular expertise or craft. Even after death their contributions were recorded, as shown in the following entry:

> Received of Moses Horn three days labor at eight and a half shillings per day = $3.00. As per A. P. Rockwood's timebook. In full on his tithing to the time of his death, which occurred on the 14th day of March 1845 whilst working on the stone quarry. His death was occasioned by the fall of a small piece of rock about the size of a hen's egg, which was forced into the air by the blast, and at the same time he was sixteen rods and one foot from the place of the blast. This happened at twenty minutes past three o'clock in the afternoon, and he expired the same evening at five minutes before six o'clock P.M. He had been a member of the Church about one year, and was greatly lamented [by] his widow and three children.[46]

Many others contributed tithing in the materials most in need by the pioneer camps, such as compasses, oats, horses, cattle, wagons, atlases, watches, and rifles.

Those paying property tithing did so in one of two ways: by deeding over a tenth of their total owned acreages or by paying in cash, in kind, or in land-clearing labor as a repayment to the Church, which had given or sold them properties.

In addition to tithing contributions, some consecrated an additional amount—mostly in response to the call for extra help to get the pioneers away. One gentleman, for instance, gave four kegs of powder, 13,600 percussion caps, and gold at an appraised value of $438.18.[47]

Whatever the method, between January and mid-June 1846, members in Nauvoo contributed a sum of $32,867.62 in tithing and consecration funds, of which only 13 percent or $4,284 was in cash or drafts made payable at banks and merchant houses in St. Louis or other river cities. If one can assume that during the previous five years contributions had been made at a rate proportional to the city's growing population, one might argue that several hundred thousands had been contributed to the Church. If the cost of constructing the temple can be set at approximately $200,000, then it is obvious little was left over in Church coffers to fund a massive emigration of people.[48]

The largest concentration of available tithing funds should have come from the British Isles, where by 1846 an estimated 10,000 people had converted.[49] Having been instructed to postpone any further emigration until a new settlement was found, the British Saints should have made a welcomed contribution. On 16 July 1846—the very day the last company of the Mormon Battalion left Council Bluffs and when it was all but certain that an 1846 dash to the mountains was out of the question—Orson Hyde, John Taylor, and Parley Pratt, three of the Apostles, left for England to set in order a deteriorating situation and to return with as much in tithes and offerings as possible before the pioneers' planned departure for the West the following mid-March. While there they were also instructed to explore the possibility of a rumored government plan to underwrite the costs of sending thousands of penniless immigrants to Vancouver Island. Such a plan, its proponents argued, would lessen crowded conditions in London as well as lay firmer British claim to an Oregon Territory now attracting the attention of increasing numbers of American settlers.[50]

Wilford Woodruff, presiding officer over the Church in Britain in 1845, had reported earlier on the unsavory state of affairs in London. "I have been a speckled bird and stranger among them," he lamented, "until it has caused me tears and sorrow by day and night. I have grown old under it." In a tone of self-deprecation for not having attended to the problem earlier, Woodruff continued:

> Brother [Reuben] Hedlock continued to carry on business his own way, without consulting me in scarcely anything unless I dragged it out of him and knowing it was my place and duty to understand what was going on I inquired into matters until in several instances he insulted me in the office and manifested much anger in the midst of considerable company, and I quit the room. . . . He has manifested a spirit to gain all the influence possible. . . . Taking all things into consideration I do not think things will go right until Bro. Hedlock is called home and transfers the business into my hands.[51]

The trio left Council Bluffs on 31 July on a whirlwind trip that astonishes the modern reader for its ambitious and almost impossible schedule—a clear indication of their financial exigency. They arrived in Liverpool on 3 October and "found that money was daily coming into [a] Joint Stock Co. and that it was received by a set of men who ate and drank it up and squandered it away about as fast as it came in." Orson Hyde and John Taylor continued their report as follows: "The poor saints are lying up their pennies, their sixpence, their shillings etc. and remitting it to the Joint Stock Co. thinking that they were paying their passages to America. . . . They were much confused at our sudden appearance there, yet they attempted to put the fair side out, but unfortunately for them, they had no fair side to turn out, turn which way they would."[52]

Soon afterward they discharged Reuben Hedlock, Thomas Ward, and other local leaders for operating a fraudulent Joint Stock Society designed to sell members shares in a false migration company. Of the 1,640 pounds raised by the society, in what many thought to be tithing donations, 1,418 pounds had gone into the coffers of the company, most of which ended up in the private hands of its directors.[53] Little was left over to contribute to the cause of Zion. After traveling all over the British Isles setting in order the various conferences and branches of the Church, canvasing for funds, and collecting tithes, the three Apostles realized a net gain of only 469 sovereigns—some $2,500—a sum that Taylor brought back with him to Winter Quarters the following spring (see chapter 2).[54]

In support of the Vancouver Island plan, early in 1847 the Mormon leaders added their own names and those of hundreds of other British Saints to a petition—signed by more than 13,000 and measuring 168 feet long—that was laid at Queen Victoria's throne in hopes that the British treasury could be persuaded to sponsor wide-scale migration to the western shores of Rupert's Land. Her Majesty's government, however, was in no position to set such a costly precedent and promptly refused the request.[55]

The second element of their financial plan—advancing Church funds as tithing credits—moved forward while Nauvoo wagon wrights, between August 1845 and the end of January 1846, built some 2,000 wagons in preparation for the trek west. Patterned after the Santa Fe, or Joseph Murphy, wagons then being constructed in St. Louis, the "Mormon wagon" featured the same characteristics that differentiated other western wagons from their Pennsylvania forerunner—the famed Conestoga wagon. The Conestoga's floor was higher in the front and back than in the middle, and its ends sloped outward at the top. Its narrow body and small front wheels ill-suited the Conestoga for the rigors of high plains freighting.

Joseph Murphy, a wagonmaster for 14 years before coming to St. Louis in 1841, fashioned his new "monster freight wagon" as Henry Walker described it, with a bed 16 feet long and 6 feet high covered by strong canvas and with rear wheels 7 feet in diameter. It became the standard freight wagon of westering America. The typical emigrant wagon was soon patterned after it, though smaller in size, with beds 9 to 10 feet long, sides 2 feet high, and running wheels 5 to 9 feet in diameter.[56] The Mormon wagon was virtually identical to the Murphy wagon, though not often with the bright green sides of the St. Louis wagons. An often-seen adaptation for the Saints was a special bar on the back to hold small trees and saplings.[57]

In May of 1847 Joseph Murphy was selling his wagons at $65 to $75 each, depending on weight and size.[58] If the cost of a Nauvoo wagon was comparable (and considering the relative isolation of Nauvoo and the scarcity of wood, canvas, tar, and other supplies, the costs could not have been anything less), then the cost of constructing 2,000 Church wagons would have been no less than $140,000. For the individual, a reasonably good wagon with yoke, oxen, and harness cost $120.[59]

All across Iowa and beyond, many Latter-day Saints (perhaps the majority)—who were unable to dispose of their properties in an evacuated, depressed Nauvoo market—were encouraged to use Church wagons, with the explicit understanding that they either return them on request or pay back in money or in kind from the net proceeds of any future sale of their Nauvoo property. Brigham instructed the Nauvoo Trustees, soon after his departure from Nauvoo, on how to credit members' use of Church teams:

> Whenever you make sale of the property of any individual which has or may be committed to your charge for that purpose, and receive oxen, horses, mules, cows, beeves, sheep, goods, cash or any other articles in payment to make a perfect entry of those identical articles, and when you shall furnish any individual with an outfit with any of those articles, or from any church funds which are or may be in your possession, that you also make a full entry with perfect description of the same and forward us a copy . . . this course strictly adhered to will cut off much occasion of difficulty and hard feelings among the Brethren hereafter.[60]

Until they did so, they could be asked to surrender them—as did William Huntington—at any time for the benefit of those with even less provisions following on behind. Wrote Huntington: "There I had one of the most severe trials I ever had—expecting that on Monday morning my goods and family to be left on the ground and by the charity of others to be helped up to the arm [Garden Grove], as I had no team of my own, having in Nauvoo, according to council given my house and lot into the hands of the Trustees in Trust by Deed, according to the covenant of the whole Church at October [1845] conference that we would do all we could to help the Church away."[61]

The securing of adequate provisions was the responsibility of the individual family. The minimal cost of outfitting a family was $100. "I much doubt $500 would fit out a family of five persons with all the essentials," wrote William Pickett.[62] At the time, a general laborer earned $1 per day, a mechanic $1.50 to $2.00. Furthermore, work was seasonal for most laborers. "A man with not a very large family, may, during the spring and summer, with strict economy, lay by a portion of his earnings, but he must be lucky, indeed, who does not find it necessary during the following winter, to spend all he has saved, together with all he can make, until spring comes again."[63]

Their hasty winter departure, their relative poverty, and their inability to sell their properties account for so many leaving Nauvoo with insufficient provisions for the westward trek. "Adequate" meant a year's provisions, a well-built wagon, a dependable team of oxen or horses, some milk cows, 1000 pounds of flour, 100 pounds of sugar, farming and mechanical tools, cooking utensils, sufficient seeds, summer and winter clothing, a musket, and other necessities.[64] To afford it, while moving west many took jobs for a fortnight at a time in the eastern Iowa countryside, working as farmhands, building fences and barns, and playing concerts in obscure eastern Iowa hamlets as part of William Pitt's brass band, all the while impeding the forward march of the camp.

Because those in the wagons were using up Church resources as fast, if not faster, as they were contributing to them, Brigham had to look elsewhere. An ambitious request to the general membership throughout the United States and Canada and a general subscription from the public would have to wait until the fall and winter when more manpower would be available. (See chapter 11.) In the meantime, letters were sent in search of tithes and donations to places everywhere where large numbers of members were congregating. Joseph L. Heywood, for instance, was in St. Louis in October 1846, "for the purpose of soliciting aid for our destitute brethren and sisters."[65]

If the tithes and sacrifices of the people were insufficient to meet all the costs, then might not governments help? Such explains the remarkable round of negotiations that resulted in the Mormon Battalion, an invitation that can no longer be seen as an imposition on a wounded and wearied people as much as it was a generated invitation stemming from the Church itself. Not only were enlistees paid cash up-front at enlistment, but they were also promised $22,000 clothing allowance for boots, blankets, hats, and other necessities. Much of this money, though certainly not all of it, was transferred to the Church to help meet the overall migration costs.

The men gave their leaders and Jesse Little several hundred dollars to aid them on their missions and a total of $5,835 for their families back at the Bluffs. Parley P. Pratt was selected to return with John D. Lee with the money, arriving back at the Missouri on 11 August.[66] Choosing "to march barefoot and without uniforms the boys have been liberal to us," wrote

Orson Hyde in a letter dispatched with the returning Pratt. "We send you the papers of the respective companies containing the amount each man has sent and for whom it is intended. We have pledged our sacred honors that the money shall be safely conveyed to their families. . . . Now all we have to say is to put it into the hands of the proper persons."[67]

The Battalion moneys proved a godsend to the Latter-day Saints in a time of great need, but also posed a difficult challenge, particularly the fair and equitable distribution of such funds. Brigham tried to balance the need to protect and preserve the health and interests of the Battalion families with the needs of the entire pioneer camp, many of whom languished in poverty and difficulty. Despite the fact that bishops were called to care for small wards of pioneers—the first such use of bishops on a ward basis—and to tend to the welfare needs of Battalion families and others, misunderstandings and contentions were bound to arise. But at least the funds were available to pool their resources and to send Bishop Newel K. Whitney and others to St. Louis "to get such things as we want to carry over the mountains." There they could buy needed supplies and bulk foodstuffs at wholesale prices for the camps at Council Bluffs and elsewhere.[68]

Although the British Empire could not be persuaded to assist them, perhaps additional help could come from the United States. Once again Jesse C. Little made his way back East to negotiate quietly for additional government assistance and contracts. Almost anything would have been welcome—help build one or more of a proposed line of forts and supply stations along the Oregon Trail, conduct scientific expeditions, or even carry mail. However, much to everyone's chagrin, Little came away empty handed.[69]

Their fourth and final hope for financial relief lay back in Nauvoo, where whatever real wealth the Church still had remained locked up in the declining real estate values of the temple lot and town properties. Long before the pioneers had crossed Iowa, even before they had escaped Nauvoo, Brigham had decided to sell both the Nauvoo and Kirtland temples and other cherished properties in order to obtain the needed funds. Evidence suggests that he fully expected the completion of that sale long before they reached the Missouri.

As early as December 1845, the Council of the Twelve entered into serious negotiations with the Roman Catholic Bishop of Chicago to sell the Nauvoo temple as a Catholic college. In a series of secret meetings in the upper room of the temple, Reverend W. Hamilton of Springfield and Reverend Mr. Tucker of Quincy asked if the 48-room temple could be suitable for a college. Tucker said they might want many of the surrounding properties as well, because Nauvoo could become "a fine gathering spot" for Catholic immigrants coming to America from Europe via New Orleans and the Mississippi River. Brigham agreed, saying, "the Nauvoo properties would be valued at one half the going price in the western country. He then further stated their reasoning: 'Our object is to get means to assist away the poor—there are hundreds of families who are poor—looking to us and we want to get means to sustain the poor, who have been robbed of their all.'"[70]

Reverend Tucker, impressed with the potential of the temple and the layout of the city for their purposes, left Nauvoo confident that "he had men in St. Louis and New York who could easily raise the money," but unsure if he could finish the deal in time to meet the seller's timetable. "The time is so short," he concluded.[71]

All across Iowa Brigham clung to the hope that the temple would sell soon enough, before any estoppel or other legal impediment by Emma Smith, Strang, or any other could hedge up the way. Orson Hyde, writing in late April 1846 from Nauvoo, referred to "a conditional offer for the Temple" from Catholic interests and "it is believed we can get $200,000. . . . He also wishes to purchase much other property."[72]

That there was trepidation, even among the Twelve, at selling off the jewel in their crown is obvious. "We have felt much anxiety on that subject," admitted Apostle George A. Smith on 26 April, "until we all agreed in council not to sell it last winter. But if you in your wisdom should think it best to sell the same to help the poor in the present emergency we frankly concur notwithstanding we feel opposed to a Methodist congregation ever listening to a mob Priest in that holy Place; but are willing to sacrifice our feelings at times for the good of the Saints."[73]

Two days later, the Council met at Garden Grove and the subject of the temple was again taken into consideration. The conclusion of their deliberations was "that inasmuch as we were driven from our inheritances and homes and from the temple that all sales of our property were but forced sales done for the purpose of keeping a poor people from perishing and that we would be justified by our Heavenly Father in so doing."[74]

On 29 April at Garden Grove the Twelve determined to instruct the Trustees at Nauvoo to sell both temples "for the simple reason that we were going so far away that they will not be of any service to us and the money was needed to help the poor away from among the Gentiles."[75] The very next day, 30 April 1846, the Council of the Twelve authorized Orson Hyde and Wilford Woodruff to complete the sale of the temple for $200,000 and to bring $25,000 of the proceeds immediately to the camp, then in central Iowa.[76]

However, the sale of the temple to Catholic interests, or to any other party, never materialized. If the asking price was not problematic, the deteriorating social conditions certainly were. Hancock County violence, the rising tide of persecution, and the fear of possible fire and destruction all negated any realistic chance of sale. Besides, with property values plummeting, the astute buyer would bide his time.[77]

There was more to selling the temple than finances. The evidence shows that Strang was eyeing it for his own purposes. He could count no greater coup than to take possession of the Nauvoo Temple. Simply possessing it would greatly strengthen his claim to legitimacy and succession.

William Smith, who had defected from the Church, encouraged Strang to "go for it" in order "to help keep up the spirit of interest in the place and help keep possession." He went on: "I still notice that the apostates in Nauvoo are trying every art and tact possible to sell the Church property . . . Nauvoo Temple for sale, Kirtland Temple for sale. How it looks to barter the Lord's property. Perhaps you had best [take] notice a little of this in the Herald."[78]

Smith's suggestion obviously took effect: in a September article Strang refused to recognize the Nauvoo Trustees as successors to Joseph Smith or in any way representative of a First Presidency. They cannot "set up any pretense to title to the Temple, or any other Church property" he wrote in his newspaper. "All we ask of the Brighamites is that they will not burn the Temple down and lay it to the mob. We will risk the legal right."[79]

Later, at their October 1846 conference,

> resolutions were passed unanimously protesting against the sale of the temples at Nauvoo and Kirtland and expressing the opinion that the men who profess to be trustees in trust at Nauvoo are not legally in office and have no right to convey title to any property of the Church. We caution all men against purchasing church property of them.[80]

Crossing the Missouri River, *by C. C. A. Christensen*

Although nothing came of Strang's effort to acquire the temple, it was a concern in the trustees' ongoing efforts to sell.

Realizing that a late-season dash over the mountains was no longer a viable alternative and casting about for a large site to winter his people, Brigham used his newfound temporary leverage with the federal government to wrest reluctant permission for them to stay temporarily on both sides of the Missouri River at Council Bluffs. The land on the west bank, today northern Omaha (Florence), Nebraska, was then territory granted by the U.S. government to the dispossessed tribes of Otoe and Omaha Indians, who were sandwiched between the Sioux Indians on the north and the Pawnee on the south and west. For as long as the Mormons occupied the west bank of the Missouri, a claim ever opposed by the Office of Indian Affairs, they were unwitting arbitrators of intertribal Indian conflicts and offered protection to those tribes in greatest peril.

"As Jonah's Gourd" —
The City of Winter Quarters

Winter Quarters began as a city in the wilderness, a ragged Nauvoo transplanted from the eastern banks of the Mississippi to the western slopes of the Missouri, a people hounded amidst a people driven, both hated castoffs of an American society unwilling to accept either of their claims to a future. The tragic irony was that the Latter-day Saints were safer in the upper Missouri wilderness amidst so-called "savages" than they ever were among "civilized" peoples back in Missouri and Illinois.

Before year's end Winter Quarters grew, in Brigham's own words, "as Jonah's gourd." By the end of December, 4,000 people lived in Nebraska's first city, occupying 700 log houses, huts, caves, and hovels. Another 3,000 were settling down in various small groups around Council Bluffs in western Iowa Territory, and another 2000 to 3000 took up winter shelter back in Mt. Pisgah, Garden Grove, and other smaller Iowa communities as far back as Bentonsport and Farmington. More than 1,500 took winter refuge in St. Louis, Missouri, and in other river towns. "Modern Israel," scattered over 10,000 square miles, lay tired and exhausted, making for winter, waiting for spring.

One woman, writing to her family back East, gave this description of Winter Quarters and an insight into her own faith:

> Our people have built an excellent grist mill here; it cost some thousands of dollars, but does first rate business. I should like to tell you how many hundred houses we have in our city but have not lately ascertained . . . about 800. . . . Some are very good log houses, and others about the medium sort, and many poor indeed, but better than none. The land is far from being level here but the hills are really beautiful, far more so to me, than the level land could be. If you could sail up the River and take a peep at our place, you would say it was romantic and grand notwithstanding the log huts.[81]

The wintry exodus, their general lack of provisions and especially of fruits and vegetables, the inadequate medical treatment, the exposed Missouri River habitation, and the poor-camp refugees from the Nauvoo War—it was all bound to catch up with them sooner or later. A deadly scourge soon began to ravage the settlement. While some downplay the tragic story of suffering at Winter Quarters, overwhelming evidence shows the Saints were perishing in epidemic numbers. Their weakened and exposed condition made many vulnerable to the malaria-like sicknesses of such a river region as well as to scurvy and other diseases of malnutrition.

Lorenzo Snow, a future President of the Church, described the tragic scenes at Mt. Pisgah this way:

> The latter part of July and August witnessed a general and almost universal scene of sickness throughout Pisgah. Well persons could not be found to take care of the sick; it was indeed a distressing scene. A great number of deaths occurred and it was very often very difficult to get their bodies decently interred. In one or two instances bodies were put into the ground without any coffin or box. Scarcely a family escaped sickness and very few where death did not make an inroad. A general spirit of lamentation and sorrow pervaded.[82]

And the scene at Mt. Pisgah repeated itself everywhere else along the trails. By the end of 1846 at least six hundred had died, with hundreds more the following year. Lorenzo Brown, after bidding adieu to Winter Quarters in 1848, spoke of "the burial ground where hundreds of Saints have found a final resting place and to judge of its appearance," he remarked, "is large enough for the town to have been settled for at least twenty years or more."[83]

James Strang had been right when he predicted many would never reach their destination, but he miscalculated the depth of their commitment and of their devotion to their wilderness leader. "Our president don't stick [balk] at anything that tends to advance the gathering of Israel, or promote the cause of Zion in these last days," wrote Thomas Bullock, clerk to the Twelve. "He sleeps with one eye open and one foot out of bed, and when anything is wanted, he is on hand and his councilors are all of one heart with him in all things."[84]

Scattered and sick and still uncertain of where they were going, the Latter-day Saints faced an uncertain winter and an unknown future. Not surprisingly, several hundred left to follow Strang or some other leader, while others opted for a new life in Iowa's prime farmland. Their numbers, however, were relatively small. If one reads the journals and letters of those who stayed the course, one senses the enduring faith and abiding commitment of these people to their cause. "You wanted to know what we waited to move for," wrote Sidney Tanner to his parents, brothers, and sisters. "It was to go to a land of freedom where we could enjoy the peace of society and our liberty. We did not want to live in [a] country where there was no peace, no liberty and its citizens [were] not allowed their rights."[85]

In looking back on the frustrations of 1846, all had reason to ponder on an eventful year, a year of rupture and departure, delay and disappointment. Rather than ascend the mountains, they had barely reached another river. Free of their antagonists, some were falling with disease. Others were leaving. All were hurting. No one knew where they would go or how.

Despite the interruption of raising a battalion and surrendering several hundred of their most able-bodied men, and notwithstanding the need to build a new city while fending off plague and death, their energies remained committed to the pending journey. Winter Quarters and all its companion Iowa settlements would never be anything but temporary waiting places, springboards to springtime action. Their future yet lay to the West.

NOTES

1. For a fuller account of the Mormon exodus from Nauvoo to Winter Quarters and Council Bluffs, see Bennett, *Mormons at the Missouri*, 13–45.

2. Brigham Young to William Huntington, 28 June 1846, Brigham Young Papers.

3. "Life of George Whitaker: A Utah Pioneer," unpublished, Mar. 1846, Utah State Historical Society, Salt Lake City, Utah.

4. Helen Mar Kimball Whitney, "Our Travels Beyond the Mississippi," *Women's Exponent*, 1 Dec. 1883, 103, 102.

5. Brigham Young to Orson Hyde, 21 Apr. 1846, Brigham Young Papers.

6. Council of the Twelve to Orson Hyde and Wilford Woodruff, 30 Apr. 1846, Brigham Young Papers.

7. Clare B. Christensen, *Before and After Mount Pisgah* (1979), 131. See also Bennett, *Mormons at the Missouri*, 37.

8. Journal of William Huntington, 24 Mar. to 6 May 1846, LDS Church Archives.

9. *Women's Exponent* 14 (1 Oct. 1885): 66.

10. Journal of Horace K. Whitney, 21 Mar. 1846.

11. Council of the Twelve to Orson Hyde and Wilford Woodruff, 30 Apr. 1846, Brigham Young Papers. Because a large number of pioneers owed their wagons and provisions to the Church, at least until their properties in Nauvoo could be sold to allow them to buy them outright, Brigham Young spoke at liberty about confiscating teams as required.

12. Journal History, 26 Apr. 1846. For a more thorough discussion of the location, size, and development of both Garden Grove and Mt. Pisgah, see Bennett, *Mormons at the Missouri*, 38–44. See also Leonard J. Arrington, *Charles C. Rich: Mormon General and Western Frontiersman* (1974), 89–110.

13. *On the Mormon Frontier: The Diary of Hosea Stout 1844–1861*, ed. Juanita Brooks, 2 vols. (1964), 29 Apr. 1846, 1:158; cited hereafter as *Diary of Hosea Stout*. Parley P. Pratt told the same gathering that "they had been called together to ascertain the available means in the camp to outfit a company of one hundred young men to go over the mountains to put in crops" (Journal History, 29 Apr. 1846).

14. Journal History, 3 May 1846.

15. Journal History, 21 May 1846.

16. *Voree Herald*, Mar. 1846, 2.

17. *Voree Herald*, Apr. 1846; from an article previously published in the *Hancock Eagle*. Strang went on to state that at least 300 wagons had left the "grand caravan" and that several hundred Latter-day Saints were quitting, disillusioned and disappointed with Brigham Young's leadership (*Voree Herald*, Apr. 1846, 8).

18. *Voree Herald*, Sept. 1846, 1.

19. Journal History, 7 June 1846, written somewhere between Mt. Pisgah and Council Bluffs.

20. Journal of John D. Lee, 7 June 1846, LDS Church Archives.

21. Journal of Wilford Woodruff, 30 June 1846.

22. Journal History, 28 June 1846.

23. Brigham Young to William Huntington, 28 June 1846, Brigham Young Papers.

24. Journal History, 28 June 1846. Heber C. Kimball, in corroborating his leader's plea, wrote the following: "It is concluded, that the Twelve when [they] leave here shall leave their companies and with their families form one Company. Also, when we get 200 miles farther they shall leave their families and what males they don't need and go over the mountains to set up the kingdom of God or its standard yet this year" (see also Journal of Heber C. Kimball, 29 June 1846, LDS Church Archives).

25. The immediate cause of the Mexican War was the outbreak of hostilities in southern Texas over boundary disputes. Accepting the Texas claim for territory, President James K. Polk ordered General Zachary Taylor to occupy disputed lands. The Mexican forces responded in kind, crossing the Rio Grande to engage the Americans in late April 1846. A more probable cause of provocation was America's design to wrestle New Mexico and California from Mexican halfhearted control before any other power laid claim to the area. See Charles L. Dufour, *The Mexican War: A Compact History 1846–1848* (1968); Bernard De Voto, *Year of Decision—1846* (1943); David M. Pletcher, *The Diplomacy of Annexation: Texas, Oregon, and the Mexican War* (1973); and Seymour V. Connor, *North America Divided: The Mexican War, 1846–1848* (1971).

26. Report of Jesse C. Little in a letter to Brigham Young, 6 July 1846, Brigham Young Papers.

27. For a more comprehensive discussion of Kane's workings on behalf of the Latter-day Saints and the Mormon Battalion, see Bennett, *Mormons at the Missouri*, 52–67. See also Leonard Arrington, *Brigham Young: American Moses* (1985), 193–94.

28. The definitive works on the history of the Mormon Battalion are Frank Alfred Golder, *The March of the Mormon Battalion from Council Bluffs to California* (1928); Daniel Tyler, *A Concise History of the Mormon Battalion to the Mexican War 1846–1847* (1969); John F. Yurtinus, "A Ram in the Thicket: The Mormon Battalion in the Mexican War (Ph.D. dissertation, Brigham Young University, 1975); and Norma

Baldwin Ricketts, *The Mormon Battalion: U.S. Army of the West, 1846–1848* (1996). See also Bennett, *Mormons at the Missouri*, 50–67.

29. Thomas L. Kane, "The Mormons." A discourse delivered before the Historical Society of Pennsylvania, 26 Mar. 1850.

30. Journal History, 1 July 1846. The full text of Allen's authorization reads as follows: "The Mormon people now en route to California are hereby authorized to pass through the Indian country on that route, and they may make stopping places at such points in the Indian country as may be necessary to facilitate the emigration of their whole people to California and for such time as may be reasonably required for this purpose.

"At such stopping points they may entrench themselves with such stockade works or other fortifications as may be necessary for their protection and defence against the Indians. This during the pleasure of the President of the United States" (see Journal History, 16 July 1846). An earlier authorization to stay at Council Bluffs had been extended on 10 July.

31. Journal History, 7 July 1846.

32. Journal of Heber C. Kimball, 27 July 1846. For more on Indian hostilities, see chapter 3.

33. Journal History, 14 July 1846.

34. Journal of Heber C. Kimball, 16 July 1846.

35. Journal History, 1 Aug. 1846; Journal of John D. Lee, 1 Aug. 1846.

36. Journal History, 3 Aug. 1847.

37. Convers, "A Brief History of the Hancock Mob," 17–21. Convers, a non-Mormon Quincy physician, deplored the rising lawless anti-Mormon sentiment in Hancock County as did many other local leaders.

38. Journal History, 21 July 1846. The council consisted of Isaac Morley, George W. Harris, James Allred, Thomas Grover, Phineas Richards, Heman Hyde, Andrew W. Perkins, William G. Perkins, Henry W. Miller, Daniel Spencer, Jonathan H. Hale, and John Murdock.

It is interesting to note that such local high councils, as directed by the governing Council of the Twelve, had been established at Garden Grove and at Mt. Pisgah and would soon be on the western side of the Missouri River (i.e., the Winter Quarters High Council). Each was given the authority to administer in both "temporal and spiritual matters" under the direction of the Twelve.

39. Journal History, 27 Sept. 1846.

40. Journal of Thomas Bullock, 9 Oct. 1846, LDS Church Archives.

41. See Richard E. Bennett, "Eastward to Eden: The Nauvoo Rescue Missions," *Dialogue: A Journal of Mormon Thought* 19 (Winter 1986): 100–108. See also "'Dadda, I Wish We Were Out of This Country,' in *The Iowa Mormon Trail*, 155–71.

42. The law of tithes and offerings had been in practice since July 1838, when a revelation (Doctrine and Covenants 119) was received no longer requiring adherence to the previous law of consecration and stewardship of property given in 1831. See also Allen and Leonard, *Story of the Latter-day Saints*, 170.

43. Little has been written about the costs of the original departures, although much is available on the costs involved in later migrations. This is particularly true of the Perpetual Emigration Fund and the financing of Mormon emigrant companies to Salt Lake City up until at least 1869 and the completion of the transcontinental rail-

road. See Leonard J. Arrington's pathbreaking study, *Great Basin Kingdom: An Economic History of the Latter-day Saints 1830–1900* (1958), 77–79.

44. One source sympathetic to Emma's claims is Newell and Avery, *Mormon Enigma*, 199–209. See also M. Hamblin Cannon, ed., "Bankruptcy Proceedings Against Joseph Smith in Illinois," *Pacific Historical Review* 14 (Dec. 1945): 424–33 and 15 (June 1946): 214–15.

45. Bishops Ledger, Tithing Record Book, 1846–1852, LDS Church Archives.

46. Ibid.

47. Ibid.

48. Ibid.

49. P. A. M. Taylor, in his well-balanced study of the Mormons in England and their emigration to America, shows a phenomenal growth in membership in the British Isles during the 1840s. In the spring of 1840 membership was still less than 1,600. By the end of 1842 that figure had risen to 7,500. By the end of 1847 there were twenty-six conferences or districts containing some 250 branches. The peak was reached in 1851, with nearly 33,000 members. After that date, due to emigration, backsliding, excommunication, and death, the figure dropped dramatically so that by 1890 only 3,000 counted themselves Latter-day Saints.

Between 1840, when the first emigrating converts sailed to America, and the end of 1845 the total British migration was approximately 6,000, many of whom came to Nauvoo and its environs. After the settlement of the Church in the Great Basin, it is conservatively estimated that between 1848 and 1860 some 22,700 British Saints emigrated to America (see P. A. M. Taylor, *Expectations Westward: The Mormons and the Emigration of Their British Converts in the Nineteenth Century* [1965], 19–20, 43–48). See also Richard L. Jensen, "Transplanted to Zion: The Impact of British Latter-day Saint Immigration upon Nauvoo," *BYU Studies* 31, no. 1 (Winter 1991): 77–87.

50. Journal History, 16 and 31 July 1846. See also Journal of Wilford Woodruff, 15 July 1846, LDS Church Archives. (Where entries are from the original manuscript of the Woodruff journal, no volume and page number are given.)

Orson Hyde, at a tent meeting with the rest of the Twelve on the west side of the Missouri on 24 July 1846, "enquired what appropriation would be asked of the British Parliament in peopling Vancouver's island. Pres. Brigham Young replied, a certain number of acres to each immigrant" (Journal History, 24 July 1846).

51. Wilford Woodruff to Brigham Young, 1 October 1845, Brigham Young Papers.

52. Orson Hyde and John Taylor to Brigham Young, 22 Oct. 1846, Brigham Young Papers.

53. *Millennial Star,* 20 Nov. 1846, 149–59.

54. Journal History, 12 and 13 Apr. 1847. For one of the best discussions of the problems in Britain, see Taylor, *Expectations Westward,* and *Millennial Star.* See also the Journal of Mary Haskin Parker Richards, 18 Apr. 1847, LDS Church Archives, for an eyewitness account of John Taylor's review of the subject after his return from England.

55. For the exact wording of this "Memorial to the Queen for the Relief, by Emigration of a Portion of Her Poor Subjects," see J. B. Munro, "Mormon Colonization Scheme for Vancouver Island," *Washington Historical Quarterly,* 25, no.

3 (July 1934): 278–85. For a thorough and responsible study on British emigration, see Taylor, *Expectations Westward*, 18–47.

56. Henry Pickering Walker, *The Wagonmasters: High Plains Freighting from the Earliest Days of the Santa Fe Trail to 1880* (1966), 96.

The Murphy wagon must be considered in three parts—bed, top, and running gear. The bed or wooden box was usually nine to ten feet long and four feet wide, with two-foot sides. The bed was usually caulked for protection against river crossing seepage. Many people built a false floor, a foot or so from the bottom of the box, for use in storing supplies.

The top or cover was of waterproof canvas and the five or six bows supporting it were made of bent hickory. Flaps at the front and a "puckering-string" at the back allowed opening and closing. Inside the wagon, an adult could stand upright along the middle line.

The running gear consisted of large wooden wheels with iron tires (the front wheels smaller than those in the rear to allow for greater maneuverability); tongue or pole axletrees, front and rear; brake beam and bolsters (George R. Stewart, *The California Trail: An Epic with Many Heroes* [1962], 108–10). See also George Shumway, et al., *Conestoga Wagon 1750–1850: Freight Carrier for 100 Years of America's Westward Expansion* (1964), 155–59.

57. Lloyd Esponschied, "An Early Wagon Builder of St. Louis, Missouri: Louis Esponschied, 1821–1887 and His Family," 5; unpublished, 10 June 1960, Missouri Historical Society.

58. Joseph Murphy Day Book, 11 May 1847, Joseph Murphy Papers, Missouri Historical Society.

59. Brigham Young to the Nauvoo Trustees, 12 Mar. 1846, Brigham Young Papers.

60. Brigham Young to the Nauvoo Trustees, 15 Mar. 1846, Brigham Young Papers.

61. "A History of William Huntington," 18 Apr. 1846, William Huntington Collection, LDS Church Archives.

62. William Pickett to Brigham Young, 27 Dec. 1847, Brigham Young Papers.

63. Ibid. Speaking on the consequences of such poverty, Pickett continued: "You know, dear Brother, that the hand of oppression has swept away the substance of many of the brightest souls of the Church, whom you would be glad to have near you, and whose highest aspiration is to live under the daily sound of your voice."

64. Former Missouri governor and Mormon nemesis, Lilburn W. Boggs, in writing from his new California home in Sonoma, north of San Francisco Bay, to his Missouri friends preparing to join him, gave this commonsense list of necessary provisions:

"Prepare good strong two or four horse wagons; crooked or frame beds; obtain good stout oxen, say from five to seven years or eight old. . . . A tent with necessary tent poles, and iron pins to fasten it down. Provide—say fifty pounds of bacon . . . to the person, and about two hundred pounds of breadstuff to each person, large and small. . . . A sack of coffee to each family, and a due proportion of sugar—dried fruit, beans, a good supply of hogs lard, and plenty of soap; the last article is important. Rosin and tallow make the best article for greasing your wagon wheels, and a good jack-screw is highly necessary. . . . Bring a number of good milch cows. . . . Bring a large cedar churn, with iron hoops, and plenty of milk vessels. You will need salt, say a bushel to each family. . . . A good rifle, powder, lead and caps, pistols if you choose. . . . A small supply of medicine is highly necessary. . . . Provide plenty of good warm clothing and bedding, . . . cookery vessels, such as a family needs in the States, are the best to bring. . . . Start with a good supply of shoes or coarse boots, and any goods you bring for clothing, let them be woolen" (Lilburn W. Boggs, "Route to the Pacific," as published in the *St. Louis Weekly Reveille*, 22 May 1848, on file at the Missouri Historical Society).

65. Joseph L. Heywood to Brigham Young, 2 Oct. 1846, Brigham Young Papers.

66. Journal History, 31 July 1846.

67. Orson Hyde to Brigham Young and Council, 7 Aug. 1846, Brigham Young Papers. Each recruit was paid $42 in advance for clothing, totaling $22,000 for the Battalion. In addition, $30,000 in regular pay was included, for a grand payment in excess of $50,000. See Arrington, *Great Basin Kingdom*, 21.

68. Journal History, 16 Aug. 1846.

69. Joseph L. Heywood to Brigham Young, 2 Oct. 1846. Evidence suggests that Kane believed Little was an unqualified negotiator, ill-suited for such a political mission and a man who offended as many as he befriended. Little was replaced by Jedediah M. Grant in February 1847.

70. Nauvoo Trustees Meeting Minutes, 9 Dec. 1845, Brigham Young Papers.

71. Ibid.

72. Orson Hyde to Brigham Young, 22 Apr. 1846, Brigham Young Papers.

73. George A. Smith to Brigham Young and Council, 26 Apr. 1846, Brigham Young Papers.

74. Notes of Orson Pratt, 28 Apr. 1846, Brigham Young Papers.

75. *Diary of Hosea Stout*, 29 Apr. 1846, 1:158.

76. Council of the Twelve to Orson Hyde and Wilford Woodruff, 30 Apr. 1846, Brigham Young Papers. This communication is telling evidence that Brigham Young and his colleagues were expecting an imminent sale. See also Journal History, 25 Aug. 1846.

77. Although the Kirtland Temple sold, the Nauvoo Temple never did. Another party, Mr. Charles Millikin and Mr. Paulding from New Orleans, came close to purchasing it in the fall of 1846 (Joseph L. Heywood to Brigham Young, 20 Oct. 1846, Brigham Young Papers).

78. William Smith to James J. Strang, 20 Aug. 1846, Strang Papers. As early as March 1846, William Smith had been demanding the keys of the temple. "The guards expected an attack on the temple from the Strangs and Smithites," John D. Lee reported. "William Smith had stated that he would be giving endowments in the Temple within two weeks" (Journal of John D. Lee, 18 Mar. 1846).

79. *Voree Herald*, Sept. 1846, 2.

80. "The Temples," an undated, handwritten document, Strang Papers. Those trustees assigned to remain back in Nauvoo understood Strang's maneuverings and made sure that such pretensions never were fulfilled. For more on the trustees, see chapter 11.

81. Letter of Fanny Murray, 5 July 1847, Special Collections, Merrill Library, Utah State University, Logan, Utah.

82. Journal of Lorenzo Snow, Summer 1846, LDS Church Archives. For more

on the topic of death at Winter Quarters, see Bennett, *Mormons at the Missouri*, 131–47.

83. Journal of Lorenzo Brown, 25 May 1848, Huntington Library.

84. Journal History, 7 Jan. 1847.

85. Letter of Sidney Tanner, 13 Apr. 1847, Special Collections, Harold B. Lee Library, Brigham Young University.

ב

"THE WORD AND WILL
OF THE LORD"

Blueprint for Exodus

And it shall come to pass that the righteous shall be
gathered out from among all nations, and shall
come to Zion, singing with songs of everlasting joy.[1]

Spring could not come a day too soon for a restless "Brother Brigham"
and the rest of the anxiously waiting encampment at their Winter
Quarters on the banks of the Missouri River. After a fatal autumn,
during which hundreds had perished from malnutrition and exposure, and a
late but bitterly cold winter, which they endured in hundreds of makeshift
hovels, cabins, caves, and wagon tops, the rustle of spring promised hope
and deliverance, health and opportunity. Above all, it could mean the
fruition of their determination to send a pioneer company to the West in
search of a new home, "a stake of Zion," a place to save themselves and their
great religious enterprise. It was their long-awaited spring of everlasting
promise.

The popular winter pastime at Winter Quarters had been repeated
speculation on who would go in the advance pioneer company and when.
It had been the labored topic of discussion in council house and at dinner
table, over pulpit and in front of cabin fires. Committees were formed and
councils met to set plans and procedures. They even dreamed of leaving.
Brigham told of a dream in which he discussed their plans with Joseph

Smith, in which he and Joseph "conversed freely about the best means of organizing companies for emigration."[2]

Timing was critical. Now was the hour. Yet, as with the departure from Nauvoo, many more than could possibly afford to go wanted to join in with the advance company. Yet most were too sick, undernourished, and unprepared to reach the Elkhorn, let alone the Great Basin. For thousands still bunkered down in makeshift communities all across Iowa, just reaching Council Bluffs would be all the trek of '47 they could endure. Spring crops had to be planted at the Missouri, Mt. Pisgah, Garden Grove, and wherever else the opportunity presented itself. Their limited resources had been used to build winter shelters, and many men were still away to the western Missouri settlements in search of late winter employment and provisions for their needy families. All 22 bishops in the Council Bluffs region were hard-pressed to feed, clothe, and house the poor and the Battalion families, whose fathers and husbands were en route to California.

For many at Winter Quarters the excitement of the pending pioneer camp was tempered by their utter exhaustion. Brigham understood that they must either "stick the stake" that year or they would risk losing hundreds more to death or defection. If this was deliverance, what could bondage be? The milk and honey of their new Iowa farms at least gave hope and sustenance. What was there to the West? And yet most were still holding true to the faith that had brought them this far. It was the moment to give the signal and lead the way.

Until the snow flew their plan remained essentially the same as it had always been, just postponed one year. "Our present design," wrote Brigham in September 1846,

> is to settle our families at this point in such a manner that we can leave them one season (or more if necessity require) and fit out a company of able men with our best teams and seeds and at the earliest moment, in the ensuing spring, start for the Bear River valley, find a location, plant our seeds, build up our houses and the next season be ready to receive our families into comfortable habitations with plenty of bread.[3]

Central to the plan was reaching their destination in sufficient time to plant summer crops and erect shelter before winter. They anticipated reaching their chosen valley no later than 1 June 1847. To achieve their goal they would have to leave "one month before grass grows," certainly no later than 15 March. Following John C. Fremont's route, they would travel up the North Platte to Fort Laramie, cross over to the Sweetwater and eventually up through the South Pass.

The plan called for their families to remain back at the Missouri for one or two years and then to come en masse later in the summer of 1847 or in the spring of 1848. They argued that "a year's comfortable situation in any civilized community for women and children is far preferable to a year or two risk of starvation in the wilderness."

As if to reinforce their 1847 blueprint for action, Brigham called a special meeting in Winter Quarters in November 1846. Among several statements of assurance given then, he related a dream he had "concerning the Rocky Mountains" and promised that all "should go in safety over the mountains, notwithstanding all the opposition and obstacles government officials and others might interpose."[4]

"THE WORD AND WILL OF THE LORD"

The signal given was the "Word and Will of the Lord," Brigham's only self-proclaimed public revelation. It not only defined the authority of the exodus but also laid down a blueprint for action.[5] For a people accustomed to prophetic utterances—but who had been driven out of their homes after seeing their leaders martyred and who were witnessing opposing claimants from all sides seeking to lead the Church—the very fact that God would speak again brought redemption and vindication. Although George Miller, James Emmett, James Strang, William Smith, and others renounced it as trickery and Brigham's self-acclamation, most at Winter Quarters accepted it as divine direction. Horace S. Eldridge "felt to receive it as the word and will of the Lord and [believed] that its execution would prove the salvation of the Saints."[6] Jedediah M. Grant of the Quorum of Seventy echoed the same prevailing sentiment: "Since the death of Joseph [Smith], [I] have believed that the keys of revelation were in the church. When I heard that read I felt a light and joy satisfied that the Holy Ghost had dictated the words within."[7]

Considering its overwhelming importance, this document has received far too little attention for what it was: the manifesto for exodus. Written on 13 January and proclaimed the following day, the revelation addressed three fundamental issues: governing authority, camp organization, and personal conduct.

First of all, it placed the future course of the Church "under the direction of the Twelve Apostles," thereby countering any other leadership claims. The record shows that George Miller, a talented trailblazer, scout, and personal friend of the Prophet's, had clashed with Brigham all across Iowa. Headstrong and independent, Miller chafed at Brigham's deliberateness and authoritative rule and at his decision to winter at Council Bluffs. Furthermore, Miller believed Brigham was moving in the wrong direction, that it would be far wiser to settle in the Oregon country or even in Texas than to aim for a new desert home in the Great Basin. Always a few miles ahead of the main companies while crossing Iowa, Miller had repeatedly resisted his leader's overtures to counsel and discuss their progress. He and his reckless assistant, James Emmett, even decided to winter among the Ponca Indians on the Niobrara (Vermillion) River some 130 miles north of the main Winter Quarters encampment. Not until the late fall of 1846 did the two forceful personalities finally come together for a series of discussions.[8]

At one particularly contentious meeting held at Daniel Cahoon's cabin at Winter Quarters on 29 October, Miller railed against Brigham's plans. Just as the meeting ended,

> Brigham [Young] appeared at the door and took up the subject. He had been without and heard all that was said. He handled the case very rough. He said that Miller and Emmett had a delusive spirit and any one that would follow them would go to hell etc., that they would sacrifice this people to aggrandize themselves or to get power. . . . And that he would not clean up after him any longer. He said that they would yet apostatize.[9]

Miller, having counseled previously with Justin Grosclaude and a Mr. Cardinal, two expert trappers of the far west, persuaded almost the entire camp leadership to abandon the proposed Platte River route in favor of a route up the Niobrara River, on to Fort Laramie, and then north to establish a summer way station in the Tongue River area near the headwaters of the Yellowstone River in what is now southeastern Montana. Joseph Holbrook and James Emmett were even given permission by Brigham Young to explore up the Niobrara and ascertain the attitude of the Sioux.[10]

Brigham, however, never warmed up to the idea. First of all, he saw it as off course by hundreds of miles from where they wanted to go; a Yellowstone march would only succeed in removing the Battalion families hundreds of miles farther north from their returning husbands, fathers, and sons. Second, he thought it unwise to risk another winter stay among possibly hostile Sioux Indians and delay their journey even longer. Also, Holbrook's preliminary findings were that feed along the Niobrara had been completely consumed by large buffalo herds.

In addition, the Platte River road was better charted than any other route north of the Santa Fe Trail. Despite its deficiencies, John C. Fremont's map of the Platte and Sweetwater river valleys would provide them with far more direction and support than any map of the no-man's land of the Niobrara. Furthermore, news had just been received of the ill-fated Donner Party, which suffered a wintry terror in the high Sierra. Brigham did not want to put the Mormon venture at similar risk in the more northern setting of the Yellowstone.

But the obstacles ran deeper than when and where. There were some in camp who were convinced that Brigham was usurping authority and leading them in the wrong direction. Some members of the Council of Fifty, a political body that Joseph Smith had established in the spring of 1844 to assist in his campaign for the U.S. presidency and to look at migration possibilities, believed they had equal or even greater authority over Church policy than the Quorum of the Twelve. Although this was a minority view, men like Peter Haws, Lyman Wight, Lucius Scovil, and George Miller clung to this interpretation.[11] The latter, associate presiding bishop and a highly respected leader of the Saints, clashed with Brigham as much as he had revered Joseph Smith.

At the core of Miller's argument was his conviction that the Council of Fifty was at least equal to the authority of the Quorum of the Twelve in the matter of finding a new settlement. The declaration in "The Word and Will of the Lord" that the exodus would be "under the authority of the Twelve Apostles" was a clear signal that ultimate authority rested with the Apostles, not with any others. Furthermore, Brigham was endeavoring to show that the Twelve were following the will of Joseph Smith while others were mere pretenders. "The Church [has] been led by revelation just as much since the death of Joseph Smith as before," he said on 17 January. "Joseph received his apostleship from Peter and his brethren, and the present apostles received their apostleship from Joseph, the first apostle, and Oliver Cowdery, the second apostle."[12]

Aware of the rising tensions developing over authority, Hosea Stout recorded his impressions of the conflict: "This will put to silence the wild bickering and suggestions of those who are ever in the way and opposing the proper council. They will now have to come to this standard or come out in open rebellion to the Will of the Lord which will plainly manifest them to the people and then they can have no influence."[13]

After reading the revelation, Miller could no longer hold back his criticism. "I was greatly disgusted at the bad composition and folly of [it]," he recorded. "So disgusted that I was, from this time, determined to go with them no longer. . . . I must confess that I was broken down in spirit on account of the usurpation of those arrogant apostles and their oppressive measures."[14]

He and Emmett left the Church soon afterwards, Miller to Michigan eventually to join with Strang in Beaver Island, Michigan, and Emmett to California. Miller's loss was felt by many, even if they disagreed with him. Commented Joseph Fielding, a close friend and fellow member of the Council of Fifty: "He was dear to me in the office he held. He was indeed a fine man, and I hope to see him again in our midst."[15]

"The Word and Will of the Lord" also laid out the organization of their pending migration. "Let all the people of the Church of Jesus Christ of Latter-day Saints, and those who journey with them," the revelation proclaimed,

> be organized into companies, with a covenant and promise to keep all the commandments and statutes of the Lord our God.
>
> Let the companies be organized with captains of hundreds, captains of fifties, and captains of tens, with a president and his two counselors at their head, under the direction of the Twelve Apostles. . . .
>
> Let each company provide themselves with all the teams, wagons, provisions, clothing, and other necessaries for the journey, that they can. . . .
>
> Let each company, with their captains and presidents, decide how many can go next spring; then choose out a sufficient number of able-bodied and expert men, to take teams, seeds, and farming utensils, to go as pioneers to prepare for putting in spring crops.[16]

The relatively individualized, spontaneous, and rather democratic movement of small groups of loosely organized companies of other parties of emigrants from such towns as Independence and St. Joseph, Missouri, contrasts vividly with the communitarian, highly structured, group mentality of the Latter-day Saints. Students of the American West will find in the Mormons' departure the most carefully orchestrated, deliberately planned, and abundantly organized hegira in all of American history. Although hundreds of other emigrant trains and thousands of other overlanders made their mark along the California and Oregon trails, nothing in American history compares to the avowedly religious expression, biblical parallels, and communitarian purpose of the Mormon exodus.

Brigham immediately proposed the formation of five major companies, each under apostolic jurisdiction: his own, number 1; Heber C. Kimball's, number 2; Ezra T. Benson's and Erastus Snow's, number 3; Orson Pratt's and Wilford Woodruff's, number 4; and Amasa Lyman's and George A. Smith's, number 5. Had Parley P. Pratt and John Taylor been in camp, they also would likely have formed companies. Each company was instructed to select a president and two counselors; these then selected captains of hundreds, fifties, and tens. Each company would "bear an equal proportion, according to the dividend of their property, in taking the poor, the widows, the fatherless, and the families of those who have gone into the army, that the cries of the widow and the fatherless come not up into the ears of the Lord against this people."[17]

During the weeks afterward, company presidents and their contingent leaders enlisted virtually the entire scattered membership from Winter Quarters all the way back to Mt. Pisgah and Garden Grove into one of the five companies to come west, if not in the spring or summer of 1847, then in 1848 or later as health and circumstance allowed. As soon as a hundred men had enlisted with their wives and children, "at least 30" were to be selected as "Pioneers" to join in the advance company. With a minimum of 150 men, it was intended to be large and strong enough to thwart any possible Indian attack, yet small and healthy enough to move west as quickly as possible.[18] The various companies would also be responsible for outfitting those to join in the advance company. Thus company presidents and captains assisted the Twelve in selecting men who could contribute their particular skills and talents to make the journey and to plant crops over the mountains.

Although the 143 men, 3 women, and 2 children who comprised the original pioneer camp hold a special place in Mormon history and family lore, little has been written explaining why this particular crew came to be selected. (See Appendix I.) Some have speculated that the original number was to have been 144—"twelve times twelve men," in reference, perhaps, to the Twelve Tribes of Israel.[19]

There is no contemporary evidence, however, to suggest such an equation. It was, rather, more a case of who was selected, who was ready, and what particular skills and talents they possessed. Those in the pioneer camp either volunteered or, as in Norton Jacob's case, were asked to go by their respective company presidents.[20] Others were specifically asked by Brigham to come along. Such was the case of William Clayton, writer and clerk, who for very personal reasons gladly accepted the last-minute invitation to come along.

Needed were the kind of "able-bodied and expert men" who could bridge a continent and build a colony. Blacksmiths such as Burr Frost and Thomas Tanner; carpenters and millwrights such as Joseph S. Schofield, Norton Jacob, and Addison Everett; wagon builders such as Charles Harper; writers and clerks such as Thomas Bullock, Howard Egan, and William Clayton; skilled hunters such as Thomas Barney and John W. Norton; and good cooks such as Jesse C. Little and George Brown—each had a specific purpose.

Others brought different skills. Henry G. Sherwood, Lyman Curtis, and Albert Carrington were skilled surveyors. Philo Johnson and Charles D. Barnum were stonemasons by trade. Appleton M. Harmon was a gifted machinist. Francis M. Pomeroy was a sawmill operator. Henson Walker was a noted fisherman. And Truman O. Angell was an architect who would later design the Salt Lake Temple. Almost all were seasoned farmers and proven teamsters. There were also two medical doctors in camp, Luke S. Johnson and Willard Richards, the latter of the Thompsonian school of herbal medicines.[21]

Neither was the company void of artistic abilities. Clayton and at least a dozen others wrote careful and colorful journals of the trip, some in poetic fashion. Stephen H. Goddard, a gifted singer, went on to become the first leader of the now famous Tabernacle Choir. George Wardle was a popular vocalist and also a lifelong dance instructor. Missing, however, was the pen of an artist or sketchmaker like James Clyman, who had sketched his way

Orrin Porter Rockwell

across the wilderness to California the year before. It is a point of continuing regret that little contemporary artwork was made of their journey.

The average age of those in the camp was approximately 31 years. Excluding the two children, the youngest were 14-year-old Andrew Shumway and 16-year-old Stephen Kelsey. The oldest, Shadrach Roundy, had just turned 58. Thirty-three were from the state of New York and a total of 76, over one-half, hailed from New England; 13 came from Ohio, 17 from the southern states, 6 from Canada, 11 from Great Britain, 1 from Denmark, 1 from Bavaria, and 1 from Norway. Very few, with the exception of Albert Carrington, possessed formal college training.

Brigham also considered it wise to have along a few trusted bodyguards and law enforcers, such as Orrin Porter Rockwell and Return Jackson Redden. The colorful Rockwell, as is well known, had been one of Joseph Smith's most trusted protectors and was strongly suspected as the would-be assassin of former Governor Lilburn W. Boggs, a charge Rockwell neither refuted nor admitted.[22] Ever since the killing of Joseph Smith, Brigham had been protected by bodyguards day and night, for it was believed that a bounty of $1000 was still out in Illinois and Missouri "for the head of Brigham Young."[23] The practical need for frontier protection is probably why the Winter Quarters chief of police, Hosea Stout (who desperately wanted to join with the camp), remained behind while the notorious Thomas Brown (an alleged fugitive from justice and a known malcontent) was allowed to come along.[24] In his characteristic style, Brigham would let the evils and weaknesses of others play themselves out before making undue judgment.

In what was more a last-minute conciliatory gesture than a part of their original plan, three women and two children were allowed to make the trip. One of Brigham's younger brothers, Lorenzo D. Young, pleaded that his 43-year-old wife, Harriet Page Wheeler Decker Young, be allowed to accompany them. Severely asthmatic and convinced that she would never

live to see her husband's return if she
had to stay another season at the
Missouri, she prevailed on her husband
to plead her cause and that of their two
children, 7-year-old Isaac Perry
Decker and his 6-year-old stepbrother,
Lorenzo Subieski Young. Her daughter, Clara Decker Young, then only
18 years old and one of Brigham's
plural wives, also received permission
to come along to take care of her
mother and two younger brothers.[25]
Permission was then also given to
Heber C. Kimball to bring along one
of his plural wives, the 22-year-old
Ellen Sanders Kimball, the only
Norwegian-born member of the company.[26]

Heber C. Kimball

Heber C. Kimball—the second-most prominent leader in the camp, a
fellow Vermonter, and only thirteen days older than Brigham—joined the
Church in 1832. One of the original Apostles when the Quorum of the
Twelve was organized in 1835, Kimball was a highly successful missionary in
England. A man of strong emotion and spiritual sensitivity, Kimball gained
early the confidence of Brigham and many others.[27]

The decision to exclude family members from the pioneer company
was, as Orson F. Whitney concluded, because "the hardships and dangers
in prospect were foreseen to be such as would test the strength and
endurance of the hardiest and healthiest men."[28] Family travel would only
have slowed them down and jeopardized the health and welfare of the hundreds of women, men, and children, particularly families of the Battalion,
who were encouraged to follow later that spring.[29]

Needed also were men who knew the country and the Indians and, in
the absence of a seasoned pilot or trailmaster, could give a measure of advice
and firsthand guidance. John Brown, who the year before had led a company of Mississippi Saints as far as Fort Laramie before realizing he was one
year and 600 miles ahead of the main camp, would serve as an ideal guide
or, as Bullock described him, "a workman that Israel need not be

ashamed."[30] (See chapter 6.) After taking his people to winter at Pueblo (Colorado), Brown had returned to his home in Mississippi the previous fall to prepare for coming on to Winter Quarters. He made the trip by wagon in just under three weeks, arriving there 10 April 1847, a few days before the pioneer camp headed west.

A southerner, Brown was responsible for bringing three "black servants" or slaves with him: Oscar Crosby, Hark Lay, and Green Flake, also of Mississippi, whom Brown had baptized a few years earlier.[31]

Another prairie counselor was James Case, a former Presbyterian missionary who had spent at least a year at the Presbyterian mission station among the Pawnee at Loup Fork River (near present Genoa, Nebraska). Case would prove particularly valuable in understanding the Pawnee.

Two totally unexpected latecomers were John Tippets and Thomas Woolsey, who made a surprise appearance in Winter Quarters during an evening of food and entertainment at Brigham's home. Half-crazed and starving, the two men had just completed a harrowing two-month journey by mule and on foot from 280 miles south of Santa Fe, where they had left the Mormon Battalion. From there—in the dead of winter—they proceeded north to Pueblo and then west down the Platte River Valley to the Missouri, some 750 miles. They brought with them 137 letters, news of the Battalion and of the Mississippi Saints, and a desire to know the plans of the main camp. Paralyzed by blizzards, captured and robbed by the Pawnee though paradoxically saved by Pawnee hospitality, they stumbled into camp like two dazed prodigal sons. "Their arrival produced no small stir throughout the camp," said Woodruff, and people came "in all directions to enquire after their friends in the Army."[32] Despite their harrowing ordeal, Tippets and Woolsey summoned up the energy to join the pioneer camp and make the return journey back the way they had come, thereby proving an invaluable asset to the camp.[33]

A TRIED PEOPLE—A NEW ORDER

Beyond the matter of defining authority and camp organization, the "Word and Will of the Lord" said much about a worthy and chastened people. "My people must be tried in all things, that they may be prepared to receive the glory that I have for them, even the glory of Zion; and he that will not bear chastisement is not worthy of my kingdom."[34]

Fundamental to the history of the exodus is the undercurrent of

Brigham Young speaking at Winter Quarters, a recreation for the film Brigham Young

obedience, of behavior modification: if the Saints were to go out on the Lord's errand they must go as the Lord's people. For Brigham, mindful of their ultimate failure to establish Zion at Independence, Missouri, the pending exodus must succeed where the other had failed. It must be as much reformation as removal, as much repentance as geography; indeed, it must be a religious pilgrimage, a term many used deliberately and repeatedly in their writings.

The topic was often discussed, even before the revelation. "Unless the people humble themselves and quit their wickedness, God would not give them much more teaching," said Brigham in a December 1846 sermon. "They would continue to slide off and it would not be long before those who hold the Priesthood will be hunted by those who now call themselves 'saints.'"[35] Heber C. Kimball followed in the same vein: "Unless there was a reformation among us he was afraid that God would send a plague among us. . . . 'I want us to get up a reformation and have the Holy Ghost in our midst and not have the Twelve drove from our midst for if they were it would be the greatest curse that possibly can befall us.'"[36]

The revelation itself had specifically condemned profanity, contention,

78

evil speaking, drunkenness, and stealing. And "Zion shall be redeemed" by a proven people.[37] Whence the revelation or whither their mission, the fact is they came to see themselves on a divine errand.

"I want you to rein up all that is within you," Brigham instructed a council of leaders in characteristically blunt language in late January, soon after the overwhelming ratification and approval of "The Word and Will of the Lord" as revelation to the entire Church.

> Make up your minds one way or the other—if we penetrate into the wilderness and do not do right and keep the commandments of God it is better to tarry here. You need not think that you are going to creep into my company and commit iniquity without being punished for it. . . . Remember when you leave the Gentiles you will only have yourself to imagine evil. If one man steals, another commits adultery and another swear and curse the authorities of the church [they] had better stay here and go to Missouri for there they will be whipt . . . don't come into my company unless you can obey the Word and Will of the Lord. I want all to live in all honesty, build up temples and go and purify the people that they may build up the Kingdom on the earth.[38]

Earlier, at an outdoor Sunday service in Winter Quarters, the people had assembled "at the stand at the ring of the bell" and were addressed by their leader for two hours. "There was iniquity in the Camp of Israel," he declared, "that some of the brethren indulged in laboring on the Sabbath, some in swearing, others in taking the name of God in vain, . . . stealing wood and hay and refuse to pay their tithing or assist the poor."[39]

In writing of the same sermon, Mary Richards recorded that

> he began by speaking of several evils existing in the camp such as swearing, evil speaking, etc. Said if they did not repent and leave off their evil doings, the door of knowledge should be shut up against them, and they should be wasted by sickness, by pestilence, and the sword.[40]

Brigham went on to counsel the bishops to "get up a reformation [a term he used frequently] that all should learn to exercise themselves in the principles of righteousness." Otherwise, he warned,

> the priesthood would be taken away from their midst and the wicked would be smitten with famine, with pestilence, with sword

and would be scattered and perish on the prairies. [I] would rather cross the mountains with the Twelve and not another person with them than be accompanied by a set of wicked men and those who continued to lie and steal and swear and commit iniquity. . . . If the Saints will reform and act upon the knowledge which they now possess, flood gates of knowledge will be open to them and they will be filled with light and intelligence.[41]

And on the very eve of their departure, rather than speaking about where they were going or the routes they would follow to get there, Brigham reemphasized this theme. "Return unto the Lord and get the Holy Ghost . . . pray for me and my Brethren that we carry off the Kingdom of God. We must not," he said,

> indulge in negligence, slothfulness, coldness. . . . We are looking for glory immortal, and eternal lives. Go at it that we may turn away disease from the camp, that we may live and redeem Zion . . . pray that we may live to do a great work in the Earth. Pray for me, hang on one to another, never slacken your exertions, don't give up. Be wide awake. . . . I feel all the time like Moses . . . would to God that all these brethren were Prophets, Seers, and Revelators.[42]

This note of reformation would show itself as a dominant motif of their travels, a theme destined to be repeated at critical moments along their way (see chapter 5).

After hearing such preaching, one might wonder at the existing climate of morality among the Latter-day Saints. Like other peoples they had their troublemakers, and they knew it and wished it were not so. The call to repentance in "The Word and Will of the Lord" was not without meaning. Small counterfeit rings and illegal gambling were recurring problems, particularly on the east bank settlements as far removed from Church leadership as possible.[43] Robberies and worse were an unwelcome reality from time to time among a small number of malcontents. Little wonder Winter Quarters had its own police force. Yet these criminal activities were exceptions to the rule and were neither characteristic of nor condoned by the Latter-day Saints generally.

"The Word and Will of the Lord" also spoke of a new social order. The revelation certainly contributes to an understanding of why Brigham came to be regarded as their leader, even though the First Presidency, the presiding quorum of the Church, would not be reestablished for another ten months. Referred to respectfully as the "law of adoption," it may be as difficult for the modern Latter-day Saint reader to comprehend as it must be for those untutored in Mormon thought.

In essence the Latter-day Saints believed they were modern Israel, not merely symbolically but in actual fact. They represented more than a church or a mere collection of believers, but a newly chosen people of God, "modern Israel" destined to fulfil prophecy and prepare the way for Christ's millennial reign. As such they were related to ancient Israel, not merely doctrinally but literally, by lineage and by adoption, a modern remnant of the ancient covenant people of the Lord. Mormonism was as much an Old Testament covenant people in modern America as it was a restoration of New Testament priesthood authority, organization, and doctrine.[44]

In speaking of this, Helen Mar Kimball Whitney wrote:

> Our history is a wonder and a marvel to those who have taken the trouble to hunt us and review it in all its ups and downs. . . . And our experience, I think, comes nearest to that of the children of Israel after their departure out of the land of Egypt than any other people of whom we have record, though I believe we were a more patient people. . . . God has . . . brought us deliverance every time; and it is our wish and purpose to trust Him still.[45]

By at least the Nauvoo period, it was well understood that the restored priesthood was necessary not only for baptisms, confirmations, marriages, and other ordinances but also for a select number of sacred temple ordinances pertaining to the eternal salvation of the family unit. In the final few weeks leading up to their Nauvoo departure the previous winter, several thousand people had attended the yet uncompleted temple to make such covenants and to receive such blessings as would endow them and their families with the hope of an eternal reward. Husbands and wives were "sealed," or married, for time and all eternity according to the priesthood, dependent on their faith and personal obedience. In some cases several wives were sealed or married to one man. Children were sealed to their parents despite sickness and death, thereby making eternal family units. And in Nauvoo the practice of baptism for the dead had also been instituted. This and other saving temple ordinances were performed by proxy for deceased ancestors, forming an intergenerational link as far back as possible.

For those fortunate enough to have attended the Nauvoo Temple, it was all very wonderful. But for those others sick and perishing in the wilderness, what lay in store for them? And for those whose husbands and fathers were heading out with the Battalion to California, or for young couples wanting to marry before—or during—their westward pilgrimage, would temple blessings be denied them?

Brigham had given instructions while crossing Iowa that "with references to sealings there will be no such thing done until we build another temple. I have understood that some of the Twelve have held forth an idea that such things would be attended to in the wilderness but I say let no man hint such things from this time forth for we will not attend to sealings till another temple is built."[46]

Still, he was a man who listened to his people, particularly in their wilderness sufferings. So Willard Richards's octagon home, the Winter Quarters council house or "potato hut," became their prairie endowment house. There Brigham selectively and without fanfare sealed several couples in celestial marriage.[47]

Their understanding of how modern families could be recipients of the ancient blessings of the Abrahamic covenant and the patriarchal blessings of the House of Israel, after generations of disbelief and apostasy, was evolving. "Had the keys of the priesthood been retained and handed down from father to son throughout all generations up to the present time, then there would have been no necessity of the law of adoption," Brigham said, "for we would have all been included in the covenant without it."[48] Because an apostasy or religious falling away had interfered with such a blood link of ancestral faith, modern believers were required to receive their blessings through being "adopted" or grafted in—by being sealed to such Church leaders as Joseph Smith, Brigham Young, Heber C. Kimball, and others of the Twelve Apostles "who were entitled to the keys of the Priesthood according to blood."[49]

Unwilling to forfeit such blessings on an impending perilous journey, families everywhere stumbled over one another to be "sealed" into Brigham's family or that of another authority. Within a very few days of his proclaiming the doctrine, some 300 families—husbands and wives—were sealed into Brigham Young's family, 200 into Heber C. Kimball's, and fewer numbers into the families of other leaders.[50]

These adoptions affected their travels by causing a reorganization of the pioneer company, this time into two family divisions—Brigham Young's and Heber C. Kimball's. Once they reached their destinations, their new lands and inheritances would be divided by adopted family. Or, as Brigham put it, "When we locate I will settle my family down in the order and teach them their duty."[51] The essential point to grasp is that they would go as families, extended and expanded families, but families no less. Furthermore, the law of adoption also provided Brigham Young, Heber C. Kimball, Willard Richards and, to a lesser extent, the rest of the Apostles with personal, paternal, and spiritual authority and responsibility. This galvanized the entire migration, providing in the process a degree of moral persuasion and authority not easy to resist.[52]

While the doctrine of modern Israel still persists, the law of adoption, at least as a social order, lasted for only a short time. It was later abandoned as a clearer understanding of the doctrine of family salvation unfolded. In time the practice of being adopted into the families of Church leaders was replaced by performing saving temple work by proxy for one's direct ancestors and by a renewed emphasis on the importance of family history and genealogical research. But for a time, though poorly understood, the law of adoption provided promise and privilege, order and opportunity to a people in peril.[53]

"UNDER THE DIRECTION OF THE TWELVE APOSTLES"

The pioneer camp intended to leave Winter Quarters on 15 March, rendezvous at the Elkhorn some 30 miles west, and be on its way as soon as the first grass, certainly no later than 1 April. An early departure would ensure adequate time to cross the mountains and reach a secluded valley in time to plant late summer crops and build temporary shelter for the hundreds to follow later in the spring. Also, they would be assured of traveling at least two weeks ahead of the "Gentile" immigrant trains coming up the Blue River and the south side of the Platte. Considering the lingering animosities with Missourians, the less contact with them the better.

But they still needed the navigational instruments of travel since theirs would be as much expedition as emigration, a time to survey new routes, calculate distances, draw and revise maps, and make scientific observations and recommendations, particularly for future trains of Mormon immigrants. They would generally follow Fremont's recently published maps and the reports of his recent expeditions into the American west, as well as rely on Augustine Mitchell's maps of the area west of the Missouri. But they would often have to follow new or lesser-known trails along their intended line of march on the north, rather than the more popular south, bank of the Platte River.[54] Instruments would also be needed to survey their new settlement. Because the finest such instruments were then made in Europe, Parley P. Pratt and John Taylor were instructed to purchase them out of British tithing funds while they were in England and to bring them back upon their return from their missions in mid-March.

But all was late that spring of 1847. The weather was unseasonably cold and early grass grew weeks late. Companies were slow in organizing. Several men decided, or were asked, to go at the last moment, causing further delays. And Pratt and Taylor had too much to accomplish in England in too little time. They could not possibly make a return journey by sea and by land—over 10,000 miles—any sooner than the first week of April.

Nevertheless, everything was bustling by the third week of March. Teams and wagons were moving intermittently out to the Elkhorn to wait for further instruction. Unwilling to delay any longer, Kimball moved about four miles on 5 April with six of his teams and formed an encampment. The following day, Tuesday, 6 April, an unplanned conference convened in Winter Quarters to mark the seventeenth anniversary of the organization of the Church, but for little other reason than to buy time.[55]

On 7 April several other pioneers "started a few miles" and in the afternoon, somewhat reluctantly, Orson Pratt, Wilford Woodruff, and Brigham Young all left the city. "When we were on the top of the ridge west of the city," Wilford Woodruff recalled, "I took a view of the place and looked at my wife and children through my glass."[56] That night he and another 25 wagon loads camped together 10 miles west and suffered through a cold and a "very windy night."

Fortunately, the winds were on their side. The very next day, 8 April, about noon, Parley P. Pratt, Orson's older brother and fellow member of the Quorum of the Twelve, arrived in camp. Pratt had been blown across the Atlantic from Liverpool to New Orleans in only 35 days. He and John Taylor had deliberately sailed on different vessels in hope that at least one of them would make it back before the departure of the camp. From New Orleans Pratt had taken a steamer to St. Louis and from there had ridden horseback through the western Missouri countryside into Iowa, through the encampments at Garden Grove and Mt. Pisgah, and on to Winter Quarters.

After hearing of Pratt's return, Brigham and his colleagues rode back to Winter Quarters to confer with their weary colleague. They met in council through the night to discuss the troubled British mission and Pratt's and Taylor's successful efforts to repair matters by dismantling Hedlock's unauthorized emigration scheme. Pratt also hastened to inform his eager listeners that Taylor was somewhere close behind on the first spring steamer, bringing with him the needed scientific instruments, hundreds of letters, and 469 sovereigns of gold in tithing funds.

Five days later, at sunset on 13 April, the heavily burdened Taylor arrived at Winter Quarters, bringing with him two sextants, two barometers, two artificial horizons, one circle of reflection, several thermometers, a telescope, and the moneys.[57] The Council agreed that Brigham should have authority to dispense such funds as necessary. According to one published account, "We had much joy and satisfaction in hearing of their prosperity on their mission."[58]

Despite their happy reunion, the unpublished accounts indicate that not all was well. Parley P. Pratt was disappointed and concerned at how badly so many at Winter Quarters had fared the winter, his family most especially. "I found my family all alive and dwelling in a log cabin," Pratt would later write in his autobiography. He confessed privately, however, that they had

> suffered much from cold, hunger and sickness. They had oftentimes lived for several days on a little corn meal. . . . One of the family was then lying very sick with the scurvy—a disease which had been very prevalent in camp during the winter, and of which many had died. I found, on inquiry, that the winter had been very severe, the snow deep, and, consequently, that all my horses (four in number) were lost, and . . . out of twelve cows I had but seven left, and out of some twelve or fourteen oxen only four or five were spared.[59]

Whether Taylor's family had fared any better is not recorded, but both men, exhausted and anxious to spend time with their families, declined the invitation to join the pioneer camp. "They expressed an earnest wish for me to accompany them on the pioneer trip to the mountains," Pratt recorded, "but my circumstances seemed to forbid, and they did not press the matter."[60] Instead, they would come west in the spring migration and join up with the pioneers over the mountains later in the year.

The truth of the matter is that Brigham was deeply disturbed and profoundly disappointed in their decision to stay back. His primary concern—one that came to dominate his thinking during the impending westward migration—was the need to reorganize the First Presidency or presiding quorum of the Church. Unlike some of his colleagues, Brigham did not believe that government by the Apostles alone could possibly succeed in the long run. Though he believed that the authority to operate the Church had been given the Twelve by the Prophet Joseph Smith before his death, he did not see that active authority resting long within the Quorum of the Twelve alone.

If, as "The Word and Will of the Lord" proclaimed, they would travel "under the direction of the Twelve Apostles," then Brigham was determined that as much of the full quorum as possible go west, and this because their agenda included far more than finding a new resting place. At stake was the survival of the Church and nothing in that direction compared—in his mind at least—to the importance of establishing a new First Presidency.[61]

He felt the reconstruction of a new First Presidency would require the active support and consent of all members of the Quorum of the Twelve Apostles, or at least the great majority of them, most of whom at that time did not share his sense of urgency. With two defections from the quorum already, time was critical. Lyman Wight, that "wild ram of the mountains," had already bolted and gone south on his own to find a new Zion in Texas. John E. Page had gone with Strang. Orson Hyde, expected back from his mission to England later in the spring, would have to stay back at the Missouri to supervise later westward migrations. That left only Brigham Young, Heber C. Kimball, Willard Richards, Wilford Woodruff, Orson and Parley Pratt, George A. Smith, Erastus Snow, Ezra T. Benson, and John Taylor to carry out the business of the Church. And who knew what might happen to them in a dangerous wilderness?

Little wonder Brigham so strongly encouraged Pratt and Taylor to join the advance company. They were not needed for the later spring migrations, because Isaac Morley and Charles C. Rich had been assigned that task. Brigham's earnest expectation was that the pioneer camp, under the direction of all the Twelve, would find a new place, stake out a site for a new temple, and unanimously decide on reestablishing the First Presidency—home, temple, and priesthood government were all essential to the perma-

Lucy Mack Smith

nent reestablishment of the Church. Brigham wanted Pratt and Taylor to take part in all of these tasks.

There was one other individual they desperately wanted to come west and to show, by her support, the unity of the Church—Lucy Mack Smith, the aging matron of Mormonism and mother of the martyred Prophet. Recognizing that her time was short and fearful that the Smith family heritage might forever remain in the East and in the past, Brigham, amid his heavy schedule, still found time to dictate to his weary scribes the following plea:

> Mother Smith, we know not your particular situation only so far as God makes it manifest unto us but be assured of this that our faith and prayers have been and are and will be for your welfare. . . . There are now thousands and thousands upon thousands who are looking to us continually to open up a way for a shelter from the storm which is about to burst on a world of intelligent beings, who have almost forgotten their God and their Savior, and our time is occupied and our hands are full. [B]ut like our Divine Master we have a fulness and yet in his name and by his authority and by his power and by his wisdom we are ready and we are willing to receive all who wish to come. And if our dear Mother Smith should at any time wish to come where the Saints are . . . there is no sacrifice we will count too great to bring her forward and we ever have been, now are and shall continue to be ready to divide with her the last loaf.[62]

Alas, Lucy Smith, in declining health and under the care of her daughter-in-law, Emma Smith, chose not to go but to stay back to tend the graves of her husband and fallen sons.

It was not easy for any of the camps to say goodbye, either to those departing for an unknown wilderness or to those sick and restless ones remaining behind in poverty. It was a poignant moment of faith and fear, adventure and sacrifice. Erastus Snow confided that before blessing his wife, Artimesia, and his four children: "I loaded my wagon and prepared for starting. . . . I called my family together and dedicated them unto the Lord, and commanded them to serve the Lord with all their hearts, and cultivate peace and love, and hearken to the whisperings of the Holy Spirit and pray much; and inasmuch as they would do this they should have power over disease and death, and we should all meet again in the due time of the Lord."[63] Once all 148 members of the camp had kneeled down on the ground, Brigham "addressed the Lord by prayer and dedicated the mission and all we have to the Lord God of Israel."[64]

Tomorrow's highway lay before them.

NOTES

1. Doctrine and Covenants 45:71.

2. *Manuscript History of Brigham Young*, comp. Elden J. Watson (1971), 11 Jan. 1847. See also Richard E. Bennett, "Finalizing Plans for the Trek West: Deliberations at Winter Quarters, 1846–1847," *BYU Studies* 24 (Summer 1984): 301–20; reprinted in *Coming to Zion*, ed. James B. Allen and John W. Welch (Provo, Utah: BYU Studies, 1997), 98–125.

3. Brigham Young to the Nauvoo Trustees, 11 Sept. 1846, Brigham Young Papers.

4. Journal History, 6 Nov. 1846.

5. Doctrine and Covenants 136.

6. Journal History, 16 Jan. 1847.

7. Journal of Willard Richards, 15 Jan. 1847.

Heber C. Kimball commented further on the revelation. "A revelation was read which was the first one that has been penned since Joseph was killed," he wrote.

"The Lord has given it through the President for the good of this people as they are traveling to the west. Pres. Young said the difference between a revelation of God, a revelation of man and a revelation of the devil is this: in one of the devil you will always see some great and dark thing which you cannot understand, and in a revelation of man you will always see the man sticking out in it, but one that cometh from God is always plain and suited to the present condition of the people" (Journal of Heber C. Kimball, 19 Jan. 1847).

8. For a fuller study of this colorful personality who eventually affiliated with Lyman Wight in Texas and later with James Strang at Beaver Island, Michigan, see Richard Bennett, "'A Samaritan Had Passed By': George Miller—Mormon Bishop, Trailblazer, and Brigham Young Antagonist," *Illinois Historical Journal* 82, no. 1 (Spring 1989): 2–16. See also Richard E. Bennett, "Mormon Renegade: James Emmett at the Vermillion, 1846," *South Dakota History* 15, no. 3 (Fall 1985): 217–33. For a more sympathetic study of Emmett, see William G. Hartley, *My Best for the Kingdom: History and Autobiography of John Lowe Butler, a Mormon Frontiersman* (1993), 135–230.

9. *Diary of Hosea Stout,* 29 Oct. 1846, 1:208.

10. Bennett, *Mormons at the Missouri,* 150–53. One possible reason for examining the Niobrara alternative to the Platte River Valley was the fact that they would not have to compete with the expected large number of Oregon and California emigrants who were already preparing their western departures in the spring of 1847. There was a real sentiment to stay as far away from other overlanders as possible.

11. For more on the Council of Fifty, see Klaus J. Hansen, *Quest for Empire: The Political Kingdom of God and the Council of Fifty in Mormon History* (1967). See also Michael D. Quinn, "The Council of Fifty and Its Members, 1844 to 1945," *BYU Studies* 20 (Winter 1980): 163–97.

12. Journal History, 17 Jan. 1847.

13. *Diary of Hosea Stout,* 14 Jan. 1847, 1:229.

14. H. W. Mills, "De Tal Palo Tal Astilla," in *Historical Society of Southern California Annual Publications* 10 (1917): 111–12.

15. Journal of Joseph Fielding, Spring 1847, 5:126, LDS Church Archives.

16. Doctrine and Covenants 136:2–3, 5, 7.

17. Doctrine and Covenants 136:8. This was a reiteration of the October 1845 Nauvoo Covenant, Brigham Young's unending call and preoccupation that the poor have as good a chance at emigration as those with more provisions.

18. Journal of Horace K. Whitney, 29 Jan. 1847, LDS Church Archives.

19. See Orson F. Whitney, *History of Utah,* 4 vols. (1892–1904), 1:298–305; John Henry Evans, *One Hundred Years of Mormonism: A History of The Church of Jesus Christ of Latter-day Saints from 1805 to 1905* (1909), 440; *Comprehensive History of the Church,* 3:163; and E. Cecil McGavin, *The Mormon Pioneers* (1947), 176.

20. Journal of Norton Jacob, 1 Mar. 1847.

21. The return of Luke S. Johnson to the Church in late 1846 was particularly well received by the members. Born in Vermont in 1807, Johnson was baptized in 1831 by Joseph Smith and served several early missions to Ohio, Pittsburgh, Virginia, Kentucky, New York, and Upper Canada. A highly successful missionary and beloved by many, he was ordained an Apostle in the original Quorum of Twelve in February 1835. Later, however, during the Kirtland difficulties, he alienated himself from Joseph Smith and was excommunicated in December 1838. He studied medicine before returning to the Church at Nauvoo, where he was rebaptized by Orson Hyde on 8 March 1846. He died in Salt Lake City in 1861 (Lyndon Cook, *The Revelations of the Prophet Joseph Smith: A Historical and Biographical Commentary of the Doctrine and Covenants* [1981], 110–11).

Commenting on Johnson's return and arrival in Winter Quarters, Helen Mar Kimball Whitney wrote the following in December 1846: "Meeting was held at the stand. Brother Luke Johnson was present. He had just come on—had buried his wife at St. Joseph. There was quite a rejoicing among the old Kirtland saints to see Bro. Luke Johnson among them again" (Whitney, in *Women's Exponent,* 1 Mar. 1885, 151).

22. Harold Schindler, *Orrin Porter Rockwell: Man of God, Son of Thunder* (1983), 74–80. Return Jackson Redden, a rough and ready former riverboat worker and body-guard to Joseph Smith, although only 29 years old in 1847, already had a reputation. Later that year, Jim Bridger accused him of passing counterfeit money. He died in 1891.

23. Journal of Nelson Wheeler Whipple, 25 Feb. 1846, LDS Church Archives.

"We thus kept a sharp look out for them for we knew as they had slain Joseph and Hyrum so they would slay Brigham, Heber, and the Twelve if they could."

24. Tom Brown and Return Jackson Redden were of the same notorious crowd as Bill Hickman, Judson Stoddard, Nathaniel Levitt, and Caleb Ellsworth, who all had stained reputations as horse thieves or worse in the upper Missouri valley. "Something has to be done with these men or we shall all be thrown up," complained Orson Hyde the following spring. Convinced that they were the worst of thieves, Hyde, known for his excitability, was told by Brigham to calm down and wait for conclusive evidence. Tell the Saints "to smooth down those angry feelings that are strolling about you," Brigham said (Orson Hyde to Brigham Young, 11 Mar. 1848, and Brigham Young to Orson Hyde, 14 Mar. 1848, Brigham Young Papers).

For insight into Bill Hickman's reputation, see Joseph Young to Brigham Young, 26 June 1848; Brigham Young Papers.

25. McGavin, *The Mormon Pioneers*, 176–77. Lorenzo S. Young died in 1924, the last survivor of the pioneer camp. Isaac Perry Decker died in 1916. See Andrew Jenson, "Day by Day with the Utah Pioneers," *Deseret News*, 25 June 1947. See also "History of the 1847 Pioneer Companies," *Deseret News 1997–1998 Church Almanac* (1996), 114–59.

A reluctant convert to plural marriage, Brigham took as his first plural wife Lucy Ann Decker in 1842. The following year Harriet Cook and Augusta Adams were added to his family and in 1844, Clarissa Decker, sister of Lucy Ann. By the time he left Nauvoo in February 1846, 26 women had been sealed to him, many of whom were widows or older women whom he merely cared for or gave the protection of his name.

For an excellent study of his family life, see Dean C. Jessee, "Brigham Young's Family: The Wilderness Years," in *The Exodus and Beyond: Essays in Mormon History*, ed. Lyndon W. Cook and Donald Q. Cannon (1980), 24–48.

26. See Clara Decker Young, "A Woman's Experiences with the Pioneer Band," *Utah Historical Quarterly* 14 (1946): 173–76. See also *Comprehensive History of the Church*, 3:163–64, and Jenson, "Day by Day with the Utah Pioneers," *Deseret News*, 10 Apr. 1947.

Ellen Sanders Kimball was born in Ten, Thelemarken, Norway in 1824 and died near Salt Lake City in 1871. Harriet Page Wheeler Decker Young was born in Hillsborough, New Hampshire, in 1803 and also died in 1871 in Salt Lake City. Clara Decker Young, born in Freedom, New York, in 1828 died in Salt Lake City in 1889.

Roberts, in speaking of these special provisions, which if they caused any charges of favoritism are never mentioned in any contemporary account, argues nevertheless that "it speaks well for the discipline of the people that the rule that men only should constitute the Pioneer company, thus infringed, was not further violated."

27. See Stanley B. Kimball, *Heber C. Kimball: Mormon Patriarch and Pioneer* (1981).

28. Whitney, *Utah*, 1:302.

29. They intended that a minimum of half, preferably "7/8" of the Battalion families be taken west later that spring, even if husbands of other families had to leave their own families and take over those "who are in the army" (Journal of Willard Richards, 12 Feb. 1847; see also Journal History, 25 Jan. 1847).

30. Thomas Bullock to John Brown, 6 Nov. 1847, Brigham Young Papers.

31. *Autobiography of Pioneer John Brown, 1820–1896*, arr. John Zimmerman Brown

(1941), 72–73. See also Jenson, "Day by Day," *Deseret News*, 31 May 1947. Lay and Crosby later died in California. Flake lived in Salt Lake City for most of his life, dying in Idaho Falls in 1903 at the age of 75.

    Although slavery was countenanced by the early Mormon pioneers as the legal right of southern members, most converts were New Englanders, not inclined to condone the practice. Orson Hyde's attitude was representative:

    "A respectable minority of the citizens of the Salt Lake Valley are Southern men, and have their slaves with them, but as our creed teaches us more the principle of holding men, either white, red or black by moral power than by any legal ties, it matters little to us whether slavery or abolitionism prevail" (Orson Hyde, Ezra T. Benson, and George A. Smith to the First Presidency, 12 June 1849; Brigham Young Papers).

    See also Newell G. Bringhurst, *Saints, Slaves, and Blacks: The Changing Place of Black People within Mormonism* (1981), chapters 1–4.

    32. Journal of Wilford Woodruff, 12 Feb. 1847.

    33. The perilous, frightful journey of John Harvey Tippets and Thomas Woolsey belongs in that category of western American history reserved for the incredible and heroic. Their overland journey was fraught with danger and hardship. Several times they almost perished from the cold or from starvation only to stumble on deserted wigwams or wandering buffalo at the most propitious moments. A faithful pair, they attributed their preservation to divine providence. One entry, written by Tippets, from somewhere on the Platte on 17 January 1847 is indicative of their experiences.

    "We rode till two o'clock when we saw the wind a long ways ahead of us it meeting in the face and was so cold and blew so hard we had to get off from our mules and get down in the grass we sat awhile it grew so cold we dare not stay no longer for there was no wood in sight nor within our knowledge we see we must find wood or freeze to death. . . . It turned cold so fast that it froze over 12 feet of water in twenty minutes the prospect of freezing to death was very fair for us and our animals our minds was filled with serious and melancholy meditations fearing it might be the last night with us. . . . But considering there was a God and his goodness extended to them who loved him we took a bite to eat and laid down our buffaloes and blankets. . . . After lying down went to sleep being kindly preserved by our father in heaven in answer to our prayer . . . I thought of home I thought of wife and our children I thought of the church I thought of the Twelve I thought of the Priesthood I thought of my [temple] garments" (Journal of Harvey Tippets, 17 Jan. 1847, LDS Church Archives).

    34. Doctrine and Covenants 136:31.

    35. *Diary of Hosea Stout*, 15 Dec. 1846, 1:218.

    36. Ibid.

    37. Doctrine and Covenants 136:18.

    38. Journal of Willard Richards, 18 Jan. 1847.

    39. Ibid., 20 Dec. 1846.

    40. Journal of Mary Haskin Parker Richards, 20 Dec. 1846.

    41. Journal of Willard Richards, 20 Dec. 1846.

    42. Journal of Willard Richards, 14 Mar. 1847. It is interesting to note that in the dreams which Brigham Young said he had of Joseph Smith while preparing for the exodus, Joseph "stepped toward me, and looking very earnestly, yet pleasantly, said 'Tell the people to be humble and faithful, and be sure to keep the spirit of the Lord and it will lead them right. . . . Tell the brethren to keep their hearts open to

conviction, so that when the Holy Ghost comes to them, their hearts will be ready to receive it'" (Journal History, 23 Feb. 1847).

In a second, similar dream recorded almost ten days later, Brigham asked Joseph about the sealing powers and the law of adoption. Joseph said to "tell the brethren that it is all important for them to keep the spirit of the Lord" (*Diary of Hosea Stout*, 28 Feb. 1847, 1:238).

43. Minutes of the Pottawattamie High Council, 3 July 1847, LDS Church Archives. Counterfeiting seemed to be the biggest problem among a small cell of noted criminals. "If I had been governed by the spirits of some who claim to be orthodox saints or Mormons," Hyde later indicated, "I could have had a hell for you to come to from the Great Salt Lake" (Orson Hyde to Brigham Young, 27 Apr. 1848; Brigham Young Papers).

44. Jan Shipps, *Mormonism: The Story of a New Religious Tradition* (1985).

45. Whitney, in *Women's Exponent*, 1 May 1884, 182; originally written 15 June 1846. Much of what Helen Whitney wrote was commentary to the splendid unpublished journal of her husband, Horace K. Whitney.

John D. Lee said much the same thing, deferentially referring to their doctrine of modern Israel: "We are sojourning to a land west not knowing whether they go just as it was with the ancient covenant people of the Lord. Hence we have taken upon [us] the same appelation because we follow their steps when they were led by the Spirit of the Lord. Their paths were strait and difficult to tread in—and so it is for us" (Journal of John D. Lee, 7 June 1846).

46. Journal of John D. Lee, 9 Aug. 1846.

47. Journal of Willard Richards, 24 Jan. 1847. See also Bennett, *Mormons at the Missouri*, 188–90.

48. Journal of John D. Lee, 16 Feb. 1847.

49. See D&C 86:8–10.

50. "I had application made to me to receive a man and his wife into my family," recorded John D. Lee, himself an adopted member of Brigham Young's family. "After speaking freely upon the Law of Adoption, I accepted James Woolsey and Sevina his wife into my family by the Law of Adoption, he choosing to retain his surname for the present and to have mine named upon him. This, however, was a prerogative that I gave to him" (Journal of John D. Lee, 11 Jan. 1846).

51. Journal of Wilford Woodruff, 16 Feb. 1847.

52. Brigham Young himself did not claim to understand fully the law of adoption, nor did he feel he had to. In mid-February 1847 he reported on a second dream in which he again conversed with Joseph Smith and "was very anxious to know about the law of adoption, and the sealing power." Joseph said to tell the people one thing: "That it is all important for them to keep the Spirit of the Lord. . . . When the still small voice speaks always receive it, and if the people will do these things, when they come up to the Father, all will be as in the beginning, and every person stand as at the first. [He] saw how we were organized before we took tabernacles and every man will be restored to what he had then, and all will be satisfied."

Brigham concluded: "I want you all to remember my dream for I know it is a vision of God and was revealed through the spirit of Joseph" (Minutes of the Winter Quarters High Council, 28 Feb. 1847, LDS Church Archives. Brigham said his dream had actually occurred a few days earlier, on 24 February).

53. For a fuller explanation of the law of adoption in Mormon history, see Bennett, *Mormons at the Missouri*, 190–94. See also Gordon Irving, "The Law of Adoption: One Phase of the Development of the Mormon Concept of Salvation, 1830–1900," *BYU Studies* 14, no. 3 (Spring 1974): 291–314.

It should be noted, however, that as early as Nauvoo the Saints had begun to recognize the value of temple ordinance work for deceased ancestors. Some in Nauvoo before the exodus and others along the way were constant in writing nonmember family members for genealogical information. "I wish you would get the births and deaths of all our kindred," Isaac Rogers wrote to his son, Lester Rogers, then living in Waterford, Connecticut. "And if you cannot get all their births, get all their deaths. Get all the Rogers, Leuters, Tinkers and Bebees [family names]. . . . You will have to go to the Bibles and to the graveyards. It is of great consequence. I wish you would go to the oldest men living and see how near you can get back to John Rogers [who was] burned at the stake" (Isaac Rogers to his son, Lester T. Rogers, 19 July 1846).

54. Carl I. Wheat, in his study *Mapping the Transmississippi West, 1540–1860* (1959), has argued that the Mormons utilized the recently available Mitchell map. Contemporary evidence fully supports his view as well as his argument that they made use of the map of the road to Oregon by Preuss, Fremont's brilliant cartographer (see Wheat, 3:31–32).

55. One important item of business conducted at this unexpected conference was the sustaining of Brigham Young as "President of the Church and of the Twelve Apostles" (*Manuscript History of Brigham Young*, 6 Apr. 1847, 546). This action should not be confused with the later reorganization of the First Presidency in December 1847. The action taken here was merely to recognize formally Brigham Young's position as senior member of the Quorum of the Twelve Apostles. As Woodruff explained: "We met in public conference this morning in Winter Quarters. Not much business was done. . . . The conference voted to sustain the Quorum of the Twelve in their place, the Presidents of the Seventies, the Bishops, etc." (Journal of Wilford Woodruff, 6 Apr. 1847).

56. Journal of Wilford Woodruff, 7 Apr. 1847.

57. *Manuscript History of Brigham Young*, 13 Apr. 1847, 548. In comparison, John C. Fremont, for his 1843–1844 expedition to Oregon and California, had brought along the finest instruments available for that era, most of which were likewise from Europe. His package included one refracting telescope, one reflecting circle, two sextants, two pocket chronometers, one syphon barometer, one cistern barometer, six thermometers, and a number of small compasses (*The Expeditions of John Charles Frémont*, ed. Donald Jackson and Mary Lee Spencer, 2 vols. [1973], 1:428). The favorable comparison between Fremont and the Latter-day Saint camp gives credence to the argument that the exodus was as much expedition as it was emigration.

58. *Manuscript History of Brigham Young*, 13 Apr. 1847, 548.

59. Journal History, 8 Apr. 1847; see also Parley P. Pratt, *Autobiography of Parley P. Pratt* (1938), 357.

60. Journal History, 8 Apr. 1847.

61. Samuel Taylor argues in his controversial book *The Kingdom or Nothing: The Life of John Taylor, Militant Mormon* (1976) that both Taylor and Pratt had married plural wives during their return voyages, which was further cause of Brigham's unhappiness. If such was indeed the case, it only represented the conviction in fellow

apostles' minds that they were all equal in authority, while underscoring Brigham's concern that until a new First Presidency was established, regulation of this and other practices was virtually impossible to control.

62. Brigham Young for the Council of the Twelve to Lucy Mack Smith, 4 Apr. 1847, Brigham Young Papers.

63. Journal of Erastus Snow, 6 Apr. 1847, as printed in *Utah Humanities Review* 2, no. 2 (Apr. 1948): 107.

64. Journal of Norton Jacob, 16 Apr. 1847.

3

"A GREAT
AMERICAN DESERT"

Here was an immense wilderness of arid plains,
rugged mountains, and burning deserts, to be crossed
before you reached Oregon or California.[1]

The well-traveled reader of the late 20th century may find it difficult to identify with the uncertainties, perils, and personal sacrifices characteristic of a mid-19th century march across the vast
trans-Mississippi west, which Stephen H. Long termed the Great American
Desert.[2] Overland immigrants were risking their fortunes and their very
lives on a journey to an unseen new somewhere. Some went on to fortune
and a new life; others turned back or died in the attempt.

For Brigham Young and the Latter-day Saint pioneers, even more was
at stake. The future of the Church was in danger if they were routed by
Indians or by Missouri discontents, especially if the leadership were killed,
or if they were unable to find a suitable place. This was not a group of individuals bent on fulfilling their personal needs and dreams as much as it was
an organization making an expression of faith. The destiny of the Church
would go in those wagons, in queen bee fashion, in search of a distant hive.
Nothing was certain.

Also uncertain was what would happen to the hundreds of families
planning to start their trip in May if the advance company were to fail in its
objective: Salvation or starvation? Discovery or dissolution? For them all

there were a thousand questions and very few answers. And the ante was up as never before.

The purpose of this chapter is to review briefly the changing dynamics of the American West on the eve of the Mormon departure, to evaluate the dangers and risks, and to try to recreate the tenor of the time.

THE ENDING OF AN ERA

As the vanguard companies rolled west, they saw several wagons laden with fur belonging to Peter B. Sarpy, longtime trader of the American Fur Company, en route from the Pawnee hunting grounds to his post at Bellevue, near Council Bluffs.[3] Though trade for deer, buffalo, raccoon, and other skins endured for a few more years, Sarpy's wagons symbolized the twilight of an era—a symbolic exit from a colorful stage, for years dominated by the Spanish, French and British fur companies, and mountain men.

By 1847 the great fur trade era in the western wilds of North America was in steep decline after a half century when furs had defined the history and economy of the American West. It had been the fur trader, as historian Ray Billington put it, who had

> spied out the secrets of all the West, plotted the course of its rivers, discovered the passes through its mountains, and prepared the way for settlers by breaking down Indian self-sufficiency. No single group contributed more to the conquest of the trans-Mississippi region than those eager profit seekers.[4]

Though the Spanish had been trading with the Plains Indians since before 1700, the fur trade era in American history began in earnest the moment President Thomas Jefferson signed the Louisiana Purchase in 1804. This compact with Napoleon, in one stroke of a pen, doubled the land mass of America by adding the area from the

A New Map of Texas, Oregon and California
(1846), by S. Augustus Mitchell

96

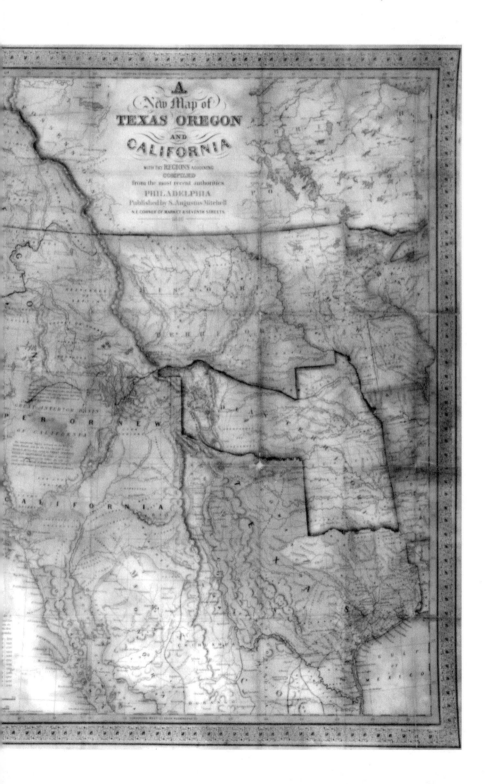

Mississippi Valley to the Rocky Mountains. The subsequent expedition of Meriwether Lewis and William Clark in 1805–1806 to the mouth of the Columbia River and back to St. Louis proved the existence of navigable waterways to the great Northwest and thus the viability of a profitable fur trade with Europe.

Within a year of the return of Lewis and Clark, Manuel Lisa, a Spanish explorer turned American trader, set out on the first of his many fur-trading expeditions up the Missouri to the Yellowstone River. Lisa was directly responsible for the establishment of the short-lived St. Louis Missouri Fur Company, soon reorganized in 1814 as the Missouri Fur Company. At a time when the two great Canadian rivals—the Hudson's Bay Company and the Northwest Company—were jockeying for control among native tribes all across Prince Rupert's Land (western Canada) and south into the yet ill-defined American northwest, Lisa was instrumental in preventing the Plains Indians from aligning themselves with the expanding British and French-Canadian interests.

But mismanagement, undercapitalization, and Indian hostility, especially among the Blackfoot and the Sioux, spelled the demise of Lisa's enterprise. In its wake, Jacob Astor's American Fur Company, begun in 1808, planned a series of forts across the West to capture the fur trade and dominate markets of the Far East, halting his aggressive Canadian rivals in the process. His famous post on the Columbia, Astoria, was a blatant challenge that American interests would take on any and all competitors.

The War of 1812 interrupted the American challenge, however. For a generation the Canadians dominated, especially after the merger of the Hudson's Bay and Northwest Companies in 1821 under the brilliant administration of Governor George Simpson and such able superintendents as John McLoughlin. In turn, McLoughlin hired a team of intrepid explorers and traders, including the man who discovered the Great Salt Lake in 1825—Peter Skene Ogden.

Henry Ashley, founder of the new Rocky Mountain Company, chose new tactics and new territories. Rather than erect a series of forts that would only irritate the natives and invite attack, and rather than rely on Indians who were better hunters than trappers anyway, Ashley hit on a new idea—the rendezvous system. The plan called for his own trappers to ply the high mountain streams for beaver in the safer central Rockies, cache or seclude their winnings, and then, heavily laden, rendezvous once or twice a year at a downstream site with caravans from St. Louis. At such spirited gatherings, pelts and skins would be exchanged for presents, guns, powder, flour, clothing, and more to trade with the tribes. Jedediah Smith, Thomas Fitzpatrick, James Bridger, Milton Sublette, and Robert Campbell, names now synonymous with the Rocky Mountain West, were just some of the mountain men who made the new system succeed. Rendezvous sites they set up included Fort Pierre and Fort William (later renamed Fort Laramie).

Jedediah Smith, perhaps the most famous of all fur trappers, joined Ashley in 1822. A legend in his own time, this "Knight of the Buckskin" opened the first two overland routes to California—from South Pass to Los Angeles and from the San Joaquin through central Nevada to the Great Salt Lake. He was the first to travel the Pacific coast from San Diego to the Columbia and drew the first maps of the central Rockies and of the Great Basin. Killed in 1831 at the age of 32 by Comanche warriors, Jedediah Smith remains a human monument to the era of the Mountain man.[5] In 1834 the Rocky Mountain Company sold its interests to the American Fur Company, which soon dominated the American fur trade through its monopoly on trappers, steamboats, and the liquor trade among the natives.

By the 1840s, with European prices for beaver hats and fur-trimmed outerwear declining, and with the number of fur-bearing animals diminishing, the fur trade was in clear decline—just as the era of overland migrations was beginning in earnest. Courageous missionaries, such as Marcus Whitman and his wife, Narcissa, had made it all the way to Oregon's Willamette Valley, signaling a grand new country open for settlement. The subsequent rise in "Oregon Fever" throughout the Missouri and Mississippi Valleys was directly proportional to the business collapse or "Panic of 1837." This economic disaster, coupled with poor transportation networks and inadequate living quarters in frontier communities, motivated many farmers in Illinois, Missouri, and other western states to head to Oregon for a new life.

Colonel John C. Fremont, that "Pathfinder of the West," embarked on his famous explorations of the Rocky Mountain West in 1842. In 1843 and 1844 he pushed on to Oregon and California in search of passageways through the West, exploring the Platte River Valley, the Sweetwater, and other routes. In immediate demand, his detailed summaries were studied by almost every overland company after 1842. In 1842 the migration was only a trickle, but a thousand followed in 1843 and another three thousand in

The Rocky Mountains, *by A. C. Warren*

1845, greatly strengthening America's claim to Oregon in the face of McLoughlin's benign opposition. Facing the reality of a strong and vigorous American settlement, Britain agreed to sign the Oregon treaty in June 1846, securing for the United States the 49th parallel for a northern boundary. Manifest Destiny was in the air and the West was America's to own.

Meanwhile, in the Southwest, the Spanish influence had been on the wane for decades. Mexico had declared its independence from Spain in 1821. Shortly thereafter the famous Santa Fe Trail opened the Southwest from St. Louis to Santa Fe. Etienne Provost is still regarded as one of the foremost traders and explorers of the area. In 1845, Texas declared its independence from Mexico, becoming its own republic for a short time before affiliating with the Union. Within a year, the U.S. and Mexico were at war; the Americans hoisted the Stars and Stripes over New Mexico in March 1847 and over California by that summer.

Overridden and then overlooked, scorned and then scattered in the rising rush of American migration were the many Indian tribes east of the

Mississippi—the Choctaw, Cherokee, Sauk and Fox, Chippewa, Iowa, Ponca, Omaha, and others. These were removed from their homelands and forced to live within the ill-defined borders of the Great American Desert and to fend for themselves against indigenous native populations and oncoming settlers. Such enforced deportation fanned bitter warfare, sickness, and disease. Some of the Plains tribes, particularly the Sioux, blamed the fur trappers and the new emigrants for the outbreak of a devastating smallpox epidemic in 1837, a scourge that wiped out some 15,000 Sioux and many in other tribes. They also blamed the fur companies for establishing the ruinous liquor trade, for introducing overland emigration with its damage to the Platte and other river valleys, and for the decline of the buffalo on the great plains.

As early as 1841 the Ogalala Sioux warned D. E. White and other emigrant parties not to pass through their lands. The threat of hostilities became so grave by 1845 that President Polk dispatched Colonel Stephen W. Kearny up the Platte with a large company of dragoons to quiet the tribes and to threaten retaliation for any attack on emigrant trains. And in 1847, Marcus and Narcissa Whitman and several others were killed in an Indian uprising in Oregon. The Latter-day Saints were about to enter an American West where the culture and economy were in rapid transformation and where the Indian tribes were increasingly defensive, restless, and volatile, themselves an unwitting party to the coming tide of American Manifest Destiny.[6]

A LAND UNKNOWN

The dangers and risks of an overland migration in 19th-century America cannot be overestimated. Merrill J. Mattes, one of America's most respected historians of the westward migrations, measured the cost of overland travel:

Here was an immense wilderness of arid plains, rugged mountains, and burning deserts, to be crossed before you reached Oregon or California. Aside from thirst and starvation, there were other perils lurking to strike down the emigrants—drownings at river crossings, getting run over by wagon wheels, caught in a stampede of oxen or trampled by onrushing buffalo, killed—or worse, yet, captured—

by Indians, afflicted with Asiatic cholera, smallpox, mumps, measles, or scurvy, getting stabbed or shot by a fellow emigrant, or more often accidentally shooting yourself through carelessness or dying from fatigue and exposure.

Mattes concluded that between 1845 and 1870, as many as 10,000 emigrants lost their lives: an average of five graves every mile.[7]

The most obvious intimidating factor and an absolute barrier to thousands was geography—first a desert, then a mountainous wall. Since Zebulon M. Pike's early expeditions of 1806–1807 through present day Kansas, Colorado, Texas, New Mexico, and beyond, Americans had been reading about vast "internal deserts" stretching between the Missouri and the Pacific. Lamenting the aridity of the area, the lack of plant production and the barren soils, Pike compared the region to the "sandy deserts of Africa . . . on which not a speck of vegetable matter existed."[8] In 1819, E. Dana observed in his book, *Geographical Sketches on the Western Country*, that the whole prairie region "is a wild waste, in a manner devoid of wood or water."[9]

This concept of a desert wasteland gained even wider credibility in the writings of Stephen H. Long, who had led a well-appointed expedition westward from Council Bluffs along the Platte River Valley in 1819–1820. His four-month tour of the plains, the most exhaustive scientific expedition up until that time, led him to conclude that the entire region was "a Great American Desert," inhospitable, uninhabitable, and an absolute barrier to civilization.[10] The domain of the wolf, the rattlesnake, and the Indian, the American West was a fearful and uninviting wilderness.

By the 1840s, however, it was becoming more well-known that crossing the plains was not impossible. In fact, the Platte River Valley probably afforded the most direct route west to the Pacific. Furthermore, explorers had indicated that the north bank of the Platte River was likely the most desirable route. The first fur traders of record to use the north bank route were four men led by Thomas Fitzpatrick in 1824 on their way east from South Pass. Missionaries, including the Whitmans and Eliza Spalding, followed the same route in 1835 and 1836. However, in 1847 the only acceptable maps of the region were Augustine S. Mitchell's and John C. Fremont's, both of which left large areas uncharted and were particularly deficient in distance calculations. That the Mormons would utilize the work of both cartographers is obvious; seeking to improve on them became one of their primary objectives.

Nothing in their experience with American geography, not even the Alleghenies or the rugged Appalachians, could have adequately prepared the pioneers for the sheer heights and depths of the Rocky Mountains. One wrong step and a wagon team could meet with instant disaster. Winter could come on early and unexpectedly in the high altitudes. Word of just such a disaster—the ill-fated Donner party—had already reached the Missouri River by February 1847. This group chose the southern or Hastings Cutoff route (see chapter 7) through the Great Basin and over the high Sierra, and then met with tragedy, death, and terror late in the fall of 1846.

"MORMON STORIES"

Of even greater concern to the Latter-day Saints than desert or mountain was the possibility of armed conflict along the way. They knew they were not the only ones preparing to head west that fateful spring of 1847. Scores of other companies were preparing for their own journeys west from various jumping-off places further south along the Missouri River.[11] Mormons and Gentiles would have to share the Platte River road all the way west, although the Latter-day Saints planned to use the less-traveled north bank route and get a good jump on the coming spring migrations. John D. Unruh, in his classic study of westward migration, estimates that as many as 4,450 headed west in 1847, the largest annual migration up to that time.[12]

Bound more for the green valleys of Oregon than for the yet-to-be-discovered gold mines of California, most of the other 1847 overlanders hailed from Illinois and Missouri. One of the year's largest trains, the "Chicago company" headed by Thomas Cox and Joel Palmer, boasted 99 wagons, 400 persons, and a wide assortment of professionals, tradesmen, and common laborers. "I think that camp was a good average of the pioneers of 1847," remembered Ralph C. Geer at a later reunion of his Oregon pioneer associates.

> We had preachers with their bibles and psalm books, doctors with their medicine chests, lawyers with their law books, school teachers, . . . merchants with their goods, nurserymen with their

trees and seeds, stockmen with their fine horses and cattle, millers, millmen, millwrights, wheelwrights, carpenters, cabinet makers with their chest of tools, blacksmiths with anvils, bellows, hammers and tongs ready and willing to do all kinds of repairing at any time and place, gunsmiths and silversmiths with their fine tools, tailors . . . , shoemakers with the lasts, awls, hammers and bristles, saddlers with their tools, dressmakers and milliners with their needles, thimbles and patterns, . . . and . . . farmers with and without families . . . ; all determined to go to Oregon.[13]

However, many also carried with them a suspicious and nagging fear of Mormon leaders and their intentions, particularly of their rumored alliances with western Indian tribes in order to wreak havoc on the plains. Wrote G. M. Goddard in Clay County, Missouri, in May 1846: "There is a great deal of excitement here about the [Mexican] war, as we are near the frontier. The people are afraid of the Mormons and Indians. The Mormons are persuading the Indians to embrace their doctrines and then use them to annoy the Missourians."[14]

Many such rumors circulated widely and in vivid detail, colorful enough to scare any would-be traveler. One particularly notable story then making the rounds was that

a party of Mormons in spangled crimson robes of office headed by one in black velvet and silver, had been teaching a Jewish pow-wow to the medicine men of the Sauks and Foxes. Another averred that they were going about in buffalo robe, short frocks, imitative of the costume of Saint John, preaching baptism and the existence of the Kingdom of Heaven among the Ioways. To believe one report, ammunition and whisky had been received by the Indian braves at the hand of an elder with a flowing white beard, who spoke Indian, he alleged, because he had the gift of tongues, this as far north as the country of the Yanketon Sioux. According to another . . . the Mormons had distributed the scarlet uniforms of H.B.M.'s [Her British Majesty's] servants among the Pottawattamies and had carried into the country twelve pieces of brass cannons, which were counted by a traveller as they were rafted across the east fork of Grand River.[15]

Since 1832, Mormon efforts to establish their Zion headquarters at Independence, Missouri (a major Oregon Trail departure site on the

Missouri River), and their simultaneous attempts to convert the Indians (in Book of Mormon parlance, the Lamanites, descendants of ancient Israel) had been misinterpreted and misunderstood, even among Latter-day Saints themselves. Volumes have been written on the failure of that enterprise and on the subsequent years of bloodshed between a rough and tumble frontier population set on resisting Mormon migration and expelling the Indians and a zealous religious people determined to fulfil prophecy.[16] The line of misunderstanding and violence stretched all the way from the massacre at Haun's Mill to the door of Carthage Jail six years later. Hatred and fear still filled the air and cast a pall of suspicion and animosity over their respective westward movements.

The forced exodus from Nauvoo had spawned a whirlwind of speculation and distrust. Edwin Bryant, while waiting at Independence in May 1846 for his company's departure, wrote of "the various rumors connected with the several expeditions. One of these," he later recorded,

> was that five thousand Mormons were crossing, or had crossed, the Kansas river; that they marched with ten brass fieldpieces, and that every man of the party was armed with a rifle, a bowie-knife, and a brace of large revolving pistols. It was declared that they were inveterately hostile to the emigrant parties; and when the latter came up to the Mormons, they intended to attack and murder them, and appropriate to themselves their property.[17]

Francis Parkman, a well-known writer of his day on a fact-finding mission among the Plains Indians in 1846, further fanned the fires of apprehension. "At St. Joseph's," he said, "the prevailing impression was, that these were Mormons, 2300 in number, and a great alarm was excited in consequence. The people of Illinois and Missouri," he continued,

> who composed by far the greater part of the emigrants, have never been on the best terms with the "Latter Day Saints"; and it is notorious throughout the country how much blood has been spilt in their feuds. . . . No one could predict what would be the result when large armed bodies of these fanatics should encounter the most impetuous and reckless of their old enemies on the broad prairie, far beyond the reach of law or military force.[18]

Even neutral travelers soon picked up on the anti-Mormon rhetoric of the time. Phebe Stanton, while on the road just east of St. Joseph, Missouri, in early May 1847 noticed that "there is a great deal said about the Mormons. They say they have gone on and joined three tribes of Indians," she recounted in a letter to her sisters,

> and are going to cut us all off. They are raising a company of volunteers, and 300 have volunteered to go and guard us through. . . . We are asked a great many times if we are Mormons. When we tell them 'no' they say 'I know you are, but you won't own it. Your wagons look like it.' And then they will say, 'I hope you are not; for their road is marked with stolen property and all manner of wickedness.' We could not get any kind of accommodations if we were known to be Mormons. Some would tell us the Mormons will rob you before you get half way through; but we are not afraid of them. We tell them there is a great deal done on their credit.[19]

It was significant how little authentic intelligence was available about the Latter-day Saints, which led to such falsehoods and rumors.

Spawning many such suspicions were the writings of Mormon apostates and defectors—a small number of disenchanted, yet vocal, men and women—who taught that Mormon doctrine and temple rites went beyond reclaiming the Indian to the point of condemning America and its leaders. Such a theory of a Mormon conspiracy against America was influenced by the feelings of many that they had been betrayed by their political leaders, although most were loathe to denounce the Constitution, which they had always accepted and revered.

In one particularly acidic anti-Mormon pamphlet, published in 1847, Increase McGee Van Dusen gave vent to such accusations. "The Mormon Bible claims to be the Indians' record," he wrote.

> And they are told this American land is legally theirs, and that the whites have an unlawful possession, and the Indians are finally to drive off the whites and possess their father's land. We are told that this ceremony [temple endowment] is the commencement of the Law of God and the laws of the land are no more binding on us, but we must at present submit for want of strength and power; but after strengthening ourselves and getting our own people, the American Indians, with us, by the same initiation, we shall have power eventually to effect the final overthrow of this whole nation by their secret stratagem.[20]

The Latter-day Saints themselves, or at least some of them, were convinced that Joseph Smith and other leaders had been murdered by a ruthless, godless, bigoted, and degenerate people who would one day suffer the overflowing scourge of divine retribution (see Introduction). Wilford Woodruff, in an outdoor sermon designed to dissuade desertion from Winter Quarters in January 1847, remarked as follows:

> If there was any under the sound of his voice who felt as if the journey was too great for them, or the trials too hard for them to endure, his advice to such would be to go into their waggons and . . . pray the Lord to take away their lives and grant them a burial with the Saints . . . and when the servants of God should return to the places where they had buried their dead, in the morn of the Resurrection, and sound the Trumpet that should shake the earth and call them from their slumbering tombs, then they would receive a resurrection and come forth. Whereas if they should go into Missouri and be buried there, he did not know who would [take] the trouble to go there and hunt them up for they would never once think that a Saint of God would be buried there.[21]

John Pulsipher, still smarting from Governor Lilburn W. Boggs's Mormon extermination order of nine years before, was even more critical: "The inhabitants of Missouri are an indolent, filthy race of human beings. . . . They have possession of one of the choicest lands in the world, yet they have no spirit of enterprise—no desire to make buildings which are considered convenient and comfortable for civilized and enlightened people."[22]

The antagonism many Latter-day Saints felt toward their once beloved America cannot be denied. Some could never be convinced, even by their own leaders, that the call for the Mormon Battalion was not a sinister plot by a United States government bent on destroying them. Others believed America, and most certainly Missouri and Illinois, were involved in a blatant conspiracy to destroy their religion. As the first pioneer wagon teams rolled far enough west to be out of sight of the Missouri River, then the border of America, one pioneer recorded these feelings: "We came in sight of the waters of the Elkhorn. On casting my eyes back, the vision of them could not reach the Land of the Gentiles which [I] related to some that were travelling by, whereupon they shouted 'Glory Hallelujah' to the top of their voices."[23]

Notwithstanding all the rumors, the innuendoes, and the criticisms of the disaffected, it was never the intention, private or public, of the Latter-day Saints to ally themselves with the Indians and wreak havoc on Independence or on any other town or country. Though men such as Alpheus Cutler and a few other second-level leaders eventually split with Brigham Young over his denunciation of such a possible development, Brigham, while allowing many to blow off steam against their native land, never seriously entertained the idea of warring with Indian tribes against American wagons or against Missouri. They had no doctrinal provision, no intention, and no military might to do so.[24]

Although the Mormons' intended home lay outside the advancing boundaries of America, their alienation was more a matter of geography and religious freedom than of any doctrinally supported hatred of the United States. Let them say and think what they will, reasoned the shrewd Mormon leader. Their plan was to keep their detractors off guard long enough to negotiate as many concessions and treaties as possible without risking military intervention. This policy eventually secured his people and their Zion within America but on their own terms.

THE WOUNDED PRIDE OF THE PAWNEE

The Mormons were as fearful of the Indians as anyone else that spring of 1847—and with ample reason. Their proposed line of march from the Elkhorn to the Platte led right through the heartland of the Pawnee, who for centuries had dominated the eastern Platte regions. Lewis and Clark had estimated that the Great Pawnee nation numbered at least 10,000. The Commissioner of Indian Affairs had reported in 1843 that there were 12,500 Pawnees and 25,000 Sioux.[25] Showing slightly more interest in farming than did the other tribes, the Pawnee were growing beans, corn, melons, and tobacco with mixed results. Their primary interest still lay with the buffalo hunt, a wandering treasure to which they laid almost exclusive claim. At least twice yearly their best warriors left their villages and traveled up the Platte in search of the buffalo. Expert horsemen, the Pawnee were arguably the best hunters of the Plains.[26]

The Latter-day Saints were probably unaware that a century before the Pawnee had annihilated an entire Spanish regiment of some 60 soldiers under the command of Lt. Col. Pedro de Villasur. Just where and why the conflict occurred remains a mystery, but the Spaniards, on a march from New Mexico into French territory in search of the fabled silver mines of the

Missouri, were destroyed. It was, as one scholar has noted, "the worst defeat Spain ever suffered in battle against Plains Indians."[27]

The Pawnee remained the terror of the eastern Plains up until the Medicine Arrow fight in 1829, in which the Pawnee killed an entire war party of Cheyenne near the forks of the Platte some 200 miles west and captured their sacred medicine arrows.

For reasons yet unclear, the Medicine Arrow fight drew the attention of the Teton Sioux to the Pawnee and began an increasingly savage, unremitting warfare between the two tribes. At first the two tribes seemed at rough parity, with first one tribe and then the other loudly celebrating a victory. One overland writer described a Pawnee victory dance:

> We found out that there was to be a great war dance that night by the Pawnee Indians, as they had been successful in a battle with the Sioux and had carried off a number of scalps and wished to celebrate the victory. . . . When that dance was started, if ever a boy wished he was somewhere else, I was certainly that boy. I was certain we would all be killed. I do not think anyone could describe that performance so that one could realize what it looked like. There must have been 300 or 400 jumping, writhing, yelling and twisting and waving those Sioux scalps which were held on the end of sticks about four feet long.[28]

But most celebrations went the other way around. The proud Sioux, in all their tribal varieties, were a "restless, roving active people, numerous and brave, difficult of restraint and careless of consequences."[29] By 1832 the Pawnees had been so badly mauled by the Sioux that they were compelled to abandon the Loup Fork country for new villages south of the Platte. But the United States government, fearful that they would attack fur trading companies and the increasing numbers of westbound travelers using the south bank Platte road, induced the Pawnee to return to the Loup Fork with a promise of protection. This pledge was on paper only, however, for in 1839 the Sioux returned to kill at least another 110 Pawnee while their warriors were away on a hunting expedition. As late as June 1845, the Sioux attacked the Pawnee village at Loup Fork and killed scores of women and children.[30] Just weeks after the Mormon pioneer camp passed through their territory, the Pawnee were again attacked by the Teton Sioux, with further loss of life and property.

The Sioux continued to make senseless sport of warring on the other tribes. By 1851, the Omaha had so suffered from both illness and the Sioux that they could enlist barely 80 warriors.[31] And for the next 25 years, the Pawnee were victimized year after year. As late as 1873, a war party of 1000 Sioux attacked a relatively helpless Pawnee camp, killing over 100 men, women, and children. "The wounded, dead and dying women and helpless children were thrown into a heap and burned in a most barbarous manner possible."[32]

Clearly the greatest threats to native life on the prairies were disease (particularly smallpox), alcohol and its attendant ills, and intertribal warfare. According to one noted authority, during this period many more Plains Indians "were killed by other Indians in intertribal wars than by white soldiers or civilians. . . . Had each of the tribes of this region continued to stand alone, fighting all neighboring tribes, it is probable that many of the smaller tribes . . . would have been exterminated."[33]

So the Pawnee were agitated and defensive, fearful of the Sioux, distrustful of Washington, and in no mood to put up with wanton destruction of the buffalo by careless passersby. Although the Pawnee and most other tribes were not prone to murderous attacks on passing wagon trains (only 362 emigrants were killed by Indian attacks during the entire period from 1840 to 1850),[34] the potential for conflict had definitely increased. The tension had so increased that, by order of President Polk, in 1845 Kearny was dispatched west at the head of a column of 300 United States dragoons to intimidate the Indian warriors and to guard various emigrant companies all the way west to South Pass. "I think it was a good act of President Polk," commented one emigrant in 1845, "as we believe it came very timely as the Indians are getting very jealous of the whites, believing as they say the whites will surround them and take all their country from them, but while the dragoons are in the neighborhood there is nothing to be feared from them."[35]

However, more important to the cause of peace than a show of force were the artful negotiations of Thomas Fitzpatrick, an Indian agent and the most trusted white arbitrator and peacemaker among the various Plains Indian tribes. His efforts kept 1847 from being a year of bloodshed among a score of emigrant trains.

Though there had been agents among the tribes immediately west of the Missouri for several years, prior to 1846 no agency had existed among the tribes of the far western plains. But in that year, the Upper Platte and Arkansas region was given agency designation, and Thomas Fitzpatrick became its first agent. For 25 years Fitzpatrick, whom the Indians called Broken Hand, had been one of the West's outstanding fur traders and guides. He joined Ashley's enterprise in 1822 or 1823, and by the early 1840s was generally acknowledged as the most famous guide in the West, held in high regard by both Indian and emigrant. He possessed an uncanny ability to understand the Indian psyche and to defuse potentially explosive conditions.[36] Using his enormous influence among the Indians, in late 1846 he began moving from village to village throughout the vast territory from Fort Laramie and Bent's Fort in the west to the Missouri River on the east, talking with chiefs to allay their resentment of the annual migrations. Because of his work, Indian depredations in 1847 and 1848, at least throughout the Platte River Valley, were limited principally to horse stealing.[37] The year 1847 seems to have been, as one noted scholar has concluded, "a dull year on the Upper Platte."[38]

Brigham Young and his followers could not have picked a better year to travel the Indian country.

NOTES

1. Merrill J. Mattes, "The Council Bluffs Road: A New Perspective on the Northern Branch of the Great Platte River Road," *Nebraska History* 65, no. 2 (Summer 1984): 193.

2. See Terry L. Alford, "The West as a Desert in American Thought Prior to Long's 1819–1820 Expedition," *Journal of the West* 8, no. 4 (Oct. 1969): 515–25.

3. Peter Sarpy had been an employee of the American Fur Company for many years and knew the upper Missouri River country as well as any man of his times. He owned property on both sides of the Missouri River and operated a flourishing trading post at Bellevue and at Council Point, just south of present-day Council Bluffs. He proved sympathetic to the Mormons, providing assistance in the building of ferries, offering fur contracts, and giving advice about the West.

4. Ray Allen Billington and Martin Ridge, *Westward Expansion: A History of the American Frontier*, 5th ed. (1982), 395.

5. See LeRoy R. Hafen, "Mountain Men before the Mormons," *Utah Historical Quarterly* 26 (1958): 305–16. There are many fine histories of the American fur trade. Few, however, match the excitement, color, and romance of Robert Campbell's own handwritten account on file at the Missouri Historical Society. Entitled "A Narrative of Colonel Robert Campbell's Experiences in the Rocky Mountains Fur Trade from 1825 to 1835," this 48-page holograph is a classic document of the time.

6. The standard work on the American fur trade is still Hiram Martin Chittenden, *The American Fur Trade of the Far West*, 2 vols. (1901).

7. Merrill J. Mattes, "The Council Bluffs Road: A New Perspective on the Northern Branch of the Great Platte River Road," *Nebraska History* 65, no. 2 (Summer 1984): 193.

8. Zebulon M. Pike, *An Account of Expeditions to the Sources of the Mississippi and through the Western Parts of Louisiana* . . . (1810), part 2, appendix, 8.

9. E. Dana, *Geographical Sketches on the Western Country, Designed for Emigrants and Settlers* (1819), 14.

10. See Terry L. Alford, "The West as a Desert in American Thought Prior to Long's 1819–1820 Expedition," *Journal of the West* 8, no. 4 (Oct. 1969): 515–25.

11. Some of the earliest Oregon-bound companies of 1847 included Edward Long's Oskaloosa Company that left Oskaloosa, Iowa, 4 April; P. F. Blair's company, that started out from Lee County, Iowa, 15 April, in a train "of about 100 wagons" with 65 grown men; Joel Palmer's train; and Thomas Smith's company, that left the Missouri River on 26 May. See *Transactions of the Annual Reunions of the Oregon Pioneer Association, 16th Annual Reunion* (1888), 145–47; *18th Annual Reunion* (1893), 213; and *23rd Annual Reunion* (1895), 39 and 76.

12. John D. Unruh Jr., *The Plains Across: The Overland Emigrants and the Trans-Mississippi West, 1840–60* (1982), 84. Unruh estimates the following migration figures for the pre–gold rush era:

1840	13	1843	913	1846	2,700
1841	58	1844	1,528	1847	4,450
1842	125	1845	2,760	1848	1,700

13. Ralph C. Geer, "Occasional Address," in *Transactions of the 4th Annual Re-Union of the Oregon Pioneer Association for 1876* (1877), 33–34.

14. G. M. Goddard to his sister, Lucretia C. Fruit of Lewisburg, Pennsylvania, 25 May 1846; photostat, Goddard Family Papers, Missouri Historical Society.

15. Henry Mayhew and Samuel M. Smucker, *The Religious, Social, and Political History of the Mormons or Latter-day Saints* (1858), 232–33.

16. Two of many fine accounts of the Missouri difficulties are Warren E. Jennings, "The Expulsion of the Mormons from Jackson County, Missouri," *Missouri Historical Review* 64 (Oct. 1969): 41–63 and Richard L. Bushman, "Mormon Persecutions in Missouri, 1833," *BYU Studies* 3 (Autumn 1960): 11–20. A recent full-length monographic study is Stephen C. LeSueur, *The 1838 Mormon War in Missouri* (Columbia: University of Missouri Press, 1987).

17. Edwin Bryant, *What I Saw in California; Being the Journal of a Tour . . . in the Years 1846, 1847* (1848), 15.

18. Francis Parkman, *The Oregon Trail* (1930), 35–36.

Parkman, in his colorful literary style, was as instrumental in extolling the cultures and virtues of the Ogalala Sioux as he was in condemning the Mormon ways and beliefs. His book, *The Oregon Trail*, went through nine editions in his own lifetime and many more since, even though Parkman traveled only a few miles west of Fort Laramie. When referring to the departure of the Mississippi Saints from Pueblo in early 1847 (see chapter 6), Parkman wrote: "After remaining with them an hour we rode back to our camp, happy that the settlements had been delivered from the presence of such blind and desperate fanatics" (page 279).

19. Phebe Stanton to her sisters, Benazah and Cyntha Stanton, 9 May 1847, Stanton Family Collection, mss #475, Oregon Historical Society, Portland, Oregon. Also printed in *Transactions of the Oregon Pioneer Association, 40th Annual Reunion* (1912), 622–23.

20. Increase McGee Van Dusen, *"Sketch of the Rise, Progress and Dispersion of the Mormons," by John Thomas . . . To Which is Added An Account of the Nauvoo Temple Mysteries and Other Abominations Practised by the Mormons Previous to Their Emigration for California* (1847).

21. Journal of Mary Haskin Parker Richards, 12 Jan. 1847.

22. Diary of John Pulsipher, 12, typescript copy at the Utah State Historical Society.

23. Journal of Albert P. Rockwood, 10 Apr. 1847, LDS Church Archives.

Though the Mormons and Missourians were quick to castigate and defame one another, they had freely traded together along the western frontier. Scores of Latter-day Saints left Winter Quarters and found temporary work in western Missouri farms and villages. And Missouri merchants were more than pleased to trade with Mormon overlanders. For more on this topic, see Richard Bennett, "Mormons and Missourians: The Uneasy Truce," *The Midwest Review*, second series 9 (Spring 1992): 12–21.

24. Alpheus Cutler, president of the Winter Quarters Municipal High Council, became convinced that God had a mission for him to fulfill among the Indians in Missouri. He and a few others left the Church and proclaimed the new doctrine of "Lamanism," which was aimed at inciting local Indian tribes and reclaiming Jackson County as the center stake of Zion. His radical scheme may have owed its origin to a blessing Cutler claimed he received from Joseph Smith.

For more sympathetic studies of Cutler, see the writings of Danny L. Jorgensen, a descendant. His "Cutler's Camp at the Big Grove on Silver Creek (Iowa), 1847–1853" and given at the Annual Meeting of the Mormon History Association, 23 May 1997, may soon be published.

There is evidence to show that Cutler later regretted his leaving the Church, being influenced by lesser men. "I know that Joseph Smith was a prophet of God, and I know that Brigham Young is his legal successor and I always did. But the trouble with me was I wanted to lead and could not be led" (Reminiscences of Abraham A. Kimball, 22).

Ample evidence shows, however, Latter-day Saint belief that if America were to be scourged, it would eventually be done by the displaced and wounded Indian tribes acting on their own accord. As "to the sufferings of the gentiles when the Lamanites go forth," Eliza R. Snow wrote in her diary after conferring with others on the coming calamity, "language cannot describe the scene" (Journal of Eliza R. Snow, 1 June 1847, LDS Church Archives).

25. T. Hartley Crawford's report to J. M. Porter, Secretary of War, 25 Nov. 1843, estimated the combined Indian populations west of the Missouri as follows:

Chippewas, Ottawas, and Pottawattamies	5,779
Sioux	25,000
Sacs and Foxes	2,348

Omahas	1,600
Otoes and Missouris	931
Pawnees	12,500
Poncas	800

("Report of the Commission of Indian Affairs," 28th Congress, 1st Session, vol. 1, serial 431, Senate Documents, 277–78).

26. The Pawnees consisted in reality of four tribes: the Chaui or Grand Pawnee, then located on the south bank of the Platte (near Schuyler, Nebraska); the Kitkahaki or Republican Pawnee, on the south side of the Republican River (near Red Cloud); the Skidi or Loup (Wolf) Pawnee, on the Loup Fork north of the Platte; and the Pithauret or Noisy Pawnee, near Grand Island (see Bert Webber, *Indians Along the Oregon Trail* [1989]).

Another observer noted: "The Pawnee [is] a nation of four tribal units bound together by ties of blood and language and custom and religion" (Addison E. Sheldon, "The North Brothers and the Pawnee Nation," *Nebraska History Magazine* 15, no. 4 [Oct.–Dec. 1934]: 299).

27. George E. Hyde, *Indians of the High Plain: From the Prehistoric Period to the Coming of Europeans* (1959), 76–77.

28. William A. Hockett Reminiscences, 1847, 6, mss #1036, Oregon Historical Society.

29. "Report of the Commissioner of Indian Affairs," 469.

30. "The Sioux would charge into the village, kill some Pawnees, set fire to a few lodges and ride back to their ridge, taking many captured horses with them; then form up and charge again. Most of the Pawnees had taken refuge in the head-chiefs' house, a very large earth-lodge, and cutting loop-holes in the walls they fought desperately against the overwhelming force of Sioux. . . . This fight went on for hours, and when the Sioux finally drew off with their plunder the Pawnees were so badly frightened that they threw their dead into corn-caches and ravines, gathered up a few of their belongings and fled from the village" (George E. Hyde, *Red Cloud's Folk: A History of the Oglala Sioux Indians* [1937], 48).

31. *Journal of Rudolph Friederich Kurz: An Account of His Experiences Among Fur Traders and American Indians on the Mississippi and Upper Missouri Rivers During the Years 1846 to 1852*, trans. Murtis Jarrell, ed. J. N. B. Hewitt, Smithsonian Bulletin 115 (1937), 66.

32. Report of William Burgess, U.S. Indian Agent, to Barclay White, Superintendent of Indian Affairs, Omaha, Nebraska, 9 Aug. 1873, as published in "Indian Office Documents on Sioux-Pawnee Battle," *Nebraska History Magazine* 16, no. 3 (July–Sept. 1935): 148.

33. John C. Ewers, "Intertribal Warfare as the Precursor of Indian-White Warfare on the Northern Great Plains," *Western Historical Quarterly* 6, no. 4 (Oct. 1975): 402.

34. Unruh, *The Plains Across*, 185.

35. James Taylor to his father, 21 May 1845 from near the Vermillion River, papers and letters of James Taylor, mss #1006, Oregon Historical Society.

36. LeRoy R. Hafen, "Thomas Fitzpatrick and the First Indian Agency of the Upper Platte and Arkansas," *Mississippi Valley Historical Review* 15 (1928): 374–75.

37. Remi Nadeau, *Fort Laramie and the Sioux Indians* (1967), 60. The definitive biography of Fitzpatrick is LeRoy R. Hafen's *Broken Hand—The Life of Thomas Fitzpatrick: Mountain Man, Guide and Indian Agent* (1931).

John C. Fremont credits Fitzpatrick's skill as negotiator for saving the lives of many emigrants from almost certain destruction at the hands of various western tribes. His "name and high reputation are familiar to all who interest themselves in the history of this country" (*Expeditions of Frémont*, 1:222–23).

38. Hyde, *Red Cloud's Folk*, 61.

4

WAGONS WEST

From the Elkhorn to Ash Hollow

The great cause of Zion, taken en masse, swallows up
all minor or personal considerations, and wife and children
and relatives appear lost, as it were, and we are obliged
to forsake them all to build up the Kingdom of God
and bring about a reign of peace upon the earth.[1]

The Latter-day Saint errand into the wilderness hardly began on a positive note. Pent-up excitement was soon tempered by such harsh realities as bitterly cold nights, windswept prairies, stubborn animals, stolen horses, careless accidents, quicksands, and sandbars. Each of these tribulations were amply documented by a score of diarists, whose surviving writings frame a memorable portrait of a faith in exile.

British-born William Clayton (who the year before in Iowa had composed the hymn "Come, Come, Ye Saints," which had gained instant popularity) found the early going a painful experience, literally from head to foot. A last-minute recruit, Clayton started out suffering from a throbbing toothache. "Tonight I went to bed about 7:30 o'clock suffering severely with pain in my head and face," he recorded on 18 April. Two days later he asked Luke S. Johnson, medical doctor and would-be dentist, "to draw my tooth. He willingly agreed," noted the sufferer,

> and getting his instruments, I sat down in a chair, he lanced the gum, then took his nippers and jerked it out. The whole operation

116

Wagons crossing the Platte

did not take more than one minute. He only got half the original tooth, the balance being left in the jaw. After this my head and face pained me much more than before. I ate but little supper and then lay down, but could not sleep for pain till near morning.[2]

Several days and sleepless nights passed before the best scribe in camp fully recovered.

But toothaches were not his only problem. After three days of walking an average of 12 to 15 miles per day alongside his wagon, Clayton admitted that his "feet were so sore and blistered he could not walk for some time."[3]

The weather at that early season in the Elkhorn Valley alternated between winter and summer, with winds that almost blew loaded wagons onto their sides. "In the night there was a very strong wind, accompanied with frost," complained 30-year-old Thomas Bullock, official camp historian. "When I arose [I] found the ice one inch thick in the water buckets, the guard complained much of the severity of the weather, and the brethren generally wrapt themselves in their buffalo skins and blankets."[4]

At other times, afternoon temperatures rose as high as 80 degrees, a fluctuation that spawned the sudden storms so well known in those parts. "About 2 thunder was heard," Bullock remarked a few days later, "which was soon followed by lightning and rain, and continued to descend very prettily until about 4 o'clock, when a strong East wind arose and assisted to blow us forward on our journey."[5] A careful look at "Professor" Orson Pratt's daily recordings of temperature and barometric readings, as well as a careful review of the diaries, indicate that the weather remained unseasonably cold all the way to Fort Laramie.[6]

Other pioneers faced different difficulties, all in keeping with the hazards of life on the trek. Apostle George A. Smith, 29-year-old cousin of Joseph Smith and a seasoned rider, was almost crushed to death by his own horse. While being watered near the Loup Fork, the animal startled and "sprang suddenly," Bullock recorded, "throwing George against the bank, the horse having his hind foot on G. A.'s foot, and his fore foot on G.'s breast, in which situation he continued until the brethren took the horse off him. It was very fortunate that the place was muddy, so he escaped with only a few bruises."[7]

During their first 10 days on the trail they lost four of their best horses: one to an accidental gunshot blast, two to Indians, and one to a hole in the ground. During the predawn hours of 24 April, while tied to a stake with a chain near a steep ravine, a horse belonging to Phineas Young (one of Brigham Young's two brothers making the trip) rolled over, fell into the hole, and strangled to death. This was "a grievous loss," as one put it, "for there are no more teams in the camp than what are absolutely necessary, and in fact, there are hardly enough to get along very comfortably."[8]

It was the river crossings, however, that caused most of their initial stress and turmoil. Although the Elkhorn had proved an easy conquest, with all 72 wagons crossing the 150-foot wide river on a raft with ropes on either side drawn by cattle, the Loup Fork, 133 miles west of Winter Quarters, proved a much more formidable task. Its 400 yards of swiftly flowing, ice-cold spring runoff hinted at the much larger mountain streams and rivers they would eventually have to confront. The current was so rapid that their makeshift rafts almost capsized. The shallow sandbars proved problematic for rafting and the quicksand a potentially fatal quagmire for horses and livestock. Commented Albert Rockwood: "The bottom is quicksand which renders it very difficult and sometimes dangerous to cross. A man on a horse standing a few moments in one place will settle in, and if they do not exert themselves immediately, they will sink to rise no more until the resurrection of the just or unjust."[9]

Pratt dared to go first with a lighter carriage, but his horse promptly swamped in the mud; only with great difficulty did five or six men get them out. Three other wagons got by, but only by doubling teams and "with a good deal of difficulty." "The brethren were about discouraged with regard to the rafting business," 42-year-old Norton Jacob, a captain of 10, confessed, because they had concluded the only way across was to empty their wagons and raft their provisions over on the "revenue cutter." This was a leather skiff belonging to Alanson Eldridge, which his son, John, brought along with them; it could serve as a fishing boat or double as a wagon bottom when not in use.[10]

How it all worked out makes for colorful reading. After conferring for some time, Jacob recalled,

> a council of officers was called in the evening to consult upon the best method to adopt for crossing the river. . . . It was finally concluded to build two rafts in the morning out of the dry poles at the [Pawnee] village and at the same time commence crossing the goods in the boat; and the Colonel [Stephen Markham] would direct the crossing of the teams. He proceeded the next morning to set stakes in different places across the stream so as to follow one track and thereby pack the sand and make it more firm. President Young commenced crossing his loading in the boat. Brother Heber proposed to his boys to double the teams and take our loads in our wagons as we could not all go over in the boat today. So at it we went and put on three and four teams to a wagon, and took over all our effects long before the first division got theirs over with the aid of the boat. I crossed my ten in about 3 hours. By the time half of us had got over the road had become tolerably firm. At 4 o'clock the whole camp had passed over without any accident, for which we felt truly thankful to our Heavenly Father.[11]

Even more than toothaches and river crossings, the fear of the unknown wilderness, of an extended separation from loved ones, and of a possible imminent Indian attack proved too much for some. Tempers flared and oaths were exchanged. One teamster, 58-year-old Solomon Chamberlain, an 1830 convert and early missionary, was out of sorts with almost everyone for awhile. Sensing the need to let the camp "blow off steam" from time to time, Brigham nominated the less quarrelsome Henry G. Sherwood as "chief grumbler for the Camp": if anyone had a complaint he would first have to go through Sherwood, "the only man that had a legal right to find fault and murmur."[12]

Likewise, Thomas Bullock, constantly frustrated with the lack of time to complete his writing assignments, vented his frustration over one of his disagreeable wagon mates. "There is one thing I do know positive," he complained in a letter to his wife.

> And that is this. I shall be very glad when I shall change both my bed and bedfellow. I suppose you think I sleep with the Dr. [Willard Richards], but it is no such thing. I believe I have slept with him in his wagon twice. I sleep in the wagon I drive, and George Brown is my bed fellow and the most uncomfortable one I ever slept with. If it was night only I could do well . . . but he is a disagreeable, saucy, idle fellow by day. I am tired of him and I pray God, my return journey may be by myself or another person, not him.[13]

Another disaffected soul, Ellis Eames, was the only one to "see the Elephant," a contemporary term for those who turned back. For whatever reasons, whether sickness or a lack of faith and commitment, he left the pioneer company.[14]

In these ways, the first 10 days on the trail took their toll on both man and beast.

IN THE LAND OF THE LAMANITE

As indicated in the preceding chapter, the pioneers expected trouble from the Pawnee, who felt justified in extorting a ransom from any camp passing through their territories, regardless of the cautions Thomas Fitzpatrick had placed on them. The accounts of Pawnee thievery in 1846 and 1847 are multiple. Joseph Bissonette, a trader at Fort John, had written John B. Sarpy at St. Louis just nine months before about the Pawnee penchant for stealing. "I regret to inform you," he said,

> that on my way here I was detained by the Pawnees and that to avoid being robbed to a larger extent, I had to give up several articles of value. . . . They have behaved shamefully to some parties of emigrants and killed one of them, after robbing them of cattle and

horses. Unless the attention of government be called to that nation, it will be impossible for travellers to follow the road along the Platte, unless they keep in large numbers.[15]

Other emigrants experienced similar treatment. Catherine Margaret Haun aptly described the Pawnee art of stealing:

> The emigrants were often sorely tried and inconvenienced by losses more or less serious for in spite of the most alert guard it was almost impossible to see the advancing thief crawling . . . on the ground up to his intended prey.
>
> Horses and mules seemed always to be uneasy and fearing danger. Their keen sense of smell and hearing caused them often to sound the danger alarm, by snorting or being very restless, at the approach of Indians or wild animals. However, even their vigilance was often defeated by the sly enemies. If the wind or gentlest motion of the air was coming from the direction of the intruder they were apt to detect his approach—the Indians knew this and laid their plans accordingly.[16]

An Oregon company crossing the plains the same year as the Mormon pioneers did not fare so well in their encounters with the Pawnee. Their accounts are almost comical, were they not so painful—and embarrassing—for those involved. William Hockett remembered one incident his uncle, and a few others in pursuit of several stealing Pawnee, never forgot nor forgave:

> After awhile they found them [cattle stampeded by the Indians], but the Indians had found them [the Oregon company] first and robbed them of their guns and clothing, leaving them nothing but their hats and boots. My uncle resisted so stubbornly about being robbed that they bent him over until his head was on his knees, and then the chief beat him over the back with his bow. Some places the skin was split four or five inches. . . . So we travelled on. . . . We saw many bands of Indians, always moving the same direction we were, but gave us no more trouble. My uncle's back gave him so much trouble that the Widow Fisher took in a young man . . . to drive her team. . . .[17]

After reuniting with the main company patiently waiting at the Elkhorn, Brigham lost little time organizing the pioneer camp "into a travelling capacity," selecting a military profile, establishing rules for safe conduct, and setting strategy to deal with the Indians. Knowing that the Pawnee would observe their every move from the moment they crossed the Elkhorn (that unmarked boundary line separating the Omaha from the Pawnee), Brigham pursued a definite strategy—much the same as the one they had adopted in Winter Quarters when dealing with the Omaha and the Otoe.

First, the camp had to be well armed, with guards multiplied at night to prevent theft or loss of life. Second, there must be no unnecessary provocation, with communication preferred over confrontation. Third, hunting, especially of buffalo, elk, and other game, had to be kept to a minimum.

Stephen Markham and Albert P. Rockwood were appointed the two captains of 100s; Addison Everett, Tarleton Lewis, James Case, John Pack, and Shadrach Roundy were chosen captains of 50s. Fourteen others were selected as captains of 10s.[18] Markham was then elected captain of the guard and directed to draw out 50 men for a standing guard that was divided into companies of 10 with a guard captain to each 10.[19]

The following day the rigid camp structure was further overlaid with military formation or, as Jacob put it, "in a military point of view," clearly in anticipation of possible imminent hostilities. The camp had a regimental structure, with Brigham Young elected general, Stephen Markham colonel, John Pack and Shadrach Roundy first and second majors respectively, and all the former captains of 10s, plus Wilford Woodruff, made military captains. Though it may seem an overregulation of a very small host, their penchant for organization insured safety for themselves, plus a certain saving distance between the Quorum of the Twelve Apostles and camp leaders in case of disagreements over minor trail concerns. The fear of an unknown wilderness, of probable Indian thievery and potential attack, and of confrontations with other emigrants all contributed to a desire for keen preparation and order.[20]

The Council of Captains promptly drew up a list of rules and regulations for the pioneer camp, a sort of prairie constitution that would be their pattern of travel for the next three months.[21]

1. The bugle to be blown at 5 A.M. for prayers; after which, each is to attend to his team, prepare breakfast and be ready to leave by the sound of the second bugle at 7 A.M.

Mormon Train in Camp, *sketch by George Simons*

2. With usually two men to a wagon, the driver is to keep his gun close by while his partner walks on the off side of the team with his gun on his shoulder fully loaded—caps and powder flask ready.

3. The camp to stop at noon for about an hour to feed and graze the animals—dinner to be ready cooked.

4. Upon making camp for the night, all 72 wagons to be drawn in a circle with the front wheels on one interlocking with the rear wheels of the other with all horses and other animals remaining inside the corral with the pioneers sleeping in their wagons or tents outside the circle.

5. The bugle to be blown again at 8:30 P.M. for evening prayers and all fires out by 9 P.M.

6. The camp to travel in close order, usually in two columns by division with no one allowed to wander more than 20 rods without permission of his captain.

7. Every man is to put as much interest in taking care of his brother's cattle, in preserving them, as he would his own, and no man will be indulged in idleness.

8. All guns and pistols to be in good working order.

9. All to start together with the cannon in the rear and to see that nothing is left behind at each stopping place.[22]

Furthermore, the camp would honor the Sabbath and lay aside, wherever possible, on that day for rest for both man and animal, repairs, worship, and letter writing.[23]

The purpose of the cannon, in this case a small three-pounder, was to ward off Indian attack. Fremont and Kearny had learned that Indians had great respect for the roaring fire of cannon shot. As a preventive mechanism, a cannon added that extra measure of defense.

Military organization was, however, only the first plank in their Indian policy; the second was communication and understanding. This priority motivated a calculated gamble—to veer deliberately north to the Loup Fork and proceed directly towards the Pawnee village, despite the risks. They wanted to establish goodwill and understanding between them and the Pawnee, not only for the present camp but also for the many wagon trains to follow.

The decision to pass near the main Pawnee village was both deliberate and dangerous, and was prompted, no doubt, by those in camp who had firsthand experience with the Pawnee. James Case, a former employee at the government-operated farm near the Pawnee village who was dismissed after his conversion, had spent much of the past year at the now-abandoned farm and adjacent Presbyterian mission. Case knew the area and the Pawnee well. He also knew that his farm associates had stored a large cache of hay and provisions, which might still be hidden from the Pawnee.

Tippets and Woolsey had spent several weeks among the Pawnee as grateful, if unwilling, winter captives. Before their release, they had told the Pawnee about Mormon intentions; one of the chiefs had even pledged two of his daughters in marriage to the two sojourners. The pioneers hoped to build on this friendship.

Furthermore, George Miller, on contract to move furs for Peter Sarpy, had transported several Presbyterian missionaries the summer before, along with a few Pawnee children, out of the way of the warring Sioux and over to Bellevue on the Missouri River.[24] So both Pawnee and pioneers anticipated one another.

Shortly after 9 A.M. on the morning of 21 April, the pioneers met the first Indian on a pony, then a "dozen or so" of the Loup Band, among whom was their chief, Sisketuk, riding on a mule. Exceedingly friendly, they walked between the wagons, shaking hands enthusiastically with everyone in sight. Their heads were shaved with the exception of a strip about two inches wide and two inches high from a little back of their foreheads to the neck and, in the words of Levi Johnson, "stuck straight up and resembled a rooster's comb." They wore breechcloths and buffalo skins or a blanket. Some few had leggings.[25]

About noon they came in sight of the new Pawnee village, across the river on the south side of the Loup Fork. It consisted of approximately 100 lodges "set pretty close together" and built in the characteristic Pawnee fashion—a village of some 4 to 5 thousand Pawnee. At that very moment Peter Sarpy, whom the Mormons knew well, was in the village trading for furs. While they were arranging their wagons in a semicircle fronting south on the river, approximately 200 Pawnee came down to the riverbank; about 75 of them waded across, including the grand chief of the Pawnee nations. With a personal letter in his hand addressed to Brigham—evidence that they knew who the Mormons were and where they were going—in which Sarpy certified the Pawnee's good intention, Chief Cheffolan demanded a large present of goods.[26]

While camp leaders saw to it that the chief received four pounds of tobacco, fifteen pounds of lead powder, fishhooks, caps, flour, and meal, Charles Shumway told the Indians (through an interpreter) that "we were not like the other 'pale faces,' rich, but that we were poor, and had been driven from among other white people because of our religion and that we believed in the 'Great Spirit' like unto themselves" and that "if we had more we would cheerfully give it."[27]

Shumway's explanations fell on deaf ears; the chief suddenly turned visibly angry at what he considered an insufficient pile of gifts, "considering our numbers" and how rich "Americans were." He demanded that the whites go back, loudly complaining that they would kill or drive away the Pawnees' buffalo. "Keep! Keep! More!" he cried out, as Addison Everett recalled the scene, "and refused to shake hands with President Brigham Young and signified his displeasure at our travelling through his land."[28]

Disregarding the outburst, ascribing it to Sarpy and to other traders who feared the coming emigrants, Brigham and his companions nervously harnessed up their teams and "were rapidly in motion." That night, eight miles west, in consequence of the obvious Indian dissatisfaction, a guard of

125

100 men was enlisted, half of whom were put on duty from 9 to 1 o'clock and the other half till 5 A.M. The cannon was also readied for firing to show the Pawnee, and whatever Sioux may have been in the neighborhood, what firepower they controlled.[29] For their part, the Pawnee would wait to strike at a less guarded moment.

Anxious to put as much distance as possible between them and the disgruntled Pawnee, the camp traveled 17 miles the next day, arriving at the deserted Presbyterian missionary station, or Pawnee mission house. At that time it consisted of two double log houses, six smaller single ones, two racks of good hay, several cattle yards, and two fenced-in fields. Begun some years before by Reverend John Dunbar, it now lay vacated, a victim of intertribal warfare. Case knew the place well and lost little time finding the hidden provisions of good hay and corn fodder, which the cattle seemed to think was very good for a change. He even prevailed upon his superiors to sell off the iron plows, wagon boxes, wagon tin, and other items strewn around the site as partial payment for wages he had never received from the government and for the debts he was owed by the missionaries.[30] After the sale, Case wrote the missionaries in Bellevue, canceling their debts.

Beautifully situated on a small eminence, bounded on the south by the Loup Fork and on the north, east, and west by a range of hills or bluffs "from the height of which a person can command a view of the whole adjoining country up and down the river for miles," the calm of the deserted station masked the horrors of recent massacres and played host for a night to its westbound visitors. Almost in sight a few miles further west was the abandoned Pawnee village of over 200 lodges—some of which were 45 feet in diameter—on the north side of the Loup Fork, victimized and destroyed by the Sioux. The village invited no end of curiosity visits and lengthy descriptions in camp journals.[31]

Two nights later, despite the best efforts of tired guards, the invisible Pawnee made their move. They stole two of the best horses in camp, one of which belonged to Willard Richards and the other to Jesse C. Little, a loss neither man could afford. Richards, 42, arguably the third most influential leader in camp, was an unwell man, but highly respected and revered.[32] Despite the immediate pursuit of a large posse, the horses were never found.

The following day they dispatched their best sharpshooters and horsemen—Orrin Porter Rockwell, Joseph Mathews, John Eldredge, and Tom

Brown—back some 20 miles for one last try. Of their nearly fatal exploit, Bullock recorded the following:

> Followed the trail to within about 1 1/2 miles of our Saturday night camping ground; when Porter Rockwell thought he saw a wolf, determined to shoot it, descended from his horse, levelled his gun to fire, which brought up the resurrection of 15 Pawnee Indians, who running to seize his and Mathews' horses; Rockwell jumped on his horse and levelled his pistol, which caused them to draw back. The 15 Indians were armed with bows and arrows and guns, ready for fight, but were bluffed by the 4 brethren. The Indians got enraged, retreated about 50 yards, and fired six guns at the brethren, sending the balls whistling close by their heads. Not being able to gain the two stolen horses, they returned and fired the Prairie to purify it by fire.[33]

Their horses not retrieved, the solemn quartet returned to camp empty-handed.

"ONE CONTINUED DESOLATE VIEW": TRAVELING UP THE PLATTE

By the time they reached Grand Island, 214 miles west of Winter Quarters, near the end of April, the pioneers were leaving Pawnee country and the rolling, wooded hills of the Elkhorn. Averaging 12 to 15 miles per day, they were well on their way up the great Platte River Valley. Although the countryside made speedy travel possible, overlanders—Mormon and otherwise—spoke freely of the intimidating vastness of this windswept, treeless landscape. "The eye is tired of the one continued desolate view of the earth," lamented Albert P. Rockwood, "as it stretches itself on our right as we are passing up the wide cold sandy river."[34] Levi Jackman put it even more succinctly: "The sight of a tree is out of the question."[35]

"No place in the world looks more lonesome and discouraging than the wide prairies of this region," wrote James Clyman, while passing through the area three years before Brigham Young's company.

> Neither tree, bush, shrub, rock, nor water, to cherish or shelter; and such a perfect sameness, with a delusive ridge all around you meeting the horizon in all directions. You suppose your course to be over some one of these horizontal ridges, when after several

hours of anxious fatigue, you suppose you are about to ascend the highest pinnacle and some known landmark. What is your disappointment to find ridge rise beyond ridge, to the utmost extent of human vision.[36]

It had become a journey without beginning or end.

In the absence of any landmarks other than sky, ridge, and river, the slow-moving Platte—their companion and guide to the foothills—received its full share of comment and derision. Called the Nieborahka, or "shallow river," by the Indians and La Platte by French-Canadian trappers, the Platte was often called the Nebraska and sometimes the Flatwater. Woodruff said that it was unlike any other river "that I have any knowledge of in the world." He continued:

> It is much of the way a mile in width and generally covered with water but very shallow. When a south wind blows hard the water all rushes to the north shore until one would suppose there was a great rise in the water. Let the wind shift and blow hard from the north and the water immediately leaves the north shore until one can walk across two thirds of the river on bare ground. And the river constantly ebbs and flows like the tide just according as the wind blows.[37]

Another more disappointed observer said that it "counterfeits the majesty of the Mississippi, and even surpasses it in width, but it is a counterfeit sure enough, a complete burlesque in all the rivers of the world! It is a wide sheet of water only three or four feet deep, running over a vast level bed of sand and micah that is continually changing into short offsets like the shingled roof of a house and which thus eternally creeps along."[38]

Despite the fact that it had, in Jackman's words, "the appearance of dirty soap suds occasioned by the sand, the water is healthy and good," and provided the camp with water for drinking, washing, and cleaning.[39]

The other irritating constant in this dreary land was the dust, an almost suffocating, never-ending billow of sand from the passing of the emigrant trains. "You in the States know nothing about dust," recalled one non-Mormon emigrant who also made the overland journey in 1847. "It will fly so that [you] can hardly see the horns of your tongue yoke [and] it often seems that the cattle must die for want of breath."[40] "This is the coldest and most dusty journey I have ever travelled," complained Thomas Bullock in a letter to his wife, Henrietta, herself preparing for the journey. "I wash my hands and face some days twice and three times and yet I have been as dusty as a sweep in two hours. I would advise you to save your veils for you and the children next spring."[41] Despite wearing scarves and handkerchiefs across their mouths, "the clouds of dust were almost sufficient to suffocate everyone."[42]

Teamsters patiently waited for their turn when, on a rotating basis, their company of 10 might lead all the others. If fortunate, their wagon would lead their group of 10 (usually seven wagons) and the entire column of 72 wagons, giving them the rare opportunity—once in 72 days—of breathing the pure air of the vanguard wagon. Otherwise those following, especially at the far rear, on windy days could barely see in front of them. As punishment, banishment to the dusty end of the line was sometimes reserved for the troublemaker. "If any man should stop his team in the road, without due cause," Kimball warned, "thereby detaining the whole camp from proceeding with his team, [he] should be obliged to travel in the rear of the hindmost wagon the whole day."[43]

Under these conditions they understandably looked forward to Sundays, when they almost always laid over for rest, letter and journal writing, religious services, and washing. "Soon as the camp was formed," Clayton recorded somewhere west of Grand Island, "I went about three quarters of a mile below to the river and washed my socks, towel and handkerchief as well as I could in cold water without soap. I then stripped my clothing off and washed from head to foot, which has made me feel much more comfortable for I was covered with dust."[44]

Dust and cold notwithstanding, as they plodded up the Platte Valley, these overland caravans portrayed an unforgettable image of the frontier history of the West. "It is a singular sight," wrote one Missouri traveler, "to rise a hill and see the long trains winding along over the hills and through the valleys while a cloud of dust at times envelopes them in its haze then is swept away and reveals the teams toiling under the crack of the unmerciful whip."[45]

And from the pen of another, earlier overlander traveling on the south bank:

> Had a fair view of our camp travelling, as seen from the bluffs about a mile distant. The appearance was quite picturesque. First

came a few straggling foot and horse men ahead, and on the left flank, the right being on the river; next a thick squad of horsemen in front, followed by a long string of white-looking wagon covers, flanked with gentlemen and ladies, occasionally; in the rear a long string of loose cattle, horses and mules, the tout ensemble being rather unique.[46]

"THE CATTLE ON A THOUSAND HILLS: 'THE FAT BULLS OF BASHAN'"

Even trail dust and tedium, however, could not dampen their rising expectations—and appetites. For days many had been living on corn bread, water, and porridge. Their plan had always been to supplement their diet with fresh meat. Though many were hunters, most had only read about the buffalo. Day after day they scanned the horizon in hope of glimpsing the great beast. For the Latter-day Saints, that day came early on 1 May, when they saw three buffalo grazing on the top of a bluff five or six miles "to our right." Orrin Porter Rockwell, Thomas Brown, Luke Johnson, Heber C. Kimball, and two other "designated hunters" bolted off in the direction of the buffalo, with everyone else in camp scanning the bluffs with eyeglasses. "The brethren's feelings who were left with the wagons," reported Clayton, "were now strung up to the highest pitch, a feeling of exciting interest appeared to prevail throughout the camp, they having heard and read so much of the mad ferocity of the buffalo when hotly pursued, and knowing that all the hunters were inexperienced in regard to hunting the wild buffalo."[47]

Their expectations for hunting buffalo came from the varied animated descriptions of predecessors such as William Anderson. "Nothing can be more revolting, more terrific, than a front view of an old bull buffalo," he had written in 1834.

His huge hump, covered with long wool, rising eighteen or twenty inches above his spine; a dense mat of black hair, padding a bullet-proof head; a dirty drunken beard, almost sweeping to the ground, and his thick dark horns and sparkling eyes, gave him altogether, the appearance and expression of some four-legged devil, fresh from Halifax. But nevertheless, and notwithstanding all this, his meat is good eating. Bosse, hump-ribs, side-ribs, tongue and marrow bones. "Sufficient for the day is the fatigue and rest thereof."[48]

Setting his glass on Aaron Farr's shoulder, Clayton discovered Rockwell riding into a herd numbering over 200, which began to scatter in all directions as the hunting party approached. After wounding one cow, Rockwell ran off after others; Kimball rode close to her with his "fifteen shooter" and fired over his horse's head as she dropped helpless. At the report of the gun, Kimball's horse "sprang and flew down the bluff like lightning and he having let go the lines to shoot, her sudden motion overbalanced him and his situation was precarious to the extreme." An experienced rider, Kimball soon regained the lines and reined in the horse without accident. When it was ascertained that one had been killed, the revenue cutter was unloaded and sent to bring the buffalo into camp. By 4 P.M., after a three-hour hunt, one bull, three cows, and six calves had been taken, "far exceeding our expectations and best hopes."[49]

Joseph Hancock, nicknamed "Nimrod" by Joseph Smith for his hunting skills, was not quite so fortunate. Perhaps wanting to live up to his reputation, the 46-year-old Hancock left the main hunting party to kill a large bull back of the bluffs. Because he was unwilling to leave his prize to the wolves, he opted to stay alone with it overnight. After making a fire, he scattered gunpowder around him and the buffalo to ward off wolves and other invaders and passed the night under the stars. Though the wolves kept up their howling all through the night, the fire kept them at bay. Early in the morning, Hancock hastened back to the camp, but by the time he and his friends returned, the wolves had already devoured most of the buffalo.

Rockwell, quick with both word and gun, was soon claiming bragging rights for having felled the first buffalo. But John Pack felt constrained to paint a slightly different version of the story: "There was considerable anxiety in the camp who should kill the first buffalo," he later wrote to his family back at the Missouri.

We had none ever killed any except Bro. Wooley and Tippets that came from the army. I said but very little for fear I might not kill one at all. One afternoon about 3 o'clock we came in sight of about 300 buffalo in one herd. 11 of us which had previously been chosen for hunters prepared for the chase on horse back. . . . We started off on a slow walk the buffalo being 3 miles off. There was much bragging by the way. I told them I did not expect to kill any. I was going along behind to skin with my big jack knife. However we got up within 1/4 mile and the buffalo started. We put spurs to our horses and as they ran around a hill I cut across and came in ahead of all the hunters and along side of the buffalo. I fired away and killed one dead on the spot. . . . Porter had shot at one of them once but did not touch them then rode on and left them. I spurred up my horse and came alongside and fired away and shot the largest one through the shoulder. . . . He fell dead on the spot. This one is allowed to be much the largest of any that has been killed. . . . I killed 2 alone and helped Bros. Kimball and J. Redden kill one. They had to all give up. But well you must know that I felt first rate.[50]

The camp soon took on the appearance of a "meat market" as the pioneers cut, stripped, and prepared the meat and made good use of whatever was left over. "The meat was unloaded in the semi-circle opposite the President's wagon and placed on the hide which was spread on the ground for the purpose of keeping it clean. The brethren's faces beamed with joy to see the meat begin to come into camp."[51] The meat was then divided into 14 parcels, one to each company of 10. Cleaned from the bones and laid out in strips, the meat was then cooked and salted—"jerked"—over a small fire.[52] Hides were cut into lengths to make ropes, halters, lariats, and thongs. The hair was used for stuffing beds and pillows. The bone marrow was used in lieu of butter for cooking. Buffalo robes, in demand for outerwear, were usually made from animals killed later in the year because buffalo shed much of their hair in the spring.

As the days passed, the number of buffalo increased, until by 7 May they were uncountable. It was still many years before the near extinction of the buffalo from the great American plains, and the Mormon descriptions of the bison were probably no less awe-inspiring than those of their contemporaries. "I rode forward today with the Twelve," penned Woodruff,

and of all the sights of buffalo that our eyes beheld, [this] was enough to astonish man. Thousands upon thousands would crowd together as they came from the bluffs to the bottom land to go to the river and slues to drink until the river and land upon both sides of it was one dark spectacle of moving objects. It looked as though the face of the earth was alive and moving like the waves of the sea. Bro. Kimball remarked that he had heard many buffalo tales told but he never expected to behold what his eyes now saw. The half had not been told him.[53]

During the forenoon of 8 May, the camp traveled through one continuous buffalo herd for eight miles. Estimating herds at 100,000 or more, Clayton, who was seldom without words, could only say: "No pen nor tongue can give an idea of the multitude now in sight continually, and it appears difficult to keep them away from the wagons. . . . Truly, the Lord's cattle upon the thousand hills are numerous."[54] Worried that cattle would stray and be lost in the immense herds, the pioneers worked extra hard to corral their own without inciting a thunderous stampede, which could easily have destroyed them.

The accounts of buffalo herds and buffalo hunting are so numerous in the writings of other emigrants that they defy retelling. The travelers witnessed a thundering prairie phenomenon of immense proportions, awesome to those who observed it and bewildering to the 20th-century writer who can only imagine it. Captain Benjamin L. E. Bonneville, writing 15 years before the pioneer camp but on the same north bank of the Platte, was overwhelmed by the roving spectacle. "As far as his eye could reach, the country seemed absolutely blackened by innumerable herds. No language . . . could convey an adequate idea of the vast living mass thus presented to his eye."[55]

Meanwhile the Pawnee were not amused. Aware that Brigham's party was succeeding in the hunt, as a warning they deliberately set fire to the luxuriant spring bluegrass of the north side prairie immediately and for miles ahead of them. This common but dangerous Indian tactic tried to drive off the buffalo and dissuade emigrant hunting. Such "buffalo grass," as it was called, resembled bluegrass and grew as high as six inches. "One would think," one journalist recorded, "he was in an old pasture, the grass is cut short and the ground is well covered with dung but the fence is missing."[56] But once set on fire, the spring green of the plains turned into a barren, black wasteland. "The wind blew the ashes of the burnt grass in all directions, which soon caused us to look like sweeps; however, by washing, after our halt, we were enabled to discern each other again."[57] For several subsequent days camp members, blackened and sunburned at the same time, had precious little feed for their animals.

Things might have been worse than a blackened prairie. Brigham sent a company of scouts ahead to see how far the fires extended. William Empey of Upper Canada (Ontario), one of their finest horsemen, rode on ahead of the others. On a bluff, he looked "down on the flat in a large hollow and saw a large number of Indians he supposed about 300. Some was on their poneys and some was a standing by them with the bridles in their hands waiting (as he supposed) for the brethren to come up. He then returned to the rest . . . and told them the circumstances." Brigham immediately recalled his hunters and set out extra guards in anticipation of a possible charge; but no attack materialized.[58]

"IT WAS INDEED BEST TO MAKE A TRACK OF OUR OWN"

While struggling through seas of buffalo, the pioneers met the first of what would be a string of eastbound trappers. The first was Charles Beaumont, one of Sarpy's traders with eight or nine others in his three-wagon camp, coming down from Fort Laramie on the south side of the Platte.[59] Claiming he had not seen a white person or tasted milk or flour for two years, Beaumont gladly traded three buffalo robes for needed foodstuffs. In return the congenial French-Canadian offered to carry back a small bundle of letters to Sarpy and on up to Winter Quarters; he even turned down $20 in silver offered to him for his kind services. With only a few minutes available, the camp became a writing frenzy. They produced 54 instant letters, including the following never-before published letter from 28-year-old Horace K. Whitney to his pregnant wife, Helen. Though hurried, it remains an affectionate account of their progress, and historical evidence that Beaumont kept his pledge.

Head of Grand Island May 4 1847

My dear wife

I improve the opportunity to write you, we having just met a trader who is on his way back from Fort Laramie, . . . Excuse me, dear Helen, for not writing to you before from Pawnee village, as there was no opportunity of sending it back. I have to write (as you can discover) as fast as I can hurry my hand over the paper, because the man is waiting to take the letters back, as most of all of the brethren in the camp are improving this opportunity.

We are now, according to my reckoning, 240 miles from Winter Quarters, still going on. My beloved, true and faithful Helen, be of good cheer, for I feel in my heart that we shall see each other again in the Lord's own due time. You may be assured that no opportunity that I have for prayer for you is neglected. . . .

On Saturday last, 10 or 12 hunters went out in pursuit of a herd of buffalo which we saw grazing on the side of a hill, and at night they had killed 12 buffalo . . . so you need not be alarmed but what we are doing well as far as living is concerned, for almost every man has got as much meat as he can "pack along" . . . From all appearances we shall have but few, if any chances of communication one with another as the country which we now are is infested with Sioux Indians, and it would be dangerous to send back a single messenger. But be of good courage for we shall meet again and enjoy each other's society in circumstances of greater comfort and pleasure than we have ever yet enjoyed, for I feel to say it in the name of the Lord. Dear wife, I write everything indiscriminately as it comes into my head, for the trader, a Frenchman, is very impatient and in a great hurry to pursue their journey. I have scarcely time to be lonesome, as I have the horses to attend to, and Orson [Pratt] does the cooking, and it is only at the lone hour of midnight, when I am on guard, or laying in my wagon, that memory flies back over the span between us and hurries me back to thee.

Farewell dear wife for the man is just starting.

I remain as ever your affectionate husband,

Horace K. Whitney[60]

Beaumont indicated that the Mormons were ahead of any other west-bound company on either side of the river. He also strongly recommended that, rather than follow the north bank of the river over a poorly marked trail with little feed, they cross over to the south bank of the Platte and follow the Oregon Trail. Considering their recent difficult circumstances with buffalo congestion and burned-over prairie, Beaumont's suggestion gave them reason to reconsider their commitment to stay on the north side. A travel council was called and all members of the company given a chance to speak; many different opinions were expressed. Brigham, himself, felt inclined to cross over, if only for a few days, because of the burnt prairie.[61] The majority, however, determined to stay on the north side at least until they reached Fort Laramie.

Their reasoning reaffirmed their essential purpose—to prepare a way for those who would follow. The scorched prairie was a tactic they themselves had practiced, and they would soon ride it out. The burned-off grass would become a fine pasture by June. They also reasoned that roving

Indians bent on plunder would probably focus more on the south side, where they knew more travelers would be coming. Finally, by sticking to the north bank they would remain apart from their Missouri and Illinois counterparts on the Oregon Trail for as long as possible. "When we took into consideration the situation of the next company," Woodruff summarized,

> and thousands that would follow after and as we were the Pioneers and had not our wives and children with us, we thought it best to keep on the north side of the river and brave the difficulties of burning prairies and make a road that should stand as a permanent route for the saints independent of the old emigration route and let the river separate the emigrating companies that they need not quarrel for wood, grass, or water[. A]nd when our next company came along the grass would be much better for them than it would on the south side as it would grow up by the time they would get along.[62]

The foregoing travel council illustrates several key elements of their journey. The careful observer will note that even in their travels the Mormons were making an argument for their uniqueness. First, they were abundantly, if not overly, organized, but with room for freedom of expression, dissent, even democratic expression. Once a decision was made, however, all fell in line. Second, they went as one, meaning there was no safety outside the camp. Individuality was sacrificed for the cause of the larger body. Finally, they saw themselves as pioneers preparing the way for thousands to follow.

This pattern of preparation reveals itself in two other ways: communication and expedition. The "prairie post office"—that unique system of employing eastbound travelers as letter carriers and of leaving signposts, notes, letters, and other information for those coming behind—did not originate with the Latter-day Saints, but they certainly magnified the use of it. One of their few breaks from boredom was to read on the skulls of buffalo and other animals the news and comments of other companies. "There is one thing peculiar on this route," recorded Silas Newcomb, "the practice of writing on buffalo skulls scattered along beside the track—names of men and companies and dates of their passing that their friends who follow may read."[63] Even a cursory examination of Brigham's letters and those of his colleagues shows that, even amidst their daily difficulties, communication with their following friends was both a need and a passion. The clerks were among the busiest people in camp, another reminder that this was a Church in the wilderness, perhaps the first case of a full-fledged organization on the roll across the plains. By staying on the north side, chances were better that such written communiques—left in conspicuous, yet hard to dislodge places—would reach their intended readers.

For instance, not far from the junction of the North and South Forks of the Platte, Willard Richards left the first such written communique in a small box, 18 inches wide by 6 inches long, on the top of a 15-foot pole firmly set about 5 feet into the ground. On the outside, written in red chalk, were the following instructions: "Look at this—316 miles from Winter Quarters—Camp of Pioneers, bound Westward—May 10, 1847." Inscribed on the reverse side of the board was the following: "Look in this and you will find a letter."

The letter, written for the Council of the Twelve by Richards, with Bullock as scribe, was directed to Charles C. Rich, whom they expected to be leading the soon-to-depart Emigration Company. It contained an encouraging account of their journey and, more especially, the "laws regulating the pioneer camp, for the benefit and comfort of the Saints who should follow after." After rereading it and before nailing it inside the box, Brigham remarked, "That's scripture."[64] Such elaborate prairie post boxes were reserved only for official communication from the Twelve and were not for the common or familiar. Along their journey, the pioneer camp left several other such letters beside the trail. Clearly they were setting a pattern of organization and direction for those who would follow.[65]

A more frequent form of communication was the mileage post pioneered by William Clayton. Possessed of an active mind and given to both poetry and precision, Clayton was a perfectionist. In a camp where they were always concerned, if not arguing, about how far and how fast they were traveling and how far they had yet to go, most overrated their daily accomplishments and were quick to criticize Clayton, who they felt underestimated their daily achievements. Clayton, ever since the Elkhorn, had been suggesting some sort of mileage meter or roadometer that could be fixed either to the side of the wagon near the wheel or to the wagon wheel itself.

Convinced that his estimates were most accurate, Clayton measured the circumference of the hind wheel of Heber C. Kimball's wagon and discovered it to be exactly 14 feet 8 inches. He then calculated that 360 revolutions would equal precisely one mile—5,280 feet. Into one of the wagon spikes he drove a nail that, once per revolution, struck a saw projecting from the wagon bed. On 8 May, he counted each revolution during the entire day's travel—surely a most unique and dizzying occupation—and found the distance traveled to be a little over 11 1/4 miles. His tenacity now proven, Clayton became the mileage authority in camp. That night he boldly erected the first of his many mileage posts—some on poles, some on rocks, and some on buffalo or antelope skulls—just west of Grand Island. It read: "From Winter Quarters, two hundred ninety-five miles, May 8 '47. Camp all well. Wm. Clayton."[66]

Clayton's preoccupation with measuring mileage eventually elicited the interest, if not sympathy, of his colleagues. Orson Pratt approached Appleton Harmon, a master carpenter and former apprentice in Shadrach Roundy's Nauvoo carpenter shop, to see about constructing a device with a spiral shaft and toothed wheel with a system of interlocking gears, not unlike the internal workings of a large clock. By the morning of 12 May, the ingenious Harmon had completed the wooden machine to the point that it required only counting miles, not individual wheel revolutions. Four days later he completed his wooden masterpiece, using Pratt's blueprints, by adding another set of wheel gears. These revolved once in 10 miles, showing each mile and also quarter mile traveled. He then positioned it right on the wagon wheel. There must have been camp-wide celebration at its successful operation. And certainly Clayton was much relieved: "We are now prepared to tell accurately, the distance we travel from day to day which will supersede the idea of guessing, and be a satisfaction not only to this camp, but to all who hereafter travel this way."[67]

Clayton's precision, Pratt's persistent scientific measurements, Bullock's careful recording of the flora and fauna along the trail, and the recurring references to the cartographic deficiencies of both Mitchell and Fremont—these all clearly point to their journey as expedition. Without government commission, they nevertheless improved on the maps and guides they had been following and in the process made a new guide and new maps of their own. For example, after very nearly being bitten by a large rattlesnake in a creek bed that did not show in any of their maps, Brigham christened the stream Rattlesnake Creek. To ensure a more accurate map for the rest of the journey, he called Pratt and Clayton to a meeting in Dr. Richards's wagon. "A consultation took place about delineating the pioneer road on the topographical map sent by Col. Kane," recorded Bullock, when it was decided that "Clayton should get Professor Pratt's observations that he had taken; then the course of the road by Brother Clayton's measurement showing the bluffs and each creek as found we them, in order."[68]

In this manner the concept of making their own emigrant guide was born, an idea that Clayton carefully nurtured, later developed, and eventually published as one of the West's most reliable tools—*The Latter-day Saints' Emigrants' Guide*, first published in 1848.[69]

NIGHTFALL UNDER THE PRAIRIE SKY

Signposts, roadometers, the prairie post office—all indicated that they were moving west as fast as they could manage. From the time they left Loup Fork, traveling west along the Platte River Valley and on up the North Fork of the Platte to Cedar Island (that junction with the Oregon Trail just a few miles north of Ash Hollow) the pioneer camp averaged a rather slow 13 miles per day, exclusive of Sundays.[70] After more than a month on the trail, the challenge and routine had become manageable. Their confidence was increasing with every passing mile and, if it was not yet time to celebrate, they certainly felt to congratulate one another that they had come thus far without mishap, loss of life, or serious conflict.

"The Spirit of God rules over the camp," wrote a confident Wilford Woodruff in his private journal, and "peace, quietness, and contentment seem to pervade almost every breast."[71] At a special outdoor Sunday meeting two days and 39 miles northwest of Ash Hollow, Brigham complimented the entire camp, "satisfied that the Lord was with us and leading us. [He] had never seen a company of people more united than the camp had been thus far."[72] Addressing the concerns of some that they might not reach their destination in time for planting, he replied, "Well, suppose we did not. We [have] done all we could and travelled as fast as our teams were able to go, and when we had done all [we] could he felt just as satisfied as if we had a thousand acres planted with grain. The Lord would do the rest."[73] "I never felt clearer in mind," he said, "than on this journey. My peace is like a river between my God and myself."[74]

A contented George A. Smith bore testimony that "the prayers of this camp have been heard all the time," and that "we shall get to the right place in due time. I feel first rate. I never lay down but I felt there is a good spirit in the camp. The elders will look back at this journey as one of the greatest schools they were ever in our lives."[75] Albert P. Rockwood, though hardly a poet, was inclined to express their collective optimism in rugged verse anyway.

> An other weeks journey is done
> An other hour of rest has come
> My soul retires
> Humbled in prayers,
> On my god I calls
> For blessings all in all.[76]

In the early evening, after supper and after camp had been made, they began to relax. With beds ready and gear put away, it was still possible to play the violin and the harmonica and listen to the crackling of the evening buffalo chip fire. Some nights, under the prairie moon, they danced, as traders and trappers had been known to do, in groups to keep warm. At other times they conducted mock trials on one another, such as "The Camp vs. James Davenport" for blocking the highway and turning ladies out of their course.[77] All in fun, they danced and played until the fires began to fade, the wagon candles grew dim, and the last sounds of life fell away into much-needed slumber.

As one overlander described it, these were the quiet moments so well deserved:

> The men, except those on guard duty, would form circles around the fires . . . recounting the incidents of the day's travel, singing songs, telling jokes at each other's expense; while in another part of the camp, the violin would enliven the air with notes, to which young and agile feet were keeping time in the merry dance on the soil of the plains. . . . Gradually the stock would lie down and the people retire to dream of home and the dear ones left behind; the camp would become quiet and the fires grow dimmer until its flickering flames expired; no sound would be heard except the low talk of the guards as they made their rounds or the lonesome howl of the prairie wolf.[78]

But like the gusts of a sudden prairie storm, their contentment would not last long.

NOTES

1. Willard D. Richards to George D. Watt, 16 Apr. 1847, Willard Richards papers, LDS Church Archives.

2. *William Clayton's Journal: A Daily Record of the Journey of the Original Company of "Mormon" Pioneers from Nauvoo, Illinois, to the Valley of the Great Salt Lake* (1921), 20 Apr. 1847, 85.

3. *William Clayton's Journal,* 23 Apr. 1847, 92. A fine biography of Clayton is James B. Allen's *Trials of Discipleship: The Story of William Clayton, a Mormon* (1987).

4. Journal of Thomas Bullock, 17 Apr. 1847.

5. Journal of Thomas Bullock, 21 Apr. 1847.

6. Orson Pratt was born 19 September 1811 in Hartford County, New York. He was baptized into the Church by his older brother, Parley P. Pratt, on his 19th birthday. A member of Zion's Camp in 1834, Orson became one of the original Twelve Apostles in February 1835. Though provided with little formal training, Pratt was highly regarded for his mathematical and scientific mind. He died in Salt Lake City in 1881.

7. Journal of Thomas Bullock, 22 Apr. 1847.

8. *William Clayton's Journal,* 24 Apr. 1847, 94.

9. Journal of Albert P. Rockwood, 23 Apr. 1847. Actually quicksand was a misnomer for what they encountered in this region; true quicksand was almost nonexistent anywhere along the Oregon or Mormon trails. The Platte was known for its thick mud, but that could compact fairly easily and had a relatively firm bottom. While the overland journals tell of scores of drownings, there are no accounts of death by quicksand.

10. Journal of Norton Jacob, 20 April 1847; see also Journal of Erastus Snow, 20 Apr. 1847.

11. Journal of Norton Jacob, 24 Apr. 1847.

12. Journal of Norton Jacob, 26 Apr. 1847.

13. Thomas Bullock to his wife, 14 May 1847, Bullock letters, Thomas Bullock Papers, LDS Church Archives.

14. Brigham Young said Eames returned to Winter Quarters on account of ill health. Horace K. Whitney gave it a different slant. "Ellis Eames went back in consequence of sickness, as he said, but I think he is weak in the faith" (Journal of Horace K. Whitney, 17 Apr. 1847).

It is significant to note that camp members were at total liberty to remain or to quit the camp. Eames did come west with a later train.

15. Joseph Bissonnette to John B. Sarpy, 5 July 1846, unpublished letter in the Pierre Chouteau Maffitt Collection, Missouri Historical Society. The matter of Indian thievery, from the Pawnee perspective, takes on an entirely different meaning. To them, the whites were trespassers who had no right to travel or to hunt. As payment for permission, the passerby had to pay tribute.

16. Catherine Margaret Haun, "A Woman's Trip Across the Plains in 1849," Huntington Library; later published in Lillian Schlissel, *Women's Diaries of the Westward Journey* (1982), 165–85.

17. Hockett, Reminiscences, 4, 6.

18. *William Clayton's Journal*, 30 Apr. 1847, 115. The captains of 10s were Wilford Woodruff, Ezra T. Benson, Phineas H. Young, Luke S. Johnson, Stephen H. Goddard, Charles Shumway, James Case, Seth Taft, Howard Egan, Appleton M. Harmon, John S. Higbee, Norton Jacob, John Brown, and Joseph Mathews.

19. One reason for the several layers of organization was to preserve the authority of ecclesiastical leaders from the inevitable compromises of prairie travel. They felt it better to delegate responsibility for daily travel plans, rather than dilute their authority over minutia. This attempt at distancing moral authority from daily routine may not have always worked in practice, because Brigham Young as "general" reserved the last word for himself, but it is significant how often Markham and Pack made the everyday decisions.

20. It may be constructive to compare the layers of organization in the pioneer camp with other 1847 companies, most of whom were far simpler and less regimented than the Latter-day Saints, in large part because of the much looser affiliations between members. It appears that most other emigrant trains preferred as little organization as possible. Isaac Pettijohn, in describing his Oregon-bound company from Missouri, provides this contrast: "We completed our organization last night. A young man whose name is Nathaniel Bowman who returned from Oregon last season was elected captain, pilot, and camp master. Richard Miller was elected guard master. Those are all the officers we have" (Diary of Isaac Pettijohn, 5 May 1847, Bancroft Library, Berkeley, California).

21. See the Journal of Thomas Bullock, William Clayton, Newel K. Whitney, Wilford Woodruff, 18 April 1847.

22. The basic rifle of the Mormons was the single-shot, flintlock muzzle-loading Kentucky rifle. They also used the early versions of the Browning rifle. Browning, a recent convert to Mormonism, had set up a gun shop in Nauvoo. In 1845, Orson Pratt was directed to purchase with tithing funds $400 worth of six-barrelled pistols for self-defense. These "pepperboxes" were gradually replaced by the Colt-type revolver. The pioneers also brought along a cannon, probably a three-pounder, 25 extra pounds of powder, and 20 extra pounds of lead.

For more on the Mormon arsenal, see Harry W. Gibson, "Frontier Arms of the Mormons," *Utah Historical Quarterly* 42 (Winter 1974): 4–26.

23. The Mormons were not, of course, the only emigrant company to have such rules and regulations. In fact, it was the custom of most companies to devise a written constitution to which all members would affix their names or marks. Joseph Wood, an 1849 traveler to California, told of eight articles his company agreed to, including the responsibility of the captains, the method of calling meetings, dispensation of prairie justice ("All cases of misdemeanors shall be tried by the Company and the decision of a majority shall be conclusive"), and conduct of morality ("Inasmuch as immoral conduct and the use of profane language are useless and have an evil tendency and are hurtful to the feelings of many . . . all shall refrain from either)" (Journal of Joseph W. Wood, 15 May 1849, Huntington Library).

24. Bennett, *Mormons at the Missouri*, 85–86.

25. Journal of Levi S. Johnson, 21 April 1847, LDS Church Archives.

26. Such "begging letters," as they were called, were fast becoming a common tool for the Indian tribes to demand tribute.

27. Journal of Horace K. Whitney, 21 Apr. 1847.

28. Journal of Addison Everett, 21 May 1847, LDS Church Archives. A carpenter by trade, Everett was 41 years old and a native of New York.

29. The pioneers learned from Fremont and others how to put their cannons to good use. Wrote Nathan Tanner Porter, of the pioneer camp, when confronting Sioux Indians nearing Fort Laramie: "The wagon bearing the field piece was drawn out and placed in position outside our lines to which their attention was called. They gathered around to see the curious wagon and on motioning to them they stepped back. The torch was applied, and off she went, resulting in a general stampede on the part of the Indians. Men, women, and children were struck with consternation for a minute or two. But the smile on our faces dispelled all fear. We learned that the impression went out among them that all our wagons would shoot. No one wished to dispel the impression as it answers well to deter them from molesting us" (Reminiscences of Nathan Tanner Porter, Summer 1847, 57, LDS Church Archives).

30. Journal of Norton Jacob, 23 Apr. 1847. As early as 1830, Reverend Moses Merrill of the Baptist Missionary Society had been ministering among the Otoe and other Missouri Valley Indian tribes. In 1835 Dr. Marcus Whitman and Reverend Samuel Parker offered their services to the American Board of Commissioners for Foreign Missions to proselyte the western tribes. Parker, in turn, enlisted the services of John Dunbar. While Whitman and Parker went west to Oregon, Dunbar and a Reverend Samuel Allis spent their time among the Plains Indians near Council Bluffs. They had been responsible for erecting the Pawnee missionary station some years before.

For more on Indian missions, see Ray H. Mattison, "Indian Missions and Missionaries on the Upper Missouri to 1900," *Nebraska History* 38, no. 2 (June 1957): 127–54. See also John Dunbar, "The Presbyterian Mission Among the Pawnee Indians in Nebraska, 1834–1836," *Collections of the Kansas State Historical Society* 11 (1909–1910): 323–32.

31. Young Horace K. Whitney was just one of many who described the Pawnee village in vivid detail: "Before going over [the river]," he wrote, " Orson [Pratt] and myself went and took a view of the ruins of the Pawnee village which was an interesting sight, indeed. . . . The village is situated on the northern bank of and immediately fronting the river. It is irregularly formed . . . and comprises upwards of 200 lodges, a great share of which have been burnt down. . . . We visited 2 or 3 of those which were standing, and were much struck with the ingenuity manifested in their formation. The largest one that we visited is about 45 feet in diameter. Around the inside are 16 posts, which uphold the fabric, also 8 large ones in the center, and a man can stand upright in any part of the room. Across the roof are laid transversely cottonwood or willow poles, all verging towards the center. To these straw is bound with withes, and on the top of this is a layer of dirt, a hole being left in the center of the roof through which the smoke can escape and the fire being in the center of the lodge" (Journal of Horace K. Whitney, 24 Apr. 1847).

32. Born in Massachusetts in 1804, Willard Richards was baptized in 1836 by his cousin, Brigham Young. After serving as a missionary in England with Heber C. Kimball and Orson Pratt, he was ordained an Apostle and appointed clerk to Joseph Smith. He was with Joseph Smith during the martyrdom at Carthage Jail, miraculously escaping unharmed.

33. Journal of Thomas Bullock, 27 Apr. 1847.

34. Journal of Albert P. Rockwood, 21 May 1847.

35. Journal of Levi Jackman, 19 May 1847, LDS Church Archives.

36. Journal of Colonel James Clyman, 13 July 1844, Bancroft Library.

37. Journal of Wilford Woodruff, 13 May 1847.

38. Journal of James W. Evans, 1 June 1850, Bancroft Library.

39. Journal of Levi Jackman, May 1847.

40. Overland Journal of Elizabeth (Dixon) Smith Geer, 29 Aug. 1847, Oregon Historical Society.

41. Thomas Bullock to Henrietta Bullock, 14 May 1847, Bullock Letters.

42. *William Clayton's Journal*, 29 Apr. 1847, 113.

43. Journal of Heber C. Kimball, 18 May 1847.

44. *William Clayton's Journal*, 9 May 1847, 138.

45. Journal of Joseph W. Wood, 18 May 1849.

46. Journal of James Clyman, 12 July 1844.

47. *William Clayton's Journal*, 1 May 1847, 118.

48. William Marshall Anderson, "Anderson's Narrative of a Ride to the Rocky Mountains in 1834," 30 May 1834, 4, mss #1508, Oregon Historical Society.

49. *William Clayton's Journal*, 1 May 1847, 119–20.

50. John Pack to his family at Winter Quarters, 1 June 1847, as quoted in Davis Bitton, *The Redoubtable John Pack: Pioneer, Proselyter, Patriarch* (1982), 220.

51. *William Clayton's Journal*, 1 May 1847, 122.

52. Journal of Albert P. Rockwood, 3 May 1847. Jerking, as one overlander described it, "is a process resorted to for want of time or means to cure meat by salting. The meat is sliced thin, and a scaffold prepared, by setting forks in the ground, about three feet high and laying small poles on sticks crosswise upon them. The meat is laid upon those pieces, and a slow fire built beneath; the heat and smoke completes the process in half a day; and with an occasional sunning the meat will keep for months" (Joel Palmer, *Journal of Travels over the Rocky Mountains, to the Mouth of the Columbia River* [1847], 15 June 1845, 53).

53. Journal of Wilford Woodruff, 8 May 1847.

54. *William Clayton's Journal*, 8 May 1847, 137.

55. As quoted in Frank Gilbert Roe's monumental study *The North American Buffalo: A Critical Study of the Species in its Wild State*, 2nd ed. (1951), 553.

If the leading scholars on the topic are correct, by 1847 the number of buffalo on the Great Plains—stretching from what is now Saskatchewan to Texas and from the Loup Fork to the foothills—numbered almost 40 million (see Roe, *North American Buffalo*, and Thompson Seton, *Life Histories of Northern Animals*, 1:259, 292 as quoted in Roe, 493). The rapid decline and near extermination of the buffalo occurred in the years following 1865—one of America's greatest environmental tragedies.

56. Journal of Levi Jackman, 2 May 1847.

57. Journal of Thomas Bullock, 5 May 1847.

58. Journal of Levi S. Johnson, 3 May 1847.

59. There is some dispute over the name of this passerby. Most of the records refer to him as "Beaumont," although some refer to him as Charley Barkham (see Brigham Young letters, 5 May 1847). Erastus Snow records that the leader of the Beaumont company was a "Mr. Papan" who stayed on the other side of the river (see

also Journal of Levi S. Johnson, 4 May 1847, Special Collections, Lee Library, Brigham Young University).

60. Horace K. Whitney to Helen Mar Kimball Whitney, 4 May 1847, Whitney Collection, Special Collections, Merrill Library, Utah State University.

Brigham found time to scratch out a letter that provided a string of details about their travels thus far and about future plans. After Fort Laramie, "we shall take the most southern route to the Salt Lake that we can find" (Brigham Young to John Smith and the Saints at Winter Quarters, 4 May 1847, Brigham Young Papers).

61. Brigham Young to John Smith, 4 May 1847, Brigham Young Letters.

62. Journal of Wilford Woodruff, 4 May 1847.

63. Journal of Silas Newcomb, 31 May 1850, Huntington Library.

64. Journal of Thomas Bullock, 10 May 1847.

65. It is interesting to note that most, if not all, such communications reached their intended audiences (see Arrington, *Charles C. Rich*, 117).

66. *William Clayton's Journal*, 8 May 1847, 136–37.

67. *William Clayton's Journal*, 16 May 1847, 152. There has been disagreement over who actually invented the famous pioneer roadometer. Howard Egan was sharply critical of what he perceived as Harmon's claim to invention. Clayton also took offense at Harmon, who he thought was "trying to have it understood that he invented the machinery, . . . which makes me think less of him than I formerly did. He is not the inventor of it by a long way, but he has made the machinery" (*William Clayton's Journal*, 14 May 1847, 149). But Harmon says nothing whatsoever about the matter in his journal.

The definitive article on the topic is Guy E. Stringham, "The Pioneer Roadometer," *Utah Historical Quarterly* 42 (Summer 1974): 258–72. Stringham argues that to Orson Pratt must go whatever credit is due, because it was he who Brigham Young suggested should "give this subject some attention." His concept of a continuous screw amongst a series of cogs and wheels doubtless reflected his mathematical genius and ability. However, it was Clayton's stubborn insistence and sense of precision that initiated it all. According to Stringham, the original was long ago lost or destroyed, although a duplicate of the original is on display at the Church Museum of History and Art in Salt Lake City, Utah.

68. Journal of Thomas Bullock, 18 May 1847.

69. William Clayton, *The Latter-day Saints' Emigrants' Guide: Being a Table of Distances . . . from Council Bluffs, to the Valley of the Great Salt Lake* (1848). For more on Clayton's guide, see chapter 11.

70. In contrast, according to Isaac Pettijohn, who was part of a non-Mormon emigrant train hard on the heels of the pioneer camp, their company averaged 16.98 miles per day over a two-month period (Journal of Isaac Pettijohn). The Mormon camps began to move faster once past Ash Hollow. They had lost time crossing the Elkhorn River, visiting the Pawnee villages, searching for lost horses, and hunting buffalo. No doubt the various rules and routines took time to master sufficiently as well. That they refused to travel on most Sundays seems to show that they were not overly concerned about time, at least not at this point.

71. Journal of Wilford Woodruff, 9 May 1847.

72. Journal of Wilford Woodruff, 23 May 1847.

73. Journal of Norton Jacob, 23 May 1847.

74. General Church Minutes, 23 May 1847.

75. General Church Minutes, 23 May 1847.

76. Journal of Albert P. Rockwood, 22 May 1847.

77. *William Clayton's Journal*, 22 May 1847, 176.

78. Autobiography of J. Henry Brown (1878), 4, Bancroft Library.

5

"I AM ABOUT TO REVOLT"

Mormon Thunder at Scottsbluff

I felt all the cares and perplexities of this camp and when a man feels as though his flesh and bones would melt away, he knows it.[1]

In late May, as the Mormon pioneers pushed forward northwest of Ash Hollow, both the surrounding scenery and the mood of the camp began to change. The newness of the journey, their success with the Pawnee, the excitement of the buffalo hunt, and the almost comforting sameness of the lower Platte River Valley had all given way to a restless realization that with each passing day time was becoming critical. They were now advancing deeper into the lands of the hostile, unpredictable Sioux and far removed from the ample food supplies in the vast buffalo herds of just a few weeks before. One senses from their writings a change in tone, an increasing sobriety, a growing awareness of their smallness in the face of a vast and expansive wilderness, a waning confidence tempered and cooled by the quiet immensity of their newfound isolation.

"ONE OF THE WILDEST LOOKING PLACES"

High up the North Fork of the Platte River, on a ridge separating the North Platte Valley from Pumpkin Creek, the monotony of the prairie landscape at last began to give way. "A menagerie of enormous natural forms, monolithic clay and sandstone shapes," came into view: a domain of massive rock formations such as Courthouse Rock, Chimney Rock, Castle

Pioneers Crossing the North Platte River, *by C. C. A. Christensen*

Rock, Dome Rock, and Scottsbluff. "It was one of the wildest looking places I ever passed through," wrote the Oregon-bound James Field during his 1845 travels through the area.[2] And the traveler, wrote another earlier observer, "imagined himself in the midst of the desolate and deserted ruins of vast cities, to which Nineveh, Thebes, and Babylon were pygmies in grandeur and magnificence."[3]

Soon after noon on 22 May, Porter Rockwell reported that he had ascended a nearby bluff and had seen in the distance the fabled Chimney Rock. To satisfy their curiosity, William Clayton, Horace K. Whitney, and John Pack grabbed a telescope and scampered up the nearby hillside like excited children to view the surrounding country. Said Clayton: "Northeast, north, and northwest, alternately, appeared high swelling bluffs and valleys as far as the eye could see or the glass magnify. . . . At the distance I should judge of about twenty miles, I could see Chimney Rock very plainly with the naked eye, which from here very much resembles the large factory chimneys in England, although I could not see the form of its base."[4]

Whitney, a talented writer, was even more descriptive: "The scene to

148

us was truly one of magnificence and grandeur and almost baffles description," he penned.

> The whole scene was one of romantic solitude and inspired me with singular feelings and reminding me forcibly of the descriptions I had read in my boyish days of the fortified castles and watchtowers of the older time. We had an opportunity of viewing it to the greatest advantage, as the setting sun, throwing its lengthening rays upon hill, dale, mound and river, made the sight inexpressibly grand and solemn.[5]

Between 23 and 31 May, the pioneer camp passed by Courthouse and Jail Rocks, Castle Rock, Chimney Rock, and Scottsbluff—all in a stretch of thirty-five miles. These physical features towered over the passing canvas-covered caravan like "huge rocks that had been rolled out of their natural place by the wash of the heavy rains or the convulsive throes of nature at the crucifixion of our Saviour."[6]

"This is a barren, desolate country," wrote a subdued and weary John Pack in a letter to his wives, realizing, perhaps, how far they yet had to go. "There is but little or no wood. We have cooked our victuals with buffalo chips [dried dung] for weeks. . . . Our teams are reduced for the want of grass. We cannot travel only about 75 miles a week. We hope that Fort Laramie is about half way." Then he admitted the loneliness and homesickness many were beginning to feel:

> This is quite a lonesome journey to me. In fact I never am happy when absent from my family and kindred. The enjoyments of life are but vanity and if it were not for the sake of my kindred and the kingdom of God I never would leave home again but I would spend my remaining days in the sweet society of my family.
> . . . I am not sorry that I came on the journey but I miss my bosom friends. It will probably be late in the fall before I get back.[7]

The separation was similarly wearing on their families and loved ones back at Winter Quarters. "The time seems long, very long, since I saw you," wrote Louisa M. Lyman, wife of Amasa Lyman.

> I have been left many times but never did I realize my incapability of getting along without you to lean on or to advise me. I always had more directions about matters, and understood how to get

along better than I do at the present time. For awhile after you left I was very much broken up. I could not content myself anywhere at home or abroad, night nor day. I was miserable. Let me be where I would I had lost my companion and with him all my enjoyment. I would have given almost everything to have seen you and received your counsel . . . and I shall be thankful, very thankful, if the Lord will be merciful to me and spare our lives that we may meet again, I hope never to part.[8]

The country, however, was as dangerous as it was spectacular. Their first concern was the weather. They had earlier learned from Sarpy that several years before at this very time of the year "at about this place," a sunny, warm afternoon turned into a rainy and cold evening; before morning 16 of his best horses were frozen to death by the side of the wagons and his boats were frozen into the ice of the river.[9]

While passing through the same valley in 1842, another California-bound emigrant, John Bidwell, had noted the hailstorms that often accompanied the "water spouts" or thunderstorms of the high plains. "The hailstones were so large and heavy that we thought they would kill our animals," he recalled. "Some of the stones measured two and a half inches in diameter. Some were found yet unmelted on our next day's travel."[10] And from the pen of another traveler near Scottsbluff: "Those hail storms are great 'bugieboos' here—they are really dangerous, sometimes setting teams afright."[11]

Both the intensity and the speed of such storms caught the attention of most emigrants. Another traveler

discovered a small black cloud in the west, and immediately ordered twenty men to saddle horses and remain on them while the rest were securely tied to the wagons, tents extra pinned, the cattle herded closely by horse and footmen. The storm could now plainly be seen coming by the flashes of lightning and the rapidly increasing roar of the thunder. . . . When the storm struck us, it was quite dark, which of course added to the confusion. It seemed as if the very elements were at war with each other. The blinding brightness of lightning as it apparently covered acres, followed instantaneously by the deafening crash that seemed to shake the earth, accompanied by large hailstones and a terrific wind, when all combined was well calculated to throw everything into confusion. Tents were prostrated, thus increasing the fright of the occupants; cattle bellowing as they rushed by with the storm; horses struggling frantically to break their fastenings to the wagons, mingled with the shouting of men, made an hour's experience that can never be forgotten when once endured. But the storm went by as rapidly as it came.[12]

A hint of just such a storm hit the camp late in the day on Sunday, 23 May. A sudden gust of wind struck Heber C. Kimball's hat, blowing it across a ravine. Soon afterward, at "about five o'clock, the wind blew a perfect gale and continued till seven when it commenced to rain very heavily, large drops descending, accompanied with hail. . . . We saw the necessity of having good stout bows to our wagons," Clayton recorded, "and the covers well fastened down, for the very stoutest seemed in danger of being torn to pieces and the wagons blown over. When the wind commenced blowing so strongly it turned very cold and long before dark I went to bed to keep warm."[13] By morning snow lay on the ground, with a cold east wind blowing.

Throughout such nights on the prairie, if the winds were not howling, then the wolves were, and the cries and sounds of other wild animals seemed to echo for miles. Recalled Joseph Wood of their encampment near Chimney Rock two years later:

> Last night I stood as guard from eleven to one and saw four grey wolves prowling around the encampment. I snapped my gun at them when they cleared out [and] were joined by others. [They] kept up a serenade on every side of us for some time noises of all kinds from wild animals were heard through the night even to the yowling of cats.[14]

"In the Land of the Sioux"

Of far greater concern than inclement weather or the incessant howls was the unpredictability of the nearby Sioux. They posed the single greatest threat, not only to the forward camp but also to future trains of emigrants. From their observations of recent buffalo slaughters and abandoned campgrounds and from occasional sightings, the pioneers knew that a very large band—from five hundred to one thousand—of Sioux was in the area, likely watching their every move. As with the Pawnee, it would be in their mutual interest to make friendly contact soon and to establish some kind of positive dialogue.

Fortunately that opportunity came quickly. As their trail bent toward

Chimney Rock in the afternoon of 24 May, they saw a "drove of Indians" on the other side of the river riding in the direction of the camp. A messenger went ahead while the camp immediately began to stake their horses and form a circle for defense. The Indians waved a flag from their side of the river, signaling their desire to visit. The pioneers answered by hoisting their own "white flag of peace" and sent Albert P. Rockwood and Henry G. Sherwood to receive the natives and learn their intentions. The Sioux, some thirty-five men, women, and children, began to sing and cross the river in single file. Their chief, Owashtecha, wore around his neck a large medal that he had obviously obtained from earlier trades. Inscribed, on one side it read "Pierre Chouteau Jr. and Co. Upper Missouri Outfit," and on the other, "Brave Bear." In his hand he carried an American flag, the first seen in a Mormon camp since James Allen's invitation for the Mormon Battalion. It had the standard stripes, but in place of the stars there was an eagle, emblematic "of America scourging the Indians but giving no star of glory to the sons of the prairie."[15] The chief also brought two letters of introduction—both in French—from fur traders at Fort Laramie. Unlike the poorly clad Pawnee, the Sioux presented a striking and noble appearance. "They were all dressed in their richest costumes," Erastus Snow recalled. "Some had fur caps and cloth coats, others had cloth pants and shirts, and the rest were neatly dressed in skins ornamented with beads, feathers, paints, etc. and they were by all odds the most cleanly, orderly, and best appearing of any Indians we have seen west of the Missouri River."[16] Their women were beautifully adorned and noble in stature; Jacob noted that "some of their squaws are pretty brunettes,"[17] a description seconded by Whitney. "There were some very fine looking men and women among them."[18]

Clearly on a peaceful, fact-finding mission, the Sioux were kindly escorted around the camp, shown the cannon, and given tobacco, bread, meal, and other presents in abundance. Invited to dinner, the chief sat in a circle with Brigham and other camp leaders and proceeded to pass around the peace pipe. That night the chief amused himself by looking at the moon through the telescope; then he and his squaw stayed the night in a special tent provided for them. Early the next morning, all the other Indians came over and went about "just as their curiosity led them, some to get bread and other things, some trading moccasins, blankets, horses, etc." One of the chiefs, Washteha, was very pressing for a written paper"—a character reference which he could use to advantage with later wagon companies.

Bullock was quick to oblige. "This is to certify that Washteha of the Dacotah tribe of Indians, with O Wash te cha the principal chief, and thirty-three other men, women, and children, visited our camp on the 24th and 25th May 1847, behaved themselves civilly and peaceably; we gave them bread. They were very friendly to us, and the best behaved Indians we have yet seen. W. Richards—Thomas Bullock, scribe."[19]

The Sioux then shook hands, mounted their horses, and rode away toward the river. Throughout the rest of their outbound journey, at least, there would be no trouble with the Sioux.

Although the Sioux caused no disturbance, one of their ponies most certainly did. Ohio-born John S. Higbee had exchanged one of his ponies for another belonging to the Indians, one not "broken in" for the rigors of wagon travel. For no apparent reason, on the following day just before noon, the pony suddenly

> ran away with a singletree to his heels and gave a tremendous fright to the cows, oxen, and horses that were attached to the wagons. And in an instant a dozen or more wagons were darting by each other like lightning and the horses and mules flying as it were over the ground. Some turned to the right and some to the left. Some ran into other wagons. The horse and mule that Bro. [John S.] Fowler was driving leaped with all speed. With Bro. [John C.] Little hold of the lines and Br. Fowler hold of the bits they darted by my carriage like electricity and came within one inch of a collision with my wheels. . . .
>
> A person can hardly conceive of the power that is manifest in animals, especially mules, when in such fright.[20]

Woodruff and the rest had just witnessed the closest thing yet to a stampede, surely one of the most frightening experiences during an overland journey.[21] It was the kind of hair-raising experience emigrants prayed would never happen or, at least, never happen again.

PRAIRIE PRAYERS AND SAGEBRUSH SERMONS

Religious exercises on the trail have yet to receive the scholarly attention they deserve. Neither ordained ministers nor reverent sabbaths fared especially well on the Oregon or California trails. Sundays may have been layover days for most parties but for very practical, not only religious, reasons. And although ministers, most of whom were Protestant, often accompanied camps, they preached with sporadic, intermittent results.

The wagon pulpit of westbound America was something more needed than heeded, an almost reluctant consent to social conscience. Prayers were more from fear than from sabbatarian duty. And some travelers considered their goals too crass for the blessings of heaven. A gold seeker, J. M. Wood, put it this way: "In the states millions of prayers are being addressed to the throne of grace for mercy for themselves and for others, but few there are who think of us in the wilderness or pray for blessings to rest upon our heads, but why should they care for those who care not for themselves."[22]

For most overlanders Sunday was usually a day set aside for needed chores and restless recuperation, time begrudgingly given by impatient company captains for their members to rest and feed the animals, to clean clothes, to mend and repair, and to do the numerous other things not possible any other day of the week. "This day is a day of rest," Solomon Gorgas, an 1850 emigrant observed, "that is, a day of general bustle and confusion—washday, bakeday and reposing day."[23]

Catherine Haun, an 1849 overlander, gave her description of a typical Sabbath day. "When the camp ground was desirable enough to warrant it we did not travel on the Sabbath," she observed and

> although the men were generally busy mending wagons, harness, yokes, shoeing the animals etc. and the women washed clothes, boiled a big mess of beans to be warmed over several meals, or perhaps mended clothes or did other household straightening up, all felt somewhat rested on Monday mornings, for the change of occupation had been refreshing.[24]

In such busy company, ministers, or more usually lay preachers, could not always be assured of a ready audience. "If we had devotional service," Haun remembered, "the minister—pro tem—stood in the center of the corral while we all kept on with our work. There was no disrespect intended but there was little time for leisure or what the weary pilgrim could call his own."[25]

A Reverend M. Stevens, a young Baptist minister from Ohio who was moving his family to Oregon, found that one had to work just about as hard "when stopping in looking after the cattle as when moving." Stevens laid by the first Sabbath, "but found there was no such thing as keeping it anyway and that he might as well be moving as lying by."[26]

Charles G. Gray, on his way to California in 1849, told of another forlorn preacher. "At about 10 o'clock a clerical looking young chap invited us to church in a grove about a mile distant and one of our men did actually attend. In the afternoon he preached in a grove quite near us and I believe no one condescended to pay their respects to him."[27]

Nevertheless there were times and places, depending on personalities, abilities, and circumstances, when the preaching of the word took good effect. There was enough wilderness and enough fear of the unknown to prompt some to listen, despite the many distractions of trail life. "In the afternoon we were summoned together by a blast from the horn to listen to a sermon by an old preacher named Liseville[?]," Joseph Wood recalled of one 1849 sermon.

> He is a good man. I listened with pleasure. His text was 'watch and pray.' He was practical in his remarks and preached appropriately to the occasion. The audience were lounging about in the corral with heads uncovered and listened respectfully. . . . A sermon on these prairies is listened to attentively by those who at home would not do so.[28]

Another emigrant, on his way to fame and fortune in California two years later, told of a certain sermon on the imminent end of the world that caught the ear of his companions. "We had also with us another offshoot of the Baptist Church who had become a Millerite," he wrote,

> Ascension Day being then near at hand, the stirring oratory of this man tended to damper our enthusiasm for gold hunting, seeing how foolish and futile was our mission if we had to ascend in so short a time; and I cannot yet see why he should endure all these hardships to get to California, knowing (as he pretended) that the world would end in a few years at most.[29]

There must have been several memorable sermons in overland history. Unfortunately, few have survived in historical documentation. That prize may well belong to the Latter-day Saints and to the sermonizing thunder of Brigham Young.

Unlike the practices of many of their fellow overlanders, Mormon devotion to the Sabbath was a mixture of Puritan devotion and New England practicality. Invariably they rested on Sundays, except when travel for a better campground made it necessary to move on. Hunting was not allowed, unless they were totally without food. And worship services, complete with makeshift pews, choirs, and speeches, were held as occasion allowed. Admitted Isaac Pettijohn, part of an Illinois company that later caught up to the Mormons west of Fort Laramie: "I saw and talked with [William] Vance, a son of Mr. Vance from McDonough Co. Illinois. Unlike us they had stopped to spend the Sabbath."[30]

As with most other companies, it was expected that preachers would sermonize in the sagebrush and sing hymns of praise on a prairie highway.[31] What distinguished the Latter-day Saints, in keeping with the earliest Puritans, was more than mere sermons: it was a developing sense of divine mission. And they believed that to accomplish it, God would have a chastened and a contrite people. Burdened and blessed by such faith and expectation, it was only a matter of time before their own Jonathan Edwards would speak boldly of their Pilgrim's Progress to a new Mount Zion.

While much counsel and many sermons were given along the trail in 1847, most of them were of the kind and supportive variety. Yet the one that will stand out forever came not on a Sunday, but on a Saturday in the shadow of Scottsbluff, and from a man they had already begun to call "the Lion of the Lord." Brigham's prairie-borne jeremiad of 29 May is as much a landmark in pioneer history as Chimney Rock was to the overland trail—not merely because of its quick and colorful chastisements (for which Brigham Young was already well known), but more significantly for what it revealed about how they viewed their journey, how they would define success, and on whose errand they believed they were.

Obviously the spoken word had already borne fruit. Thomas Bullock said as much in a letter to his wife in mid-May. "I expect you will think there is a reformation in me," he said, "when you know that I have commenced reading the Bible through. I have already read as far as the 7th chapter of Judges and express my gratitude to God . . . that I have already received much light and intelligence in things of which I have been a long time dark."[32]

"I AM ABOUT TO REVOLT FROM TRAVELLING WITH THIS CAMP"

Perhaps it had something to do with the place. Scores of earlier travelers had already commented on the towering presence and stark desolation of Scottsbluff. "The whole viewed altogether has the appearance of a stu-

Scottsbluff, *sketch from the Appleton Milo Harmon Journal,*
27–28 May 1847

pendous city in ruins with broken walls," J. E. Howells recorded in 1845. "The peculiarities of this land is its sterility, its extensive level plain, large dry basins without outlets, large tracts extremely broken."[33]

Some travelers considered that a curse had been about the place since 1828, when a wounded Hiram Scott was left to die of sickness and starvation by his two notorious companions. "His death has left here a traveller's landmark," wrote an 1834 visitor to Scottsbluff,

which will be known when the name of the canting hypocrite and scoundrel who deserted him will be forgotten, and remembered only in hell. . . . The unburied corpse of poor Scott was found at this spot, having crawled more than two miles towards his father's cabin and his mother's home. His only witness, the only watcher in his death-agony, was the dark raven and the ever hungry wolf. And keen, sharp and eager was his watch. I know the name of the soulless villain, and so does God and the devil.[34]

Not given to committees, advisors, or leadership by consensus, Brigham independently spoke his mind when he wanted and where he wanted. Passionately committed to the success and purpose of their present journey, he showed little patience with sinners or fools, with the proud or the excuse maker. Erastus Snow had learned that lesson the hard way two weeks before when, after trying to justify himself for losing Brigham Young's field glasses, he had borne his leader's blistering rebuke.

> This is a school to us all. . . . The advice is good that we had better chew india rubber than talk. The last dressing was the only regular built dressing that I had for fifteen years and I intend it shall be for the next fifteen years to come. I would not expose myself for such a chastisement again for all the horses in the land of God. I do not mean to aim all my remarks at President Young. I had no business to have spoken. I had suffered my feelings to be overcome. I am very sorry for it, and I have been the target. . . . If I cannot get a piece of india rubber, I'll chaw something else next time.[35]

Some few days later, unhappy with what he thought was needless and careless killing of animals by camp hunters, Brigham gave instructions to the captains "not to let their men kill any more game, as we had more on hand now than we could take care of." He also stated

> that life was as dear to the animal . . . as it was to us. That if the horsemen hunters would go ahead and hunt out the road they would be of more utility to the camp than pursuing every band of antelope that passed the camp; . . . that the spirit of the hunter as was now manifested would lead them to kill all the game within a thousand miles as inconsistently as the butcher would apply the knife to the throat of a bullock.[36]

Unlike the ministers of most other camps, who usually came along for the ride as a reminder of heaven, Brigham was a dominant figure, convinced that the success of their journey depended less on maps and wagons and more on personal obedience. And as for his fellow sojourners, they should have seen it coming.

Ever since Nauvoo, his periodic admonitions carried with them the theme of self-improvement, repentance, and obedience. Back in Mount Pisgah, Iowa, almost a year ago to the day, he had told his people that "now is the time to prove to be the Lord's, or else go into the world or to hell like other fools. . . . If this people will continue as they have done, their own prayers will bring a curse upon them and they will be blown up and scattered."[37]

Later, at Winter Quarters, after presenting "The Word and Will of the Lord," with its theme of personal improvement, he returned to the same topic. "If we penetrate into the wilderness and do not do right and keep the commandments of God, it is better to tarry here. You need not think that you are going to creep into my company and commit iniquity without being punished for it. . . . I want every family to break off from all iniquity and turn unto the Lord."[38]

And on 15 April, back at the Elkhorn, he had said, "We go as Abram of old; where we stop we now know not; we want the brethren to cease every [light-]hearted speech, levity, nonsense and childish notions and to act as servants of God."[39]

His message was as clear as it was consistent: They were on a divine errand; the success of the journey depended on their obedience to covenant; they were being tried and tested; a scourge awaited the rebellious; and the Church was in dire need of a reformation.

It is relatively certain what triggered his immediate concerns. The threat of Indian attacks was real. The country lay vast and intimidating. Some persisted in wanton hunting and killing against specific instruction. And because of weather delays, they were running behind. It is far more demanding, however, to probe the deeper causes.

The obvious trigger was an incident on Friday evening, 28 May, just 17 miles north of Scottsbluff. Only five days after commending the camp for good behavior, Brigham walked over to Woodruff's wagon; a large number of the company were dancing about. While standing by the fire, he commented to Norton Jacob, Woodruff, and others "upon the spirit that prevails and has the ascendancy in the camp—levity, loud laughter, whooping, and hallooing among the elders." He then went on:

> There is no harm [that] will arise from merriment or dancing if brethren, when they have indulged in it, know when to stop, but the devil takes advantage of it to lead the mind away from the Lord.

159

They forget the object of this journey, and all feel well together. But if we travel in this way 500 miles farther, it will lead to the shedding of blood, and some will seek to destroy the priesthood. It would be far better for three or four to go away together to pray than to engage in playing cards and thus forget the Lord. . . . We are the pioneers for the whole Church of God on the earth, seeking for a place to establish the kingdom, but we have not found it yet.[40]

Woodruff, who "felt the force of his remarks and thought them necessary," sensed the coming storm. Retiring to Willard Richards's wagon (which served as Church headquarters on the trail because as apostle, historian, and post office agent Richards supervised the writing and receiving of all official communications), Woodruff read in the Book of Mormon before praying. Then, moving over to Brigham's wagon for a late night meeting of the Quorum of the Twelve, he heard him reread "The Word and Will of the Lord." Brigham "expressed his views and feelings concerning the camp that they must speedily repent or they would be cursed, that they were forgetting their mission and he had rather travel with 10 righteous men who would keep the commandments of God than the whole camp while in a careless manner and forgetting God."[41]

Thus it came as no surprise, to the Twelve at least, that in the cold and rain of the following morning, Saturday, 29 May, at about 10:30—having not advanced further because of the inclement weather—the bugle sounded as a signal for the teams to come together. After harnessing their teams, all were called together in a semicircle around the wagon boat, or revenue cutter, where Brigham stood above the crowd. After getting a roll call from each captain of 10, he launched forth.

"This morning I feel like preaching a little, and shall take for my text, 'That as to pursuing our journey with this company with the spirit they possess, I am about to revolt against it.'" He then proceeded, to the discomfort of all:

I have said many things to the brethren about the strictness of their walk and conduct when we left the gentiles, and told them that we would have to walk upright or the law would be put in force. . . . If you do not open your hearts so that the Spirit of God can enter your hearts and teach you the right way, I know that you are a ruined people and will be destroyed and that without remedy, and unless there is a change and a different course of conduct, a different spirit to what is now in this camp, I go no further. Give me the man of prayers . . . the man of faith . . . the man of meditation, and I would far rather go amongst the savages with six or eight such men than to trust myself with the whole of this camp with the spirit they now possess.

Pinpointing the immediate cause of his frustration, he said:

They will play cards, they will play checkers, they will play dominoes, and if they had the privilege and were where they could get whisky, they would be drunk half their time and in one week they would quarrel, get to high words, and draw their knives to kill each other. . . . I have played cards once in my life since I became a Mormon to see what kind of spirit would attend it, and I was so well satisfied, that I would rather see in your hands the dirtiest thing you could find on the earth, than a pack of cards. . . . If any man had sense enough to play a game at cards, or dance a little without wanting to keep it up all the time, but exercise a little and then quit it and think no more of it, it would do well enough, but you want to keep it up till midnight, and every night, and all the time. You don't know how to control your senses. . . .

Some of you are very fond of passing jokes and will carry your jokes very far. But will you take a joke? If you do not want to take a joke, don't give a joke to your brethren. Joking, nonsense, profane language, trifling conversation and loud laughter do not belong to us. Saints, a resting place, a place of peace where they can build up the Kingdom and bid the nations welcome, with a low, mean, dirty, trifling, covetous wicked spirit dwelling in our bosoms? It is vain! vain!

Finally, he concluded with these warnings: "If you do not stop it you shall be cursed by the Almighty and shall dwindle away and be damned. Such things shall not be suffered in the camp. . . . If we don't repent and quit our wickedness we will have more hindrances than we have had, and worse storms to encounter."[42]

Dominoes, card-playing, light mindedness—surely there was more that was troubling him. Calm one week and explosive the next, he was obviously deeply disturbed. Some might attribute it to other things, such as an uncomfortable night's sleep, a personality clash, or an upset stomach. But there was obviously more, much more on his mind.

There was a worry—and many in camp were already writing about it—
that despite their good progress they were falling behind schedule, that they
should have then been well beyond the Black Hills.[43] In the back of everyone's mind was the fact that many of their own families had already begun,
or soon would begin, their march to a home the pioneer camp could then
only imagine. The risks and dangers their families would encounter in the
following emigration camp, coupled with their concern about reaching a
suitable valley soon enough to plant late-summer crops, put a strain on
everyone. And Brigham, as leader, was ultimately responsible. All was at risk
and nothing certain was yet at hand.[44]

Filed away in their wagon-borne Church headquarters were countless
other reminders of the pressures they faced. Representing the widow and
the poor was the following letter of Aurelia Spencer, pleading for assistance.
"It is with feeling of sorrow and bitter disappointment," she had written
from St. Louis in early April 1847 in a letter probably delivered by John
Taylor,

> Having done all that lay in my power to go to the camp as it is the
> only place to fly to, but what more can I do. I have begged and
> plead with the Lord to open the way and with brethren until my
> spirit is weary, but I cannot give it up. St. Louis is no place for me
> or my family . . . now Brother Brigham what am I to do? There is
> no blame to be attached to me. . . . My three big girls are keeping
> company with gentile young men. What am I to do? If I could get
> them to the Bluffs they will be saved but I have not the means to
> do so. . . . If I don't succeed in getting to the Bluffs before you leave
> will you remember me and my family? I have no one to look to.[45]

From late reports out of Voree, Wisconsin, they also knew that James
Strang was still claiming prophetic revelations for his people and that his
emissaries were converting entire branches of Latter-day Saints to his brand
of Mormonism.[46] Reuben Miller, an on-again off-again Strang supporter,
wrote in April that Strang was sending John E. Page, a former Apostle, and
"one or two others" on a mission of reclamation to England.[47]

Of even greater concern, however, was their undeniable conviction,
spelled out in so many of their writings, that the success of their present
journey, and the safety and well-being of those now coming behind, were
in direct proportion to their adherence to covenant and commandment.

Though no one had died so far, a near-fatal rattlesnake bite to Nathaniel Fairbanks and the nearly fatal stampede had reminded them of another march long before—Zion's Camp. The Lord had chastened them then with many deaths and with failure to reach their goal; was it not possible it might happen again?

The careful student of Mormon history will appreciate the fact that Brigham Young, Heber C. Kimball, Wilford Woodruff, George A. Smith, Erastus Snow, and others in camp saw in their present expedition a very close parallel to, if not a repeat of that overland march led by Joseph Smith 13 years before from Kirtland, Ohio, to near Independence, Missouri. That grueling experience had tried the faith and endurance of men who either left the Church or went on to become leaders in the faith. Though it ended in the death by cholera of 18 men—a sign, Brigham Young and others had always maintained, of divine displeasure at the criticisms and bickerings of many in camp—it nevertheless established the faith of a coming generation of Mormon leaders. It was more than a march: it was a proving ground, a school. The pioneer camp believed the Lord was involved in this pilgrimage as well, and he would prove the faith and obedience of his leaders and his people. As much as their exodus must find a place, it was also about a people finding themselves. Brigham would return to this theme over and over again. Zion's Camp of 1834 was fast becoming Zion's March of 1847.[48]

George A. Smith saw the same parallels. Referring specifically to their earlier experience, he said:

> I went up in the camp of 1834. There came among the leaders of that camp some division, growling, etc. I have noticed that those who murmured there murmured since. Joseph mounted a wagon wheel and told us a scourge would come upon us for murmuring. The cholera came and sixteen or eighteen died. . . . I wonder now if we will suffer ourselves to follow the such like snares. If we go on in union we shall accomplish our journey and return in peace.

Then, in rebuking the camp for excessive hunting and killing beyond their necessities, he reminded them all that "if you will not kill the rattlesnakes they will not bite you."[49]

Repeatedly speakers referred to their journey as "a school," "a mission," and a testing ground. "We are now in a place where we are proving ourselves," said Woodruff.[50] "The elders will look back at this journey as one of the greatest schools they ever were in [in] our lives," added George A. Smith.[51] "Our little children will look upon this camp as angels," said Heber C. Kimball, "and will rank us the first Elders in this Church because they have learnt from the Servants of the Lord and been instructed by them and received their knowledge from their own mouths and camped night after night, and month after month with them."[52] And from Amasa Lyman: "My idea is to go right through right side up with care. . . . We shall get fat on short feed building the foundation of a work where millions will be benefitted by this campaign, and our names will be hallowed for this very journey by million yet unborn."[53]

Erastus Snow defined their exodus-mission as clearly as any of the others:

> We have been chosen out of the world and are delivered from this world but as we have been chosen and set apart as elders of Israel let us show ourselves approved in all things. Let us not falter in our course until we accomplish all we have undertaken. And although Satan may test us to try our energies he [God] will enable us to overcome. It appears to me that all kinds of snags, trials and troubles ought to be put in a way to prove us. Had not our Martyred Prophet everything to contend with and yet in every trial there was an almighty fixation brought to bare upon it that enabled him to overcome all his trials. . . . I feel that the little school that we have passed through has been useful to us and I feel that we shall have new things to call for our attention from this time henceforth and forever.[54]

Constantly referring to Joseph Smith and his teachings and deliberately patterning his style, even to the point of standing on wagon wheels as Joseph had done thirteen years before, Brigham stressed the same point. "Many of these my brethren have been with me from the commencement," he said.

> Yet this very mission will soon be considered as one of the first acts of the church. The principles that have come to us from Joseph are very easily circumscribed. Suppose Joseph were here, and you take the whole knowledge in this camp of created things. Joseph would circumscribe and wound it round his finger. What knowledge had Joseph in comparison to one of the angels that have been myriads of years with God. I feel my weakness, my littleness.[55]

Brigham and his colleagues had used the word *reformation* deliberately and repeatedly since they received "The Word and Will of the Lord." They knew certain patterns of conduct had to change. This reformation was tied most closely to behavior in their adherence to the Word of Wisdom.

The evidence suggests that the Mormon leader felt a growing sense of frustration over the fact that his people were not yet living the Word of Wisdom, a code of living they believed had divine sponsorship. It prohibited the consumption of liquor, the use of tobacco, and the taking of hot drinks. Given by revelation in 1833, this Word of Wisdom was still viewed as advice, not commandment, and the general attitude of increasing noncompliance concerned Brigham.

In December 1846, back in Winter Quarters, the High Council voted that "all ardent spirits now in the camp or shall be hereafter brought in for sale, shall be delivered up to the Bishops of the ward to be sold by them alone and the net proceeds be applied to the poor."[56] And despite their efforts, coffee, tea, brandy, and other spirits were a fairly common sight.[57]

Later Brigham said, "I am going to a stake of Zion with fasting and prayer and the Word of Wisdom has got to be kept, and quit tobacco, snuffing, drinking and swearing and if this people will be humble and prayerful the Spirit of the Lord will be increased a hundred fold. But if you neglect this you will be afflicted more than ever. I wish every man to say 'Just you say what I must do and I will do it.'"[58] "Will the Latter-day Saints at this time [for] once think [of] the Word of Wisdom and take the money that we pay for tobacco, spirits, etc. and come over and clothe your children." He went on:

> I think to propose to the pioneers to leave out ten pounds [of] coffee and take twenty of flour. . . . The Word of Wisdom says tobacco is good for cattle . . . is temperance in all things, this eating and drinking in a great measure is the misery of men. . . . There is no food, drink, vegetable, mineral or anything that is not attached to it without his death in it, but tobacco, opium—the end thereof is worse than the beginning. . . . When you go to a Stake of Zion you will have to quit it. . . . I am for a reformation. You don't go to a stake of Zion and prosper with these habits.[59]

In early Nauvoo days the Word of Wisdom had been prominently taught with some successful results, but in the ensuing periods of heavy migration, conflict, and strife the principle had suffered neglect.[60] Under better circumstances than a forced exodus, leaders might have restored the principle to a higher level of behavioral application, but they reluctantly accepted that such a reformation of all the people could come only after their physical safety and well-being were assured. Brigham spearheaded that reformation in 1856, after the Latter-day Saints were settled in the West, a belated attempt to improve a more settled people.[61]

Brigham's Scottsbluff sermon was, then, both rebuke and admission. In the moment of chastisement, he seemed to be admitting to himself that a deeper reformation would have to wait for a more appropriate time and place.

Immediately after completing his remarks, Brigham did something not seen since perhaps the final days of the Nauvoo temple. He called on all the camp to assemble in rows by quorum—8 Apostles, 15 high priests, 4 bishops, 78 seventies, 8 elders, the remaining members and nonmembers (of which there were a few). He then asked each member by quorum, starting with the Twelve, to show by uplifted hand if they were willing "to covenant, to turn to the Lord with all their hearts, to repent of all their follies." All covenanted without a dissenting voice. Then Brigham "very tenderly blessed the brethren and prayed that God would enable them to fulfil their covenants."[62] He turned some time over to Heber C. Kimball, Orson Pratt, and Wilford Woodruff, and Elder Woodruff took deliberate pains to remind the camp that they would be scourged, as was Zion's Camp in 1834, if changes were not forthcoming.[63]

The results were dramatic. Colonel Markham, whose sometimes careless arrogance had caused some of the immediate irritation, acknowledged that he had "done wrong in many things." While asking for forgiveness, "he was very much affected indeed and wept like a child." Many others "were in tears and felt humbled."[64] So great a change was manifested that William Clayton made this astute observation:

> It seemed as though we were just commencing on this important mission, and all realizing the responsibility resting upon us to conduct ourselves in such a manner that the journey may be an everlasting blessing to us, instead of an everlasting disgrace. No loud laughter was heard, no swearing, no quarrelling, no profane language, no hard speeches to man or beast, and it truly seemed as

though the cloud had burst and we had emerged into a new element, a new atmosphere, and a new society.[65]

The next day, Sunday, 30 May, the camp fasted and prayed and for the first time in many weeks partook of the sacrament.[66] Later in the day members of the Twelve, with a few others, "went into the valley of the [nearby] hills and according to the order of the priesthood," an obvious reference to a sacred temple ordinance, "prayed in a circle."[67] It was a day of deep reflection and earnest soul-searching. Two days and 23 miles later, a subdued and somber pioneer camp rolled into sight of the first sign of civilization since leaving the Loup Fork: Fort Laramie.

NOTES

1. From a statement made by Brigham Young, 5 Sept. 1847, General Church Minutes.

2. Overland Diary of James Field, 8 June 1845, 12, Oregon Historical Society.

3. As quoted in Ric Burns, "Never Take No Cutoffs: On the Oregon Trail," *American Heritage* 44, no. 3 (1993): 71.

4. *William Clayton's Journal,* 22 May 1847, 171.

5. Journal of Horace K. Whitney, 12 May 1847.

6. *Appleton Milo Harmon Goes West,* ed. Maybelle Harmon Anderson (1946), 22.

7. John Pack to his family at Winter Quarters, 1 June 1847, in Bitton, *The Redoubtable John Pack,* 221–22.

8. Louisa M. Lyman to Amasa Lyman, 13 June 1847, Amasa Lyman Collection, LDS Church Archives. Although written in June, this letter did not reach Lyman until later in the summer.

9. Journal of Wilford Woodruff, 23 May 1847.

10. John Bidwell, "California, 1841–8. An Immigrant's Recollection of a Trip Across the Plains and of Men and Events in Early Days Including the Bear Flag Revolution," 19, Bancroft Library.

11. Journal of Solomon A. Gorgas, 26 May 1850, Huntington Library.

12. Autobiography of J. Henry Brown, 6.

13. *William Clayton's Journal,* 23 May 1847, 179–80.

14. Journal of Joseph W. Wood, 8 July 1849.

15. Journal of Thomas Bullock, 24 May 1847.

16. Journal of Erastus Snow, 24 May 1847.

17. Journal of Norton Jacob, 25 May 1847.

18. Journal of Horace K. Whitney, 25 May 1847.

19. Journal of Thomas Bullock, 25 May 1847.

20. Journal of Wilford Woodruff, 26 May 1847.

21. Stampedes were a much dreaded occurrence in overland travel. One of the most chilling accounts is that given by a California forty-niner, Charles Edward Pancoast, while traveling up the Platte River in 1849: "In an instant, as if by magic, all

the animals started simultaneously with a grand leap and flew down the river to the plain, the men in front shouting and scrambling to escape the solid mass of teams coming down upon them. Men could be seen dropping from the rear of wagons in all directions as they rumbled over the sands; I myself slipped through a two foot space between two wagons going at lightening speed. Some of the teams ran into a small creek and could not extricate themselves; others stopped from sheer exhaustion; still others ran two or three miles and were halted by the owners of tied horses that had not gotten away. Strange to say, no serious damage was done, except to the wagon of two Germans, which turned over and was irreparably smashed; the owners barely escaping with their lives. This was our first experience of a genuine stampede, not uncommon in the mountain countries of the west" (Charles Edward Pancoast, *A Quaker Forty-Niner* [1930], 198–99).

22. Journal of Joseph W. Wood, 17 May 1849.

23. Journal of Solomon Gorgas, 9 June 1850.

24. Haun, "A Woman's Trip Across the Plains in 1849."

25. Ibid.

26. Journal of Addison M. Crane, 23 May 1852, Huntington Library.

27. Journal of Charles G. Gray, 17 June 1849, Huntington Library.

28. Journal of Joseph W. Wood, 20 May 1849.

29. Pancoast, *A Quaker Forty-Niner*, 184.

30. Journal of Isaac Pettijohn, 6 June 1847.

31. The Latter-day Saints differed from their emigrant counterparts in their preference for choir music. Wrote German-born Rudolph Kurz, while visiting the Mormon encampments at the Missouri in 1847: "I enjoyed, especially, too the singing of [their] choirs. When they met together for choir practice one evening in every week, I found real pleasure in hearing them sing. What made this particularly enjoyable was the fact that in the western part of the United States choir music was so seldom heard. Whatever singing one hears in the West is usually among the negroes. The American, who is not of a musical temperament as are the French and German, rarely devotes his vocal powers to anything more than psalms, unless he should indulge in light or ribald songs" (*Journal of Rudolph Friederich Kurz*, Mar. 1847, 13).

32. Thomas Bullock to Henrietta Bullock, 14 May 1847, Thomas Bullock Letters.

33. Journal of J. E. Howells, 22 June 1845, 14, Oregon Historical Society.

34. Anderson, "Narrative of a Ride to the Rocky Mountains," 29 May 1834, 3. For more on this historical-topographical landmark, see Merrill J. Mattes, "Hiram Scott, Fur Trader," *Nebraska History* 26, no. 3 (July–Sept. 1945): 127–61.

35. "Platte River, twenty-five miles from the forks," General Church Minutes, 9 May 1847.

36. *Pioneering the West 1846 to 1878: Major Howard Egan's Diary*, comp. William M. Egan (1917), 18 May 1847; cited hereafter as *Howard Egan's Diary*.

37. Journal of Heber C. Kimball, 24 May 1846.

38. Journal of Willard Richards, 18 Jan. 1847.

39. General Church Minutes, 15 Apr. 1847.

40. Journal of Norton Jacob, 28 May 1847.

41. Journal of Wilford Woodruff, 28 May 1847.

42. *William Clayton's Journal*, 29 May 1847, 189–91, 193–94.

43. Their concerns were expressed in a prairie letter, written later for the oncoming emigration company, admitting that the pioneer camp would not arrive at their destination as scheduled and warning them to take all necessary precautions against possible deprivations. "As in all probability we shall not arrive at the place of destination in time to raise a summer crop, we would advise the emigration saints to lay in large quantities of dried buffalo meat as much as they can conveniently bring. . . . Make no unnecessary delays but endeavor to get through to the place of destination in time to put in extensive fall crops and also to make every necessary preparation for winter" (Orson Pratt to Emigration Company, 2 July 1847, Brigham Young Papers).

44. Had Brigham Young known that the train behind him was four times larger than he had directed or anticipated, their concerns would have been that much greater. But there was no way any of them could have then known this fact.

45. Aurelia Spencer to Brigham Young, 8 Apr. 1847, Brigham Young Papers.

46. Journal of Willard Richards, 10–11 Mar. 1847.

47. Reuben Miller to Brigham Young, 21 Apr. 1847, Brigham Young Papers.

48. For more information on Zion's Camp, see the sources listed in Introduction, note 53.

For more on the comparison to Zion's Camp, see Therald N. Jensen, "Mormon Theory of Church and State" (Ph.D. dissertation, University of Chicago, 1938), 43. Jensen quotes Brigham Young as saying: "I have travelled with Joseph a thousand miles, as he has led the camp of Israel. I have watched him and observed everything he said or did. . . . I watched every word and summed it up, and I knew just as well how to lead this kingdom as I know the way to my own house" (see also Arrington, *Great Basin Kingdom*, 429). Considering the above, there may have been another purpose in Brigham's discourse: to make conscious connection with Joseph Smith.

49. General Church Minutes, 23 May 1847; see also entry for 25 Apr 1847.

50. Journal of Wilford Woodruff, 16 May 1847.

51. General Church Minutes, 23 May 1847.

52. General Church Minutes, 25 Apr. 1847.

53. General Church Minutes, 9 May 1847.

54. General Church Minutes, 23 May 1847.

55. General Church Minutes, 23 May 1847.

56. Minutes of the Winter Quarters High Council, 24 Dec. 1846.

57. Journal of Patty Sessions, 4 Feb. 1847, LDS Church Archives.

58. Minutes of an outdoor sacrament service held at Winter Quarters, 11 A.M., 21 Mar. 1847, Brigham Young Papers.

59. General Church Minutes, 26 Mar. 1847.

60. Addison Pratt, who left on a mission to the South Seas from Nauvoo in 1843 and did not return to his family, then in the Salt Lake Valley, until 1848, provides a revealing insight into the temporary lapse among the people in living the Word of Wisdom. On entering the valley, he found that "there seemed to be but two articles . . . and they were tobacco and coffee. The rule with some for selling tobacco was lay a silver dollar onto a flat plug and cut out the bigness of it for the dollar. I don't remember of ever seeing such a hankering after anything in my life as there was after that, and coffee was not much behind it. Notwithstanding, Br. Grouard and myself had urged an observance of the Word of Wisdom so strongly upon the natives of the South Sea Isles, I was surprised to see so little notice paid to it at the gathering place of

the Saints" (*The Journals of Addison Pratt*, ed. S. George Ellsworth [1990], 368). For a full study of the history and development of the Word of Wisdom, see Paul H. Peterson, "An Historical Analysis of the Word of Wisdom" (master's thesis, Brigham Young University, 1972). It took almost a century before the Word of Wisdom took on the status of commandment within the Church.

61. Paul H. Peterson argues that the "Utah Reformation," characterized by rebaptisms, interviews, recommitments to covenants and more, "began in September 1856" (Paul H. Peterson, "The Mormon Reformation" [Ph.D. dissertation, Brigham Young University, 1981], 55). What Church leaders launched in 1856 had actually begun back in Winter Quarters and along the trail nine or ten years before. It was a reformation already planted while in transit, but waiting for a more appropriate place to blossom and take root.

62. *William Clayton's Journal*, 29 May 1847, 197–98.

63. Ibid., 198–200.

64. Ibid., 200–201.

It has been suggested from time to time that Mormon leaders used force to ensure obedience. Certainly Brigham Young did not mince words. Back in Winter Quarters, for instance, he had warned that "those who lied and stole . . . would have their heads cut off, for that was the law of God and it should be executed" (*Manuscript History of Brigham Young*, 20 Dec. 1846). On another occasion he said: "The wicked in camp had better go to Missouri and spend the rest of their time with the gentiles for . . . if they go with us and continue their wickedness, their heads shall be severed from their tabernacle and the devils that are in them shall go out and have no tabernacle to dwell in" (Journal of Wilford Woodruff, 15 Dec. 1846). And from the journal of Heber C. Kimball: "We were told that the Law of God would be executed upon the sinners and upon the hypocrites; wherefore, such was told that they would be far better off to not start another inch with this people" (19 Jan. 1847).

Whatever the wording, no evidence has ever shown that Brigham Young or any of the Mormon leaders ever carried through on such apparent threats. The record has already shown one defection back at the Elkhorn. Others defected later, yet never at the risk of life or limb.

65. *William Clayton's Journal*, 29 May 1847, 201.

66. Journal of John S. Higbee, 30 May 1847, LDS Church Archives.

67. Journal of Wilford Woodruff, 30 May 1847.

6

"IT'S A LONG ROAD
THAT NEVER TURNS"

From Fort Laramie to Fort Bridger

> The air at sunrise is clear and pure, and the morning extremely
> cold, but beautiful. A lofty snow peak of the mountains is
> glittering in the first rays of the sun, which has not reached us.
> The long mountain wall to the east, rising two thousand feet
> abruptly from the plain, behind which we see the peaks, is still
> dark and cuts clear against the glowing sky. . . . The scenery
> becomes hourly more interesting and grand, and the view here
> is truly magnificent; but, indeed, it needs something to
> repay the long prairie journey of a thousand miles.[1]

Situated at the junction of the North Platte and Laramie Fork, Fort
Laramie had been an ideal fur trading center since 1834, when Robert
Campbell and William Sublette erected a fur trading post, a mere
stockade of logs, on the now famous historical site. Campbell christened it
Fort William after his friend and partner. The next year, Milton Sublette,
Thomas Fitzpatrick, and Jim Bridger bought the post for the American Fur
Company as an ideal rendezvous site with the Ogalala Sioux to purchase
both beaver furs and buffalo skins.

In 1841, the company erected a more substantial post—a new fort made
of New Mexican adobe on the original site—renaming it Fort John and
improving on it in the year afterward. By 1847 it had become a well-
established, fully fortified commercial trading post complete with high-

Fort Laramie, *from an engraving by Frederick Piercy*

timbered walls, corner towers, and two massive doors looking out over the vast plain before it. Though still officially referred to as Fort John by its owners, most travelers called it Fort Laramie after the river. This designation was not officially recognized until the fort was purchased by the United States in 1849.[2]

Fort Laramie marked the first sign of civilization in 600 miles. Beautifully situated on a small eminence on the banks of Laramie Fork, about 1 1/2 miles above its confluence with the Platte, the fort commanded an extensive view of the whole adjacent country, with the dusky outlines of the Black Hills towering far above the surrounding scenery. It measured 168 feet long by 116 feet wide, with 15-inch thick walls, and boasted 16 rooms, 10 for dwelling and the rest for storage, a trading room, and a blacksmith shop. Cattle and horses were secured within an interior corral. Over the main entrance stood a square tower and at two of the corners, diagonally opposite each other, were large square bastions.

Brigham and his pioneers were surprised to find there were already Mormons at Fort Laramie before they arrived. Since the middle of May, Robert Crow had been scanning the rugged North Platte landscape south of the fort with his looking glass, anxiously waiting for a glimpse of the first emigrants of the season to come up the valley. Finally, after two weeks of daily searching, on the morning of Tuesday, 1 June, he made out in the far distance four men on horseback who, on closer examination, turned out to be none other than Brigham Young, Heber C. Kimball, Wilford Woodruff, and William Clayton. Crow shouted out the news to his brother, William Parker Crow, his son-in-law, George W. Therlkill, and their wives and children. This company of 17 men, women, and children was part of the Mississippi company, whose 12-month, 1600-mile search for the pioneer camp was finally coming to a happy conclusion.[3]

Crow reported that his small contingent was part of the original Mississippi company spearheaded by John Brown and William Crosby and their families and friends. It consisted of 43 souls (including two slaves) who had left Monroe County, Mississippi, 8 April 1846, with instructions "to proceed through Missouri and fall in with the companies from Nauvoo in the Indian country." Reaching Independence, Missouri, they were joined by Robert Crow and William D. Kartchner, both Mormons from Perry County, Illinois, with their families.[4]

After hearing rumors that the Mormons were active on the trail west, robbing caravans and killing emigrants, they decided to keep their religion to themselves and joined an emigrant company outbound up the Oregon Trail. At Ash Hollow they learned from John Reshaw, another trader, the disheartening news that there were no Latter-day Saints west of that point. Disappointed, the company of about 100 moved on to Fort Laramie separately from the Oregon emigrants who, after learning their fellow sojourners were Mormons, had gone ahead. To escape the harshness of a Laramie plains winter, Crosby and his grumbling band took Reshaw's advice and detoured south some 250 miles to winter at Fort Pueblo on the Arkansas River.[5]

Crow also reported that almost one-third of the Mormon Battalion enlistees, after reaching Santa Fe, had been too ill and otherwise exhausted to complete the grueling overland march to San Diego. Colonel Doniphan, commandant at Santa Fe, and Lt. Col. Philip St. George Cooke agreed to send a "sick detachment" of 89 men, 18 women laundresses, and some children on a 300-mile detour to Pueblo, 75 miles west of Bent's Fort, in time to winter with their fellow Latter-day Saints. Their orders were to intersect with the main body of the Church in the spring of 1847 somewhere near

Fort Laramie and then to move westward—all at government expense.
Meanwhile the main body of the Battalion, as Mormon leaders would later
learn, continued their continental march westward, reaching the welcome
shores of the Pacific in January 1847 just in time to celebrate Mexico's capit-
ulation and the surrender of California.[6]

The Pueblo detachment had weathered the winter reasonably well,
reported Crow, and most of them were presently en route from Fort Pueblo
for Fort Laramie. However, because of dissension over Mormon versus
non-Mormon authority within their ranks, as well as rumors and reports on
how their families were faring at Winter Quarters, the detachment had so
soured in morale that some were talking openly of mutiny and desertion.
Almost "half of the men rebelled and entered into obligation to leave the
company at Laramie, take their portion of teams and provisions and go to
the States."[7] "Nothing in the world would have held us together," wrote
John Steele, a member of the disenchanted company, "but the gospel and
some were fast forgetting that."[8]

Upon hearing such happy as well as disturbing news, Brigham
requested that Apostle Amasa Lyman and Roswell Stevens, plus John
Tippets and Thomas Woolsey (who were enlistees in the Battalion), head
south through dangerous Indian country with a large mail, intercept the
oncoming party, and douse the smoldering discontent. Lyman was then to
bring the detachment west, hard in the wake of the pioneer camp. On the
morning of 3 June, Brigham Young, Willard Richards, Heber C. Kimball,
and Orson Pratt accompanied the Pueblo-bound quartet to Fort Laramie,
where they "took seats on a large tree fallen on the banks of the river."
Before kneeling with and blessing each one, Brigham

> read some instructions . . . and gave them to Amasa Lyman [in
> which] he told the [Battalion] brethren that they had accomplished
> their designs in getting the Battalion to Mexico but the brethren at
> Pueblo must not follow Brown to Mexico, but go to California. If
> the officers will not do right, he instructed Amasa to call out the
> men, and choose officers who would do right . . . and throw all the
> Gentile officers out of the Battalion when you come up to it.[9]

After visiting with the rest of the Mississippi company who had camped
outside the fort, Brigham and company went inside the fort. There they
were welcomed by James Bordeaux, the 32-year-old principal, or fort super-

visor, whose young years belied his almost 20 years' experience as trader, voyageur, hunter, and explorer of the intermountain West. With him at the fort were his Sioux Indian wife, Marie, and two of their children, along with some 20 other Sioux men, women, and children.

A supervisor at the fort since 1842, Bordeaux proved an excellent host—"a Frenchman and a gentleman" in Woodruff's words. "He received us kindly and invited us into a large setting room on the north side of the Fort . . . a flight of stairs leading to it."[10] It "looked very much like a bar room of an Eastern hotel. It was ornamented with several drawings [and] portraits. A long desk, a settee, and some chairs constituted the principal furniture of the room."[11]

Bordeaux informed his visitors that they were the first emigrants in what was expected to be a very busy season, and that they had arrived almost too early in the spring because the snow was "middle deep ten days ago" in the Sweetwater country. He then offered them the use of the fort's flatboat, which was large enough to ferry over a swollen Platte River, now 100 yards wide, two wagons at a time—all for the most reasonable price of 25 cents per wagon. In addition he offered them liberal use of his smithies and any other needed facilities.[12]

Brigham welcomed his new host's kindnesses. Further travel on the north bank was impossible because of the steep river banks, so the pioneers needed to ferry their wagons over the Platte. While this happened, they would use the time to wash, mend wagon covers, repair broken rims, and unload for trade heavy iron plows and other unnecessary items to lighten their loads for the mountain climbs ahead. And they would learn as much as possible about their future course of travel.

So for the next two or three days, everyone was busily engaged. "We . . . made fires to do our washing. Bro. Burnham done my washing today," recalled one pioneer, "the first time I have washed my clothing since I left Winter Quarters. Bro. Frost set 6 shoes for me today and 2 for Bro. [William C.] Smoot."[13]

If most overlanders cheered when seeing the fort, those on the inside never knew what to expect. From Bordeaux's perspective, the emigrant traffic was a rich source of income, a captive audience anxious to trade off their wares at discount prices and willing to buy robes, blankets, and foodstuffs at inflated prices. But their profiteering came at a price. Francis Parkman wrote of one emigrant visit just the year before:

The emigrants were preparing their encampment; but no sooner was this accomplished, than Fort Laramie was fairly taken by storm. A crowd of broad-brimmed hats, thin visages, and staring eyes appeared suddenly at the gate. Tall, awkward men, in brown homespun; women with cadaverous faces and long lank figures, came thronging in together, and, as if inspired by the very demon of curiosity, ransacked every nook and corner of the fort. . . . They penetrated the rooms, or rather dens, inhabited by the astonished squaws. They explored the apartments of the men, and even that of Marie and the *bourgeois*. . . . Being totally devoid of any sense of delicacy or propriety, they seemed resolved to search every mystery to the bottom.[14]

Convinced that the French were common instigators of Indian attack on the wagon trains, many emigrants treated Bordeaux and his wife with both prejudice and disdain. Whether or not former Missouri governor Lilburn W. Boggs had been part of the above-described company when he had passed that way in 1846 is impossible to prove. One thing, however, is certain: he had tried hard to abuse Bordeaux's mind about the Mormons and their intentions.

Boggs vilified the Mormons as thieves and murderers, a brutal element in a savage land. Yet according to Bordeaux, Boggs and his fellow travelers had acted so ungentlemanly and irresponsibly while at the fort that he had been relieved to see them go. "He informed us that Gov. Boggs and his men had much to say against the Mormons," wrote Woodruff, "and cautioned him to take care of his horses, cattle, etc. lest we should steal them. [He tried to prej]udice him against us all he could. He said that Boggs' company was quarrelling all the time and most of the company had deserted him. He finally told Boggs and company that let the Mormons be as bad as they would, they could not be any worse than he and his men were."[15]

Such a recounting was just another indication that, along with the prairie wind, rumors blew wild across the trails that spring of 1847—and it took some historians decades to sift the truth from the error. One persistent misconception had it that Boggs was on the trail in 1847, just ahead of the pioneer camp.[16] Although they had unconfirmed reports that Boggs had passed by the year before, some Mormons believed he was just ahead of them, returning with troops to block their progress to the West.[17] Boggs's rumored intervention was a primary topic of discussion at the fort. And if

Lilburn W. Boggs

Boggs had maligned the Latter-day Saints the year before, many returned the favor.

Actually, as one of his own fellow travelers wrote, Boggs was running scared and had been since the failed attempt on his life just a few years before. "I heard them talk in camp about Boggs' troubles," reported one A. B. Robbison, an Oregon-bound traveler with Boggs in 1846.

It was just after the death of Joe Smith. I heard Boggs and others speak about the Mormon difficulties. I was satisfied from what I saw and heard that that was his object in leaving the country, although of course he denied it. It was generally understood and believed by everybody at the time that that was his object—that he was afraid of the Mormons. There was nothing in California to induce him to go there at that time. There were no settlements. It was before it was occupied by the United States. He simply wanted to get away from the Mormons and to take his family all out of danger.[18]

Bordeaux and his Mormon visitors could not then have known it, but Boggs had very nearly gone with the ill-fated Donner party to their inglorious end in the high Sierra in late 1846. William Montgomery Boggs, a son of the former governor, along with other family members, had accompanied his father overland the year before. He told of their meeting with Lansford W. Hastings in Sweetwater County and their near decision to follow his new and untried cutoff to California. Donner decided to follow Hastings, but Boggs chose to go to Oregon and separated from his co-travelers at Independence Rock. Once at Fort Hall, however, Boggs was convinced by Applegate and Godfrey, bearing news of the recent Mexican defeat, to come to California over the more proven trail down the Humboldt Canyon. Boggs arrived at the Pacific late in 1846 and settled into prosperity, but forever nurtured a fear of the Mormons.[19]

Meanwhile, back at the fort, in return for Bordeaux's hospitality, Luke S. Johnson treated so many of those who were sick that Bordeaux said to me [Albert P. Rockwood] that this was the most gentleman-like company that had ever visited the establishment. Other companies took liberties to go in all and every bit of the fort with leave, whereas our people asked to examine and look over and [he] felt honoured by our society for every man of us had acted the part of a gentleman, which was not practiced by other companies. He also spoke in high terms of Bro. Crow that has camped by him several days.[20]

Bordeaux even expressed his intention of visiting the pioneers in the Salt Lake Valley, a place he had earlier visited and now strongly recommended to eager ears.

While sheltered at the fort, the pioneer camp began to receive firsthand information on the area ahead of them and on the people left behind them. Regarding the road ahead, they learned from a passing party of trappers just arrived from Fort Bridger that just two weeks earlier the snow was several feet deep on the Sweetwater and in the mountains, and that the spring runoffs were very strong. The Bear River Valley, they reported, was well timbered with plenty of grass, light winters, and very little snow.

And as for news from the east, four men from St. Joseph, Missouri, arrived on horseback just two days after the Mormons. They told of a 20-wagon express company of emigrants from Missouri, Illinois, and Iowa just three miles below and some 600 to 700 wagons further back along the Oregon Trail. "They think that there will be about 2,000 wagons leave the States this season for Oregon and California"—certainly the largest emigration yet anticipated.[21]

Anxious to keep ahead of the oncoming trains for as long as possible, the pioneer camp stayed at Fort Laramie no longer than necessary. With the last of Kimball's wagons safely ferried over and with all the necessary repairs and alterations made, they moved out, this time following the Oregon Trail on the south side of the North Platte fork.

"Twins of the Black Hills"

The enlarged pioneer camp now numbered 161 souls (148 men, 8 women, and 5 children) in a caravan of 79 wagons. Refreshed and well rested, they set out from Fort Laramie in midmorning of a partially cloudy 4 June.[22] They needed their rest, because the 397 miles of poorly marked trail from Fort Laramie (elevation 4,090 feet) to Fort Bridger (elevation

6,865 feet) would test their pioneering and road-clearing skills as never before. Despite swollen rivers, high mountain passes, cold nights, and hot travel days, they had to make Bridger by the first of July, at the very latest, in order to reach the Salt Lake by 15 July, their intended date of arrival. Though they missed their target by a few days, they averaged more miles per day through the Black Hills and beyond than they ever did on the bald prairie of the Platte—and for obvious reasons.

By now, seven to eight weeks out of Winter Quarters, they had mastered the routine of wagon travel—breaking morning camp, sorting out travel sequence, scouting ahead for Indian troubles and the best campsites, setting up evening encampments, and so forth. They had also learned, as did most other seasoned overlanders, that the ox and the mule were far more reliable means of motive power than the horse. "My large oxen have taken me through thus far," one Missourian recorded that same year. "I have been stalled in no place, and have never taken the second pull. The young oxen work all the way [and] I have been offered $100 for them several times. They are as good as when I started."[23]

Perhaps the fundamental reason for their accelerated pace was the competition. For the first time in their travels, they were competing for the best campsites and water holes, now further apart than before, with other wagon trains, mostly from Missouri. The vanguard company of these "Gentile" companies, as the Mormons were fond of describing them, caught up with them just one day out of Fort Laramie. Piloted by Gabriel Freedom, this express company was bound for Oregon, particularly for Vancouver Island to find sea shells for the coming summer season's trade with the Indians.[24]

The pioneer camp was not without a newfound pilot of their own. Lewis B. Myers, a non-Mormon trader and pilot who had thought to return to Pueblo after guiding the Mississippi company to Fort Laramie, changed his mind after an hour's journey southward and "retraced his steps to our camp, just as we had got ready to start." Having lived and traveled in the Black Hills country for the past nine years and "represented as knowing the country to the mountains," Myers quickly proved a valuable asset to the camp.[25]

To accelerate their march even more, Willard Richards appointed Albert P. Rockwood "Deputy Supervisor of the road from Fort John to Salt Lake." Facing a poorly marked trail that seemed to prefer going over the top of hills and bluffs rather than around them, Rockwood was assigned to take at least 10 or 15 men—"the Road Tax Crew"—ahead of the teams with pickaxes, hoes, and spades to remove boulders, level steep declines, "make the rough places smooth," and generally "clear a better way for the wagons."[26]

Immediately past the fort, the Oregon Trail struck west and away from the Platte, over parched hills in order to circumvent a wild river country, before reconnecting with the Platte 125 miles ahead. Such country, recorded Oregon-bound James Clyman, "make[s] a very singular appearance with shabby junts of dark-looking pine and cedars rooted in the white, dry, weatherworn lime rock, which in many places shows like chalk banks and appears to be formed of strong, white narly clay dried by the sun and formed into rough, solid masses of rock . . . affording but few springs and no brooks."[27] Consequently, for the first time, the company needed to use double teams while ascending and to lock the wagon wheels while descending.

Ten miles west of the fort and in full view of Laramie Peak, they came to a "long, steep and stony declivity." "At the foot," Clayton described,

is a short sudden pitch and then a rugged ascent for a quarter of a mile. The bluff is rocky and many large cobble stones lay in the road which made it hard on the teams. Appleton Harmon took one of his yoke of cattle and assisted George Billings to the top and Brother Johnson took Appleton's steers and put them forward of his and brought up his wagon. Appleton and Johnson then took the three yoke of oxen and fetched up Appleton's wagon. . . . After arriving on the top the road was good but still rising for a quarter of a mile farther. We travelled on this high land five and a quarter miles which was very good traveling although it was considerably rolling.[28]

Because of the difficult terrain, Clayton's guide posts, usually on wood bearing Willard Richards's familiar brand, were erected at ten-mile intervals. Still, they averaged 16.5 miles per day—25 percent faster than their travel time up the Platte.

The one ready advantage to their rigorous climb was a resplendent and changing scenery, a welcome relief from the weariness of the Platte River plains. As Fremont said of it:

"Truly magnificent; but, indeed, it needs something to repay the long prairie journey of a thousand miles."[29] When at the summit of one high hill,

Crossing the Platte, *by George L. Strebel*

they "had view of a most beautiful country, being in two directions like an immense park, without any fence, and dotted with pines; on the other side had a full view of Laramie Peak, covered with timber, and tipped with snow."[30]

Sixty miles west of Fort Laramie they stumbled on a stroke of good fortune in the presence of several eastbound mountaineers on horseback— William Tucker, James Woodrie, James H. Grieve, James Bouvoir, and six other Frenchmen with two squaws. Tucker, sick with the chills, was attended to by Luke S. Johnson. These men were all well acquainted with Lewis Myers, and in appreciation for Johnson's medical services, informed Myers that if they outran their Missourian counterparts they would find at the North Platte River crossing some 50 miles ahead a large leather buffalo boat hung up in a tree and "that we might use it for ferrying."[31] Accordingly, 19 wagons including the revenue cutter, under the direction of Tarleton Lewis, set out in express fashion along a shorter route, likewise pointed out by their unexpected benefactors. The result was that Lewis arrived at the North Platte (near present day Casper, Wyoming) just two hours before Freedom and his Oregon-bound party and earned the prize.

181

Under normal conditions, crossing the North Platte at this point, where it was usually four to six feet deep and 60 yards wide, was simple. However, the heavy snows of 1846–47 and a late but quickly warming spring had swollen the Platte far beyond its banks, causing a current so swift and swollen that a normal crossing was quite impossible. Now 100 yards wide and up to 15 feet deep, the Platte was a formidable challenge. For a full day before the arrival of the main camp, Lewis and company busily roped over the empty wagons and ferried across Freedom's small number of Oregon emigrants and their possessions at $1.50 per head, paid for in flour at $2.50 per hundred pounds. After a day's hard work (all of 11 June), they had earned $34 in provisions "which is a great blessing to the camp inasmuch as a number of the brethren have had no bread stuff for some days."[32]

Lewis and his crew were quick to argue, however, that roping or floating over one wagon at a time and having fearful cattle and balking horses swim over would take the camp at least a week, probably more.[33] After much deliberation, the decision was made to lash together several wagons at a time, using pine poles to prevent excessive pitching or rolling. On Monday morning, they put the pine pole plan into action, but with almost fatal results. "The second division then got a rope stretched across the river from shore to shore," one observer reported, "letting [the wagons] drift with the current to save breaking the rope." A few wagons floated successfully across to the opposite bank in this fashion. But because of the strong winds and current, they ended up some two or three miles downstream. At other times, "when the wagons struck on the sand on the other side the upper one keeled over and finally rolled over the other one, breaking the bows considerably and losing iron."[34]

Howard Egan almost lost his life in the attempt, after volunteering to get in one wagon and ride on the upper side to prevent its turning over. "Soon after we pushed off," he recalled,

Brother [Andrew S.] Gibbons jumped in the river and caught hold of the end of the wagon. When we got out about the middle of the river, the wagon began to fill with water, and roll from one side to the other, and then turn over on the side. I got on the upper side and hung on for a short time, when it rolled over leaving me off. I saw that I was in danger of being caught in the wheels or the bows, and I swam off, but one of the wheels struck my leg and bruised it some. I struck out for the shore with my cap in one hand. The wagon rolled over a number of times and was hauled ashore. It received no damage, except the bows were broken.[35]

A violent thunderstorm struck the area in the late afternoon, raising the river level considerably higher. By nightfall, after 16 hours of strenuous work in which several men were up to their armpits in water all day long, they had managed to get over only 11 wagons of the first division and 12 of the second.

Horace K. Whitney, although usually possessed with boundless energy, could barely write in his journal. "After eating some supper . . . Bro. Luke Johnson and myself laid down before the fire in the open air, covering ourselves with buffalo robes. After a while, Orson [Pratt], who had been over the river, came back and slept with us. I have done the hardest day's work today I ever recollect to have done in my life and this evening I feel quite worn out with cold and fatigue."[36]

The following morning the wind blew so hard and the current ran so strong that even the livestock refused to swim across. After further council, the camp decided that the only sure way to solve their problem was to construct a ferry boat large enough to carry over two wagons at a time with teams and provisions. And if they were going to spend the time and energy to do so, they should leave a ferry crew behind to operate it—not only to assist their own emigrant company coming on but also as a commercial enterprise for the many hundred Oregon- and California-bound wagons coming up the Platte.

Several of their number followed the river downstream two or three miles to find cottonwoods tall enough to fashion the anticipated ferry. And Brigham, a master carpenter by trade, removed his shirt and "went to work with all his strength, assisted by the Dr. [W. Richards] and the brethren, and made a first rate white pine and white cottonwood raft."[37]

Completed in two days, the ferry consisted of two 24-foot cottonwood canoes, 2 1/2 feet wide, placed parallel to each other, reinforced with cross timbers and cornered with puncheon. It had a rudder and good oars affixed for steering, and was promptly dubbed "Twins of the Black Hills." Both divisions were across the river by noon the following day, ending a six-day delay. As Woodruff put it: "The longest hindrance I ever saw at a ferry or crossing a river."[38]

Their new ferry soon paid handsome dividends. Even before the pioneer camp was entirely over, the ever-anxious Missouri companies were offering to pay $1.50, and some $2.00, per wagon if they could be ferried over during the night. With 108 emigrant wagons within four miles, all eagerly waiting to cross, the new Mormon Ferry was a very busy—and profitable—service indeed.[39]

Although several volunteered to remain behind and operate the ferry, only nine men, under the direction of Thomas Grover, received the assignment.[40] They were instructed to come on with their families in the emigrant camp or, if their families did not come, to return to Fort Laramie and remain there until the following season.[41]

"A REMEMBRANCER OF PAST TIMES"

As coincidence would have it, many of the Oregon-bound emigrants crossing at the North Platte ferry crossing were from Jackson, Clay, Lafayette, and Davies counties in Missouri, battlegrounds between the Mormons and Missourians during the conflicts of the 1830s. Even the well-known Lansford W. Hastings, author of the 1845 *Emigrants' Guide to Oregon and California*, was guiding several of their companies. Deep and abiding animosities still existed between the two groups. The Mormons blamed Missouri vigilantes for the needless slaughter of 18 men, women, and children at Haun's Mill, Caldwell County, Missouri, in 1838 and also for instigating the martyrdom of Joseph and Hyrum Smith, deaths many had covenanted to avenge if ever the chance presented itself.

And with the Missouri overlanders on guard against the rumored evil intents of Porter Rockwell, Tom Brown, and Jackson Redden, it was a prairie prescription for disaster. Neither armed camp welcomed the sight of the other, but fate, for one brief moment, made unwilling travel partners of them all.[42]

Mormon accounts show outright fear and disdain on the part of those who had lived through the troublesome Missouri years, but sharp curiosity on the part of the more recent converts. To Bullock and Clayton, they were the "Gentile camps." To Pratt and Erastus Snow, they were the "Oregon Emigrants." Howard Egan referred to them merely as "Missourians," and Woodruff as "the Missouri Companies." Norton Jacob got more to the point: "mobocrats."

"Four Missourians came up mounted," Clayton recorded of their first face-to-face contact, "being part of a company a little behind. Some of these are recognized by the brethren and they seem a little afraid and not fond of our company. They say the old settlers have all fled from Shariton, Missouri, except two tavern keepers, and I feel to wish that their fears may follow them even to Oregon."[43] Others, on hearing of Clayton's roadometer, came over "to see inside and looked upon it as a curiosity. I paid no attention to them," Clayton hastened to record, "inasmuch as they did not address themselves to me."[44]

Isaac Pettijohn, a traveler in the Missouri train, had been taking note of the Mormon's progress since before Laramie. "Traveled about fifteen miles today," he wrote on 4 June, the day the pioneer camp left the fort. "100 Mormon wagons crossed the river here yesterday and have gone ahead of us. 2000 more are said to be on the way."[45]

When the ferrying first commenced, the Missouri companies "were armed with bowie knives and pistols, but before the brethren had finished their work, the men had put them all away and having put away their fears also, were very civil and kind."[46] While waiting on both sides of the river, by the light of an evening fire men thought they recognized one another and carefully probed a troubled, explosive past. In one such conversation, a Mr. Bowman, one of the "gentile" leaders, said he was the father of Bill Bowman who had had custody of Joseph Smith at the time he escaped from Liberty Jail in April 1839. Bowman was ridden out of town on a bar of iron by Obadiah Jennings, leader of the mob. "The old man says it would not be good for him to see any of the mob," Bullock detailed, "but he tries to keep it out of his mind as much as possible. He also said Morgan the Sheriff is in Oregon, Brassfield and Togue he did not know."[47]

Whatever their differences, the ferry was as much a godsend to the impatient Missouri companies as it was to the impoverished Mormons. Aaron Burr, the blacksmith, repaired several of Hastings's broken irons.[48] A lost Wilford Woodruff one night found shelter and protection in a Missouri camp. Lorenzo Young's broken axle was repaired by his new neighbors. And one young Missouri lad was saved from certain drowning by the quick dispatch of the revenue cutter.[49]

By the end of the week, invitations were going back and forth to socialize and enjoy one another's company. A Captain Ashworth invited Rockwood and Bullock "to breakfast with him on bacon, warm biscuits, and light fried biscuits, good coffee with sugar and then milk." Said a thankful

Bullock: "Eating a good breakfast from a woman's cooking is a remembrancer of past times, and renews the desire for such times to come again."[50]

"This Is Uncle Sam's Day of Independence"

The pioneer camp finally bid Grover and his men farewell early in the morning of 19 June. From the Platte they rolled out cross-country to connect with the Sweetwater River some 50 miles west. "In good health and spirits," they were anxious to make up lost time. "It was remarked by several that their stock had fattened so much while stopping at the ferry, they hardly knew them."[51] They set a record for distance traveled in a single day—21 1/2 miles—over high bluffs, steep pitches, and crooked descents before finding sufficient spring water.

Unfortunately it turned out to be a miserable, dangerous place. "Its banks are so perfectly soft that a horse or ox cannot go down to drink without sinking immediately nearly overhead in thick, filthy mud, and is one of the most horrid, swampy, stinking places I ever saw."[52] Said Norton Jacob: "Such a country! Mire holes on the mountains, frost in July, salt water, and no wood to cook with."[53]

They could not have chosen a worse campground. Close to the Poison Springs, or Poison Pond, the camp might have met with disaster if it were not for the high moisture content still in the ground because of recent heavy snow melts. Other travelers in the same place fared much worse, as a later passerby explained:

> This morning we came to Poison Spring or the Poison Pond; it is the first water we saw since leaving the [N.] Platte River. . . . Here are the graves of some five or six persons who drank of the water and died in a few minutes. Notices are stuck over the graves and at the road side, and on each side of the spring giving warning to the Emigrants in every conceivable form: "He drank of this water and died." "Drank at this spring and died." "This water is poison." "Death!" "Poison!" "Beware! For God's sake do not taste this water! Happy is the man who can read!"[54]

As they approached the Sweetwater, the whole countryside began to take on the appearance of a moonscape—with high hills and ridges of granite rock starkly rising above desert desolation. Due to the high concentration of alkaline soil, even sagebrush grew sparsely. "I can describe their

Independence Rock, *from a painting by Barna Meeker*

appearance," wrote Clayton, "only by saying that it seems as though giants had in by-gone days taken them in wheelbarrows of tremendous size and wheeled up in large heaps, masses of heavy clay which has consolidated and become solid, hard rock."[55]

Along the way they passed between small lakes ringed with wild saleratus, a yeastlike alkaline substance which they collected by the bucketful to leaven bread and light cakes. They soon learned, however, that it had to be used with care; it was so much stronger than common saleratus that if the same quantity was used it made the bread quite green.[56]

On 21 June they reached the Sweetwater and the famed Independence Rock (or Liberty Rock as Rockwood termed it) nearly a half-mile long, 80 feet high and "shaped like an oblong loaf of bread." It had already become a well-marked trail attraction—that Great Register of the Desert—whereon the names of hundreds of persons were "painted upon these rocks . . . with red, black, and yellow paint."[57]

After inscribing a few names of their own and erecting a guidepost indicating 175 1/4 miles from Fort Laramie, they moved on, camping four miles further near Devil's Gate. Never content to trust Fremont's calculations, Pratt measured the two high rocky ridges to be 379 1/2 feet high and almost 200 yards long. Beyond Devil's Gate, the scenery dramatically improved, "a romantic appearance," in the words of Howard

Egan, "very sublime," as the Wind River mountain chain burst clearly into view.[58]

From Devil's Gate they pressed on through the valley, which varied in width from five to ten miles. They had to stay close to the banks of the Sweetwater, which was still shouldered with immense banks of snow, and constantly forded the stream for a better trail. Living off antelope, Missouri flour, sagebrush, and mountain water, the camp neared the base of South Pass, that "Cumberland Gap" of the West since its discovery in 1812. Named South Pass to distinguish it from Lemhi Pass in present-day Montana, through which Lewis and Clark had earlier traveled, by the 1840s it had become the favored passage over the Continental Divide.

The pioneer camp crossed over the pass, at an altitude of 7,220 feet, without difficulty, but always wondering precisely when and where they had reached the summit. Fremont had expressed the same imprecision a few years before:

> The ascent had been so gradual that, with all the intimate knowledge possessed by [Kit] Carson, who had made this country his home for seventeen years, we were obliged to watch very closely to find the place at which we had reached the culminating point. This was between two low hills, rising on either hand fifty or sixty feet. . . . From the impression on my mind at this time, and subsequently on our return, I should compare the elevation which we surmounted at the pass to the ascent of the Capitol Hill from [Pennsylvania] Avenue at Washington.[59]

Although the Mormons crossed over South Pass before the 4th of July, other travelers "from the states" usually reached the Sweetwater country just about the time to celebrate the nation's birthday. In fact, Independence Rock was likely so called because of earlier celebrations by those passing by who were eager to remember the glorious Fourth. John H. Brown, in an Oregon-bound camp just two weeks behind Brigham's, tells of how his group arrived at Independence Rock. "As we camped there and celebrated the 4th of July, our company also added their names, with dates, etc. We here read the names that had been placed there for years before ours."[60]

Charles R. Parke, part of the vast number of later California gold-seekers who passed this way two years later, told of how he and his company celebrated the nation's birthday at South Pass in a most resourceful way. "Having plenty of milk from the cows we had with us," he remembered,

> I determined to [do] something no other living man ever did in this place and on this sacred day of the year, and that was to make ice cream at the South Pass of the Rockies. . . . I procured a small tin bucket which held about two quarts. This I sweetened and flavored with peppermint—had nothing else. This bucket was placed inside a wooden bucket or "Yankee Pole" and the top put on. Nature had supplied a huge bank of coarse snow, or hail, nearby, which was just the thing for this New Factory, with alternate layers of this and salt between the two buckets and with the aid of a clean stick to stir with I soon produced the most delicious ice cream tasted in this place. In fact the whole company so decided and as a compliment drew up in front of our tent and fired a salute.[61]

Joseph Wood, another 1849 overlander, enjoyed a similar special South Pass celebration.

> I fired three rounds with my rifle—one for liberty, one for home and one for success. We had a few homespun extras for dinner of which we all partook heartily. They consisted of fried cakes, fried pie and apple sauce. . . . The celebration began in earnest in the pass at evening, fireworks were displayed and many large guns were fired. Companies of men would discharge their guns in rapid succession and among the hills they sounded very loud. . . . After a while all sounds died away save that of the wolves as they howled over the body of some dead ox.[62]

Another party, just after crossing the pass, also marked the day. "We have enjoyed ourselves quite as well as could be expected," a traveler reported, "in a country like this, with little else but wild sage for our cattle to eat. It is true we did not have the 'Star Spangled Banner' to wave over us, but in its absence might be seen 'floating over the breeze' a cravat, handkerchief, or something else, almost anything for an imitation. Until a late hour . . . the boys in our camp were quite merry, making Fourth of July speeches."[63]

In stark contrast, for the Mormons the glorious Fourth was a painful reminder of broken dreams and promises. There were no gun salutes, no banners, and no ice cream. Only Norton Jacob made even passing reference to the day, and then only critically. "This is Uncle Sam's Day of Independence. Well, we are independent of all the powers of the gentiles; that's enough for us."[64]

Nor were there any celebrations and flag-waving ceremonies back at Winter Quarters. "Spent the evening at Bro. Leonard's," wrote Eliza R. Snow. "[He] spoke of the American government—its fall, etc. after which the Lord manifested the centers of the happiness of the Saints and the sufferings of the Gentiles when the Lamanites go forth. Language cannot describe the scene."[65]

The day the Latter-day Saints did remember and record was 27 June, the third anniversary of the martyrdom of Joseph and Hyrum Smith. The enduring grief and deep sense of loss cannot be minimized. It signaled more than a tragic loss: it reminded Brigham and others that for the Church to survive the wilderness of both geography and ruptured Church government, much work had yet to be done—but at a more convenient time.

Perhaps Clayton expressed their anguish best:

> It is three years today since our brethren Joseph and Hyrum were taken from us and it was the general feeling to spend the day in fasting and prayer. But the gentile companies being close in our rear and feed scarce, it was considered necessary to keep ahead of them for the benefit of our teams, but many minds have reverted back to the scenes at Carthage jail, and it is a gratification that we have so far prospered in our endeavors to get from under the grasp of our enemies.[66]

This community grievance permeated their thinking for years to come, overshadowing any allegiance to a nation many once had loved and revered. It was a reflection of the esteem they held for their former leaders and of the well-nigh impossibility of ever replacing them. And if they had a flag with them, it was not that of the United States of America but a banner of their own making, a multicolored, oversize "ensign to the nations" which at some future time and place might be unfurled over a great new land of religious freedom.

Evidence shows that the pioneers were very serious about a flag, a very large banner, of their own, an "ensign to the nations." Writing in behalf of the Twelve, Willard Richards instructed Jedediah M. Grant, then on his way

190

to St. Louis one month before the departure of the Camp from Winter Quarters,

> to procure on your journey . . . a sufficient quantity of the best and most suitable cloth or fabric by whatever name you may find it called, to manufacture or form a flag, or colors, for the camp, not less than 35' in length and 15' in width, composed equally of white, blue and red. Of the same or similar material as your judgment shall dictate you will get—in addition to the above—one half the amount of cloth of either the foregoing colors—in scarlet and also in purple, for insignia . . . be sure to select such articles as will long buffet the wind and weather; a charm to your own eye whenever you behold it; an honor to the union, a praise to the Saints, to be sanctioned by the Heavens and viewed with delight by all people.

The inner councils of Church leadership had earlier discussed that Joseph Smith had begun work on such a flag shortly before his death. Brigham Young picked up on the idea and called for an enormous flag, large enough to fly over a mountain top, one that would have to be hoisted by pulleys as high as 100 feet. This banner would bear the motto, in red letters shaded with blue, "Religious Toleration."[67]

"BUT WHERE WE GO, WE KNOW NOT"

Sixty miles past Fort Laramie, Thomas Bullock wrote the last of his three surviving exodus letters to his wife back at Winter Quarters. It suggests that, although chief clerk of the camp, he still could not say with precision what was their ultimate destination. "We are now about 300 miles from Bridger, but where we go we know not."[68]

Nevertheless, a careful study of their varied writings leaves little doubt that they had narrowed their options. Horace Whitney wrote the very next day: "Bro. Heber [Kimball] told me that he thought that in about five weeks we would reach the place of our destination, viz. the Salt Lakes . . . where he said there was only one inhabitant or settler."[69] John Pack had likewise written earlier that "we do not know yet where we shall settle, but think near the Salt Lake."[70]

Bordeaux had already sustained their Salt Lake plan. And from Grieve, Woodrie, Bouvoir, and others fresh out of the mountains, the camp learned that the "Utah [was] a beautiful country" and gained from them a "flattering

Jim Bridger

or good account" of the Salt Lake country.[71]

The Salt Lake plan was challenged, however, by one of the most respected mountain men of the time—Moses (Black) Harris, or as the Mormons called him, "Major Harris"—whom they encountered just past the summit of South Pass on 27 June. Then about 40 years old, Harris had explored a newer route to Oregon in 1846 and now, with two pack mules loaded with skins, was ready to trade and pilot his way through the coming season.[72]

Cache Valley was, in his opinion, far superior to the Salt Lake Valley for a serious settlement. "The Bear River runs through it at right angles," he told his eager listeners, "on the west side of which the soil is sandy and barren, except considerable wild sage, while on the east side, there is less wild sage and quite a heavy body of timber, such as cottonwood, box elder, etc." From his description, Clayton concluded, "which is very discouraging, we have little chance to hope for even a moderately good country anywhere in those regions."[73]

Harris also brought other news. Reading from a file of newspapers Harris had with him, several copies of the *Oregon Spectator* dated 4 March and one from Sam Brannan's new Mormon paper, *The California Star* from Yerba Buena, the Mormons learned all about Brannan's successful voyage on board the *Brooklyn* and his early Mormon settlements in California. They also learned more of the sordid details of the ill-fated Donner party. Before leaving the pioneer camp, then at the Little Sandy, Harris advised them to avoid Fort Bridger and to take a more northern route to their destination, "there being more feed on the one than on the other."[74]

If Harris discouraged them in their pursuit, the camp had little time to admit it. Eight hours later, they received an entirely different report from none other than Jim Bridger, another mountain man whose name is synonymous with the early West. A "pioneer, hunter, trapper and trader,"

Pioneers at Green River, *from a painting by George Ottinger*

Bridger was then 43 years old, relatively short in stature but with a thick neck.[75] Like Harris, he too was starting east as a trader and guide. In contrast to Harris, however, Bridger knew all about the country south of Salt Lake and, contrary to myth and tradition, spoke well of the Salt Lake, commending it highly. "The information obtained concerning the Utah country is very encouraging," wrote a somewhat relieved Norton Jacob.[76]

If one can discount Bridger's proprietary interest in the pioneer camp going to Salt Lake via his fort, then only a few days away, Bridger commended their tentative decisions, saying that Harris did not know what he was talking about. Wrote Whitney:

> The country of which he gave us a description is situated between the two lakes, Utah and Salt, consisting of a valley of 100 miles in extent. The soil is good, producing wild flax in abundance, also white and red clover, and is peculiarly adapted to the growth of corn and wheat. Between the two lakes, three large streams coming from the mountains traverse the valley and empty into the Salt Lake. These abound in various kinds of fish, and their banks are heavily lined with timber, consisting of pine and oak, also quite a number of groves of sugar maple. . . . Gold, silver, copper, iron, sulphur, saltpetre, etc. are found in abundance in the mountains, he

giving a description of a number of places where the above minerals were to be found.

He went on to make even more positive comments about another valley 200 miles south of the Salt Lake. "In fine, he gave a minute description of the whole country, which differed materially from the account given us by Major Harris." His only cautionary comment pertained to the possibility of early frosts, considering the high altitudes.[77]

Bridger recommended that from his fort they try the more southerly route to the valley—the Hastings route or cutoff that the Donner party had blazed just the year before. "We conversed about a great variety of things," Woodruff recalled. "He said he was ashamed of the maps of Fremont for he knew nothing about the country, only the plain traveled road, [and] that he could correct all the maps that had been put out about the western world. He said if we wanted any of his services to let him know."[78] But Bridger was more interested in going east, not west.

Forty-eight hours later the pioneers met still another eastbound messenger in what truly was a remarkable sequence of visitors. This was a fellow Latter-day Saint and now continental traveler, the colorful, 38-year-old Sam Brannan. Brannan arrived in camp while the camp was ferrying across the Green River in the afternoon of 30 June. He was accompanied by two men, one of whom was a distant cousin of Joseph Smith.

In addition to a 10,000-mile ocean voyage around the southern tip of South America on board the *Brooklyn*, Brannan had just traveled on horseback 800 miles overland from San Francisco Bay; they left there on 4 April, the same day many of the pioneers left Winter Quarters. On the way, crossing over the deep snows of the high Sierra, they met with the last of the unfortunate souls in Donner's party, before heading across the California Trail to the Great Basin and the Salt Lake Valley and on to Fort Hall and the Green River crossing.

Brannan, all aglow with the California fever, was on a mission of his own. Having just compared the arid shores of the Salt Lake with the golden coasts of California, he was convinced that the Saints should go all the way west to the Pacific. The Mormon Battalion had safely reached the coast and were in possession of the Mexican city Pueblos Angelos de los (Los Angeles). "Elder Brannan gives a very favorable account of the climate and soil of California," wrote Whitney, "and appears quite anxious that we should

Sam Brannan

immediately go there and take possession of the country, before it becomes occupied by others. . . . San Francisco . . . bids fair to become a flourishing city."[79] Brannan felt they should not settle for the sands of a desert lake when the verdant shores of the Pacific were just a few weeks farther. Besides, he said, "old Boggs is on the opposite sides of the Bay and dares not come over for fear of the Mormons."[80]

Brannan's eyewitness account of the blighted Donner party certainly held the rapt attention of his new-found listeners, especially on hearing that some in Donner's camp were Mormons. Among those listening, one or two were quick to ascribe their fate to divine retribution. "Brother Brannan fell in with a company of emigrants," Jacob reported,

> who by quarrelling and fighting among themselves, delayed time until they got caught in the snows on the mountains last fall. . . . The snows were much deeper in all this region than was ever known before. Their sufferings were incredible. Many of them perished with cold and hunger. All their cattle died, and they [were] compelled to eat the flesh of those that died among them! In fact they killed some, and among the rest a Mormon woman by the name of Murphy, who formerly lived in Nauvoo. Those people are in a wretched condition. Their teams all gone, they cannot get away until assistance shall be sent from Oregon. Quarreling is a common complaint among these emigrants, until they [are] all divided and subdivided into small parties [and] can't agree to travel together in peace, which fulfils Joseph Smith's prophecy that "peace is taken from the earth." These are the men that have mobbed and killed the Saints![81]

While all paid close attention to everything Brannan had to say about California, Brigham was as skeptical of the man as he was of the message and played the disinterested party at best. If Brigham had not yet heard of

Brannan's overbearing leadership style while sailing on board the *Brooklyn* and later in California—an approach that almost led to mutiny—he certainly suspected it. A master at reading men's minds and intentions, Brigham welcomed Brannan with less than three cheers. Brannan's importuning notwithstanding, Brigham and the Twelve put his zeal for California on hold, inviting him to come with them to the Salt Lake and to await further information.[82]

Meanwhile the pioneer camp left the Green River overland to Fort Bridger, where they finally arrived 7 July. It had taken them five grueling weeks over mountains and rivers to cover the nearly 400 miles from Fort Laramie. As Brigham himself said: " 'It's a long road that never turns' is an old maxim; and though this is a pretty long road, we expect when we have gone a little further, it will so turn as to lead us directly west."[83]

Undeterred and despite Brannan, Harris, and whomever else, they were as committed as ever to their future course of action.

NOTES

1. *Expeditions of Frémont*, 1:255. Fremont is here describing the Wind River Mountains.

2. See *Forty Years a Fur Trader on the Upper Missouri: The Personal Narrative of Charles Larpenteur 1833–1872*, ed. Elliot Coues, 2 vols. (1898), 1:23; David W. Lupton, "Fort Platte, Wyoming, 1841–1845: Rival of Fort Laramie," *Annals of Wyoming* 49, no. 1 (Spring 1977): 83–92; John D. McDermott, "James Bordeaux," in LeRoy Hafen, *The Mountain Men and the Fur Trade* (1965–1972), 5:68–69. Laramie itself was the name of an earlier French-Canadian trader, Jacques La Ramie, who had traded in the area years before. Fort Laramie, not to be confused with the city of Laramie, Wyoming, is now a preserved historical site situated 75 miles north of Cheyenne, Wyoming, near the Wyoming-Nebraska state line.

A second post, Fort Platte, a large adobe fort situated a mile north of Fort Laramie on the North Platte River, had been built in 1841 by competitors of the American Fur Co. but was sold in 1845. By 1847, Fort Platte was in ruins, although well described by every civilization-starved overland journalist.

3. Journal of Levi S. Johnson, 1 June 1847.

4. See William E. Parrish, "The Mississippi Saints," *The Historian* 50 (August 1988): 489–505. See also Leonard J. Arrington, "Mississippi Mormons," *Ensign*, June 1977, 46–51; and *Autobiography of Pioneer John Brown*.

5. "Diary of the Mormon Battalion Mission: John D. Lee," 14 Sept. 1846, ed. Juanita Brooks, *New Mexico Historical Review*, 42, no. 3 (July 1967): 188. See also *Journals of John D. Lee 1846–47 and 1859*, ed. Charles Kelly (1938), editor's note, 31.

John Brown, who had been dispatched to Winter Quarters for clarification and directions and who had become a member of the pioneer camp, was especially glad to meet his old friends, although only a portion of their wagons and teams had been able to make the return trip to Fort Laramie. The rest remained back at Fort Pueblo.

6. For more information on the Mormon Battalion, see the sources listed in chapter 1, note 26.

7. Report by Captain James Brown, Journal History, 29 July 1847, written 10 Nov. 1859.

8. "Extracts from the Journal of John Steele," *Utah Historical Quarterly* 6, No. 1 (Jan. 1933): 15. For a more thorough study of the authority question, see Eugene E. Campbell, "Authority Conflicts in the Mormon Battalion," *BYU Studies* 8 (Winter 1968): 127–42.

9. Journal of Thomas Bullock, 3 June 1847.

Lyman accomplished his mission. A few days later he intercepted the soldiers and "laid before them the instructions from the council which had the effect to quell the spirit of mutiny that was among them. Instead of leaving at Fort John, as they had calculated, they concluded to follow the counsel and a good spirit prevailed" (Amasa Lyman to Brigham Young and Council, 28 June 1847, Brigham Young Papers).

10. Journal of Wilford Woodruff, 2 June 1847.

11. *Appleton Milo Harmon Goes West*, 2 June 1847, 27.

12. Known as Mato (bear) by the Sioux, James Bordeaux was born near St. Charles, Missouri, 22 August 1814, of French-Canadian descent. In 1826, at the age of 12, he joined an American Fur expedition to trade with the Kickapoos. In 1829, he signed on with Pierre Chouteau Jr. and stayed in the West in the employ of the American Fur Co. for most of the next 20 years, trapping and trading in and around Fort Union, Fort Pierre, and Fort Laramie. He was promoted to supervisor of Fort Laramie in 1842. Parkman described him as a "stout, bluff little fellow" who treated most visitors well. Even after Fort Laramie was sold two years later, Bordeaux traded in the area, although with new employers. He died in 1878 after a life of continuous involvement in the fur trade (John D. McDermott, "James Bordeaux," 5:65–80).

13. Journal of Wilford Woodruff, 3 June 1847.

14. Parkman, *The Oregon Trail*, 101–2.

15. Journal of Wilford Woodruff, 2 June 1847.

16. See Edward W. Tullidge, *History of Salt Lake City* (1886), 39. Several other writers have accepted Tullidge's research seemingly without question.

17. Journal of Erastus Snow, 24 June 1846, LDS Church Archives.

18. A. B. Robbison, "Growth of Towns: Olympia, Fernwater, Portland and San Francisco," handwritten manuscript, 1878, Bancroft Library.

19. Statement of William Montgomery Boggs taken 27 January 1886 at Napa, California, 12-page handwritten manuscript, Bancroft Library.

20. Journal of Albert P. Rockwood, 4 June 1847.

21. *Howard Egan's Diary*, 3 June 1847, 64. Other Mormon diarists varied in their estimates of 1847 oncoming traffic.

22. The new members of the company included Robert Crow, Elizabeth Crow, Benjamin B. Crow, Harriet Crow, Elizabeth Jane Crow, John McHenry Crow, Walter H. Crow, George W. Therlkill, Martilla Jane Therlkill (then seven months pregnant), Milton Howard Therlkill, James William Therlkill, William Parker Crow, Ida Vinda Exene Crow, Ira Minda Almarene Crow, Archibald Little, James Chesney, and Lewis

B. Myers. Accompanying Myers were two Indian wives and a number of children (see *William Clayton's Journal*, 4 June 1847, 215).

23. H. Warren to the editor of the *St. Louis Daily Union* dated 4 July 1847, published 5 Aug. 1847 (found in Dale Morgan Newspaper Collection, "Mormons and the American West," Huntington Library).

24. Journal of Norton Jacob, 5 June 1847. Further evidence that the Latter-day Saints had been first across the plains in 1847 can be found from a report appearing in the *St. Louis Daily Union* for 12 June 1847: "Mr. Richards [with the Beaumont Co.] arrived here yesterday from Fort Laramie, which place he left on the 26th of March, in company with two other traders. He brought in more than 30 packs of robes. The upper Indians have been very quiet during the winter. . . . He met the advance party of Mormons at Big Island, about 250 miles from the settlements. There were 180 wagons [an obvious exaggeration]. The next party of emigrants were those who left St. Joseph and were met on the great Nemaha, and numbered 64 wagons. They were getting along well, with fine cattle and horses—travelling from 20 to 25 miles each day. They were bound for Oregon and California" (Dale Morgan Newspaper Collection).

25. *William Clayton's Journal*, 4 June 1847, 215, and Journal of Horace K. Whitney, 4 June 1847.

26. Journal of Albert P. Rockwood, 5–8 June 1847.

27. Journal of James Clyman, 3 Aug. 1844.

28. *William Clayton's Journal*, 5 June 1847, 217.

29. *Expeditions of Frémont*, 255.

30. Journal of Thomas Bullock, 7 June 1847.

31. Journal of Horace K. Whitney, 9 June 1847.

32. *William Clayton's Journal*, 12 June 1847, 234–35.

33. The crossing of a typical river by a pair of horsemen was often no small accomplishment, as described in the following account: "The halters were taken from the horses and tied into a line, which was found to be in length double the width of the river. The horses were then driven across; after which two of the men swam over, carrying one end of the line with them. Those who remained tied the luggage in a bundle to the rope on the edge of the shore, then holding the rope behind, and letting it slip through their hands as those on the opposite side pulled, both parties keeping the ropes well stretched as to hold it above the water. The next minute the two remaining men were over and all soon under way again" ("The Oregon Expedition of Obadiah Oakly," pamphlet reprinted from the *Peoria [New York] Register*, 1914 [1842–45], 8, Oregon Historical Society).

34. *William Clayton's Journal*, 14 June 1847, 237.

35. *Howard Egan's Diary*, 14 June 1847, 74.

36. Journal of Horace K. Whitney, 14 June 1847.

37. Journal of Thomas Bullock, 16 June 1847.

38. Journal of Wilford Woodruff, 17 June 1847.

39. Woodruff saw it all providentially, "as much of a miracle to me to see our flour and meal bags replenished in the midst of the Black Hills as it did to have the Children of Israel fed with manna in the wilderness" (Journal of Wilford Woodruff, 13 June 1847).

40. *William Clayton's Journal*, 18 June 1847, 242. The crew left at the North Platte River crossing included some of the best carpenters and blacksmiths in camp: Thomas Grover, captain; John S. Higbee, assistant; Benjamin F. Stewart; James Davenport,

blacksmith; William Empey; Luke S. Johnson; Appleton Harmon; Francis M. Pomeroy; and Edmund Ellsworth. Eric Glines decided, against counsel, to stay back with Grover's crew; he later changed his mind and hurried on by himself at considerable danger, catching up with the main camp several miles west.

41. Brigham remarked that if they would obey counsel, they should all be blessed, "for I promise you that in the name of the Lord" (Journal of Horace K. Whitney, 18 June 1847).

Between 19 June and 11 July, Thomas Grover and his busy crew ferried over a minimum of 23 emigrant companies, 489 wagons, and approximately 1,956 souls, earning almost $600 in the process (see table below). On 13 July, after the river had receded sufficiently to allow travelers to cross on their own, Grover left William Empey and three others in charge while he and the others left for Fort Laramie. For more on the ferry operation, see Dale S. Morgan, "The Mormon Ferry on the North Platte," *Annals of Wyoming* 21 (July–Oct. 1949).

The Mormon Ferry: 25 June–11 July 1847

The approximate number of emigrant wagons (excluding Latter-day Saints) that made full use of Grover's ferry are as follows:

Date	Company	Wagons	People	$ Earned
to June 20		64	256	$256.00
June 25	John Battice	3	12	3.00
	Wm. Vaughn	5	20	5.00
	Capt. Hodge	11	44	5.50
June 27	Mr. Cox	11	44	16.00
June 29		75	300	
June 30	Capt. Higgins	23	92	23.00
	Capt. McClay	10	40	10.00
	Capt. Taylor	12	48	12.00
	Cpt. Patterson	16	64	16.00
	Others	12	48	12.00
July 1	Capt. Collard	18	72	18.00
	Capt. Turpen	23	92	23.00
	Capt. Bidwell	56	224	56.00
July 2	Capt. Snook	17	68	17.00
	Capt. Dodson	11	44	11.00
	Daniel Putnam	11	44	11.00
July 3	Cpt. Ingersoll	12	48	12.00
July 4	Cpt. McKinney	27	108	27.00
July 5	Capt. Retford	6	24	4.00
July 6	Capt. Ward	18	72	9.00
July 7	Capt. Magone	36	144	36.00
July 11	Capt. Basner	12	48	10.55
Totals		489	1,956	$593.05

Source: *Appleton Milo Harmon Goes West*, 20 June to 11 July.

42. The reader need only remember the notorious Mountain Meadows Massacre of 1858 in southern Utah, in which many Missouri emigrants were killed by Indians and Mormon malcontents, to appreciate the potential for conflict (see Juanita Brooks, *Mountain Meadows Massacre* [1962]).

43. *William Clayton's Journal*, 6 June 1847, 219.

44. *William Clayton's Journal*, 6 June 1847, 220.

45. Journal of Isaac Pettijohn, 4 and 6 June 1847.

46. Journal of Thomas Bullock, 13 June 1847.

47. Ibid. These riverside chats throw a slightly different light on the traditional accounts. Obadiah Jennings was, indeed, a most despicable character. Leader of the mobs that murdered at Haun's Mill, he had a dreaded reputation. Meanwhile, William Morgan, sheriff of Daviess Co., and William Bowman, ex-sheriff, were convinced of the unjust jailing of the Mormon leaders and participated in freeing Joseph and Hyrum Smith and their fellow inmates from Liberty Jail in 1839. Because of it, they received harsh treatment from the locals—in frontier vigilante style.

According to one early county history, quoted by B. H. Roberts, the people were "greatly exercised, and they disgraced themselves by very ruffianly conduct. They rode the sheriff on a rail, and Bowman was dragged over the square by the hair of the head. The men guilty of these dastardly acts accused Sheriff Morgan and ex-Sheriff Bowman of complicity in the escape of the Mormon leaders; that Bowman furnished the horses, and that Morgan allowed them to escape, and both got well paid for their treachery" ("History of Daviess County" [1882] as quoted in *History of the Church*, 3:321, note). Jennings, who led the charge against Bowman and Morgan, was never brought to trial.

48. Journal of Lansford B. Hastings, 10 July 1847, Oregon Historical Society.

49. *William Clayton's Journal*, 12 June 1847, 235.

50. Journal of Thomas Bullock, 18 June 1847.

51. *William Clayton's Journal*, 19 June 1847, 242.

52. *William Clayton's Journal*, 19 June 1847, 245.

53. Journal of Norton Jacob, 19 June 1847.

54. Journal of James W. Evans, 22 June 1850.

55. *William Clayton's Journal*, 21 June 1847, 252.

56. A later Oregon emigrant described saleratus this way: "I examined a white substance that sprouts up out of the ground about the size and shape of a watermelon. It is familiarly called Indian Bread and looks precisely like a loaf of raised bread, except that it is white and much finer. It is perfectly solid and lays very near to the ground, with a root as large as a man's thumb, running into the earth. Many of them are dry; on breaking a thin crust of a dry one, you find it full of a very light and fine dust of a snuff color, rather inclined to green. I threw one up and it filled the air as if with a valley of smoke" (Journal of James W. Evans, 12 May 1850).

57. Journal of Wilford Woodruff, 21 June 1847.

While descending from the rock, they noticed a short distance away the burial ceremony of a 25-year-old woman, Rachel Morgan, who had died of poisoning.

"Independence Rock is an isolated outcropping of the granite which forms the mountains enclosing the Sweetwater Valley; it is, thus, part of the Sweetwater Range. The rock stands 6,028 feet above sea level; its northern summit is 136 feet above terrain. With a circumference of 5,900 feet, its mass covers an area of 24.81 acres"

(Robert L. Munkres, "Independence Rock and Devil's Gate," *Annals of Wyoming* 40 [Apr. 1968]: 24–25).

58. *Howard Egan's Diary*, 21 June 1847.

59. *Expeditions of Frémont*, 253.

60. Autobiography of J. Henry Brown, 10.

61. Journal of Dr. Charles R. Parke, 4 July 1849, Huntington Library.

62. Journal of Joseph W. Wood, 4 July 1849.

63. The Autobiography of Samuel Hundsaker, 4 July 1853, Oregon Historical Society.

64. Journal of Norton Jacob, 4 July 1847.

John Smith, of the emigration camp following behind, expressed a similar sentiment: "We do not feel to celebrate the birthday of the Independence of the United States, as we have been driven from its boundaries because we worshiped God according to his laws" (Journal History, 4 July 1847).

65. Journal of Eliza R. Snow, 1 June 1847.

66. *William Clayton's Journal*, 27 June 1847, 272. And from another: "Shall we believe the cracking asunder of the union of the United States? Yes, sooner or later the Lord will avenge the blood of his martyred Prophets and persecuted Saints, unless they repent and restore their right."

67. Willard Richards to Jedediah M. Grant, 25 Feb. 1847, Brigham Young Papers. Richards went on to say that if Grant could not find cloth in sufficient quantity, a "lesser flag" 18 feet in length would suffice. (See also Minutes of a Special Meeting, 26 Feb. 1847, Brigham Young Papers.)

Whether Grant ever succeeded in his mission is not clear. Certainly there is no reference to such a monstrous flag in any of the camp journals. Because of weight restrictions, it was probably not brought along that summer of 1847, if ever. It would appear that the purpose of such a flag was not only to herald a religious society, but also to be "an honor to the union," perhaps the antecedent to a future territorial or state flag.

68. Thomas Bullock to his wife, 9 June 1847, Thomas Bullock Letters.

69. Journal of Horace K. Whitney, 10 June 1847.

70. John Pack to his family at Winter Quarters, 1 June 1847, in Bitton, *The Redoubtable John Pack*, 222.

71. Journals of Wilford Woodruff and Thomas Bullock, 8 June 1847.

72. Moses "Black" Harris, so named because of his swarthy, dark complexion, was a native South Carolinian born approximately 1804 in Union County. In all likelihood he was a member of W. H. Ashley's first fur trading company up the Missouri in 1822 and in another Ashley party in 1825 led by Jedediah Smith. He had circumnavigated the Great Salt Lake as early as 1825, visited the headwaters of the Yellowstone in 1826, and traveled through the Wind River Valley in 1828 and 1829. He later led several expeditions of rendezvous parties west from St. Louis. After 1840 he became a trusted, if rather expensive, guide for Oregon emigrant trains. A stranger and an enigma even to his fellow mountain men—"a bird alone" in the wilderness—he was known for his tall tales and colorful yarns, the West's most famous entertainer around a campfire. He died in St. Joseph, Missouri, in May 1849 (see Jerome Peltier, "Moses 'Black' Harris," in Hafen, *The Mountain Men*, 4:103–17).

73. Journal of Horace K. Whitney, 27 June 1847.

74. Journal of Horace K. Whitney, 27 June 1847. Brannan's newspaper, *The California Star*, may well have been the second newspaper published in California. Robert Semple's *Californian* first appeared 29 August 1846.

75. P. W. Crawford, "Narrative of the Overland Journey to Oregon," handwritten, 26, July 1847, Bancroft Library.

76. Journal of Norton Jacob, 28 June 1847.

77. Journal of Horace K. Whitney, 28 June 1847. Clayton corroborates and expands on Whitney's account and from the two of them, one is hard pressed to believe any longer in the time-honored myth that Bridger was so down on the valley that he offered, the vanguard company at least, $1,000 for the first bushel of corn grown there (see also *William Clayton's Journal*, 28 June 1847, 272–78).

Bridger's alleged statement may have originated not with Bridger but with Harris, who was much less kind in his comments about the Salt Lake. Or it may have derived from a less well-documented conversation between Bridger and oncoming members of the Mormon Battalion, some of whom were unhappy they were bound for a desert valley and not the gentler climates of California (see "Extracts from the Journal of John Steele," 17).

Bridger's positive comments are further witnessed in the General Church Minutes for 28 June 1847, as recorded by Thomas Bullock. In certain parts of the valley, Bridger had eaten "the best wheat I ever saw" and instead of a desert, "it rains at the Salt Lake at all times of the year."

78. Journal of Wilford Woodruff, 28 June 1847.

79. Journal of Horace K. Whitney, 30 June 1847. For a firsthand account by Brannan of his overland journey, see his letter to "Brother Newell" dated 18 June 1847 from Fort Hall and published in *Millennial Star*, 15 Oct. 1847, 305–7.

80. Journal of Horace K. Whitney, 28 June 1847.

81. Journal of Norton Jacob, 30 June 1847. No diarist other than Jacob attributed the horror of the Donner camp to any other influence but their own lack of judgment and poor advice. It is generally conceded that Lansford W. Hastings, more than any other man, was responsible for their miserable, but avoidable, fate.

82. Brannan (1818–1889) converted to Mormonism in 1833 in Kirtland, Ohio, at the age of 15. Although active in building the Kirtland Temple, he left the Church for several years, not resurfacing until the Nauvoo years. First a follower of Joseph Smith, he later became associated with William Smith (the Prophet's rebellious brother) and his claim to succession, a move that resulted in his being disfellowshiped from the Church. A printer by trade, after his reinstatement he went to New York to assist Orson and Parley P. Pratt in defending the faith through his publications. He there conceived the idea of leading a group of Saints to California by sea and received Orson Pratt's approval. On 4 February 1846 the ship *Brooklyn* left New York with 238 new converts aboard under Brannan's leadership. Six months later, after a voyage of 24,000 miles by way of the Sandwich Islands (Hawaii), the *Brooklyn* landed at San Francisco on 30 July 1846, just three weeks after the Mexican surrender.

Brannan failed to organize a branch of the Church at the Bay as he had been instructed to do, but succeeded in publishing one of California's first newspapers, *The California Star*, which first appeared on 9 January 1847. Soon after his return from Utah to California in the late summer of 1847, and still carrying a grudge against the Mormon leaders, he quit Mormonism and embarked on his own career. He amassed a fortune with the discovery of gold at Sutter's Fort in 1849 and became California's first great landowner and millionaire and later a state senator. Later his fortunes turned sour and he lost his wealth in a spectacular series of misfortunes and mismanagement. He died in ruin and abject poverty in 1889 in San Diego. For lack of money even to bury him, his remains lay unclaimed for a year (see Eugene E. Campbell, "The Apostasy of Samuel Brannan," *Utah Historical Quarterly* 27 [1959]: 157–67). For more on Brannan and his colorful career, see Paul Bailey, *Sam Brannan and the California Mormons* (1943); William Glover, *The Mormons in California*, ed. Paul Bailey (1954); Reva L. Scott, *Samuel Brannan and the Golden Fleece: A Biography* (1944); Annaleone D. Patton, *California Mormons by Sail and Trail* (1961); and Douglas S. Watson, "Herald of the Gold Rush: Sam Brannan," *California Historical Society Quarterly* 10 (1931): 298–301.

83. Brigham Young and Council to Amasa Lyman, Journal History, 8 July 1847.

7

"HURRA, HURRA, HURRA— THERE'S MY HOME AT LAST"

Fort Bridger to the Great Salt Lake

> . . . When we turned round the hill to the right and came
> in full view of the Salt Lake in the distance, with its bold hills
> on its islands towering up in bold relief behind the silvery lake.
> A very extensive valley burst upon our view, dotted in 3 or 4
> places with timber. . . . I could not help shouting "hurra, hurra,
> hurra, there's my home at last." The sky is very clear, the air
> delightful and all together looks glorious.[1]

The final stage of the pioneer company's march, from Fort Bridger to the Salt Lake, was the most difficult of the entire journey and also the most rewarding. It began in murmur and complaint but ended in triumph and discovery, although not before they had endured more sickness and suffering than yet experienced on the trail. There would be one last obstacle more formidable than the Rockies, one final test of their faith and endurance, this time in the form of the smallest of enemies, the active agent of a serious disease that hindered their progress as no mountain pass ever could.

Because they were running two weeks behind their appointed schedule, their stay at Fort Bridger, consisting then of nothing but "two or three rudely constructed log cabins," was as brief as possible.[2] They arrived in the afternoon of 7 July and left only 40 hours later. Their time was used for essential blacksmith repairs, mapping the route to the Great Basin, trading

Fort Bridger, *from a sketch by Frederick Piercy*

for buckskin and horses, and as time would tell, insufficient rest and recuperation. Used more as a trading lodge with the Snake Indians than as a fort, Bridger's trading post was "a shabby concern" built of poles and dogwood. It was situated on a beautiful site on the Black Fork of Green River, with trout-laden streams running in several channels. George A. Smith described it as consisting of "two long, low, rough cabins built in the form of an L with a small enclosure for stock built of upright poles. The surrounding country was beautiful, but the fort itself was an unpretentious place."[3]

Some still found time for diversion. None enjoyed the respite more than Wilford Woodruff. "The calculation was to spend the day at the fort," he recalled. So,

as soon as I got my breakfast I rigged up my trout rod that I had brought with me from Liverpool, fixed my reel, line, and artificial fly and went to one of the brooks close by camp to try my luck catching trout. The man at the fort said there were but very few trout in the streams. And a good many of the brethren were already at the creeks with their rods and lines trying their skill baiting with fresh meat and grasshoppers, but no one seemed to catch any. I went and flung my fly, . . . it being the first time that I ever tried

205

the artificial fly in America, or ever saw it tried. I watched it as it floated upon the water with as much intense interest as [Benjamin] Franklin did his kite. . . . And as Franklin received great joy when he saw electricity or lightning descend on his kite string, in like manner was I highly gratified when I saw the nimble trout dart my fly, hook himself, and run away with the line.

By noon he had pulled in a dozen fish while his fellow anglers looked on in jealous surprise—"proof positive to me that the artificial fly is far the best thing now known to fish trout with."[4]

Meanwhile, the restless Sam Brannan, upset with Brigham's lack of interest in his California Eldorado, jumped at the chance to head back east. He quickly accepted the assignment to take mail for Amasa Lyman and for the oncoming Battalion contingent and then to pilot them on to Salt Lake Valley. And for those of the sick detachment anxious to collect their muster-out pay, he likewise agreed to pilot them all the way back to California. On Friday morning, 9 July, he, his two sidekicks, Sergeant Thomas Williams, six other Battalion soldiers, and Thomas Brown headed back along the trail, leaving five soldiers to go on ahead with the pioneer camp. Anxious to rid the camp of a detracting influence, Brigham was as relieved to see Brannan go as Brannan was to get away.

THE HASTINGS CUTOFF

While some fished, others fretted. Bullock, who always saw himself more overworked than appreciated, spent several hours copying out at least two important items Brannan had loaned them. The first was handwritten directions by Lansford W. Hastings giving directions from Fort Bridger to the Great Salt Lake, the first part of the "Hastings Cutoff" to California. The second was a map of the proposed shortcut, apparently embellished by Brannan during his recent trip east from California. Brannan knew the trail firsthand.

They already had a copy of Hastings's guide, so what Bullock copied were likely more detailed descriptions of the trail that Brannan got earlier from Hastings himself and from his own recent experiences. If they had not decided on the Hastings Cutoff before they met Jim Bridger and Sam Brannan, they certainly did afterward. Both men had advised it unequivocally, it being much better marked than the year before. The other route—

up the Oregon Trail, north to Bear Lake, and down the Bartleson Trail to the Great Salt Lake—was at least three times longer than the Hastings Cutoff. They also knew that Fremont had successfully taken the route to the Valley in 1845.

A young, ambitious Ohio lawyer, Hastings made his first journey to Oregon in 1842 and on down to California in 1843. Seizing a chance to make fame and fortune for himself in California, he returned east in 1844. There he lectured extensively and wrote a book called *The Emigrant's Guide to Oregon and California* (1845). Although he never followed the entire route himself until 1845, this newcomer to Rocky Mountain geography confidently pronounced that the most direct route to California left the Oregon Trail "about two hundred miles east from Fort Hall; thence bearing west, southwest to the Salt Lake; and thence continuing down to the bay of San Francisco."[5] So long as travelers properly prepared for a long, but manageable, trek across a salt desert to Pilot Peak and the valleys beyond, Hastings simplistically argued, overland companies should save 200 or 300 miles and several weeks hard travel time on their way to California.

The first white man to follow what essentially was an Indian or pack trail from Fort Bridger to the Salt Lake Valley was Fremont, during his third expedition in 1845. The following spring, Hastings, James Clyman (an experienced trapper), James M. Hudspeth, and a few others left San Francisco on mules to prove the theory by traveling east to the Salt Lake, northeast up Mountain Dell Creek to Big Mountain, through East Canyon, up the Red Fork (Echo Canyon), and eventually to Fort Bridger.

There they met a small pack party led by William H. Russell (later founder of the Pony Express) and Edwin Bryant who, listening to the newly-arrived enthusiasts, chose to follow Hastings's route to the Pacific. This time Hudspeth was determined to find a passage down the mountainous Weber Canyon rather than follow the Indian trail over the Wasatch Mountains. At great cost to animal life and human endurance, they miraculously made their way down the Weber Canyon gorge, learning the hard way that a large wagon train could never hope to follow in their footsteps.

Behind the Russell-Bryant party came a second pack company on the southern route—the Harlan-Young party—with Hastings himself as their guide; a third party, of Swiss emigrants led by Heinrich Lienhard, was close behind. All reached the Salt Lake via Weber Canyon and in reasonably good time.

A fourth party to take the same route belonged to James Frazier Reed, William Pike, and Charles T. Stanton (better known as the Donner Company), who reached Fort Bridger only eight days after Hastings had gone ahead with Russell. Seven days getting over the mountains to the Weber Canyon, they there found a handwritten note from Hastings advising them to take their heavy wagons down the pack trail over the mountains instead of through the dreadful canyon.

Bewildered at such nebulous instructions, Reed and two others rode ahead on horseback, eventually catching up with Hastings somewhere west of Salt Lake. Hastings and Reed returned to a summit somewhere in the Oquirrh Mountains from where Hastings, by means of hand pointing, explained to Reed as best he could the Big Mountain Indian trail from East Canyon to the valley. Reed returned to his waiting company and in due course found the trail. They then proceeded to cut and hack a roadway from the base of Echo Canyon to Big Mountain, then west to Little Mountain, and eventually down into Emigration Canyon. Historians concluded that the 30 days spent by the Donner party clearing a sad semblance of a wagon trail through the Wasatch underbrush cost them far more time than they could afford.[6]

One day out from Fort Bridger, the Mormon pioneers thus became the fifth company in less than a year to try the Hastings road. Only 115 miles from the Salt Lake Valley, with ten times as many able-bodied men to clear a trail as their predecessors the year before, they planned to be planting crops in ten days.

Almost immediately, however, following Three Mile Creek on a barely visible trail, they encountered some of the most difficult mountain trails they had yet encountered—or as one later emigrant put it, "a worse and worse continuation of a bad beginning."[7] Climbing over the ridge dividing the waters of the Colorado from those of the Great Basin, they climbed 750 feet in two days, reaching an altitude of 7,700 feet on 10 July—over 300 feet higher than South Pass.

Hauling wagon trains through dense willow underbrush, up steep climbs, and down precipitous, life-threatening descents was surely the challenge of the entire trek. "The last 100 miles is some of the worse road you can imagine," wrote one traveler, "over mountains 3, 5 and 7 miles from the top to the bottom, and so narrow are the passes you would almost think to look ahead of you, that you could travel no farther, but a narrow passage always opens out before you."[8]

Doubling or even tripling ox teams for a single wagon while on a climb, with men out clearing stones and cutting tree branches on one side and pulling on extended ropes on the other, was a common, backbreaking scene. The constant fear that a wagon might tip over and plunge far down a mountainside exacted their most skillful efforts.

And the descents were even more hazardous. Locking the wheels of a one-ton wagon was only a partial answer to the frightening proposition. Usually, a dozen or more men held on tightly to ropes attached to the back of the wagon to ease the descent. Occasionally even a team of oxen were hitched to the back end of the wagon and held back in order to keep it from "ending over." The occupants tumbled or slid the best they could to get down the steep declivities. It's "like jumping off the roof of a house," a frightened Bullock complained of one particularly steep descent near Muddy Creek, in what others described as "the most mountainous course we have yet seen."[9]

Yet in just two days, they made 31 miles. Orson Pratt, ever scouting the trails ahead, soon discovered smoke rising from a nearby camp. Pratt soon found himself in company with the first white settler of the Great Basin, the redheaded mountaineer Miles Goodyear, who was heading east with a corral of California horses to trade with the oncoming Oregon immigrants.

The 30-year-old, Connecticut-born Goodyear and his associate, John Craig, were quickly beholden to Pratt for his information on the earlier than usual Oregon emigration. As a result, Goodyear changed his course to the northwest toward Fort Hall to intercept as many of the earliest spring companies as he could. In return, Goodyear and Craig were generous with their advice on the best of the three poorly marked trails to Salt Lake, sketching yet another map and pushing hardest for the road that would lead to Goodyear's own encampment, Fort Buenaventura, a primitive cottonwood log cabin and small farm acreage at the mouth of Weber Canyon.[10]

If Goodyear was encouraging about a future settlement, Craig took an opposing view. Having recently settled near San Francisco Bay, this former resident of Ray County, Missouri, was hard pressed to say anything positive about the Salt Lake. "Notwithstanding all we had heard of the richness of the country," Whitney recorded, "we would find it vastly overrated and that if we had formed an idea of its superiority, we should be disappointed."[11]

The only hope for settlement, Craig argued, was irrigation, and any success in settling would come at a terrible price.

Craig, in a 7 October letter to a George Bossinger, confirmed the coming of the Mormons and their intent to plant crops around both Salt Lake and Utah Lake. "About seventy-five miles this side the Lake," he wrote,

> on the 11th of July we met 83 wagons being an advance party of the Mormons on their way to the lake intending (as they informed us) to sow buckwheat and establish a colony around this and the Uataw Lake intending to sow a large quantity of wheat. They having all kinds of seeds with them together with implements of husbandry. The party numbered about two hundred men with eight or ten females. They informed us that their was about six hundred more wagons on their way from the Council Bluffs that expected to reach these Lakes and there spend the winter and the Spring. Such as could not be suited here would proceed to California proper.[12]

Craig's bluntness seems to have struck a negative chord in the minds of an increasing number in the camp. Some were beginning to question their ultimate destination and the treacherous route they were following to get there. Perhaps Brannan and Craig were right after all and California should be their ultimate goal. Why go to all this trouble over so poorly marked a trail? And even if they did get to wherever it was they were going, the season was getting so late they might never get in sufficient crops. What's more, many were coming down sick with the mountain fever. Confided Bullock: "As I lay in my wagon sick I overheard several of the brethren murmuring about the face of the country."[13] Echoed Clayton: "There are some in camp who are getting discouraged about the looks of the country but thinking minds are not much disappointed."[14]

It was the first vocalization of any real dissatisfaction during the entire journey, and they expressed it by accepting Goodyear's advice to follow a route to the Red Fork (Echo Canyon) which the Twelve had rejected. "But let the Camp decide," said a frustrated Woodruff, "so that none may have room to murmur at the Twelve hereafter."[15]

ROCKY MOUNTAIN FEVER

The very next morning, within hours of Goodyear's departure, Brigham came down so violently sick that the entire camp was forced to halt in the

Bear River Valley. Seized with the most excruciating pain in his hands and back, and suffering a sudden fever that spiked to 104 or 105 degrees within hours, their leader by nightfall lay raging and delirious.

Before this time he had counted himself fortunate to have been spared what many in camp had been suffering during the past two weeks. The first hint of trouble came back at the Green River crossing. Tired and exhausted, Erastus Snow came down with a fever on 3 July; and at least half the camp had been sick since. "Its first appearance is like that of a severe cold," he warned,

> producing soreness in the flesh, and pains in the head and all parts of the body; and as the fever increases the pains in the head and back become almost insufferable. But an active portion of Physic accompanied with warming and stimulating drinks, such as ginger and pepper tea, cayenne, etc. taken freely before and after the operation of the Physic, seldom fails to break it up, though it left the patient sore, weak and feeble. All are now recovering except some fresh cases.[16]

It was well-known among trail-goers that Rocky Mountain Fever stalked the Oregon Trail, particularly from where it joined the Sweetwater back at Independence Rock.[17] A springtime disease of the higher North American altitudes, it was wrongly attributed either to contaminated melted snows or to the seasonal swarms of flies and mosquitos at river crossings.

That they all began to suffer at more or less the same time points to a decisive contaminating moment. Passing the Sweetwater ahead of season, the pioneers' first brush with the problem probably began on Saturday, 26 June, just two miles below South Pass. There they first encountered the tall, fresh grasses of the high Rockies plain, which were infested with tiny wood ticks, no larger than the lead end of a blunt pencil, waiting for the passerby.

Modern research has shown that the brand of mountain fever they suffered from may have been typhoid related, but more likely was Colorado Tick Fever caused by a tick-borne virus. Within three to fourteen days, the illness would often show itself with a rash on the hands and feet that looked very much like the black measles. This was followed by, as Snow correctly described, chills, a hacking cough, severe headache, acute pain in the calves and lumbar regions of the back, rapid temperature rise, restlessness, and delirium until the body's immune system had received sufficient strength to destroy its attackers. Among those over 40 years old who were infected, as many as 20 percent died from the disease; and in some companies, 10 to 15 percent of the entire group perished from it.[18]

Brigham (46 years old) and Albert P. Rockwood (41 years old) had carried the virus for up to 17 days; when it hit, it did so with sudden vengeance and held on with a tenacity not seen among others in their camp. After suffering for 19 days, barely able to write and smarting from every jar and jolt of the wagon, Rockwood recorded what he thought was his death wish on 14 July: "Brigham Young is a little better. The fever rages harder than ever on me. Br. Lorenzo Young and many others look upon me as dangerous ill. I so considered myself and so told the brethren that if no relief came in 24 hours they might dig a hole to put me in."[19]

The standard medical treatment of the time for such advanced cases was to purge the body of all foreign substances by inducing vomiting and flushing the bowels with enemas. The former came by way of lobelia and the latter, as Rockwood explained, with "emetick and cathartics." If that failed, doctors prescribed bleeding, in the mistaken belief of that pre-immunization era that health was restored through balancing the four humors of the body—blood, phlegm, yellow bile, and black bile.

But like many others of their time, the Mormon pioneers put little trust in the traditional medical practices of the age (or "poison doctors" as they were often called).[20] Instead they preferred the so-called Thompson school of medicines, of which their own Willard Richards was a licensed practitioner. The Thompsonians usually prescribed mild herbs and emetics and warmed the blood with cayenne pepper (hence Snow's reference to a "physic," or enema) "accompanied with warming and stimulating drinks, such as ginger and pepper tea, cayenne, etc."[21]

Confident in Richards's prescriptions and in the power of healing through the laying on of hands by the priesthood, camp leaders fully expected a quick recovery. Heber C. Kimball thought they were seeing an improvement in Brigham's weakened condition, but he decided that the prudent course of action would be to send Orson Pratt and several others on ahead, down Echo Canyon to ascertain for themselves if the Weber Canyon was at all passable. If not, they were instructed to find "Mr. Reed's route across the mountains."[22]

So on the afternoon of 13 July, with 23 wagons and 42 men from both the Brigham Young and Heber C. Kimball divisions, Pratt left the main company on Coyote Creek, near the top entrance to Red Fork or Echo Canyon. He was to explore the country, find the trail, go over the mountains, and leave trail instructions for the rest to follow so they could eventually reassemble prior to entering the Salt Lake Valley. Meanwhile, with Brigham and Rockwood using the comfort of Woodruff's carriage, the main camp would descend the canyon as best they could and await word from Pratt's various messengers.[23]

The following evening Pratt's company made it down Echo Canyon. While exploring and evaluating the upper reaches of Weber Canyon and ruling out all possibility of that route (as Rockwell described it, "blocked up by the rocks, some places could not see two wagons ahead"), Pratt discovered the Hastings's trail or "Reed's Route."[24] From there he traveled up the divide called Hog's Back (Reed's Pass), crossed Dixie Creek southwest of present Hennifer, Utah, reached East Canyon Creek on 17 July and the top of Big Mountain two days later.

The main camp, meanwhile, spent the time passing slowly down Echo Canyon with its "wild and melancholy red rocks frowning down upon us with sullen majesty," and was forced to lay over repeatedly because of sickness, much to the chagrin of some. "Quite dull business this, lying by," wrote a frustrated Horace K. Whitney. But he had enough time on his hands to see how such a ravine might someday work in their favor: "Indeed, this pass is so well fortified by nature, that I have no doubt but that 10 men could successfully dispute its passage for a long time, against 100 men."[25]

By the time they reached the Weber River at the foot of Echo Canyon—despite the comforts of Woodruff's carriage and all the prayers, blessings, and medicines in camp—Brigham had suffered a serious relapse and appeared worse than before, totally incapable of further travel. Fearing the worst, all the Apostles in camp, with a few selected others, ascended a nearby high mountain, where in a special circle of faith they prayed to Almighty God for their leader and all the other sick in camp.[26]

Uppermost in their minds was that daunting "what if." Who would lead them if Brigham died? Where would they go? Who would follow them? And above all, what would happen to the Church?[27] Brigham eventually rallied, but not before unwillingly testing the faith and allegiance of a once more tried and humbled band.

213

"A Resting Place for the Saints"

Sunday, 18 July, with Brigham's sick camp still navigating the twisting creek of Echo Canyon, Kimball proposed further that a planting party go on ahead to join Pratt's exploring company, "find a good place, begin to plant potatoes, etc., as we have little time to spare." All voted to sustain Kimball's proposition.[28]

Consequently the next morning the planting party, consisting of Willard Richards, Erastus Snow, George A. Smith, and the majority of the camp, in 41 wagons under John Pack's command, started out ahead. They left Heber C. Kimball, Wilford Woodruff, Ezra T. Benson, and a few others in 8 or 10 wagons to care for the sick. Prior to their departure, a slightly stronger Brigham Young counseled Erastus Snow to go ahead on horseback and overtake Pratt's vanguard company with specific instructions that once in the valley they were to "halt at the first suitable spot after reaching the Lake Valley, and put in our seed, potatoes, buckwheat, turnips, etc. regardless of our final location."[29]

The critical point was to start planting. They would decide later if the valley would be their permanent home.

> Pres. Young gave us his views concerning a stopping place in the Basin, by saying that he felt inclined for the present not to crowd upon the Utes [Ute Indians] until we have a chance to get acquainted with them, and that it would be better to bear toward the region of the Salt Lake rather than the Utah Lake, and find some good place for our seeds and deposit them as speedily as possible, regardless of a future location. . . . And begin to judge where will be the best spot to put in the plows. . . . It matters not where it is. The President thinks the Utes may feel a little tenacious about their choice lands on the Utah Lake, and we had better keep further north towards the Salt Lake, which is more of a . . . neutral ground, and by so doing we should be less likely to be disturbed.[30]

Pratt, however, was hard to catch. That very day, he and his riding companion, John Brown, ahead of their own road-clearing company, had ascended Big Mountain, from where they first saw the Salt Lake Valley. Not given to dramatic expression, let alone exaggeration, Pratt could only mention "an extensive level prairie, some few miles distant" and must give way

Pathway to Zion, *from a painting by William Maughan*

to the following, more literary account by a later, non-Mormon traveler at the same point:

> We then ascended up a very long and steep mountain, over a horrible road over stumps, holes, rocks, logs, etc. and the greatest care being required to prevent the upsetting and breaking of the wagons. Our progress consequently was very slow. At last . . . we gained the top where we were fully and more than fully compensated for all our days' toil and trouble by a splendid view which burst upon us in an instant. . . . And when on the summit of the mountain . . . ahead of us for some 30 or 40 miles the splendid valley of the Great Salt Lake bathed in golden sunshine and we could see mountain tops far above it.[31]

From the peak, Pratt and Brown rode down the eastern slope of Big Mountain into Mountain Dell Canyon (still following Reed's trail), over a steep divide (Little Mountain), and down into a narrow ravine later known as Emigration Canyon. They then returned to their own company, which through strenuous labor had moved over six miles up East Canyon. On 20 July, Pratt's company of 23 wagons worked its way through to Parley's Park and camped in an area now inundated by Mountain Dell Reservoir.

The final 35 miles from Big Mountain to near the mouth of Emigration Canyon were by far the most difficult of the journey. At times the groves of aspen, poplar, willow, shrub oak, and balsam were so thick there was "scarce room to pass through." And where the timber had been cleared, the path was so cluttered with stumps that it kept every teamster busy clearing them away. Boulders loomed everywhere out of the dense brush, and the descents were as precipitous as the large rattlesnakes and curiously big black crickets were abundant. Dropping at the rate of 130 feet per mile, their wagons descended 4,000 feet in two days. Frightened oxen, worried teamsters, suspended wagons, blistering heat, worry, and confusion mingled with restless anticipation everywhere. Lorenzo Young's wagon lost control while in steep descent and crashed down the mountainside, but his two young boys survived uninjured by cutting out a hole in the canvas to escape. Obstacles notwithstanding, George A. Smith, Willard Richards, and their planting crew managed to camp within a mile or so of Pratt's company on the evening of 21 July, having covered in three days what the Donner party had taken 16 days to travel.

The next day, rather than follow the Donner trail over the precipitous mountain that now bears its name, the newly-combined parties inched their way down Canyon or Emigration Creek. They found it "practicable" to make their own road down the creek bed "thus avoiding the strenuous Donner Mountain climb" before coming into full view of the valley.[32] As Levi Jackman described it: "The mountains came almost together at the bottom. But when we got through it seemed like bursting from the confines of a prison."[33]

Meanwhile, Snow, with his additional counsel from Brigham, had ridden horseback express all the way from Echo Canyon and finally reached Pratt at the foot of Little Mountain in the afternoon of 21 July. Riding on ahead of the struggling road builders, and after climbing Donner hill, they suddenly came in full panoramic view of the Salt Lake Valley. "We involuntarily, both at the same instant," recorded Snow, "uttered a shout of joy at finding it to be the very place of our destination."[34]

Sharing a common dream but a single horse, the excited pair proceeded down into the valley, descending a gradual slope some four or five miles before returning in the evening to their eagerly waiting but weary canyon company.

Most others in the forward companies got their first full view of the valley on 22 July, and their comments, after months on the trail, are a kaleidoscope of color and reaction. To some, it was Zion in a moment; to others, how could such a desert bleakness ever prove a paradise? Common to all, however, was a certain relief and a sense of discovery, a hope for a possible promised land but tempered by the stark reality of a timberless desert stretching for miles below them. "I could not help shouting 'hurra, hurra, hurra,'" wrote Bullock. "There's my home at last."[35]

To tired eyes accustomed to the timbered hills of New England and the vast prairie green of Illinois and the Missouri River Valley, the sight of such an arid plain gave pause for soul-searching reflection. "We at length engaged from the pass," wrote Horace K. Whitney, "and were highly gratified with a fine view of the open country and the Great Salt Lake whose blue surface could be seen in the distance with a lofty range of mountains in the background."[36]

William Clayton, wanting to be more excited than he was, could not but notice the scarcity of timber. "And that is mostly on the banks of creeks and streams of water, which is about the only objection which could be raised in my estimation to this being one of the most beautiful valleys and pleasant places for a home for the Saints which could be found. . . . For my own part," he concluded, choosing to take the long-term, optimistic view, "I am happily disappointed in the appearance of the valley. . . . But if the land be as rich as it has the appearance of being, I have no fears but the Saints can live here and do well while we will do right."[37]

But for many, these were the very qualities they were looking for in a new mountain home. Those diarists with long memories of past persecutions were quick to perceive the natural defenses such a valley could afford, ringed with snowcapped mountains and difficult valleys. "From what knowledge we have of it at present," penned Howard Egan, "this is the most safe and secure place the Saints could possibly locate themselves in. Nature has fortified this place on all sides, with only a few narrow passes, which could be made impregnable without much difficulty."[38]

Regardless of reaction, little time was spent in sightseeing. On the morning of 22 July, Orson Pratt, George A. Smith, Joseph Matthews, John Brown, John Pack, Orrin Porter Rockwell, Jesse Little, and one other explored the valley further. Following a line west of north, they explored the eastern reaches of the Great Salt Lake, discovered several hot springs, and eventually, after conferring with Willard Richards, selected a place for a temporary campground. Pack and Matthews, meanwhile, rode back with letters to the sick company still on the eastern side of Big Mountain.

The following morning, 23 July, at a special meeting Orson Pratt prayed to God, returning thanks for their preservation and consecrating the land to the Lord. Several project committees or work crews then began the task of planting. A "committee of five" was appointed to locate a place for planting potatoes, corn, and beans. Other committees were also formed, including "the committee to stock plows and drags," "the committee to superintend the moving and seizing up of scythes," "the committee for cir- culating teams," and "the committee for making a coal pit."

Before noon they reported on a spot 40 by 20 rods in size (near a point where Main Street now intersects First South Street), where the first fur- row was turned by Captain Seth Taft at 12 noon. The sunbaked, brittle ground broke Taft's and several other plows on the first run. Undaunted, by two o'clock they had erected a small dam diverting what was later called City Creek into several small trenches "to irrigate the land." As Clayton put it: "This land is beautifully situated for irrigation, many nice streams descending from the mountains which can be turned in every direction so as to water any portion of the lands at pleasure."[39]

Meanwhile the sick camp had sufficiently recovered to pursue their journey, crossing Big and Little Mountain on 23 July. The following morn- ing, Saturday, 24 July, after coming down the last six miles of Emigration Canyon in Woodruff's carriage, Brigham (still sick with a low-grade fever) saw the full valley, from near Donner Mountain, for the first time.

There is limited contemporary evidence that Brigham ever expressed himself in these familiar terms, "This is the right place; drive on," as he sur- veyed the valley before him. His own account leaves everything to be desired, sick as he was. And of the handful of men who were in the rear- guard company, none referred to such a pronouncement. Albert P. Rockwood, his nearby companion in sickness, made no reference, even ret- rospectively, although this comes as no surprise given his sparing and parsi- monious style of writing. Neither did the more careful writer, Horace Whitney. More surprising is the fact that Heber C. Kimball, who must have shared the moment near his file leader, if he did hear him say such words, never said so at the time.

The only reliable witness comes from Wilford Woodruff, in whose car- riage Brigham rode. He alone captured their poignant moment of discov- ery and decision. From his comments, it is incontestable that if Brigham did not then utter such a proclamation, he surely meant the same.

First Glimpse, *sketch of the initial sighting of the Salt Lake Valley, by Charles B. Hall*

We came in full view of the great valley or basin of the Salt Lake and land of promise, held in reserve by the hand of God for a resting place for the Saints upon which a portion of the Zion of God will be built.

We gazed with wonder and admiration upon the vast rich fertile valley. . . . Our hearts were surely made glad . . . to gaze upon a valley of such vast extent entirely surrounded with a perfect chain of everlasting hills and mountains covered with eternal snow, with their innumerable peaks like pyramids towering towards Heaven presenting at one view the grandest and most sublime scenery probably that could be obtained on the globe.[40]

He concluded: "President Young expressed his full satisfaction in the appearance of the valley as a resting place for the Saints and was amply repaid for his journey."[41]

If Brigham felt a pang of disappointment on looking at that barren, desert expanse—as Harris, Craig, and the California-bound Brannan predicted he surely would—that, too, went unrecorded.

The two men gazed on the scene for some time, long enough for a weakened but rallying leader to feel the kind of profound relief and gratitude that comes only with recovery from a near fatal illness. Perhaps their long and tiresome journey was, finally, at an end and he and others could find the rest they craved so desperately.

More clear-minded than he had been for days, Brigham's feelings centered on more than just the moment or himself. For all their obstacles and delays, it was not yet too late to plant and prepare some late summer crops for the hundreds now on the trail behind them. Surely this must have been a brief moment of exhilaration, even victory, that none had perished along the way (as he himself had predicted at the outset), and that their march had been spared the tragedy of Zion's Camp.

He might also have mused of other times: of Joseph and Hyrum Smith who had died that such a moment of promise might come; of the message of Cumorah which he and many of his companions in camp had taken to Canada and overseas to England as early missionaries. Perhaps it would yet survive the misunderstandings, disruptions, and persecutions that had marred and hindered its way since those Palmyra beginnings a short seventeen years before.

He also understood that there must be more to the valley than planting crops and building shelter. For the Church to survive, it needed more than a safe and isolated habitat, timberless or otherwise. It required a home where, through dint of continued hard labor, it could restore itself, rebuild, and heal its collective wounds and divisions, and a place from where it could send out a message and a beacon to its far-flung membership that the destructive storm of the past three years was over. A new temple would have to be erected. Doctrines and practices needed time and space to be tested and developed. And a new First Presidency must be organized. In short, there was a church to save and to mold, and here lay their place and opportunity.

After a journey of three and a half months and 1,073 miles, the Mormon pioneers had finally reached a potential settlement site. They still needed time to ascertain if it would be a permanent spot, but for now they would plant first and explore and decide later. The season was already well advanced. Their very lives and those to follow lay in the seeds they were now planting. But surely it had the makings of a new mountain Zion. Perhaps Egan said it best: "My heart felt truly glad, and I rejoiced . . . that [it] may yet become a home for the Saints."[42]

NOTES

1. Journal of Thomas Bullock, 22 July 1847.

2. Fred R. Gowans and Eugene E. Campbell, *Fort Bridger: Island in the Wilderness* (1975), 13.

Another 1847 visitor to Fort Bridger, Lansford B. Hastings, described the fort as follows: "The buildings that constitute the fort are two double log cabins. One is used for a trading house and the other for a dwelling house. He [Bridger] has a very high yard for his horses. The fort is situated on the head waters of Blacks Fork of Green River in a valley 4 or 5 miles wide covered with thick grass. The mountains on the south and west are covered with snow. This fort is a few miles acrost the line into California" (Journal of Lansford B. Hastings, 31 July 1847, mss #660, Oregon Historical Society).

3. Gowens and Campbell, *Fort Bridger*, 31.

Elizabeth Geer, passing by Fort Bridger in 1849, described the area as "a pretty place to see in such a barren country—perhaps there is a thousand acres of level land covered with grass interspersed with beautifully stoney brooks and plenty of timber such as it is quaking asp" (The Overland Journal of Elizabeth Dixon Smith Geer, 9 Aug. 1849, Oregon Historical Society).

4. Journal of Wilford Woodruff, 8 July 1847, 3:225.

5. Hastings, *The Emigrants' Guide to Oregon and California*, 137.

6. I have relied heavily on Dale L. Morgan's *The Great Salt Lake* (1947), 148–75, for an understanding of the early trails from Fort Bridger to the Salt Lake Valley. See also Charles Kelly, "The Hastings Cutoff," *Utah Historical Quarterly* 3, no. 3 (July 1930): 67–82. For a more recent, revisionist interpretation of Hastings, see Thomas F. Andrews, "Lansford W. Hastings and the Promotion of the Salt Lake Desert Cutoff: A Reappraisal," *Western Historical Quarterly* 4 (Apr. 1973): 133–50, and "The Controversial Hastings Overland Guide: A Reassessment," *Pacific Historical Review* 37, no. 1 (Feb. 1968): 21–34.

7. Journal of Charles G. Gray, 13 July 1849.

8. William Greenwood to his family, 17 Oct. 1847, William Greenwood Papers, Harold B. Lee Library, Brigham Young University.

9. Journal of Thomas Bullock, 10 July 1847, and *William Clayton's Journal*, 10 July 1847, 289.

10. For more on Goodyear, see Eugene A. Campbell, "Miles Morris Goodyear," in Hafen, *The Mountain Men*, 2:179–88. See also Dale L. Morgan, "Miles Goodyear and the Founding of Ogden," *Utah Historical Quarterly* 21 (1953): 195–218, 307–29. Goodyear is credited by historians as the first white settler of Ogden and of the state of Utah. Goodyear had taken part in western expeditions since the Whitmans' in 1836, but he did not erect his fort in the Weber River country until the early fall of 1846. One of his assistants, Captain Wells, ran the fort in his absence. Goodyear died in 1849.

Levi Riter, a member of the emigration camp, and many others were surprised to hear of Goodyear's establishment: "When we arrived in this valley we supposed that no civilized man had ever entered it for the purpose of settling it, but to our astonishment we soon learned that a man by the name of Miles Goodyear and a Mr. Wells born in the city of Boston had formed the nucleus of settlement 40 miles north of us. They came here from Arkansas in 1846 bringing with them a large number of cattle, horses and goats" (Levi Evans Riter letter, 15 Jan. 1848, Levi Riter Collection, LDS Church Archives).

11. Journal of Horace K. Whitney, 11 July 1847. John Craig is not mentioned much in any other contemporary Mormon journal and remains a shadowy figure. Dale Morgan is one of the few to have noticed his appearance, but even he seemed to have overlooked Craig's comments (see Morgan, "Miles Goodyear," 309–10).

12. John Craig to George Bossinger, 4 Oct. 1847, Papers of F. Bossinger, Huntington Library.

13. Journal of Thomas Bullock, 11 July 1847.

14. *William Clayton's Journal*, 11 July 1847, 290.

15. Journal of Wilford Woodruff, 11 July 1847. This was another illustration of the hands-off approach of the Twelve from everyday trail decisions.

16. "Journal of Erastus Snow," 3 July 1847, 270–71.

17. Coming two weeks behind the Mormon pioneers, the Oregon-bound Joel Palmer Company (about 400 persons) started coming down with Rocky Mountain Fever just past Independence Rock. "Our captain told us we might expect sickness in our camp on [the] Sweetwater," Ralph C. Geer later wrote. Later, near Fort Bridger, they discovered the grave of one Elias Brown, who had recently died of the ailment ("Occasional Address," 35–36).

18. "Mountain fever" seems to have been given most fevers and sicknesses experienced while emigrants crossed over the mountain country. Although it is still not certain to diagnose precisely what it was that 150 years ago afflicted so many in the Pioneer Camp, modern research has narrowed the disease to one of two likely possibilities: Rocky Mountain Spotted Fever or Colorado Tick Fever.

Both are caused by the bite of the wood tick *Dermacentor andersoni* found in Colorado, Oregon, Utah, Idaho, Montana, and Wyoming. The more deadly Rocky Mountain Spotted Fever, particularly prominent in Montana's Bitterroot Valley, south of Missoula, is a form of typhus caused by a *Ricketsia bacteria*. Its symptoms are usually longer and more severe than those manifested by the Pioneer Company. For excellent studies on Rocky Mountain Spotted Fever, see Victoria A. Harden, *Rocky Mountain Spotted Fever: A History of a 20th Century Disease* (1990) and Jerry K. Aikawa, *Rocky Mountain Spotted Fever* (1966). Harden suggests in passing that the Mormons "may have seen cases of Rocky Mountain Spotted Fever" (Harden, p. 11).

It is more likely most of them suffered from a tick-borne virus, rather than a bacteria, and were afflicted with the milder Colorado Tick Fever. Jay A. Aldous (M.D.) and Paul S. Nicholes (M.D.) have both made recent convincing arguments that the mountain fever Brigham Young and his colleagues suffered from lacked the prominent skin rashes, longer duration, and higher mortality rate associated with Spotted Fever. See Jay A. Aldous and Paul S. Nicholes, "What is Mountain Fever?" *Overland Journal* 15, #1 (1997): 22–23.

19. Journal of Albert P. Rockwood, 14 July 1847. Rockwood did not fully recover from the disease for at least another two weeks.

20. Charles R. King, "The Woman's Experience of Childbirth on the Western Frontier," *Journal of the West* 29, no. 1 (1990): 76–84. Years later, one observer could still say, "The learned profession was not so very learned. [Doctors were] to be sent

for only as a last resort" (A. Britt, *An America That Was: What Life Was Like on an Illinois Farm Seventy Years Ago* (1964), 135, as quoted in King, 83).

21. See Joseph R. Morrell, "Medicine of the Pioneer Period in Utah," *Utah Historical Quarterly* 23 (1955): 127–44.

Samuel Thompson (1769–1843) was the original botanic physician and father of the popular 19th-century school of medicine that bore his name. His patented system of treatment, in its simplest form, was to (1) cleanse the body with lobelia (an emetic) and other enemas; (2) restore lost body heat with cayenne pepper, hot packs, and sweat baths; and (3) carry away the residue of infection by doses of bayberry, sumac, and red raspberry. Spiteful of the regular medical professionals and their habit of bleeding patients and clogging human bodies with laudanum, mercury, and opium, Thompson patented his medical approach in 1813. He sold the right for others to use his approach at $20 a diploma. His medicines soon swept the northeast, especially Ohio (see Blanche E. Rose, "Early Utah Medical Practice," *Utah Historical Quarterly* 10 [1942]: 14–33, 44–48). For the manual on the standard medical practices of the age, see *Gunn's Domestic Medicine* (1830), reprinted by University of Tennessee Press (1986).

Willard Richards's interest in medicine did not develop until he was about 29, because of the severe illness of his beloved sister, Rhoda. He studied the Thompsonian system of medicine and received a "Thompsonian Certificate" in 1833. Realizing he had only a diploma and no training, he moved to Boston to enter the Thompsonian Infirmary and practiced for some time under Dr. Samuel Thompson himself; this was just before his conversion to Mormonism through his cousin, Brigham Young. Though his duties and responsibilities in the Church gave him little time to practice, he never abandoned his medical beliefs and was later instrumental in organizing the Council of Health in Great Salt Lake City. Luke S. Johnson, on the other hand, apparently had a more traditional medical training.

22. Journal of Orson Pratt, 13 July 1847.

23. The following are the names of those who went ahead as part of Orson Pratt's exploratory company, as recorded in the Journal of Horace K. Whitney, 15 July 1847.

S. Markham	Lewis B. Myers	Norman Taylor
O. P. Rockwell	John Brown	A. P. Chesley
J. Redden	Shadrach Roundy	Seth Taft
N. Fairbanks	Hans C. Hansen	Horace Thornton
Joseph Egbert	Levi Jackman	Stephen Kelsey
John M. Freeman	Lyman Curtis	James Stewart
Marcus B. Thorpe	David Powell	Robert Thomas
Robert Crow	Oscar Crosby	J. D. Burnham
Benjamin B. Crow	Hark Lay	John S. Eldridge
John Crow	Joseph Matthews	Elijah Newman
W. P. Crow	Gilburd Summe	Francis Boggs
Walter Crow	Green Flake	Levi N. Kendall
Geo. W. Therlkill	John S. Gleason	David Grant
Alex. Chesney	Charles Burke	

1st Division	7 wagons	15 men
2nd Division	16 wagons	27 men
Total	23 wagons	42 men

24. Journal of Thomas Bullock, 16 July 1847.

25. Journal of Horace K. Whitney, 14 and 16 July 1847.

26. Journal History, 17 July 1847.

27. See the journals of Thomas Bullock, Howard Egan, William Clayton, Horace K. Whitney, Erastus Snow, and Wilford Woodruff, 17 July 1847. Concluded Egan after their special mountain experience: "We had a glorious time, and I thank the Lord for the privilege."

28. *William Clayton's Journal*, 18 July 1847, 300.

29. "Journal of Erastus Snow," 19 July 1847, 275.

30. Journal History, 21 July 1847. Brigham Young was clearly relying heavily on the advice tendered him earlier by Jim Bridger, who had counseled the pioneers to stay clear of the Utah Lake area, at least for the time being. Brigham's instructions certainly would not have come as a surprise to his chief scout.

31. Journal of Charles G. Gray, 13 July 1849.

32. "Journal of Erastus Snow," 22 July 1847.

33. Journal of Levi Jackman, 22 July 1847.

34. "Journal of Erastus Snow," 21 July 1847, 277; see also Journal of Orson Pratt, 21 July 1847.

35. Journal of Thomas Bullock, 22 July 1847.

36. Journal of Horace K. Whitney, 24 July 1847.

37. *William Clayton's Journal*, 22 July 1847, 309.

Dale Morgan argues that they were awed by a sense of desolation and infinite remoteness, because "the wide empty valley was filled with a loneliness in which a whole people might disappear like a stone dropped in still waters." (Morgan, *The Great Salt Lake*, 198.)

38. *Howard Egan's Diary*, 24 July 1847, 105.

39. *William Clayton's Journal*, 23 July 1847, 313.

40. Journal of Wilford Woodruff, 24 July 1847.

41. Ibid.

42. *Howard Egan's Diary*, 24 July 1847, 103.

8

"IT IS AN EXCELLENT PLACE
TO SERVE THE LORD"

We have now fulfilled the mission on which we were sent,
by selecting and pointing out to you a beautiful site for
a city, which is destined to be a place of refuge for the
oppressed, and one that is calculated to please the eye,
to cheer the hearts and fill the hungry soul with food.[1]

Having reached the Salt Lake Valley behind schedule, the Mormon
pioneers had much to accomplish—and in short order. The burden of their moment was to prove the purpose of their entire
westward journey—to lay stake to their future in this desolate and remote
wilderness, to raise an ensign to waiting Latter-day Saints everywhere, to
signal the construction of a new temple, to blunt the pretensions of Strang
and others, to explore the territory, and to plant sufficient crops to test the
soil and preserve the lives of coming settlers. To succeed they needed speed
of action, decisiveness, and abundant industry, qualities they manifested in
rich supply. Now was the time and this was the place.

PLOWING, PLANTING, AND IRRIGATING

The valley had withheld its secrets long and well. The Great Salt Lake,
some 100 miles long and up to 40 miles wide, had lain undiscovered by
modern civilization until Jim Bridger first looked on it in 1824. Not until
Captain B. L. E. Bonneville and his crew explored the lake eight years later,

225

in 1832–33, was it proven that the Salt Lake was part of a vast geological basin without outlet to the Pacific. The valley's reputation as a great wilderness desert, incapable of cultivation, had only recently begun to surrender to the plow of Miles Goodyear and to the sanguine observations of other recent passersby.

Writing in 1846, Heinrich Lienhard, on his way west to California, remarked on the majesty of the scenery and the richness of the soil in the land east of the Salt Lake as few fur traders and mountain men ever did. "The soil is deep, rich, black, and mixed with sand," he confided to his journal,

> and is doubtless potentially highly productive. The clear sky-blue surface of the lake, the warm, sunny atmosphere, the high mountains with the beautiful countryside at their base . . .—all this put me in a very happy mood. All day long I felt like singing and whistling; and if there had been a single white family there, I believe I would have stayed. What a pity that the magnificent countryside was uninhabited.[2]

The scarcity of timber throughout the valley floor masked the fact that it was "clothed with a heavy garment of vegetation" and that wheat grass grew 6 to 7 feet high, in some places as high as 10 or 12 feet. The lines of small bush growth and greenery following the creeks from the canyons onto the floor of the valley led Clayton and others to defy the arid, desert sight with their optimistic predictions: "We can easily irrigate the land at all events, which will be an unfailing and certain source of water, for the springs are numerous and the water appears good."[3] What nature had long withheld, perhaps ingenuity and irrigation could now provide.

Orson Pratt, Willard Richards, and Erastus Snow took to the task of planting with both dispatch and alacrity. The first earthen dams were thrown up on City Creek, one of two creeks flowing down through their chosen site seven and a quarter miles from the mouth of Emigration Canyon. And despite broken plows and large, shiny black crickets, the parched and hardened soil soon surrendered to the spreading, life-giving waters. Their misgivings, if any, gave way later that afternoon when a light shower passed through, which lasted almost two hours, "not quite enough rain to lay the dust" as Clayton recorded, but proof enough that the desert could be tamed and "that [God] listens to and answers the prayers of the Saints."[4]

By the time Brigham arrived in camp in the early afternoon of 24 July, still unwell and riding in Woodruff's carriage, they had already planted a few acres of potatoes. Even before eating his first meal in the valley, Wilford Woodruff planted half a bushel of potatoes in the widening potato patch. Of his early planting efforts, he later wrote:

> Of course we had no experience in irrigation. We pitched our camp, put some teams onto our plows . . . and undertook to plow the earth, but we found neither wood nor iron were strong enough to make furrows here in this hard soil. It was like adamant. Of course we had to turn water on it. We would have done anything. We went and turned out the City Creek. We turned it over our ground. Come to put our teams on it, of course they sank down to their bellies in the mud. We had to wait until this land dried enough to hold our teams up. We then plowed our land.[5]

And although all publicly ceased from their labors on the Sabbath, some, like Albert Carrington, found the temptation too great and in between meetings managed to plant some corn, beans, and peas.

For the next several days, starting with the 4 A.M. bugle call and Stephen Markham's daily instructions, the order of business for almost everyone was planting, plowing, and irrigating. With five prairie oxen teams plowing in constant four-hour rotations and another three teams harrowing, within the week they had cultivated a 53-acre public farm; 35 acres were sown in buckwheat, corn, and oats; 8 acres in potatoes and beans; and another 10 in various garden vegetables. Although it was a public, or community, farm, a careful accounting was made of which seeds and furrows belonged to each of the two grand divisions in camp—Brigham's or Kimball's. Those with any leftover energy managed to plant smaller, temporary vegetable plots of their own three miles south of the big farm. Within the week, thanks to their ambitious irrigation efforts, good weather, and hard work, corn was already sprouting two inches high and the potato sprouts were showing above the ground.

Much has been written about their use of irrigation, some even crediting them for its introduction to America. The practice, however, was not at all new, and several in camp had observed similar irrigation efforts in

Mexico, the Holy Land, and elsewhere. It really took "no leap of the imagination to see that water, if it can be brought to the fields, might save a withering crop." As prominent scholars have concluded, "Immediate necessity more than lofty vision forced the Mormons to pioneer the arts of irrigation."[6]

"Shall This Be the Spot?"

Although "highly satisfied" with their discovery and their newly cultivated farm, none yet knew precisely where in the valley they would permanently settle. "We shall go tomorrow," remarked an enthusiastic Heber C. Kimball during his first Sunday sermon in the valley, "if Brigham [Young] is well enough, in search of a better location—if indeed, such can be found."[7] Come Monday morning, exploration parties fanned out in all directions to determine if a better location existed elsewhere.

While John Brown and Joseph Mathews followed the emigrant road (the Bartleson-Bidwell Trail of 1841) across the valley west to the mountains and other parties scouted areas to the north and south, Brigham's party made a "short exploring expedition" five miles north to a lookout hill they promptly called Ensign Peak. From this vantage point, they had, in Bullock's words, "a splendid view of the Salt Lake, [the] islands thereon, and the surrounding valleys."[8] And the more they viewed, as Clayton recorded, "the better we were satisfied that it is as handsome a place for a city as can be imagined. . . . The more I view the country, the better I am satisfied that the Saints can live here and raise abundant crops."[9] Though still feeble and barely able to navigate the climb, Brigham "considered it [Ensign Peak] a good place to raise an ensign" and looked out with obvious satisfaction on the valley below.[10]

The party then traveled southwest some 20 miles to explore the southern shores of the Salt Lake where they discovered the Utah inlet. This they later renamed the Jordan River, an obvious parallel to biblical geography, in which the River Jordan joins the Sea of Galilee to the Dead Sea. Like children in gleeful discovery, they enjoyed "a fine bathing frolic," discovering that they could not sink in this landlocked ocean brine. Calling it the eighth wonder of the world, they found it "so warm that no one had a desire to retreat from it."[11]

Returning to camp on 28 July, they were of the unanimous opinion that they had seen enough to know they had probably made the right decision four days before. "After returning from this trip," wrote Howard Egan, "the brethren were more satisfied than ever that they were already encamped upon the spot where their contemplated city should be built."[12] Brigham put it this way:

> Some of the brethren talked about exploring the country further for a site for a settlement. I replied that I was willing that the country should be explored until all were satisfied, but every time a party went out and returned, I believed firmly they would agree that this is the spot for us to locate.[13]

That evening they moved their wagons across the creek and slightly northeast to the intended site of the city.

With a confident air belying his fragile condition, Brigham strode out from their wagons at about 5 P.M. to a center spot between the two creeks and declared to his fellow Apostles, as he waved his hands in the air: "Here is the forty acres of the temple lot." He then went on to give instruction on how to build the basement and the baptismal font of the proposed new temple. Spreading out from the temple lot and in all directions, he envisioned a city "two miles east and west" and "as large as we have a mind to north and south." The Twelve then alternately moved and approved that each lot be one and a quarter acres in size, that the streets be eight rods wide, that the sidewalks be 20 feet wide, that the houses be built 20 feet back from the street, that all the people on a block could choose a school for themselves, and that there be four public squares.[14]

Later that evening, the entire camp attended a special council meeting on the proposed temple site. Enjoying the warm evening air and obviously pleased with their planting efforts, "cheerfulness and a general hilarity prevailed in [the] little company." Brigham then asked the question: "Shall we look further or make a location upon this spot and lay out and build a city? . . . Shall this be the spot or shall we look further? I want all to freely express their minds and feelings."

All but William Vance, who "felt as though we should go farther, perhaps on the other side of the lake," commented in favor of the site. Brigham replied that "if we were on the other side of the lake we should not have the benefit of the warm north and west winds from the lake. I knew this spot as soon as I saw it," he continued, and "up there on that table ground [Ensign

Peak] we shall erect the Standard of Freedom!" Invoking the memory of Joseph Smith, as he was prone to do at such critical moments, he persuaded:

> Well, I know it is the spot, and we have come here according to the suggestion and direction of Joseph Smith who was martyred. The word of the Lord was, "Go to that valley and the best place you can find in it is the spot." Well, I prayed that he would lead as directly to the best spot, which he has done, for after searching we can find no better.[15]

Another eyewitness noted the militant rhetoric and vengeful talk sure to stir the hearts of his followers and gain their support.

> He hoped to lead forth the armies of Israel to execute the judgments and justice on the persecuting Gentiles and that no officer of the United States should ever dictate him in this valley, or he would hang them on a gibbet as a warning to others. He showed the spot where the Ensign would be hoisted, and never have any commerce with any nation, but be independent of all.[16]

The entire company then voted in favor of a committee to superintend the management and layout of the new city on the site as approved earlier by the Twelve.

And so their city—a new city on a hill—was born.

"A WELCOME ADDITION"

But Brigham was not one to let rhetoric get in the way of practical requirements. He knew that the arrival of a United States army was imminent. The very next day the combined company of Mississippi Saints and the Pueblo detachment of the Mormon Battalion, some 240 souls in all, arrived in camp with 60 wagons, over 100 horses and mules, and some 300 head of cattle, more than doubling their numbers.[17] Marching to fife and drum, the soldiers, now looking like mountaineers, sunburned and weather-beaten, entered the valley in smart military procession—council and officers first, infantry next with martial music, then the cavalry, with the baggage wagons bringing up the rear. "The brethren were very much rejoiced at getting once more among their friends," Bullock noted, "and a general congratulation took place."[18]

Praising the Battalion boys enthusiastically, Brigham assured them that all their families were well and many of them were already on the overland road. Shouting "Hosanna, Hosanna, Hosanna, give glory to God and the Lamb," he congratulated the Battalion for having "saved the people by going into the Army. If they had not gone, Missouri was ready with 3,000 men to have wiped the Saints out of existence."[19] It was better to have a beholden army, still on government payroll, than an opposing one. He closed his comments by asking the Battalion to erect a bowery 40 feet long by 28 feet wide for Sunday preaching.

The truth of the matter was that many of the new arrivals had almost mutinied on their way to Fort Laramie, wanting to return to their families. Many were unhappy with how some of their enlistment pay and later wages had been appropriated and were convinced that their wives and families were getting less than their due. While some made secret arrangements to leave for the East in a day or two, others wanted assurances that their families were indeed part of the emigration camp (or "Big Company") that was following the advance camp. Some had the "California fever" and were anxious to follow Sam Brannan to the Pacific, there collect their muster-out pay, and set out on their own.

Anxious to keep the heavily armed Battalion in camp, particularly in case of possible Indian attack, Brigham instructed them to "quarter here until their captain could go over to the Bay [of San Francisco] and obtain their discharge."[20] In the meantime they would help in getting their oncoming families over the mountains, build houses, make their farms, and lay out a city. A little over a week later, on 9 August, Captain James Brown, a disgruntled Sam Brannan, and several others started for the Pacific by way of the Bear River. Convinced that the Mormon desert experiment was doomed to failure, Brannan was once again as glad to leave as Brigham was to see him go.[21]

"They Say They Own This Land"

Throughout all their busy activities, the new arrivals had been carefully observed by the aboriginal populations native to the valley. First to show, on 27 July, were two Ute Indians "of moderate size, pleasing countenance and dressed in skins."[22] They arrived in camp ostensibly to trade ponies for rifles and muskets but privately anxious to scout out the numbers and assess the intent of their industrious new neighbors. Four days later, 30 more came

Utah Indians in Utah Valley, *engraved by Charles B. Hall,*
after an etching by John Hafen

to trade horsepower for firepower, no doubt to gain an upper hand in their long, continuous intertribal warfare.

Later that same afternoon, obviously observing both Mormons and Utes, approximately 20 Shoshone Indians converged on the scene. They came not just to trade but to demonstrate their dominance over the Utes and their ownership of the land. In short order they redressed a grievance of a stolen horse, which one of the young Ute Indians had already traded with the unsuspecting Mormons earlier in the day. After learning of his identity, four Shoshone started out in wrathful pursuit, "shooting him dead while another one shot his horse. They returned and made this report to the others of the tribe at the camp at the same time exhibiting fresh blood on one of the rifles. They appear to be much excited," wrote Clayton, "and continually on the watch. When the men returned, they sat down and made a meal of some of these large crickets."[23]

Later that evening, Brigham advised

us of the folly of trading with the Indians here for if we continued to do so, we would always be molested with them, therefore, we should give them to understand that we were not permitted to trade at this place, but appoint a distant place for that purpose. He also admonished the brethren not to buy Indian and Californian horses, as they were not near so good as our American ones, neither did we wish to be overstocked with horses, for they were only a trouble to us.[24]

Once again the place the Latter-day Saints were intent on settling lay between warring tribes. As they had done back at Winter Quarters the year before—when they had settled between the Sioux on the north and the Ponca, Otoe, and Omaha on the south—the Mormons were here following the counsel of Jim Bridger, deliberately or otherwise, to choose a settlement in a buffer zone, a disputed area, between two unfriendly tribes.

And here again they followed a similar policy with respect to the Indians: be friendly but impartial; be firm and fair but trade sparingly; provide food where absolutely necessary; and finally, avoid conflict wherever possible. The last thing they could afford was armed conflict with the Indians. It was a deliberate policy Brigham had forged back at the Missouri with some success and one he now was determined they follow.[25]

The coming of the Latter-day Saints and of other white settlers to the area marked the beginning of the end, for both tribes, of their nomadic lifestyle, which had endured for centuries, if not millennia. The Utes had been accommodating to modern culture as soon as the Spanish had settled New Mexico in 1598. The most dramatic change to Ute culture came as a result of the Pueblo Revolt of 1680, which freed many of their slaves, made an equestrian lifestyle available to them on a far wider scale than ever before, and allowed the Utes to extend hunting rights to the high plains east of the Rockies. Eventually driven from the Plains by other tribes, the Utes retreated to their traditional mountain setting.

Unlike their Colorado cousins to the east, change came more slowly to the Utes of the Great Basin. As late as Father Escalante's visit in 1776, they owned no horses and many lived in "little huts of willow" in abject poverty and filth, even by native standards. By the 1840s, their northern boundary with the Shoshone was vaguely drawn at the Point of the Mountain, some 20 miles south of the Mormon camp. Most still traveled on foot and already had been labeled "diggers" for their propensity to live off ants, grasshoppers, crickets, roots, seeds, and weeds.[26] As the respected Roman Catholic priest and explorer, Father Pierre de Smet, had written: "There is not, perhaps, in the whole world, a people in a deeper state of wretchedness and corruption . . . their habitations are holes in the rocks, or the natural crevices of the ground."[27]

The Shoshones—related to the Snake Indians of the northern plains, Montana, and Wyoming—occupied much of the upper Great Basin regions as far north as the Snake River and as far south as the Great Salt Lake. Unlike the Plains Indians, who made handsome garments of buffalo, antelope, and elk skins, the Snakes and Shoshones west of the mountains spent their lives in little more than searching for something to eat. "The very names they gave to their groups," argues one authority, "indicate their absorption in the quest for food. The Snakes or Shoshonis were divided into Root Eaters, Rabbit Eaters, Squirrel Eaters, Salmon Eaters, Seed Eaters, Pine Nut Eaters, and one poor group was known as the Earth Eaters." Barely able to live in their parched and desert surroundings, neither Utes nor Shoshones had organized themselves into strong tribes.[28]

At first accepting of white emigrants on their way east, by the mid-1840s the Shoshone and Paiute Indians had turned hostile and aggressive, especially near Fort Hall and other sites on the Oregon Trail to the north. A saving grace in the Mormon migration had been the selection of a trail and a settlement in an area not heavily populated by either Shoshones or Utes and, moreover, in an area of ill-defined ownership.[29] Nevertheless, it was the Shoshones, not the Utes, who claimed that the Mormons were occupying their lands and who demanded compensation in the form of powder and lead for selling. "They appear to be displeased because we have traded with the Utahs," wrote Clayton, "and say they own this land. . . . They signified by signs that they wanted to sell us the land for powder and lead."[30]

The Mormon response was consistent with how most new emigrants of the day were treating Indian claims—without serious consideration. However, just as there were variations in the Mormon's attitudes towards the United States government, there were subtle differences among them toward the "Lamanites." Orson Pratt, for instance, anxious that they start off on a good basis and a strong advocate for preaching the gospel to the tribes in due course, was of the opinion that "we should not [even] feed them at all until they had done something for it so as to begin right with them and teach them industry."[31]

Kimball, meanwhile, was concerned about favoring one tribe above another and discouraged "the idea of paying the Indians for the lands, for if the Shoshones should be thus considered, the Utes and other tribes would claim pay also. . . . The land belongs to our Father in Heaven, and we calculate to plow and plant it."[32]

Brigham, who had gained the respect of the Omaha, Ponca, and other tribes back at the Missouri, would not have disagreed with either man but perhaps struck a more expansive tone. His view was that "we should not buy any land of the Indians, but as the Lord made the land there was enough for both them and us, that we would teach them to labor and cultivate the earth."[33] He could not be persuaded that the Shoshones owned the surrounding lands even though they had occupied portions of it for a very long time. Neither tribe pressed the issue or countered in stubborn conflict, although in later years, as Mormon settlements extended to the north and south, conflicts did erupt.[34]

"The Land of Their Inheritances"

At their outdoor services of Sunday, 1 August, under the hastily-erected bowery, there was much to talk about. First of all, because they had made such good progress in planting during the past week and because so many new women and children had recently joined them with many more on the way, it was proposed "that we build houses instead of living in wagons this winter; that we go to work immediately putting up houses; . . . that the houses form a stockade or fort to keep out the Indians; . . . and that we let the Indians alone."[35] A stockade, a corral, and a fort—all would be necessary to shelter and protect the settlement throughout the coming winter.

Recognizing the scarcity of timber and having seen the Spanish-style adobe construction native to the American southwest, the Battalion took the lead in recommending adobe brick construction for the proposed settlement. Cheaper and quicker to build than log houses and better insulated and less susceptible to fire, the adobe home was well-suited for the valley. "To those unacquainted with this kind of building," argued Erastus Snow from his new desert pulpit, "dobies are brick made of gravelly soil and dried hard in the sun instead of being burned with fuel."

It was then unanimously resolved "to go jointly to enclosing one of the public squares of the city, containing 10 acres or 40 rods square, by a wall of log and dobie houses, to be joined together with the exception of a gate on each of the four sides; buildings to be 14 feet wide, 9 feet high on the outside, roofs to slant a little inwards."[36]

Illustrating the kind of instant response and diversity of talent characteristic of the pioneers, Samuel Gould and James Drum reported in as lime burners and Sylvester H. Earl, Joel J. Terrill, Ralph Douglas, and Joseph Hancock offered their brick-making skills. Albert Carrington promised to set out in the morning with a party to look for limestone and others signed up to find and bring down spruce and pine logs from nearby valleys and ravines for floors, roofs, and some log houses.[37]

The next day the Mormon hive was busy with activity, virtually every person part of one committee or another. Many were still planting while others were out exploring. Some were laying out the adobe square while others were preparing a saw pit. Blacksmiths, hot and sweaty, were busy hammering out wagon repairs while careful tailors trimmed their cloth. Mothers tended to their makeshift wagon homes while children played everywhere, all the while with dogs barking, cattle lowing, and sheep bleating. A whole new sound of industry and a budding sense of excitement dented the daunting silence of the sprawling valley floor. It was the sound of new life and a new future.

Others, impatient at how long it was taking to haul the needed limestone and to dry the adobe mud, decided to head for the hills to cut down as many logs as possible. Soon several hands were chopping down fir and pine with almost careless energy. "This made 77 logs in two days that we cut and drew home," a tired and winded Wilford Woodruff recorded. "In two days we got timber sufficient for two buildings, each of us one. But I had labored so hard during the two days I could hardly stand upon my feet. I went to my wagon and flung myself upon my bed to rest."[38]

No committee took its responsibility more seriously than did Henry G. Sherwood's city survey crew. Starting out from the proposed temple lot with survey chains, his first priorities were to locate the public square on the southwest quarter of the city that would serve as the fort and to locate the "dobie square" four blocks south and three blocks west of Temple Square. The size of the proposed temple lot was eventually reduced, after considerable discussion, from 40 to 10 acres as the Twelve concluded that they "could not do justice" to such a large acreage.[39] With the survey completed on the northwest and northeast corners of the temple block, Thomas Tanner and Burr Frost were free to erect their blacksmith shop.

Meanwhile the adobe pit was soon churning out large quantities of material—some 1,600 adobes per day by 6 August and 4,000 per day a week later. And by mid-August, they had completed 30 log houses and had erected a perimeter adobe wall about four feet high on two sides of the proposed fort, with materials ready for the third side (log houses formed the fourth side).[40]

The history of the early building of what they soon called "Salt Lake City—Great Basin of North America" (still a part of Mexican Territory) is well known and requires no further elaboration here. What merits attention, however, is their unique method of land distribution. Unlike most other settlements of the developing West, where the race was on for private property and individual ownership of the choicest locations, the Mormon distribution of land—as before in Far West, Independence, and other early communities—was Church-governed. Properties were assigned to obedient followers, a reward for commitment and endurance.[41] And those who chose not to follow counsel understood that they could forfeit everything.[42]

Furthermore, the concept of the good of the whole ruled, rather than monetary gain for the individual. Small holdings were thought best, with the general "desire to people the region with as many families as could make a living." Private speculation in land was foreign to their immediate objective. It was God's land and as God's people they would adhere to his spokesmen and take what was granted them—no land banks, no real estate offices, no land for a quick profit.[43]

Their original method of land apportionment owed everything to the apostolic adopted family and the dual divisional organization that had governed their travels across the plains. Immediately after their arrival, the soldiers "reorganized themselves" to join one of either of the great family divisions and resume their places in the families of the leading Apostles (see chapter 2).

According to their respective rank of seniority within the Quorum of the Twelve, Brigham chose first, opting for the block immediately east of the temple block "and running southeast to settle his friends [including his adopted family] around him." Kimball took the block north, and Orson Pratt selected the block opposite on the south side. Woodruff chose the block west of the temple for him and "his friends." Amasa Lyman chose the block 40 rods southwest of the temple block and George A. Smith further west still. "It was supposed Bro. [Willard] Richards would take his inheritance on the east near Bro. Young." The other Apostles (Ezra T. Benson had already returned east with mail) chose their sites later.[44] Thereafter,

48

and our lots 10 rods by 20, independent of streets.

O. Pratt motioned "that the lots contain one acre and a quarter each, independent of the streets 20 rods by 10" H. C. Kimball seconded . Carried

W. Richards motioned "that the streets be 8 rods wide" G. A. Smith seconded . Carried

B. Young motioned "that the side walks be 20 feet wide"

Pres't Young said he wanted the houses, to be put so far from the line of his neighbor's lot, & 20 feet from the front of the street, so that if one house gets on fire, it does not endanger another.

H. C. Kimball motioned "that they be placed 20 feet back". O. Pratt sec'd   Carried

G. A. Smith said he thinks it better to lay out places, or squares, for markets.

B. Young thinks it better for any man who wants a market, to have it on his own lot, & let each man cultivate his own lot.   In regard to Schools I shall have a School for my own children, & the people on a block, can chose a School for themselves. let the children be kept out of the streets, keep them on the lots or in the houses.   We will have our bathing places directly, and in three years we shall not know what sickness is .   all said "Amen"

G. A. Smith motioned "that we have four public squares for play ground & walks" E. T. Benson seconded . Carried .

Minutes of a Quorum of the Twelve meeting planning Salt Lake City, from the Thomas Bullock journal, entry for July 28, 1847, p. 48

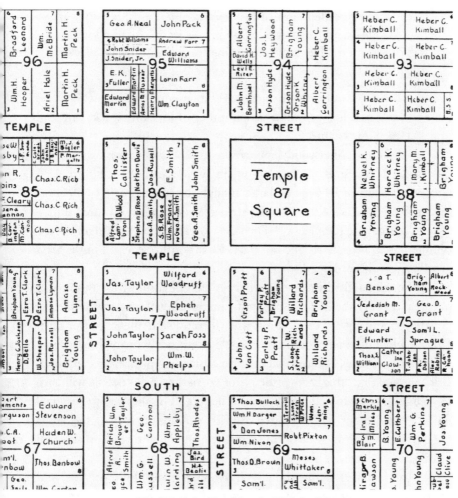

The Salt Lake Plat Map, by Nicholas Morgan

according to their adopted family affiliation and lottery selection, almost everyone else claimed their property or inheritance in turn, spreading the settlement outward from the center of the city.

Horace K. Whitney (Kimball) explained precisely how the lots were divvied up in the Kimball family.

> After [supper] we took a walk over the creek to look at the city lots, of the situation of which, etc. He [Heber C. Kimball] gave me a better idea than I had before possessed. After we had got [there], we knelt and prayed by his suggestion; after which we returned to

camp. He then called most of his boys [adopted sons] together at Bro. Wilkie's tent, when each chose his respective lot and I wrote their name on the blanks, representing the lots on the city plot or map.[45]

Two days later, at Kimball's request, Whitney copied the names of those who had selected lots as well as the number of lots and blocks selected opposite each one's name.

By 11 August, Sherwood's survey ran 15 blocks north and south by 9 blocks east and west. By 20 August his survey consisted of 135 blocks, each containing 8 lots of 1 1/4 acres, large enough to accommodate 1,080 families or from 5,000 to 6,000 people; streets 8 rods wide; and three public squares besides the temple lot.[46] The streets were named, starting from the temple block, First East, Second East; First South, Second South; First North, Second North; and so on.

Although family division of properties did not last long for a variety of practical reasons, the larger concept of communality of property endured a generation and spread throughout the Mormon settlements of the west. Believing that their new social order would lessen or eliminate the scramble for private property, reduce economic jealousies, and preserve social order, Brigham said that "this is the principle of oneness that this people will have to go into in order to help build one another up." This idea was the original guide for settlement: without purchase price, a means of repaying the Saints for the loss of lands in Nauvoo and elsewhere and of putting all on an equal footing.[47]

In the midst of laying claim to brave new hopes, bold dreams, and divine directions—and as if fate itself would demand a price for their enthusiasm—came word of a tragedy, a victim of their general distraction. On Wednesday, 11 August, three-year-old Milton Howard Therlkill, son of George W. and Martilla Jane Therlkill (both non-Mormon members of the Mississippi company), fell into the deepest part of the creek near the dam on the southeast of the camp while playing with his brother. The boy was immediately taken out, but despite every frantic effort at resuscitation was pronounced dead.

"The grief of both the parents was great," Whitney sadly recorded,

but that of the agonized mother baffles all description. She laughed, wept, walked to and fro alternately, refusing all attempts at consolation from her friends, being apparently unable to be resigned to her domestic and melancholy bereavement. As for myself, I never witnessed a sight that so awakened my sympathy and I sincerely hope that I may ne'er look on its like again.[48]

Ironically, three days later this same grieving mother gave birth to a daughter, Harriet Anne.

Asked to speak at the child's funeral, Brigham used the occasion, as well as the ensuing Sunday meetings, not merely to extend comfort to the grieving family but also to speak on the principle of temples and temple sealings and of family togetherness beyond the grave. While directed to the family, it gave opportunity for him to answer the questions of his people and of detractors about the place of temple worship in their new wilderness.

"In the loss of this child . . . that was drowned, I felt that I could weep in sorrow," he remarked.

> It is true all children are saved. Their names are written in the Lamb's book of life. . . .
>
> But notwithstanding this, can Brother Crow [grandfather] get that child again or any other person their children except there is something done for them on the earth by their parents? No, they would not. They would go to God who gave them, but the parents on the earth would not have them. . . .
>
> What then can be done? I will tell you. A man that has embraced the gospel must [be] someone who has the priesthood and keys and power of Elijah and must attend to ordinances for that child; . . . have it sealed to him and . . . claim his child in the morning of the resurrection and the Lord will give it up to him.[49]

Brigham then turned his attention to the matter of both a temple in the valley and, until its completion, possibly a temporary place for conducting their sacred ordinances, this despite earlier statements that such work could never be done outside the temple.[50] He recognized here, as he had done back at the Missouri, the demands of his people, particularly of the Mormon Battalion and their concerns for their families. "As soon as we get up some adobe houses for our families," he said,

> we shall go to work to build another temple and as soon as a place is prepared we shall commence the endowments long before the temple is built. And we shall take time and each step the Saints

take, let them take time enough about it to understand it. Everything at Nauvoo went with a rush. We had to build the temple with the trowel in one hand, the sword in the other; and mobs were upon us all the while and many crying out "O the temple can't be built!"

. . . But we went at it and finished it and turned it over into the hands of the Lord in spite of earth and hell, and the Brethren was so faithful at it that we labored day [and] night to give them their endowments.[51]

Not only would they have all they realized back in Nauvoo, but as they had done back at Willard Richards's octagon in Winter Quarters, certain temple blessings would be restored almost immediately.

"A CITY SOUGHT OUT AND NOT FORSAKEN"

There was more than streams and wagons, logs and adobe, in their view at least, to what was happening. They came to believe that they were not merely leaving an old world and seeking a new, but that they were fulfilling prophecy and that their success depended again on their collective obedience to divine will. Further, they saw in their new surroundings the recovery of their relinquished Zion.

Such belief explains the decision to rebaptize as many in camp as desired to renew their covenants and inaugurate a new order in their mountain home. Performed sparingly previous to this time and place, this repeat of their original baptisms had been earlier commended as a way of reaffirming the faith, of healing, and even of remission of sins—a long-since abandoned practice in modern Mormonism.[52] But this was an exciting place of new beginnings, a promised land. Consequently, early in the morning of Sunday, 8 August, after damming up the streams sufficient for deeper pools of water,

the bishops repaired with the Twelve to the streams of water for the purpose of baptizing and confirming the whole camp who had not been [rebaptized] since we came into the valley. We felt it our privilege to be baptized and to baptize . . . for the remission of our sins and to renew our covenants before the Lord. Bros. [Tarleton] Lewis, [Stephen H.] Goddard, [Addison] Everett, [Andrew P.] Shumway, [Erastus] Snow, and H. C. Kimball baptized and the

Twelve confirmed them. There were 224 baptized and confirmed . . . making 288 in all . . . during the last three days.[53]

The above episode would not merit more than a footnote in this history were it not for two overriding considerations central to this work: first, they firmly believed that their transgressions had to be blotted out in order to ensure the permanent success of their venture; and second, they came to see with unbending conviction that they were truly on a divine errand, fulfilling prophecy, and establishing Zion.

Regarding their transgressions, the record is clear that the rumblings, murmurings, and "iniquities," more particularly among some within the Battalion ranks, would only hinder their progress. Rather than single out any one group for grievous conduct, the leaders determined to rebaptize virtually the entire camp. This perception of themselves as God's chastened, if chosen, people is evident in many of the earliest valley sermons. "The revelation tells us what to do," Amasa Lyman said,

> and if we are not a righteous people we deceive ourselves and shall defeat the very object we are laboring for and it is to begin to be holy and to build a city. It is ours because God has given it us. We must not buck at impurity in any way favorable. Go to work and be pure every wit and then if they build up a temple and the city the blessings will flow down to us as the waters from yonder hill. . . . Zion is the pure in heart and the only way to be pure is to have no will but the will of God.[54]

They likewise began to see, or at least interpret for themselves, that they were in the middle of fulfilling ancient prophecy. If while crossing Iowa and beyond they had paid at least lip service to ancient Israel's flight from Egypt, in the valley they began to proclaim that their long and tedious journey and recent establishment of a mountain city was literal fulfillment of biblical prophecy.

The importance of such a new self-perception can hardly be overstated. Such scriptural vindication would more than validate their decision to quit Missouri and Nauvoo—it would redeem it! It would give them the doctrinal ammunition they required to confront Strang and others and to convince many laboring behind in doubt and confusion. And it would come to define them as a distinct people, a religious movement with a purpose perhaps unparalleled since the Puritan arrival in the New World over two centuries

before. It was as if the enormity of
their immediate accomplishment was
only now being fully realized—a collective dawning of enormous consequence.

It was Orson Pratt, their scientist
and systematic theologian, who first
voiced this conviction. "It is with peculiar feelings I arise before so many of
the Saints in this uncultivated region,"
he announced in the bowery that same
Sunday in August, just after the choir
had sung "On the Mountain Tops
Appearing."

Orson Pratt

My mind is full of reflection on the scenes through which we
have passed and being brought through the deserts of sage to this
distant region. God's ways are not as our ways. . . . This movement
is one of the greatest that has taken place among this people.

For many years I have not read the good old book, but I
remember the predictions in it and some that are now very nearly
fulfilled by us. Isaiah says (Chapter 62) speaking of the City of
Zion, "it shall be sought out, a city not forsaken, etc." Many in this
congregation know what is meant by the garments of salvation and
the robe of righteousness. Righteousness and praise shall spring
forth before all the nations of the earth and they will not hold their
peace. . . . We have gathered out the stones out of the road and
thousands will yet fulfil this prophecy. . . . If ever there was a place
sought out it is this. We have inquired diligently and have found
it.[55]

Turning then to the second chapter of Isaiah, Pratt quoted as follows:
"It shall come to pass in the last days, that the mountain of the Lord's house
shall be established in the tops of the mountains, . . . and all nations shall
flow unto it. And many people shall go and say, Come ye, and let us go up to
the mountain of the Lord, to the house of the God of Jacob; . . . for out of
Zion shall go forth the law and the word of the Lord out of Jerusalem."[56]
With their new temple site determined and a new city soon to be built,
surely, Pratt proclaimed to his eager audience, this prophecy would soon be

fulfilled. "The wilderness shall become as a fruitful field and a fruitful field as a forest" and "the desert shall blossom as the rose."[57]

One cannot help but notice not only how soon the pioneers seeded their crops and laid claim to the valley but how quickly they regarded it as the symbol and substitute of their relinquished Missouri Zion. Not to be confused with the former "center stake," or site of the New Jerusalem, their new mountain home would nevertheless retain in them the conviction and belief that God's imprimatur was on this place.[58]

To a busy people well aware of the many earlier prophecies and predictions that their ultimate Zion or New Jerusalem was still back east, in Independence, Missouri, and to the many who still regarded Nauvoo as the center of their faith, it was reassuring, if not flattering, to know that God had been leading them all along. And despite the lack of a First Presidency, their leaders were still inspired and directed. It was, in short, a new scriptural frame of reference—a doctrinal delivery after a long night of labor. And for many, it would make all the difference.[59]

"I Wish to God We Had Not Got to Return"

The journeys back to Winter Quarters (start backs) began as early as 11 August, when Norton Jacob and his advance hunting party set out with several well-rested teams of oxen. Six days later, under the direction of Shadrach Roundy and Tunis Rappleye, 72 men, 32 wagons, and 92 more yoke of oxen began the long trek east. Both companies were instructed to wait at Grand Island for the returning Company of the Twelve.

On Sunday, 22 August, the Battalion soldiers were instructed to turn over most of their arms; then provisions were made for a new stake to be organized with John Smith as president after his arrival with the emigration camp. Finally Brigham Young, Heber C. Kimball, and the rest of the Twelve began their return journey on 26 August, none too happy at the prospect of leaving their new settlement. Said Kimball: "I wish to God we had not got to return. If I had my family here, I would give everything I have [to stay]. This is a Paradise to me. It is one of the most lovely places I ever beheld. I hope none of us will be left to pollute this land."[60]

Having accomplished so much in so little time, perhaps Wilford Woodruff can be forgiven for his hyperbole and self-congratulatory tone on the eve of their return:

We as a pioneer company have accomplished more this season than can be found on record concerning any set of men since the days of Adam. [We have] traveled with heavy loaded wagons over one thousand miles, having made our road more than one half of the way over and through the rough mountains and canyons, and searched out a glorious land as a resting place for the Saints. And in one month after our arrival [we] laid out a city two miles square and built a fort and fortification of hewn timber drawn seven miles from the mountains and of unburnt brick, surrounding 10 acres of ground, 40 rods of which was covered with block houses, besides planting about 100 acres of corn, potatoes, buckwheat, turnips, and gardens.[61]

Yet some of their greatest challenges lay before them.

NOTES

1. Brigham Young, "An Epistle to the Saints in Great Salt Lake Valley," Willard Richards, clerk, Journal History, 9 Sept. 1847.

2. Heinrich Lienhard, *From St. Louis to Sutter's Fort, 1846*, trans. and ed. Erwin G. and Elisabeth H. Gudde (1961), 103.

3. *William Clayton's Journal*, 24 July 1847, 314.

4. Ibid.

5. *Official Report of the Irrigation Congress . . . 1891* (1891), 43, as quoted in Leonard J. Arrington and Dean May, "'A Different Mode of Life': Irrigation and Society in Nineteenth-Century Utah," *Agricultural History* 49 (1975): 7.

6. Arrington and May, "'A Different Mode of Life,'" 6. See also Eugene E. Campbell, *Establishing Zion: The Mormon Church in the American West, 1847–1869* (1988), 9, and Andrew L. Neff, *History of Utah 1847 to 1869* (1940), 91–95.

7. *William Clayton's Journal*, 25 July 1847, 315, 316.

8. Journal of Thomas Bullock, 26 July 1847.

9. *William Clayton's Journal*, 26 July 1847, 319, 323. Included in the party were Brigham Young, Heber C. Kimball, Wilford Woodruff, Willard Richards, William Clayton, George A. Smith, Ezra T. Benson, and Albert Carrington.

10. The long-held tradition that this scouting party raised the United States flag on this occasion is false. There is no evidence whatsoever that they even had an American flag with them. On this date, the flag or ensign they had in mind was the ensign to the nations, or flag of the Kingdom of God, as discussed in chapter 6.

11. Journal of Thomas Bullock, 27 July 1847.

12. Journal History, 28 July 1847.

13. Ibid. This decision was made even before other scouting parties returned from the Utah Lake area in the south and the Cache Valley region in the north.

14. Journal of Thomas Bullock, 28 July 1847.
As early as June 1833, Joseph Smith had proposed a layout for the City of Zion.

The plan had specified lot, block, and street sizes, building materials, the distance houses were to be set back from the streets, and the population of each city. However, the only similarity between this new Salt Lake city and the original City of Zion plan was its grid pattern and ten-acre blocks. Perhaps the greatest departure from the original plan was in the size of the city: 20,000 with provision for at least five times that number, due no doubt to their desire to have a strong center from which they could never be driven (see Richard H. Jackson and Robert L. Layton, "The Mormon Village: Analysis of a Settlement Type," *Professional Geographer* 28, no. 2 [May 1976]: 136–41).

Brigham Young once estimated that the valley could hold one million people.

15. Journal of Norton Jacob, 28 July 1847. Brigham's use of the word "spot" rather than "place" or some other synonym may not have been coincidental, since the revelations used the same word when identifying Independence as Zion. See D&C 58:57 and 84:31.

16. Journal of Thomas Bullock, 28 July 1847.

17. According to Eugene Campbell, the Battalion consisted of 152 men and approximately 30 wives and 50 children. There were also 47 members of the Mississippi company with them (see *Establishing Zion*, 13). The new totals in the valley were 156 original pioneers, 232 Battalion folk, 47 Mississippi Saints, Sam Brannan and his two companions, for a grand total of 438 souls.

18. Journal of Thomas Bullock, 29 July 1847. John Steele described his fellow soldiers as being "mostly dressed in buckskin with fringes and porcupine quills, moccasins, Spanish saddles and spurs, Spanish bridles and jinglers at them, and long beards, so that if I looked in the glass for the young man who left the Bluffs a year ago, I would not have known myself" ("Extracts from the Journal of John Steele," 17).

19. Journal of Thomas Bullock, 30 July 1847.

20. Ibid.

21. Journal of Norton Jacob, 9 August 1847. Ebenezer Hanks, Thomas Williams, and Edward Dalton were to go to Fort Hall for provisions for the soldiers. Meanwhile, Capt. James Brown, Jesse S. Brown, William H. Squires, William Gribble, Lisander Woodworth, Gilbert Hunt, and John [?] Blackburn were assigned to go with Brannan to California via the Bear River on pack horses to get the discharges and collect the muster-out pay of the Battalion.

As a later precaution, before the Twelve headed back East, most of the Battalion rifles were confiscated "for safekeeping."

22. *William Clayton's Journal*, 27 July 1847, 324.

23. *William Clayton's Journal*, 31 July 1847, 329.

24. Journal of Horace K. Whitney, 31 July 1847.

25. For a full discussion of Mormon-Indian relationships at Winter Quarters and their policies of nonalignment and noninvolvement, see Bennett, *Mormons at the Missouri*, 91–111.

26. Omer C. Stewart, "Ute Indians: Before and After White Contact," *Utah Historical Quarterly* 34 (Winter 1966): 50–52.

27. Pierre Jean de Smet, "Letters and Sketches: With a Narrative of a Year's Residence Among the Indian Tribes of the Rocky Mountains," in *Early Western Travels 1748–1846* (1906), 17:165–67.

Silas Newcomb, traveling through the area in 1850, described the Utes as "small in stature, dark complexion and half naked and living on the flesh, feet and even entrails of cattle and horses. . . . The Utah and Snake Indians are deadly enemies" (Journal of Silas Newcomb, 16 July 1850).

28. Hyde, *Indians of the High Plains*, 118–19. See also Brigham D. Madsen, *The Shoshoni Frontier and the Bear River Massacre* (1985); Carling Malouf and Ake Hultkranz, *Shoshone Indians* (1974); and Ake Hultkrantz, "The Shoshones in the Rocky Mountain Area," *Annals of Wyoming* 33 (Apr. 1961): 19–41.

29. Madsen, *Shoshoni Frontier*, 28–29.

30. *William Clayton's Journal*, 31 July 1847, 329.

31. Journal History, 1 Aug. 1847.

32. *William Clayton's Journal*, 1 Aug. 1847, 335.

33. Journal of Wilford Woodruff, 31 July 1847.

34. Howard A. Christy, "Open Hand and Mailed Fist: Mormon-Indian Relations in Utah, 1847–52," *Utah Historical Quarterly* 46 (Summer 1978): 216–35. For a more critical view of the Mormon-Indian conflict and of the Mormon disruption of the environment, see Beverly P. Smaby, "The Mormons and the Indians: Conflicting Ecological Systems in the Great Basin," *American Studies* 16 (Spring 1975): 35–48.

The prevailing sentiment of most, but not all, Latter-day Saints toward the Great Basin Indians was one of sympathy, bordered with fear and burdened with religious responsibility. Considering their filthy, weakened, diseased, and impoverished circumstances, the Utes and the Shoshones were particularly and simultaneously repulsive and pathetic, sorry symbols to a lost glory. That was not enough to change the pervasive prejudices and biases of a largely eastern American population, but it did soften them to some degree. At the risk of choosing one comment over another, it is nevertheless a fact that Brigham always spoke more kindly, if condescendingly, about the Indians than he ever did about the policies of the American government and its Office of Indian Affairs. "We call them savages," he said on one occasion, "while at the same time the whites too often do as badly as they have done, and worse, when difference of intelligence and training are taken into account. This has been so in almost every case of difficulty with the red skins. When soldiers have pounced upon these poor, ignorant, low, degraded, miserable creatures, mention a time, if you can, when they have spared their women and children. They have indiscriminately massacred the helpless, the blind, the old, the infant, and the mother" (in *Journal of Discourses*, 10:108, 8 Mar. 1863).

35. *William Clayton's Journal*, 1 Aug. 1847, 337.

36. "Journal of Erastus Snow," 1 Aug. 1847, 280–81. This apparently would become the Old Fort erected on the site of present Pioneer Park, Third South and Second West, Salt Lake City. The earliest bricks were molded 18 by 9 inches in length and breadth and 4 1/2 inches thick.

37. *William Clayton's Journal*, 1 Aug. 1847, 337. According to Richard H. Jackson, the adobe bricks initially used by the pioneers were much larger than the conventional kiln-dried variety used in the East. Although lack of experience with unfired brick and a misunderstanding of the climate created difficulty with adobe construction in the first year, later improvements with stone foundations and slanted roof construction made adobe more attractive. It remained the dominant building material during the last half of the nineteenth century in the Mormon west (see "The Use of Adobe in the Mormon Cultural Region," *Journal of Cultural Geography* 1 [1980]: 82–95).

38. Journal of Wilford Woodruff, 6 Aug. 1847.

39. Journal of Wilford Woodruff, 4 Aug. 1847.

The temple lot eventually became Temple Square, on which the Mormon Tabernacle was completed in 1867, followed by the Assembly Hall in 1880 and the temple itself in 1893, 40 years after its groundbreaking in 1853 (see Susan Easton Black, "The Mormon Temple Square: The Story behind the Scenery" [1993]).

40. "Journal of Erastus Snow," 26 Aug. 1847.

41. In several of their early revelations, much had been said about land and the inheritance of lands in their new Zion. One revelation to Joseph Smith in 1831 had said the following:

"And I have made the earth rich, and behold it is my footstool, wherefore, again I will stand upon it.

"And I hold forth and deign to give unto you greater riches, even a land of promise, a land flowing with milk and honey, upon which there shall be no curse when the Lord cometh;

"And I will give it unto you for the land of your inheritance, if you seek it with all your hearts" (Doctrine and Covenants 38:17–19).

42. Wrote one early settler: "Every man will have given to him an inheritance of as much land as he can attend to, and it is expected every one to keep the Laws of God and live upright with his neighbor and deal honestly with every man" (William Greenwood to family, 17 Oct. 1847, Greenwood Papers).

43. Arrington, *Great Basin Kingdom*, 51–52, 93. See also Richard H. Jackson, "The Mormon Village: Genesis and Antecedents of the City of Zion Plan," *BYU Studies* 17 (Winter 1977): 233–40.

44. Journal of Wilford Woodruff, 7 Aug. 1847.

45. Journal of Horace K. Whitney, 17 Aug. 1847. As far as the records show, there was no debate or argument over the division of properties.

46. Journal History, 20 Aug. 1847.

47. See Bennett, *Mormons at the Missouri*, 192–94. That these lands or inheritances were not purchased is indication of their early conviction that the land belonged to God, or at least to the Church. In other words, it was an act of collective homesteading. As had been the case at Winter Quarters, Mt. Pisgah, and Garden Grove along the trail, there would not be, at least not now, private property. And for those who had lost everything back in Nauvoo or who would arrive penniless, the promise of free land must have been an important persuading consideration indeed. See the editorializing of Horace K. Whitney's journal by his wife, Helen Mar Kimball Whitney, 10 May 1846. For a more comprehensive study of the Mormon concept of land and its development, see Leonard J. Arrington, Feramorz Y. Fox, and Dean L. May, *Building the City of God: Community and Co-operation among the Mormons* (Salt Lake City: Deseret Book Co., 1976), 41–62.

48. Journal of Horace K. Whitney, 11 Aug. 1847.

49. Journal of Wilford Woodruff, 15 Aug. 1847.

50. One year before, Brigham had said: "With references to sealings there will be no such thing done until we build another temple. I have understood that some of the Twelve have held forth an idea that such things would be attended to in the wilderness but I say let no man hint such things from this time forth for we will not attend to sealing till another temple is built" (Journal of John D. Lee, 9 Aug. 1846).

51. Journal of Wilford Woodruff, 15 Aug. 1847, 259–60. The well-known Salt Lake Endowment House was not completed until 1855. It would appear, then, that there were temple ordinances performed in the valley well before that time. Brigham's comments about haste in the Nauvoo Temple indicate that understanding of some of these doctrines was evolving along the way. Such may explain the relatively short-lived practice of the law of adoption.

52. The practice of rebaptism had certainly occurred in Nauvoo and, on rare occasions, at other times since 1832 in Kirtland, Ohio (see D. Michael Quinn, "The Practice of Rebaptism at Nauvoo," *BYU Studies* 18 [Winter 1978]: 226–32). See also Ogden Kraut, "A Short History of Re-Baptism," unpublished, LDS Church Archives. Some had also been rebaptized at Winter Quarters (Journal of Wilford Woodruff, 8 Aug. 1846).

Until the end of the nineteenth century, it was a general custom to allow a repetition of the ordinance to adults before they first entered the temple. The practice was discontinued, however, both to preserve the sanctity and significance of one's original baptism and to discourage reliance upon rebaptism as an easy way to gain forgiveness of sins (see Joseph F. Smith, "The Repetition of Sacred Ordinances," *Juvenile Instructor*, 1 Jan. 1903, 18–20).

53. Journal of Wilford Woodruff, 8 Aug. 1847.

54. Sermon by Amasa Lyman, General Church Minutes, 1 Aug. 1847.

55. General Church Minutes, 1 Aug. 1847. See also Journal History, 1 Aug. 1847.

56. Isaiah 2:2–3.

57. General Church Minutes, 1 Aug. 1847. See also Journal History, 1 Aug. 1847.

58. That the early Latter-day Saint pioneers did not confuse the Salt Lake Valley for Jackson County is clear from the following address of this same Orson Pratt:

"But where is the spot where the city of Zion or the New Jerusalem shall stand? We answer, in Jackson County, State of Missouri, on the western frontiers of the United States. It is there that the city of Zion shall be built. All the other cities that have been built by the gathering of the Saints are called, not Zion, but 'stakes' of Zion" (Orson Pratt, "New Jerusalem or The Fulfillment of Modern Prophecy" [Liverpool, 1849], 18).

59. Many who listened were quick to grasp Pratt's message. Wrote Captain James Brown of the Battalion in a letter to his wife, Abigail: "I have quartered my company in this beautiful valley where there is salt water and sweet water, cold water and hot water [nearby hot springs] in abundance and the plain looks very much like the one the Lord speaks of in the scriptures where the Lord's house was to be built in the tops of the mountains. And I hope I shall soon see you together with the rest of our friends flowing to it" (James Brown to Abigail Brown, 6 Aug. 1847, James Brown Collection, LDS Church Archives).

60. Journal of Horace K. Whitney, 22 Aug. 1847.

61. Journal of Wilford Woodruff, 25 Aug. 1847.

9

"WE EXPECT TO SEE THE SUN RISE AGAIN"

The Emigration Camp of 1847

Our numbers far exceed what we anticipated, for instead of
numbering 100 wagons we have near 600; the cattle were
generally weak in coming off the rushes; we had to recruit
our cattle and send to Missouri for breadstuffs. You know,
brethren, that it takes a little time and labor to start a large
wheel; it has, however, commenced rolling and will, we
trust, not stop until it reaches the valley of the Salt Lake.[1]

So wrote an anxious and overburdened John Taylor in mid-August
1847, some 35 miles east of the Mormon Ferry on the North Platte,
to Brigham Young, then just leaving on his return trip to Winter
Quarters. Having modified Brigham's original instructions, which had been
given by revelation, Taylor and his immediate leader, Parley P. Pratt, knew
they were in for a fateful day of reckoning. Nonetheless, they took consolation and pride in their accomplishment—the bringing out of the single
largest train of emigrants yet to have crossed the great American Plains—
the Emigration Camp.

"I MEAN WHAT I SAY WHEN I TALK OF THE 25TH OF MAY"

Just as Brigham had learned, while crossing the mud fields of Iowa in
the spring of 1846, that it was infinitely more difficult to get away from his

followers than it was to flee from his enemies, Pratt and Taylor were learning firsthand that they, too, could not resist the press of their people. Even before the vanguard pioneer company had disappeared over the hills west of Winter Quarters two months before, the rush was on to follow "as soon as the grass grows." As Amelia Richards said in a letter to her uncle, Willard Richards: "It makes me almost sick of home to see the teams rolling out so this morning. I want to be going myself."[2]

And little wonder! Winter Quarters and the Council Bluffs settlements had proven sad and weary habitats. Hundreds had died of scurvy, exposure, and malnutrition. The long winter had been severe, and their hovels, huts, wagons, and caves had provided scarce comfort. Many were fearful of potential Indian attacks. Scores of Battalion wives and families yearned to roll out and meet their returning husbands and fathers, just as Brigham and the bishops who provided for them had promised. And if the pioneers had indeed found a new place, as they had promised, everyone wanted to be there. Surely the cost of going could be no greater than that of staying. Reluctantly they had let Brigham and his little band forge onward in April; now in June there would be no stopping them.

"There was only one thing that made [us] venture to start from the Missouri River in 1847," wrote George W. Hill, with an attitude representative of their anxious faith bordering on defiance,

> and that was the health of my wife. She had taken the scurvy in the winter superinduced by our living as we did without vegetables. And as soon as the weather began to get warm in the spring, she got worse instead of better and came very near dying. In fact, I had no hopes for her but to get on the road travelling as soon as possible, thinking a change of scenery, a change of air, and a change of water might be beneficial to her. I was determined to try it, let the consequences be what they might. . . . You may think this was a very hazardous undertaking; well, we thought so too, but the stakes were terrible we had to play.[3]

The original plan was for Patriarch John Smith (uncle to Joseph Smith) to preside over the Emigration Camp with the well-seasoned Isaac Morley second in command and all the various companies organized as per "The Word and Will of the Lord."[4] To make the trip, each family had to bring along a minimum of 300 pounds of provisions because they did not expect to find enough crops in their new mountain home to sustain them for the coming winter. Each company was to include as many of the poor as possible, as per the Nauvoo Covenant, and a large number of the Battalion families. As the last official communique of the Twelve had stated:

> It is our wish and counsel that the emigration company . . . shall follow the pioneers as soon as the grass is sufficient to support the teams, and the presidents and captains will examine and know that every soul that goes in said company is provided with from 3 to 500 lbs. of breadstuff for a year and [a] half and as much more as he can get, for we know not whether we can raise corn this summer, as we anticipate, at the place of location.
>
> Let the first emigration company take with them as many of the sisters whose husbands are in the army as can fit themselves out, or can be conveniently fitted out.[5]

As repayment for their sacrifice, Brigham had pledged the departing soldiers back in July 1846 that he would do all in his power to ensure that as many of their families as possible would meet them in the valley, rather than expect them to crisscross the continent a second time.

Their original instructions were to assemble first at the Elkhorn River no later than 25 May and then to come on in installments of smaller, more manageable companies of no more than 100 wagons each. Larger groups than this would be too cumbersome and unwieldy for everyone and make it too difficult to properly care for and feed the animals. But despite every effort at restraint, everyone who was even nearly ready began assembling at the Liberty Pole—a 51-foot high willow tree pole 6-feet deep in the ground with pins 18 inches apart from top to bottom and a white flag at the top—at the Elkhorn as early as mid-May, intent on leaving with the first companies.[6]

Pratt and Taylor, having declined Brigham's earlier invitation to go west in the pioneer company, were now, by right of their apostleship, sustained as overall company leaders. John Smith was appointed to "preside over the spiritual affairs" of the camp and John Young over "the temporal affairs," with Edward Hunter and Daniel Spencer as his counselors. Spencer was given command over the first hundred; Hunter, Jedediah M. Grant, and Abraham O. Smoot each commanded one of the other three hundreds. Charles C. Rich was appointed commander of the military unit and W. C.

Staines camp clerk and historian.[7] Those who could not obtain sufficient flour from the overworked Winter Quarters mill were detouring south to Westport, St. Joseph, and other Missouri frontier towns to acquire the needed provisions.

One of the biggest problems Pratt and Taylor had to deal with was the reorganization of those who had been assigned to Brigham's first division and Kimball's second division in this second, or emigration, camp.

> Pratt spoke on the circumstances with which we were sur-
> rounded, how that Captains of hundreds, of fifties, etc. appointed
> last winter are not here, some coming on, some not. Now I think
> it is best to act according to our circumstances; or shall we stay here
> and theorize and alter for a week or two . . . the time is now when
> we have to go and the theory is not what we will see now so much
> as the practical. Now if you belong to Heber or Brigham, shall you
> not belong to them if you do not go maybe in Brigham's but
> because we both go in the same company or the same fifty will that
> alter us any . . . now act in operation and union with us and we will
> deliver you up to those whom you belong.[8]

The result was a rising tide of the most adequately provisioned and best-prepared families but fewer of the poor and Battalion families than originally anticipated. New captains of hundreds, fifties, and tens had to be called at the last minute to replace those previously assigned who were either not yet ready or chose not to come. In a word, it became the departure of the fittest.

Such a rush of oncomers inevitably delayed their departure. Despite Pratt's warning—"I mean what I say when I talk of the 25th of May"—every family wagon had to be checked for provisions and pass a road-worthiness inspection. Besides waiting for several to return from Missouri, Pratt and Taylor waited several extra days for the late arrival of a nine- and a six-pound cannon, a leather skiff, and the rescued 700-pound Nauvoo Temple bell. This they planned to ring each morning to alert the far-flung wagons of their daily departures. Some others were detained by sickness, and others, like Hosea Stout, refused the invitation to come at all. The murder of Jacob Weatherby by Omaha Indians, just past the Elkhorn, also caused considerable consternation and delay.[9]

What finally came of the confusion was a sprawling, wagon-borne congregation numbering 1,448 men, women, and children and almost 600 wagons—or a would-be caravan some 10 miles long. In tow were 2,213 oxen, 887 cows, 716 chickens, 358 sheep, and 124 horses.[10] There were approximately 482 men and boys over the age of 13, almost an equal number of women (471), 485 children, and 50 infants under the age of three, 26 of whom had been born in Winter Quarters during the previous year. Included in the group were 77-year-old Abigail McBride, 73-year-old Hezekiah Sprague of Massachusetts, 72-year-old Priddy Meeks of South Carolina, and at least a dozen others in their 60s. Some 450 (31 percent) hailed from New England (229 from New York State alone). Almost 200 (14 percent) called themselves Southerners, with 50 from Kentucky. Another 16 percent were British or Canadian converts.[11]

Not everyone was enthusiastic about leaving. "Soon after parting from our kindred on the banks of the Missouri," wrote one young man inclined to turn back,

> and while grieving over the separation, I was gently chided by my mother who rehearsed to me the story of Lot's wife, and exhorted me never to "look back." This made a deep impression upon my mind. . . . I [was] more or less in dread all the way over the plains, for my rebellious thoughts, in spite of me, would often go back to the loved ones we had left behind.[12]

The great majority, however, were determined to make the journey, no matter what the risks, and pleaded for their nonbelieving relatives to understand. "All I ask of this world is to get comfortably out of it," wrote one woman in a letter to her unbelieving relatives back in Missouri,

> or through it. I am not deposed to hurry out by any bye path, but I wait the leisure of my Lord. I believe my sun will set in peace; I can say in truth I am weaned from the world. I do not love the world nor the things of the world. When shall we fast for Gould and Laura [relatives]? Not, I suppose until they have tried the world a little longer, and let it pierce them to the heart a few times more, for it is hard to give it up; well, stick to it as long as you can, and when you get ready, come to us; we shall be very glad to see you, and we as much expect you will come if you live, as we expect to see the sun rise again . . . and we know assuredly that everything

will work together for the good of those that love him, and put their trust in him.[13]

Despite their many problems and delays, the swollen emigration camp finally left the Elkhorn on the morning of 15 June, almost two months to the day after the departure of the pioneer camp. They were late by at least three weeks but still westward bound. It was an unforgettable sight as "the wagons went four abreast, and you can hardly imagine their appearance; some that were there declared it the grandest sight their eyes were ever blest with, their wagons all neatly prepared, and everything for their comfort."[14]

"THE WOMEN BORE THE BURDEN WITH MUCH PATIENCE"

The route of the emigration camp followed that of the pioneer company in virtually every detail. From the Elkhorn they passed by the Pawnee village without incident and followed the north bank of the Platte River. They reached Grand Island on 6 July, the Platte Forks nine days later, Chimney Rock on 29 July, and Fort Laramie on 5 August, averaging almost as many miles per day as did the vanguard company ahead of them. From Fort Laramie they followed up the North Platte, crossed over to the Sweetwater and to South Pass. There they finally met up with Brigham's returning party in early September.

The sight of such a moving entourage was something to see. "The whole camp of near 600 wagons arranged in order on a fine plain," remembered Jesse Crosby, "beautifully adorned with roses . . . our cattle are seen in herds in the distance—the whole scene is grand and delightful."[15]

Accounting for their relatively good time were better feed, little Indian interference, less time spent in hunting, easier river crossings, and the very clear instructions left them by the pioneer camp. Fifteen miles west of Grand Island, for instance, they found "the first traces of our Brethren who have gone before"—a board with the following inscription: "Apr. 29 Camp of Pioneers—grass short but plenty—watch Indians—217 miles to Winter Quarters—watch the trees near our encampment."[16] Several more directives and communiques were later located wedged into poles, written on buffalo skulls, or inscribed on rocks or boards along the way. As a further aid, pilots such as George Woodward had been dispatched to travel back to

Wagons moving out

greet the advancing party. Scattered members of the returning sick detachment of the Battalion also were welcomed into camp from time to time.

Unlike the pioneer company, the emigration camp counted large numbers of women, children, and families. Their colorful accounts, trials, and interpretations give new insights into what it meant to be a daughter of Zion—a mother, a wife, a plural wife, and child—while moving west. Most of the men had been directed by the priesthood to keep a written record of their journey; those journals kept by the women show a refreshing spontaneity, a natural willingness to record the wild adventure of it all on the one hand and the tedium of the daily grind on the other. Their several accounts make for memorable reading.[17]

"I will describe our wagons and tent as well as I can," wrote Ursuline Hascalls.

> The wagon is long enough for both our beds made on the flour barrels, chest and other things. Thales and I sleep inn thee back end and F. and Irene at the forward end. It is painted red. It has

eight bows eighteen inches apart; a hen coop on the end with four hens. We had two webs of thick drilling. We put on one cover of than, then three breadths of stout sheeting over that and then painted it. The heaviest showers and storms does not beat through, only a few drops now and then. Our tent is made of drilling sixteen breadths in the shape of an umbrella. A cord three feet long in the middle that holds it up carries it three feet from the ground, than a breadth of sheeting put on the edge to let down in cool weather and fasten with loops and pins in the ground.[18]

It took a woman, for instance, to convert a wagon into a home. Helen Mar Kimball Whitney, young wife of Horace K. Whitney, told of her attempt. "We had doors, generally, cut on the left side of the wagon covers," she recalled.

Boxes and bags of grain, etc., were packed in the rear part of our wagon, upon which our bed was made. We had our provision chest in front, which served as a table and between was just room for my chair—this being my only piece of furniture—the most of our household chattels having been left in our house in Nauvoo. I could now knit and read as we traveled. . . . None, I think, but those who had a like experience can form the slightest idea of the appreciation and happiness it gave us to have a little wagon all to ourselves, which, under the circumstances, was [the] next thing to paradise.[19]

Paradise, however, was not the word many women chose to describe their experiences, especially after a few weeks out on the trail. For one thing, it was their lot to prepare the food, to cook the meals, and, once in buffalo country, to roam the countryside in search of buffalo chips to fuel their prairie fires. Many are the accounts of women milking cows, making cheeses, churning butter, picking berries and black currants, and baking meat and berry pies over open flames to feed their hungry families. How tiring it all could be is captured well by a later emigrant traveling over the same countryside:

From the time we get up in the morning, until we are on the road, it is hurry scurry to get breakfast, and put away the things that necessarily had to be pulled out last night—while under way there is no room in the wagon for a visitor, nooning is barely long enough to eat a cold bite—and at night all the cooking utensils and provisions are to be gotten about the camp fire, and cooking enough done to last until the next night.

Although there is not much to cook, the difficulty and inconvenience in doing it, amounts to a great deal so by the time one has squatted around the fires and cooked bread and bacon, and made several dozen trips to and from the wagon, washed the dishes (with no place to drain them) and gotten things ready for an early breakfast, some of the others already have their night caps on—at any rate it is time to go to bed.[20]

Tedious or otherwise, at least when there was food none went to bed hungry. Some nights when the meat supply was low, they "went to bed supperless and what was worse got up this morning breakfastless. Some crying among the children. We churned and drank the buttermilk."[21]

No less onerous was the constant need to knit, mend, wash, and dry the clothing. Men usually wore heavy, durable trousers, woolen shirts, sturdy high boots, work gloves, and broad-brimmed hats. Women often traded in their hoop skirts for more adaptable, simple homespun or cotton dresses, large aprons, shoes, and sunbonnets. Usually all the water had to be heated in large camp kettles over open flames. At other times, creeks, rivers, and rain water sufficed as a place to wash in their attempts to keep up with the suffocating dust. Whenever the camp did stop, even on the occasional Sabbath, most of the women were busy washing the week's heap of dirty clothing. "Four of our women," recorded one diarist, "went down to the creek with a wagon and stopped there the whole day to wash and did suffer much for heat and for want of food. The water was first rate and there was also very good spring water. The women bore the burden with much patience."[22]

Some of their other experiences were anything but routine. "My first child was born in a wagon," remembered Eliza Maria Partridge Lyman of her travels back in Iowa. Although wagon companies would usually make short stops to allow for the birth of a child, the stay was always too short, giving rise to sickness and discomfort for both mother and child. Many women took weeks to recover. "I am uncomfortably situated for a sick woman. The scorching sun shining upon the wagon through the day and the cool air at night is almost too much of a change to be healthy." Lyman continued:

Sunflowers and Buffalo Chips, *from a painting by Gary Kapp*

I am now like a skeleton, so much so that those who have not been with me do not know me till told who I am. It is a fearful place to be sick with fever in a wagon with no shade over except the cover and a July sun shining every day. All the comfort I had was the pure cold water from a spring nearby.[23]

Distrustful of regular doctors in these pre-anesthesia times, most Mormon women relied either on the practitioners of Thompsonian medicine (see chapter 7) or on priesthood blessings and, like most other American women, treated themselves. It was the Mormon midwife with almost religious zeal who played the prominent role in assisting with deliveries on the prairie. Of this group, none stands out so prominently as Patty Sessions.[24] Between 25 June and year's end, Sessions delivered at least 14 babies, including two girls and two boys born along the trail and later, the first boy born in the Salt Lake Valley, a son of Harriet Page and Lorenzo Dow Young.[25]

Women were also called on to do work traditionally left to the men. With so many men away with the Battalion or the pioneer camp, several companies were left "with almost half the teams without teamsters except females. This was a scene of things that looked hard indeed but go we must at this crisis and under these circumstances."[26] Consequently several women, many of whom had absolutely no experience with driving oxen, drove their wagons all the way west, while others took an occasional turn at the reins while their menfolk were off hunting.

Wrote Mary A. Rich, one of Charles Rich's wives:

> Mr. Rich thought he would have to hire two more men or boys to drive two of the wagons, but there was one of his wives besides myself who had no children, so we volunteered to drive the wagons until we got to the Valley. He did not think we could, but we persuaded him to try us one day and see. We did so well that we had our teams every day after that until we arrived in the Valley, as regularly as the men did. We did not grieve or mourn over it, we had some very nice times when the roads were not so bad.[27]

Ann Pratt, one of Parley P. Pratt's plural wives, was a city girl, "never having seen cattle yoked together." But seeing the need, she quickly thought:

> "Well, what any other woman can do, I can do." So shouldering my whip I drove out of Winter Quarters and soon learned to manage my team first class. I learned to put on the lock chain instantly at the top of a steep hill and would jump out quickly while the cattle were going; and to take it off, so that the impetus afforded by the end of the descent would aid them in starting up the other side for we often passed through deep gullies.[28]

Many women had to learn their trade as fast as lightning. Eliza R. Snow tells of one of the most frightful experiences in overland travel—a stampede. "We had stopped to repair a dilapidated crossing over a broad slough," she remembered.

> The teams were standing two, three and four abreast; and from the top, nearly to the bottom of a gentle slope, facing the hands at work, when two men on mules, with blankets swinging, rode galloping past frightening the back teams. They started on a rush forward, which started others, and soon nearly every vehicle was in motion with fearful velocity, the drivers absent, and women and children in wagons, carriages, and others still more exposed, standing where they were in danger of being crushed by the reckless flying wheels. With fearful velocity, heedless of crossings and bridges,

those teams whirled their vehicles across the slough where it was admitted that the most skillful teamster could not have succeeded. I was sitting alone on the back seat of a carriage, holding the reins of a high-spirited *spirn* [sic]—vehicles were flitting past—the horses made several springs, and I knew very well, if they really got started, no human power could prevent them stripping everything to strings. While I held them with all my strength, I prayed with all the fervency of my soul. Mrs. Pierce and her daughter, Margaret, with whom I was journeying, being out of the carriage when the scene occurred, had been trying to stop some ox-teams, but finding they would not succeed, they came, one on each side, and caught the horses by the bits: they stopped prancing but shook all over like a person with the shaking ague. Whatever skeptics may say, I attribute my preservation at that time to the peculiar and special blessing of God. And not only mine, but that of others: in the midst of the many fearful exposures no one was seriously hurt.[29]

Sometimes even their best efforts met with injury and calamity. Ann Pratt remembered her lock chain giving out while charging down a hill. "I had to hold the nigh ox by the horn," she said,

and tap the off one over the face and keep saying, "Whoa back, whoa back," and nearly hold my breath till I got down to the bottom; then stop and draw a breath of relief, see that all was right, and then on again for others were right on our heels and we had to get out of their way. You can just imagine what a condition our skirts were in.[30]

Another woman fell from the tongue of her wagon, which weighed 1,600 pounds, and the front wheel ran across her chest as she lay prostrate on the ground. "To all appearances," her friend recorded, "she was crushed, but on being administered to by some of the elders, she revived; and after having been anointed with consecrated oil, and having the ordinance of laying on of hands repeated, she soon recovered and on the fourth day after that accident, she milked her cow as usual."[31]

Not all were as fortunate. "The burial of the dead by the wayside was a sad office," wrote Eliza R. Snow of the great intruder on the prairies.

For husbands, wives, and children to consign the cherished remains of loved ones to a lone desert grave was enough to try the firmest heart-strings. Today [4 August], a Sister Esther Ewing who had passed away after a sickness of two weeks was buried. The burial was attended with all the propriety the circumstances would permit. After the customary dressing the body was wrapped in a quilt and consigned to its narrow house. It truly seemed sad and we sorrowed deeply as we turned from the lonely grave.[32]

Of all the natural landmarks and impressive sites along the Platte River road, perhaps none were as sobering and soul-stirring to passersby of all faiths and backgrounds as these hastily made monuments to their fallen dead—wilderness reminders that their journeying often came at the supreme price. Witness the following moment of silence by an Oregon-bound emigrant wending his way up the Platte that same year:

> We have seen a number of graves along the road, five I believe. Truly it was a sad spectacle to behold the graves of those who had thus left their friends comfortless during the toils and fatigue of emigration. Thrilling and sad were the thoughts that passed through my mind as I gazed on those sacred spots in the wilderness. Where, thought I, are those who have left here their dearest and nearest friends. I asked of the silent dead: 'Where are thy friends? Where are those for thee wept? Gone, gone to a distant clime or left behind where was once my sunny home,' seemed to be the saddening answer.[33]

One woman, the wife of Jedediah M. Grant, took sick near Bear River. Before her death, she begged her husband to carry her remains for burial in the valley—a request he dutifully fulfilled.[34]

Every emigrant company developed its own mechanisms to deal with such griefs and hardships. Many of the Mormon women coped with faith and religious convictions as their solutions, referring often to a sort of working sorority on the high plains, reminiscent of the many small devotional meetings that had characterized female worship back at Winter Quarters.[35]

Several women devoted whatever free time they had while traveling overland to teaching their children. This was particularly the case with instruction on the doctrines and practices of their faith. Patty Sessions, for instance, tells of meeting "with the little girls in my wagon. Have a good time. The lord is pouring his spirit out on the youth. They spoke in tongues and rejoiced in God."[36]

If women and men shared the responsibilities and heartaches of overland travel, the children, full of excitement and adventure, often seemed oblivious to the dangers around them. "This was quite an undertaking for me as I was only 6 1/2 years old and small for my age," recalled one young boy. "It was hard for me to keep out of the way of the teams and wagons, for in fact I had my feet and legs run over two or three times by the wagon in jumping out to stop the teams."[37]

Eliza R. Snow

Others were less fortunate. William Staines recorded that one day, at the Loup Fork, "Bro. Kinyon's son, aged 7 years, and Robert Gardner, aged 5 years [son of Archibald Gardner], were run over by wagons while crossing the river. One of the wagons weighed 3,000 lbs. and the other 3,500 lbs. Both boys were administered to immediately and they soon appeared to be in a fair way of recovery."[38]

The thundering crash of a fully loaded wagon over a young body often proved fatal. Unfortunately the injury suffered by young Robert Gardner, though he tried gamefully to show otherwise, eventually killed him. Not wanting to let on to others or even believe himself how badly hurt he was, "for 500 miles, through dust and wind, over rough roads or smooth the little sufferer grew more thin and wan. He lived until he was nothing but skin and bones before expiring on 13 August at Deer Creek on the North Platte."[39]

The agony of losing children in a forlorn wilderness and of burying them in makeshift shallow graves was a constant fear. John Bennion had to write the sorrowful news to his wife's sister and family of the passing of their infant daughter. The day after her death on 7 September, they carried her dead body 13 miles "and buried it on the morning of the 9th near the campground called The Pacific Springs, on the left hand side of the road, 'Oregon Route–South Pass of the Rocky Mountains.' I put down a head board with this inscription: 'Ann Bennion, died September 7, 1847, aged 1 year, 9 months and 19 days.'" As if wanting to put such bad news far behind them, the camp traveled 21 miles that day—"the longest day's travel of any of the journey"—though of slight consolation to the grieving family.[40]

In the case of young Robert, the following year family members visited his grave during their journey back to the Missouri River. Unfortunately when they came to the place where his body had been buried, "they found that the wolves had uncovered the grave and his bones were scattered about. The sight was too much for kind-hearted [cousin] John. He wept and wailed and tore his hair. They tenderly gathered up the bones, reinterred them and sadly journeyed on."[41]

The surprising thing is that even with so large a traveling congregation, few were injured or killed. Only four people died during the movement of the emigration camp, and of that small number, two were children.

But for most children, many of whom walked barefoot the entire distance, their travels spelled a never-ending panorama of excitement and adventure. "The trip to me, as a boy, was one of interest, novelty and pleasure," recalled one of Parley Pratt's children.

> Daily new scenes burst upon our view, and now and again we would meet the hunter and the trapper or a band of Indians decked with beads, ornaments and feathers. The novelty and bustle of camp life, the neighing of the horse, the lowing of the cows with their young calves, the deer, the antelope, the buffalo and flocks of wild geese, the rocks, rills and caves [and] the wild night owls . . . all filled my young heart with delight and inspiration.[42]

Many of the boys and girls sang, whittled sticks, threw countless stones into the boring brown Platte, and played hide-and-seek and every other game dear to the hearts of the young. Ann Woodbury recalled one of their many childhood pranks:

> While they were eating, I picked some service berries and sat down by the creek to pick them over. While sitting there, I started to bleat like a sheep. The men and boys all started to run. One said, "I'll keep it if I catch it first." When they had gone as far as I thought they could hear me, I bleated again. They ran back to their dinner and saw me. They asked: "Was that you?" I laughed. It was the law then that if anybody left anything behind, the finder could keep it.[43]

Others found delight in the smallest of things. "There were a great

many ant hills along the road raised to a considerable height," Mary Jane
Mount Tanner recalled,

> where we often found beads which were, no doubt, lost by the
> Indians and collected by those indefatigable little workers along
> with the gravel of which their mounds were composed. If we were
> hardy enough to risk a bite now and then we found much amuse-
> ment in searching for the beads to string into necklaces.
>
> Another favorite pastime consisted of walking far enough
> ahead of the train to get a little time to play; when we would drive
> the huge crickets, large unwieldy insects, if they could be called
> such, that abounded in some sections of the country; and build cor-
> rals of sand or rocks to put them in, calling them our cattle. . . . In
> keeping ahead [of the train] we managed to get across if possible
> before the teams came up. If the rivers were not too deep we pulled
> off our shoes and stockings and waded through.[44]

For most children, the wide-open west was their never-ending play-
ground, or as one emigrant recalled: "In the innocence of our childhood,
we looked upon the whole affair as a great picnic excursion."[45]

But even the youngest boys were assigned as teamsters wherever
required. Inexperienced, they often made clumsy mistakes. For instance, 13-
year-old Thales Haskell managed to run a wheel onto a bank and broke an
axletree. "I heard a great many making remarks about me being a very careless boy to let such an accident happen. I felt badly, of course, and thought
if they had given me a little caution beforehand it would have done more
good."[46]

Another young man, George Q. Cannon, had the misfortune to drive
his wagon straight into the one belonging to General Charles C. Rich, military commander of the whole camp. Later in life a counselor in the First
Presidency, Cannon learned a lesson there on the high Nebraska plains
which he never forgot. "It became necessary one day for the company in
which I was traveling to pass through the line of General [Charles C.] Rich's
company," he recalled.

> My team, which I had left standing while I went back to assist some
> of the other teams in crossing a difficult place, started on, and the
> point of the hub of the wagon I drove struck the rim of the wheel of
> one of Brother Rich's wagons and broke the axle-tree. I ran up in

time to see what had been done, but not in time to prevent the damage. An axle-tree in that timberless region, and under those circumstances, was worth more than gold. I was exceedingly sorry, and bore patiently without any attempt at justification the reproof which Brother Rich gave me. The captain of our fifty (Orson Horne) told me to drive on, while he stayed behind to do what he could to repair the injury. Brother Rich was put to great inconvenience to get a new axle-tree; but by Captain Horne he sent to me his regrets for the manner in which he had spoken to me. He had learned that I was not so much to blame as appearances would indicate, and felt that he had spoken too harshly; but I thought I deserved all he said, and more too, for leaving my team in such a position where it could do such mischief.[47]

By the time the camp reached Independence Rock in late August, they had lost one-third of their cattle through stampedes, their own carelessness, and theft by Indians.

"BY THE BLAZE OF A WILLOW PATCH"

Unofficial news of the discovery of the Salt Lake Valley first reached the toiling emigration companies just west of Fort Laramie on 14 August with the arrival of the pilot party from the Mormon Ferry; it was confirmed two days later by Apostle Ezra T. Benson's advance party on 16 August.[48] In quick order the glad tidings rippled through the group, like the sudden excitement of unexpectedly seeing long-lost relatives. Messengers on ponies shouted the news up and down the lines in glad hurrah's for all to hear. Children screamed and shouted. Men hollered to their wives. Mothers beamed for joy. Excitement mounted everywhere, and happy faces black with dust burst out in cheers. Some laughed; others sang; and many wept for the fulfillment of their faith. As George B. Wallace remembered it: "In the evening Elder E. T. Benson preached to us, telling about the beautiful land that the Lord had given to the Saints. He said that he felt like a little child and that he could go by himself and weep for joy."[49] John Taylor, meanwhile, blessed with a soft and mellow singing voice, was quick to sing the song "The Upper California." "It was," as one eyewitness recorded, "a most joyful evening for all who attended."[50]

Later that night, an exuberant Taylor continued his song in a fulsome communication to Brigham Young and others of the Twelve:

We thank God, our Heavenly Father, that you have been so successful in your undertaking and that after the many wanderings, trials, persecutions, and afflictions of the Saints that you have at last found a home, and we trust that when your families and ours shall meet in Zion, you may rest from your weary pilgrimage, realize the full fruition of your hopes and rejoice with your brethren, the Saints of the Most High, in the Kingdom of God, which shall be established, and in the Lord's House which shall be reared in the mountains.[51]

Such happy times repeated themselves all along the trail, from company to company, as west met east. All were particularly anxious to talk with Brigham and the others of the Quorum of the Twelve in their returning company of 33 wagons. Perrigrine Sessions's group met them just over South Pass in late August. "We met several of the Pioneers on their way back after their families," Sessions recorded. "They gave us a brief account of the Valley with many instructions pertaining to the course that the Camp should pursue. . . . Our spirits were refreshed and it seemed as though our burdens were lightened although we were worn out with the long and tedious journey."[52]

The full story of these interesting meetings, which Woodruff called "one of the most interesting councils we ever held together on the earth," high on the plateau of the Big and Little Sandy Rivers west of South Pass has not been adequately told.[53] In them lay not only the heralding of a new Zion and a promising future for the Latter-day Saints, but also the struggle of a leader convinced that finding a new home was only a partial resolution to the challenges they faced as a Church.

In two nights of meetings, on 3 and 4 September, between the returning members of the Quorum of the Twelve and Apostle Parley P. Pratt in Willard Richards's wagon, there was less excitement and more blunt criticism of Pratt and Taylor's handling of the camps. Evident was Brigham's rising frustration that the government of the Church was still disorganized and incomplete.

First they shared the good news. Said George A. Smith (as recorded almost verbatim by clerk Thomas Bullock):

It feels well. We started out to seek a country. We came over these sages, plains and rocks and found a sweet little valley in the midst of the hills. I was satisfied we should not find the beautiful timber and prairies on the same ground—we are not afraid we can't sustain ourselves but fear the saints will not always do right, but bring down the displeasure of the Lord should we forget to call on the Lord. The scourges of the Almighty are to be feared. . . . If the valley was interspersed with groves it would be the most beautiful spot. The children of Israel built of sun-dried bricks; we have done the same. That will be the best way of building. The walls can be whitewashed. The soil is of sufficient variety to please every person. If the sisters are in want of hot drinks they can find spring water already heated for them and drink as much as they please . . . with industry, economy and prudence it will be one of the most blessed places in the world. I never was so contented as I was in that valley.

He concluded by praising the virtues of nearby Utah and Cache Valleys, convinced that it was "land enough for a million men. . . . We all feel first rate and you will all feel first rate [too]."

Orson Pratt, Parley's brother, was quick to follow with an array of meteorological and geographic descriptives and superlatives. "We had prayed for many years that we might enjoy health and escape one of the greatest enemies and sickly places. . . . We have found a land that has not been cursed by the hands and abominations of the Gentiles."

Brigham then said:

Our minds, feelings, judgements and affections are to build up the Kingdom of God on the earth in spite of all hell. The Lord has led us this summer. . . . Every man and woman that is filled with the Spirit of the Lord will see that the Lord has guided his people since the death of the Prophet. You will see thousands living in the tops of the mountains.

He talked of their successful irrigation efforts and declared their new valley motto: "Every man do his duty." He instructed Pratt and others that none of the land was to be sold but all to be divided up as needed—without price. "If the brethren will only be humble I know that this Church will never be removed. I am afraid for the brethren becoming covetous."

Erastus Snow followed with his testimony that

we have been led to the right spot. . . . There has been a oneness of feeling in the Pioneer Company. The moment our eyes caught a glimpse of the Valley we felt as though we got home. . . . You will pass through canyons where you could roll down rocks and destroy all the armies of the world. . . . We will not have to be on a combined watch. The only thing we have to fear is the corruptions of our own heart. . . . [W]e shall establish and raise a standard to all the nations of the earth.

Wilford Woodruff, ratifying everything said by his peers, told Pratt, "I never saw a site for a city better in my life," and commented on the city layout, the wide streets, the new temple block, and the richness of the soil.[54]

And so the glowing talk and valley promotion continued until Pratt and his lieutenants were called on to describe their journey, provide the company lists, review their difficulties, and, above all, explain why they had not followed counsel and "the Word and Will of the Lord."[55] It was not long before it became clear that the emigration camp was far larger than the Twelve had expected or directed it to be; that it was overpopulated with the best-provisioned but underrepresented the poor and the halt; and that it did not include nearly as many of the Mormon Battalion families as Brigham had promised his army boys back at the Missouri River the year before.

Pratt stoutly defended his actions, saying that as for the changes in leadership, the people had nominated him and John Taylor to take the lead because of their apostolic authority. Swamped as they were with so many newcomers at the Elkhorn, they had no choice but to name new captains of hundreds and fifties and form new complements of travelers. Unwilling and unable to wait any longer, because of the lateness of the season, they took what they had and reorganized everything. In a word: "We had no time to alter it."

Sensing Brigham's keen disappointment that he had not come west with the pioneer camp, Pratt defended himself: "It was not a spirit of rebellion and wickedness in regard to my not going with you last Spring. I did not feel it my duty to go and if you censure me, censure me." Moreover, he argued that his position as a coequal member of the Twelve gave him the right to act independently of Brigham Young: "We hold the keys as well as yourself and I will not be judged by you but by the Quorum."

What followed, "by the blaze of a willow patch," was a remarkable give and take that underscored the tenseness of the time, the strength of their personalities, and their differing views of mission and Church government.

Parley P. Pratt

Brigham: Our companies were perfectly organized . . . why should our whole winter's work be set at naught? Every man knew what they had to do when they got to the Horn. There was the president to appoint who should lead. This is all disarranged and disannulled. When the Quorum of the Twelve do a thing it is not in the power of two of them to rip it up. . . .

Pratt: If I have done wrong, I am willing to repent. . . .

Brigham: . . . You had no business to control, alter or direct our organization. We wanted you to bring a part of your family [with the Pioneer Camp] and leave the rest—the same as we did. If you had done right you would have come into the organization and would have assisted. I know you have had a hard time and you have brought it on yourself. . . . We've got the machine amoving and it is not your business to stick your hands among the cogs to stop the wheel. . . .

Pratt: I have done the best I could. You said I could have done better. If I am to blame in it, I have done wrong. If I am guilty of an error, I am sorry for it. I would lead them to the Twelve. I am willing that all the camps should know that I have done wrong and that I repent. I am willing to confess that I did wrong. Am I forgiven?

Brigham: I forgive you . . . if I don't do right I want every man so to live in the sunshine of glory to correct me when I am wrong. I feel bowed down to the grave with the burden of this great people and if a president [of the quorum] does not do right put him down and put another in his place. . . . Parley, you did know about the divisions and it was to get the poor, the halt, the lame and the blind. . . .

Pratt: It was at the latest moment that we organized and had not time to organize them. . . . I acknowledge the error but I did the best I could.

In the ensuing comments, Brigham hinted at the much greater concern that lay behind his rebuke of Pratt and why it was he felt so strongly about the issues at hand. "I do believe that better men [the Twelve] cannot be found on the earth who can live as we live," he said.

> I report to them my thanks for their forbearance. Before my clothes were dried on my back [baptism in 1832] I was ordained an Elder. By and by Brother [David] Patton ordained me to be a high priest. I said I had not power to magnify my calling. By and by I was ordained to the Twelve and I think as little of myself as any man can think of me. I am unworthy. I look upon myself as a weak, poor, little man who is called by the providence of God to preside. Now I tell you: we may sit here till doom's day and the word and will of the Lord will come to me before any of you. . . . I want you to go right into the Celestial Kingdom with me. . . . God bless you [Parley] forever and ever and don't think any more about it.[56]

At this same meeting Patriarch John Smith was nominated to preside over the Salt Lake Stake of Zion once the camps arrived in Salt Lake Valley.[57]

What Brigham urgently wanted was the unanimous support of his fellow Apostles to agree to the reordering of priesthood and Church government and the reestablishment of the First Presidency. As Woodruff put it while on their return trip from the Valley: "I had a question put to me by Pres. Young what my opinion was concerning one of the Twelve Apostles being appointed as the President of the Church with his two counsellors. I answered that . . . I thought it would require a revelation to change the order of that quorum."[58]

Likewise the matter of succession and reorganizing the First Presidency had been heavy on Brigham's mind while settling in the Salt Lake Valley. He had digressed from his funeral sermon to address the topic by stating that just as Joseph Smith had been the senior Apostle in this dispensation by right of his divine ordination from Peter, James, and John in 1829 before becoming President of the Church at its creation in 1830, so he, too, as president of the quorum now had both the right and sacred responsibility to reorganize the presidency. Until such work was done, others would continue to claim control. "Joseph was a prophet, seer and revelator long before he received the priesthood," he argued.[59]

The imperative in Brigham Young's mind was the pressing need to convince the rest of his colleagues, including Pratt and Taylor and perhaps most especially them, that the supreme governing quorum of the Church, the First Presidency, had to be reestablished as soon as possible. Government by the Twelve was, in his mind, no longer satisfactory, because they all felt they could rule in the place of each other. As Parley P. Pratt had said at Winter Quarters just prior to their departure:

> I don't know anything about three but I do know about Twelve men who hold the keys of this kingdom . . . all the Twelve are alike in keys, power, might, majesty and dominion and the Seventy [Quorum of] are equal, everyone in its place. So are all who have the fullness of the Priesthood. . . . There is no higher nor lower.[60]

It was for this very reason that Brigham had been so upset that neither Pratt nor Taylor had agreed to come in the original pioneer company, where the matter of place and government could be addressed as a unanimous quorum.[61]

Part of the heritage of the 1847 pioneer treks, then, was the matter of reorganizing the Church and laying the groundwork for the reestablishment of the First Presidency. Such a view leads to a more accurate understanding of why Brigham was displeased with Pratt and Taylor. With part of the Twelve now going east and another going west, the possibility of obtaining unanimous support for reorganization was impossible. And until that approval was extended, the potential for disagreement and disharmony played into the hands of opposing claimants to succession.

There is no evidence that Brigham sought such a sustaining vote from Pratt on the trail nor is there any indication the chastened leader would then have given it. Furthermore, Brigham knew that even Heber C. Kimball, George A. Smith, and Orson Pratt did not yet see the need for an imminent reorganization. It would take much more persuasion and discussion than any light from a prairie willow patch could provide. Nevertheless, the wheel was in motion.

Three days after the Brigham and Parley companies rolled out in opposite directions, the returning company of the Twelve reached John Taylor's division. On 8 September, on the east side of South Pass, Taylor was struggling west up the Sweetwater with barely enough oxen power to make it up the Pass. The weather had turned wintry cold and snow was falling heavily. Whether out of Taylor's desire to temper the moment, or simply as an expression of sheer gratitude and respect, what occurred in the evening among that poorly provisioned people is unparalleled, at least in Mormon pioneer history. Instead of giving a cold and formal greeting, the womenfolk busied themselves with preparing a sumptuous feast more fit for a banquet hall than a snowy wilderness.

"A nice fat steer was bought from Bishop Hunter," Isabella Horne recalled. "The dishes were unpacked and the sisters did the best possible to prepare a dinner worthy of the occasion. . . . It was snowing heavily . . . , which made camp cooking quite a task. The storm passed before dinner, and the brethren cleared away the brush and improvised a rude table, and I can assure you we had a feast indeed, spiritual as well as temporal."[62]

The banquet consisted of roasted and broiled beef, pies, cakes, and biscuits. Fully a hundred people dined in their improvised outdoor setting with Brigham at the head of the table and the Twelve by his side. A program followed, at which "Bishop Hunter and [Bishop] Foutz acted as masters of ceremonies. . . . A dance in the evening completed the festivities. It was a joyful occasion."[63] As Eliza R. Snow concluded: "I know not as I have set at a table better supplied with the luxuries of life in all my travels for many years than was this table set at the foot of the South Pass of the Rocky Mountains."[64]

The council meetings that followed with Taylor and his leaders were significantly less tense than the one held earlier with Pratt, in part because Taylor was junior to Pratt in command. And if there were rebukes, they were muted by the glow of a warm reception, a delicious meal, and a happy evening.

Shortly afterwards the companies left in opposite directions. The company of the Twelve reached Winter Quarters seven weeks later on 31 October, while the forward lines of the emigration camp attained the Salt Lake Valley as early as 28 September. Though once again not all were pleased, perhaps Ann Pratt should have the final word:

> I shall never forget the last day we traveled and arrived in the Valley. It happened to be my turn to drive that day, September 28, 1847. The reach of our wagon was broken. . . . I kept expecting every minute to see the poor old concern draw apart and come to grief but it held together and when my eyes rested on the beautiful entrancing sight—the Valley—oh! how my heart swelled within me. I could have laughed and cried, such a commingling of emotions I cannot describe. My soul was filled with thankfulness to God for bringing us to a place of rest and safety—a home.[65]

NOTES

1. John Taylor to Brigham Young in Journal History, 18 Aug. 1847 (written just after Ezra T. Benson had reached the camp with word of the pioneer discovery of the Salt Lake Valley).

2. Amelia E. Richards to Willard Richards, 14 June 1847, Richards Family Letters 1840–1849, LDS Church Archives.

3. "Incidents in the Life of George Washington Hill," unpublished, Joel E. Ricks Collection, "Cache Valley Historical Material, Spring 1847," 17–31, LDS Church Archives.

4. "Isaac Morley remarked on our being left here to carry on the plan marked out by the Twelve in being organized according to the Will and Word of the Lord. Let the two divisions stand together and let us equalize them as near as possible and those that have come on lately let them stand together" (Winter Quarters High Council Minutes, 10 July 1847).

5. Official letter of the Twelve Apostles to the Brethren at Winter Quarters, 16 Apr. 1847, Journal History. See also Brigham Young to Titus Billings, 25 Mar., Brigham Young Papers.

That Brigham Young confidently expected a large number of Battalion families is witnessed further in a later communication to Captain James Brown, then with the Battalion: "We expect another company of Saints are on their way from Winter Quarters, following our trail, among whom will be as many of the families of the Battalion as can possibly be fitted out, and they will be with us nearly as soon as yourself" (Journal History, 2 June 1847).

6. Journal of John Lyman Smith, 16 July 1847, LDS Church Archives. Symbolic of their march out of oppression and into freedom, this was at least the second such Liberty Pole erected by the Mormon pioneers. A previous pole had been raised on the Council Bluffs side of the Missouri River, near where the Mormon Battalion enlisted into service. On the top of it a white sheet, with an American flag underneath, had been raised. No such American flag adorned the Elkhorn pole (Journal of Jacob Whitaker, July 1846, LDS Church Archives). See also Journal of Eliza R. Snow, 19 June 1847. Another such pole was erected in the Salt Lake Valley.

7. Journal History, 15 June 1847. On the other hand, some who had been bidden to come, like Hosea Stout, refused on the grounds they were invited too late. Stout, with characteristic self-sympathy, said: "I felt insulted, abused and neglected" (*Diary of Hosea Stout*, 15 June 1847, 1:261).

8. Historical Department Journal, 15 June 1847, LDS Church Archives.

9. The killing of Jacob Weatherby is the only documented instance of a fatal encounter between Indians and Mormons in all of 1847. Having gone out after a frightened and disoriented Nancy Chamberlain (wife of Solomon Chamberlain), who was alone in a wagon west of the Elkhorn, Weatherby and three companions were fired on by three Omaha Indians. According to one account, one of Weatherby's friends "jumped out of the wagon and clinched two of the Indians [but] the third one shot Weatherby through the hip and bowels. The Indians then ran off as soon as the scuffle began." Weatherby died soon afterward and was buried in a buffalo robe near

the Liberty Pole. Hosea Stout led a posse in search of the guilty party (Patty Sessions Journal, 20 June 1847).

As late as 1850, Weatherby's grave and the Liberty Pole were noticed by passing emigrants. "A raise of earth and a board on the right [of the pole]," wrote one passerby, "marks the spot where his murdered remains are deposited. There are also two other graves aside of [Weatherby's], these are Mormons" (Journal of William B. Lorton, 27 May 1850, Bancroft Library).

10. B. H. Roberts, *The Life of John Taylor* (1892), 188. By comparison, most other emigrant companies in 1847 were much smaller. Even Joel Palmer's Oregon-bound camp of 99 wagons was thought to be "too large."

There is a slight discrepancy regarding the final numbers. Some diarists counted 1,553. The Journal History figure shows 1,490; Susan Easton Black's studies show a final figure of between 1,423 and 1,438, plus the militia (see Susan Ward Easton [Black], "Pioneers of 1847: A Sesquicentennial Remembrance," unpublished, LDS Church Archives). Brigham Young is on record as having counted 566 wagons while he returned east (Journal History, 25 Nov. 1847).

11. Easton (Black), "Pioneers of 1847."

12. M. J. Thompson, "Early Church Recollections," *Juvenile Instructor*, 15 July 1897, 431.

13. Fanny Murray to "Gould and Laura" in Atchison County, Missouri, 5 July 1847, Helen Mar Kimball Whitney Collection.

14. Ibid.

15. Jesse W. Crosby. "The History and Journal of the Life and Travels of Jesse W. Crosby," unpublished, 1 July 1847, LDS Church Archives.

16. Journal of John Lyman Smith, 5 July 1847.

17. For one of the better accounts of Mormon women on the frontier, see Maureen Ursenbach Beecher, "Women's Work on the Mormon Frontier," *Utah Historical Quarterly* 49 (Summer 1981): 276–90.

18. Ursuline Hascalls to Wilson Andrews, 19 Sept. 1846, Hascalls Papers.

19. Helen Mar Kimball Whitney, in *Woman's Exponent*, 15 Jan. 1884, 126. Isabella Horne recalls that the only household furniture she could bring was "a small cooking stove, a very rare article in the pioneer camps, and a small rocking chair" (M. Isabella Horne, "Pioneer Reminiscences," *Young Women's Journal*, July 1902, 292).

20. Journal of Helen M. Carpenter, 22 June 1856, as quoted by Robert L. Munkres, "Wives, Mothers, Daughters: Women's Life on the Road West," *Annals of Wyoming* 42, no. 2 (Oct. 1970).

21. Journal of Jacob Gates, July 1847, LDS Church Archives.

22. Journal of Heber C. Kimball, 17 June 1846. For more on women's clothing on the frontier, see Sandra L. Myres, *Westering Women and the Frontier Experience 1800–1915* (1982), 124–27.

23. Journal of Eliza Maria Partridge Lyman, 14 July 1846, LDS Church Archives.

24. Chris Rigby Arrington, "Pioneer Midwives," in *Mormon Sisters: Women in Early Utah*, ed. Claudia Bushman (1976), 51–54; Sylvia D. Hoffert, "Childbearing on the Trans-Mississippi Frontier, 1830–1900," *Western Historical Quarterly* 22 (Aug. 1991): 272–88. See also Judith Walzer Leavitt, "'Science' Enters the Birthing Room: Obstetrics in America since the Eighteenth Century," *Journal of American History* 70, no. 2 (Sept. 1983): 281–304.

25. Journal of Patty Sessions, 20 June 1847. See also her entries from 20 June to 31 Dec. 1847.

26. Journal of Perrigrine Sessions, early June 1847, LDS Church Archives. At least 30 wagons in his company of fifty had female volunteer teamsters.

27. Mary A. Rich, "Incidents of the Rich Company," in *Heart Throbs of the West*, comp. Kate B. Carter, 12 vols. (1939–1951), 4:349.

28. Ann Agatha Walker Pratt, "The Pratt Story," in *Our Pioneer Heritage*, comp. Kate B. Carter, 20 vols. (1958–1977), 17:225.

29. Eliza R. Snow, "Sketch of My Life," Bancroft Library and LDS Church Archives.

30. Pratt, "The Pratt Story," in *Our Pioneer Heritage*, 17:226.

31. Snow, "Sketch of My Life," 23–29.

32. Journal History, 4 Aug. 1847.

33. Diary of James Raynor, 26 May 1847, Oregon Historical Society.

34. John Smith, Charles C. Rich, and John Young to Brigham Young, 14 Oct. 1847, Brigham Young Papers.

35. For a more complete discussion of female worship at Winter Quarters, see Bennett, *Mormons at the Missouri*, 173–79.

36. Journal of Patty Sessions, 19 July 1847.

37. Autobiography and Journal of Gideon Allen Murdock, 47, LDS Church Archives.

38. Journal History, 1 July 1847.

39. The Autobiography and Account Book of Archibald Gardner, LDS Church Archives; and Delila Gardner Hughes, *The Life of Archibald Gardner* (1939), 39.

40. John Bennion to his wife's sister, Hannah and family, 5 May 1848, in "The Bennion Family of Utah," 1:32–33, 7–9 September 1847, LDS Church Archives.

41. Hughes, *Life of Archibald Gardner*, 39.

42. Message of Parley P. Pratt Jr., in Arthur D. Coleman, "Pratt Pioneers of Utah," unpublished, xxviii, LDS Church Archives.

43. "Autobiography of Ann Cannon Woodbury," in *Cannon Family Historical Treasury*, ed. Beatrice Cannon Evans and Janath Russell Cannon (1967), 169.

44. Memoirs of Mary Jane Tanner, 21–29.

45. D. B. Ward, *Across the Plains in 1853* (1911), 10, 12.

46. "Emigrant Pioneer Stories," in *An Enduring Legacy*, 10 vols. (1978–87), 2:324.

47. George Q. Cannon, "Topics of the Times," *Juvenile Instructor*, 15 Dec. 1883, 377.

48. Journal of Jesse Crosby, 14 and 16 August 1847, LDS Church Archives. At least 14 "Mormon soldiers" of the Battalion who had left the pioneer camp at Green River had met up with the emigration camp on 4 August, "looking heathy and in good spirits." They knew nothing, however, about the valley (Journal of Eliza R. Snow, 4 Aug. 1847).

49. "Daily History of the George Benjamin Wallace Emigrating Co.," recorded by J. C. Kingsbury, clerk, 17 Aug. 1847, LDS Church Archives.

50. Journal History, 17 Aug. 1847.

51. John Taylor to Brigham Young and Council from La Prele Creek, 35 miles east of the Ferry, Journal History, 18 Aug. 1847. Taylor went on to tell of their recent serious loss of cattle and the subsequent slower than expected progress.

52. Journal of Perrigrine Sessions, late Aug. 1847.

53. Journal of Wilford Woodruff, 4 Sept. 1847.

54. General Church Minutes, 3–4 Sept. 1847.

55. Or as Bullock put it: "Obtained from Staines his minutes and reports. Found minutes of a meeting of 25th June last, which fully corroborated the President's views of last night" (Journal of Thomas Bullock, 4 Sept. 1847).

56. General Church Minutes, 4 Sept. 1847. See also Journal History, 4 Sept. 1847.

57. Pratt's description of the proceedings is helpful. Among others things, he wrote: "A council was called, in which I was highly censured and chastened by President Young and others. This arose in part from some defect in the organization under my superintendence at the Elkhorn, and in part from other misunderstandings on the road. . . . I no doubt deserved this chastisement; and I humbled myself, acknowledged my faults and errors and asked forgiveness. I was frankly forgiven, and, bidding each other farewell, each company passed on their way. This school of experience made me more humble and careful in future, and I think it was the means of making me a wiser and better man ever after" (*Autobiography of Parley P. Pratt*, 359–60).

58. Journal of Wilford Woodruff, 12 Oct. 1847. Concluded Woodruff: "Whatever the Lord inspires you to do in this matter I am with you." (Ibid.)

59. General Church Minutes, 13 Aug. 1847.

60. General Church Minutes, 23 May 1847.

61. I have gone to some lengths to discuss these prairie council meetings for the very reason that they have been misunderstood and misrepresented in the past. Samuel W. Taylor, for instance, in his biography of John Taylor (*The Kingdom or Nothing: The Life of John Taylor, Militant Mormon* [1976]), mistakenly argues that the reason Brigham Young was so upset was "not that his authority had been flouted, but that actually he didn't *have* the authority, thanks primarily to Taylor and Pratt. Taylor reminded Brigham that he wasn't president of the church, and that the Twelve, as a body, governed the Society of Saints" (134).

Actually, as president and senior member of the Quorum of the Twelve Apostles, Brigham did have authority to direct his colleagues—and to chastise them. And they knew it. Samuel Taylor not only misread this critical point but misses on several other issues as well, including his argument that Pratt and Taylor clashed with Brigham over the need to travel up the north, rather than the south, bank of the Platte River.

Likewise, Reva Stanley, in her biography of Parley Pratt (*The Archer of Paradise: A Biography of Parley P. Pratt* [1937]), at best simplifies a complex matter. She argues that the biggest cause of debate was Pratt's earlier plural marriages without permission. While this was clearly a factor, the consent of Brigham Young, at least in the matter of plural marriages, was not yet well understood. The issue was representative of the bigger problem before them—whether or not a new court of supreme ecclesiastical authority—the First Presidency—should not now be reestablished.

62. Horne, "Pioneer Reminiscences," 293. See also Journal of Wilford Woodruff, 7 Sept. 1847.

63. Hughes, *Life of Archibald Gardner*, 7 Sept. 1847, 40.

64. Journal of Eliza R. Snow, 7 Sept. 1847.

65. Pratt, "The Pratt Story," in *Our Pioneer Heritage*, 17:226.

IO

"WE HAVE BEEN IN THE VALLEY TO SET THE BIG WHEEL TO WORK"

The cause of Zion is brightening, and the mobbing and driving of the Saints will all lend to hasten their final gathering together. Our removes thus far have tended to the diminution of our substance, and also that of many others of the brethren, but we believe the Lord will still open the way again, soon as it shall be his will for us to go, which we anticipate shall be in a short time.[1]

A s watchful eyes of relief parties dispatched from the Salt Lake Valley eagerly awaited the first canyon sighting of the jostling wagons of the approaching Emigration Camp, a thousand miles to the east, 10,000 anxious Latter-day Saints worried and waited. Their summer had been long and hot, and their rich farmland had brought them an abundant harvest of grain and vegetables that, unlike the year before, assured them of all the provisions they would need for the coming winter. The Lord had been good to them, they were quick to say. But they wondered what news lay just beyond their western horizons.

It was an excited but exhausted Phineas Young, with three companions, who arrived back in Winter Quarters first, the evening of 2 October. But he was not so tired that he could not preach to an overflow outdoor crowd the following day. After sharing the news of the discovery of the Salt Lake

Valley, he called for relief missions to help the struggling oxen team party and, further back, the company of the Twelve somewhere out along the Platte.[2]

The Twelve, meanwhile, after quitting John Taylor's wagon lines on the high Sweetwater, made the return journey in relatively good time—67 days total from the valley—without serious incident, although they were very fatigued and perilously low on provisions. Due to some misunderstanding, the returning ox and hunting parties that had been instructed to wait for them at Grand Island had gone ahead. What transpired next was little less than a prairie rescue. Some 90 miles out of Winter Quarters on 18 October, Hosea Stout and several others met up with them "with the determination to find out what was become of us." The result was, in Brigham's words, "they gladdened our hearts and caused our souls to rejoice even as much as though sixteen Heavenly messengers had come down to congratulate us in our return from the arduous enterprise and to comfort us in the hour of fatigue."[3]

Two weeks later, Bishop Newel K. Whitney, Alpheus Cutler, and a dozen others awaited them at the Liberty Pole at the Elkhorn "with abundance of provisions." "Brother Brigham looked very thin," reported one observer, "and others from their exposure and hardships felt fatigued."[4]

The next day, 31 October, the Mormon leader made his final speech of the campaign short and precise:

> Brethren I will just say to the Pioneers I want you to receive my thanks for your kind service and willingness to obey orders. I am satisfied with you as you have [labored] with me and the Twelve. The boys have done first rate. We've accomplished more than we expected. Out of 143 men, all are well. Not a man died. . . . The blessings of the Lord have been with us.[5]

Late that afternoon, their wagons rolled into Winter Quarters. The streets were crowded with people who had come out to shake hands with the returning pioneers, who were anxious to see wives and children once again. Woodruff recalled:

> Each one drove to his own home. I drove up to my own door and was truly rejoiced to once more behold the face of my wife and children again after being absent over six months and having traveled with the Twelve and the pioneers near 2,500 miles and sought

Willard Richards

out a location for the Saints and accomplished one of the most interesting missions ever accomplished at the last days.[6]

But there was no time to celebrate—that would come later. A crowded agenda awaited Church leaders as they reassembled, after a few days of needed rest, at Willard Richards's octagon house in Winter Quarters. A decision had to be made immediately about evacuating Winter Quarters and turning over their lands and improvements to the local Omaha and Otoe Indian tribes.

There was also a desperate need to raise funds, from both within and without the Church, to underwrite the costs of future migrations of as many members as possible, most of whom were more anxious than prepared to make the journey. Likewise, the call to gather to the Great Basin had to be distributed quickly by printing press and word of mouth to the entire scattered membership: all the way across Iowa; in the many branches of the Church in Illinois, Wisconsin, the South, and the East; and to the British Isles. Finally, the time was ripe to reorganize the Church, to set in place a new leadership that would free the Twelve and the Seventy to fulfil once again their missionary duties throughout the world.

These three issues—evacuating Winter Quarters, promoting the valley as the place of gathering, and the reordering of Church government— would absorb the minds and energies of almost everyone during the coming winter months.

"I AM IN FAVOR OF VACATING THIS PLACE"

The Mormon city of Winter Quarters, Nebraska's first, on a site later occupied by Florence, a northern suburb of Omaha, was never intended to be a permanent settlement. It was a necessary compromise with the wilderness and the delayed march of the pioneers across Iowa. Rather than risk the exodus of his people with too late a start, Brigham had decided to quarter his people at the Missouri River, on the west side to eliminate a springtime crossing of a river filled with runoff. His decision was made all the more compelling with the enlistment of the Mormon Battalion. And at Captain James Allen's request, he negotiated a tentative agreement with the United States government to settle temporarily on Indian lands owned then by both the Omaha and Otoe Indian tribes.[7]

Although the Mormons had negotiated a treaty with both tribes to remain on the land for two years in return for certain favors and services, the Office of Indian Affairs frowned on the idea and continually tried to terminate the agreement. While the government took more than enough criticism for its stance, in truth it seemed most concerned about the possibility of bloodshed and inciting further friction between two already angry, dispossessed tribes. The Indians themselves were insistent on the Mormon removal and the recent killing of Weatherby underscored the fact that an agreement must soon be made.

By November 1847 it was clear that Winter Quarters would have to be vacated the following spring and its 4,000 citizens choose either to go west with the 1848 migration or to move east back across the river. The prospect of moving into Iowa was made more palatable because of the recent abandonment of that area by the Pottawattamie Indians and the imminent extension of Iowa Territory to the Missouri River. "I am in favor of vacating this place," Brigham proposed in council, "and the brethren draw their houses over the river" the following spring. Or, as Orson Pratt put it: "I motion that every man and family who cannot go West, go into the state of Iowa and settle where they may until they can fit themselves out for the mountains."[8] Although some were convinced that a total evacuation might signal a Sioux massacre of the Omaha, the general consensus was otherwise and "to remove over the river as soon as they can." The new site proposed on the Iowa side was Miller's Hollow, six miles from "where four small streams descend through a table land to Keg Creek,"—a "natural place for a town," as Orson Hyde remembered it.[9]

Rather than construct a new city, however, it was determined to spread the settlements out over a much larger area and to concentrate on farming and erecting other improvements. In the process the new settlements would become a breadbasket and a fitting-out center for future migrations of incoming Latter-day Saints. And unlike Nauvoo and Winter Quarters, when time came to sell off their properties, they would realize a favorable return and even a respectable profit. "If the design is to sell improvements," said George A. Smith, "it will be best to scatter all over the country for farms; then they may be sold."[10]

At the time, Winter Quarters consisted of 700 to 800 houses of varying size and quality, "mechanical shops of sufficient kinds, shelters, stables, a water driven grist mill and one or two other mills propelled by horse power."[11] Despite the prospect of losing their many improvements, the local citizens approved the plan of abandonment unanimously at a public meeting on 14 November; they were convinced that the eastern bank would be a healthier, safer place than Winter Quarters had been.

When April came, most of the settlers who were not going west began leaving the city to resettle in one of some 40 new settlements all clustered within a radius of 30 to 40 miles of Miller's Hollow. This they soon christened Kanesville in honor of Colonel Thomas L. Kane and his ready support of the Mormon cause in the halls of political power back in Washington.[12] By the autumn of 1848, Winter Quarters was a deserted memory looking "pretty much as it did," remembered George A. Smith,

> except the roofs and floors which had been brought to this side of the river. The Indians visited it of late and feasted on the potatoes that grew in the old cellars, and also upon the Indian corn and the volunteer squash and such other vegetables as grew without culture. . . . Winter Quarters afforded more flies and fleas than anything less than a stargazer could well estimate.[13]

"THIS PEOPLE ARE CALLED TO REVOLUTIONIZE THE WORLD"

The matter of relinquishing Winter Quarters to the Indians now decided, leaders turned their attention to other pressing issues of much longer-lasting consequence. The immediate priority was to disseminate quickly and broadly the news of the valley. Despite such severe cold that the clerks could not write the exact wording of each sermon, large numbers assembled at the stand at Winter Quarters to listen to a combination of happy persuasion and heavy directive.

"We filled the mission that we were sent to do and come home humble and like little children," reported Ezra T. Benson.

The Lord God of Israel has been with us. Shall we now sit down and give up the ship? We have a good man at the helm. No, let us arise and have more perseverance than we ever did before. . . . That valley is a place reserved by the Almighty for this people. We have been tried in poverty and sickness. Now you are going to be tried in riches, in homes, farms and vineyards. . . . You may as well have it all. We have gold, warmth, salt, soil, tar and springs. We have been in the valley to set the big wheel to work and that sets all the little wheels whirling. . . . We have now laid the foundation for our coming day.[14]

Amasa Lyman referred to it "as the best place to keep the command- ments of God that we have ever been in. I have no uneasiness about the place of rest but my anxiety now is to get the people there."[15]

Brigham Young then followed.

I am perfectly satisfied with the mission. I rejoice in it. Many of the Saints have witnesses to what I told them in Nauvoo that I would lead them to a healthy country. It has been highly extolled. It is the will of the Lord for us to repair to the spot. After travelling for months through grease, wood and sage, mountains and barren rocks, the place there looks beautiful to me. . . . That country is not for any but Mormons.[16]

The picture of a healthier climate scored well. Kimball said "he was not going to flatter the country but would tell it as it is," but rushed to compare the valley with their Missouri winter settlement. "It seems to me [like] a person living in a four story building in the upper room all finished off in good style and the comforts of life and then move down in a cellar where it is damp and chilly and sickly; that is the contrast between the valley and this place here in Winter Quarters."[17]

The need was critical to promote the news to the widespread member- ship in order to dampen the continuing tide of defection and to gather the Church to the Missouri. To this end, the Twelve drafted a "General Epistle" to the Saints in December 1847 and printed it in St. Louis the month fol- lowing. Aimed at disciple and detractor alike, the document cut swiftly to the quick.

What shall we do?

Gather yourselves together speedily, near to this place, on the east side of the Missouri River, and, if possible, be ready to start from hence by the first of May next, or as soon as grass is sufficient. . . . Let the Saints who have been driven and scattered from Nauvoo, and all others in the western states, gather immediately to the east bank of the river . . . ; and let all the Saints in the United States and Canada gather to the same place, by the first spring navigation, or as soon as they can, bringing their money, goods, and effects with them. . . .

To the Saints in England, Scotland, Ireland, Wales, and adjacent islands and countries, we say, emigrate as speedily as possible to this vicinity, looking to and following the counsel of the Presidency at Liverpool; shipping to New Orleans, and from thence direct to Council Bluffs, which will save much expense. . . . And to all Saints in any country bordering upon the Atlantic, we would say, pursue the same course. . . .

For the time has come for the Saints to go up to the mountains of the Lord's house, and help to establish it upon the tops of the mountains.[18]

The above was more than invitation or mild request: it was a proclamation to gather, an expectation bordering on directive, an urgent call for Latter-day Saints everywhere to "leave Babylon" and consolidate the strength of the Church in a new mountain stronghold. Like generals in battle needing to concentrate their forces and like shepherds worried about lost and straying sheep, they clearly recognized that for its survival, the Church had to circle the wagons, to replant and rebuild and in the process reinterpret itself for another new day.

But the question was, who would bear the cost? While some might be able to afford moving west, most could not. Tithing submissions were at low ebb among a people out of work and on the move. Battalion pay was all but spent and no other government contracts were in the works, despite the best efforts of Thomas L. Kane. Neither could they expect a dime from relinquishing Winter Quarters. The only possible options were to canvass the Church membership back east and to beg for assistance from an American public clearly unsympathetic towards this strange people. It would be no small undertaking. (See chapter 11.)

Such destitute conditions called for desperate and decisive action. "To the rich saints in the United States" is how Brigham began his letter distributed 7 December, which was obviously designed to accompany their General Epistle.

> The Camp of Israel in the wilderness is in want; the hands of the servants of the Lord are stayed for lack of means; the operations of the Church are paralysed with poverty, but the time for the Lord to favor Zion is at hand. . . . Send us of your substance, that the poor may be blessed, the sick relieved, the hungry fed, the naked clothed, and the camp may move forward to their destination. Send us of your substance . . . not by farthings, by pence and by shillings, but by hundreds and thousands and by tens of thousands. . . . The time has verily come to favor Zion and help must be had, for the Lord designs it.

Characteristic of so many others of his letters, Brigham was quick to add a concluding warning: "If you refuse or neglect this our call . . . and prove not your faith by your works, . . . the spirit will take its departure from your souls; your light will be turned into darkness, and you will ere long be left to mourn that your money has perished with you."[19]

But what good is a message without its messengers? Worn out and tired though they obviously were, many of the leaders faced the daunting task of going as far east on missions that coming winter as they had just traveled west to the Rockies. They also had to call many sick and weary settlers on both sides of the river to head back as missionaries to where many of them had come from. Once more, sacrifice knew no bounds. Fortunately, with the harvest in, many could see their way to go.

There was talk of a general missionary call as early as 15 November, and likely far sooner. "I feel that we ought to keep the big wheel agoing," Brigham had said earlier and that volunteers were needed to go "apreaching" and to gather the people.[20] George A. Smith was quick to respond: "My feelings are to go over the mountains, but I am quite ready to go anywhere." Said Orson Pratt: "I feel like roaring, as I have something to roar about."[21] Five days later, the first mission calls were extended to Winslow Farr, W. W. Major, and George W. Harris to go to Terra Haute, Indiana; Phineas Young and Jonathan C. Wright to try their hand with a reconsidering Oliver Cowdery; and scores to go elsewhere.[22] Soon a list of over 30 high priests and 80 seventies was drawn up, and a general plea went out by letter and over the pulpit.[23]

And woe to those who pleaded the care of farm or family above service. Preached Amasa Lyman:

> Some men, in getting a little farm, their whole soul and entire man are swallowed up in a 160 acres of land at the footstool of the Almighty. Men do not appreciate the calling unto what they are called. . . . This people are called to revolutionize the world . . . they have to turn the world inside up, turn the veil inside out. . . . Let us wake up and if you are going to be Latter-day Saints wake up and don't be swallowed up in a little patch of 160 acres. I don't want to be swallowed up in anything less than the redemption of the world. The cause of Mormonism will wash you up on your little farm and it will run over your farm and you, too. The Lord don't care much about you or your farm if you get in the way. It is bound to travel onward and go the tops of the mountains and if Zion gets in a low place, it is the highest low place there is in the earth.[24]

By late December 100 to 125 men had heeded the call and were on the road—again.

"It Is in Me like Seven Thunders Rolling"

The other critical concern was to reorganize the Church, specifically to reinstitute the First Presidency. By late 1847, the onus was on the Quorum of the Twelve to show why Brigham Young, the oldest and senior member of the Quorum, should not be called and ordained to the office of President of the Church, a position that had been vacant since the death of Joseph Smith in 1844. As shown earlier, the issue had been discussed repeatedly but without resolution.

In a series of remarkable meetings over a three-week period between 15 November and early December the wheel turned. One reason for the change was the missions that the Apostles and others would have to serve. "From the time I have been in the Great Salt Lake till now," Brigham said, "the whisperings of the Spirit to me [are] for the Church to be now organized and it whispers to the Church if there is a God in Mormonism . . . to prove to the devils in men that we are just willing to do what the Lord wants us to do. Now is this question to be answered."[25]

The matter was very much on his mind in the Salt Lake Valley and later in the return meetings with Pratt and Taylor. And all the way back to

Winter Quarters, he had put the question to each of his traveling companions "concerning one of the Twelve Apostles being appointed as the President of the Church with his two counselors."[26]

The full account of Brigham's appointment has been chronicled elsewhere.[27] Nevertheless, it is instructive to understand the several issues involved. Of the surviving, active Apostles at Joseph's death, Lyman Wight had gone to Texas to settle his fugitive company of followers. Wight entertained no thought of returning to the Saints. John E. Page (replaced by Ezra T. Benson) was now solidly in Strang's camp. William Smith remained back in Illinois vacillating between going with Strang or combining with Brigham. Parley P. Pratt and Taylor were now in the valley. That left only eight Apostles to ratify and sustain such a major change.

Although it may always be a point of controversy between the divergent traditions of the "restoration movement," those Apostles who gathered at Winter Quarters in November 1847 fully believed that they had received the "keys of the priesthood" or governing ecclesiastical authority from Joseph Smith, as an administrative body equal in authority to the First Presidency, though held in dormancy until that higher quorum was dissolved.

What they did not understand was the urgent need to reorganize and how soon it should be done. Most felt that the Twelve were administering the affairs of the Church well enough. There was also resistance to breaking up the unity they obviously enjoyed. Some of them worried, frankly, over how their quorum president had never hesitated to chastise and correct them, in both private and public settings, and wondered what might happen if he were given more authority. Most importantly, this group of men who so devoutly believed they were on a divine errand required inspiration, if not revelation, to make such a change.

Tempering their reluctance, however, were several realities. It was understood that James Strang, the Voree prophet, was still counting points among disenchanted believers for having already organized his own first presidency. One of their first items of business once back at the Missouri was to hear briefings on Strang's progress. And despite the wording in their General Epistle that "many false prophets and teachers . . . [have] run their race undisturbed [and] have died natural deaths, or committed suicides,"[28] the matter of defection and apostasy was a real concern.

Their recent decision to send missionaries on winter assignments to the east would severely limit the decision-making powers of a depleted quorum. There was also uneasiness over abuses in the practice of plural marriage and the emerging consensus that a First Presidency was best equipped to handle these delicate matters with authority. And if there had been any hope that one of Joseph Smith's own sons might immigrate with them and perhaps take his place in the quorum, by now it was clear that no such possibility existed.

In retrospect, the tone of discussions had changed with the discovery of the Salt Lake Valley. Joseph Smith had staked his leadership by prophecy and revelation, and Brigham continued in that tradition, proving his claim through mud and mountain. None questioned his industry, integrity, or shrewd political savvy. His status grew the further west they traveled. As Orson Pratt put it: "There is no man in this Quorum who I respect more than Brother Young, and no man that I would wish sooner to be at the head. . . . He has a great anxiety on his mind and although I consider I have seen errors in him, I feel that I could lay down my life for him."[29] It may well be argued that the discovery of the valley was an essential precursor to the restoration of the First Presidency.

All things considered, none could any longer resist Brigham's arguments that as president of the quorum he was already the foremost leader in the Church, that the authority and responsibility rested in them to reorganize the Church, and that the complexities of the time demanded it. "If my lot is to preside over the church," he said, "must I eternally be asking when should I speak? If this body is the head of the church, I am the head of the Quorum, I am the mouthpiece and you are the belly."[30] Or, as he said on a later occasion, "You can't make me President because I am President. You can't give me more power because I have it." And further: "It is in me like seven thunders rolling. . . . I love this quorum as I love my eyes. . . . I know what it is to have a First Presidency. God has brought us where we are and we have got to do it, and if the devil can get us to decide we will not have a First Presidency, [or] if you throw the Kingdom into the Quorum of Fifty they can't manage it and the Seventies can't do it."[31]

Perhaps Ezra T. Benson, the junior member of the quorum, captured best the growing unanimity of feelings.

> I have not exchanged a word with Brigham on the matter. I feel now . . . that everything is right and it is hard to get it wrong. . . . I

have a testimony that he is called of God. My conscience is perfectly clear and my feelings the same as they ever have been. I am willing to lift him up a peg. That's my private and public feelings. The arguments that have been used are gone. The time has come and it may as well be done now as any other. I can act tonight [5 December] as well as any time. As the revelation says "It is of necessity."

. . . It is plain to me as the nose on my face. I have as much power as I can deal with. I will not carry any burden that grinds in here. The Kingdom of God is a Kingdom of light and truth and we have enough. . . . I came in [the quorum] like Abram going from his house not knowing why I came. I was tapped on the head like a shot of electricity. If I did not keep watch ahead as John E. Page said it's hell and damnation all around. I am tormented all the while if I did not do right. I am not concerned but that the Lord will carry on the work and that all will be right. I could not get it into my mind that God would send an angel, call one of his servants, and then suffer one ignoramus to lead away the people to the Devil. I would not worship such a God and I believe God would remove our head out of its place. I am here and I am willing to act. . . . I want to keep with the quorum of the Twelve and I mean to stick with Brother Brigham.[32]

After some further private discussion, Heber C. Kimball motioned and Wilford Woodruff seconded that Brigham Young be sustained as President of the Church. All others voted in the affirmative. To Orson Pratt's suggestion that he select two counselors, Brigham nominated Heber C. Kimball and Willard Richards. The meeting then adjourned for supper and quiet celebration until 11:30 P.M.

It was further decided not to wait until April conference, as would normally have been the case, but to hold a special assembly as soon as possible because most of them were about to disperse east on missions. Furthermore, the call to gather would be strengthened by the calling of a new President. The best time for such a conference would be around Christmas, since many of the Saints were coming to the Bluffs from further settlements then to be with family and friends.

An important ancillary question was where to convene the conference, which would surely attract a large audience. There was no building large enough in Winter Quarters, and holding a conference outdoors in January would negatively affect attendance.

Log Tabernacle, *a painting by Katie Gregory*
(Used courtesy of Katie Gregory, Omaha, Nebraska)

Recognizing that the largest meetinghouse then available, Silas Richards's double blockhouse some 10 miles southeast of Winter Quarters on the Iowa side, would be entirely inadequate, that same night the Twelve directed Henry W. Miller, a leading settler on the Iowa side, to erect a tabernacle. Highly regarded and an original member of the Pottawattamie High Council, Miller immediately went to work on an edifice large enough to fit the need. About "200 gave their names to go to work immediately at it" despite the winter cold—some cut and others hauled the large cotton-wood logs from over three miles away; the rest fashioned the construction.[33] The happy result on the evening of 23 December was that the building was completed—and with one day to spare! The finished structure pleased almost everyone. It was, for its time, a wonderfully large cottonwood log tabernacle 65 feet long by 40 feet wide, complete with newly hewn benches, stoves for heating on all sides, a large fireplace, several doors, glass windows, and a smooth floor—"an ornament to this new country."[34] As one proud settler put it: "Such is the industry and perseverance of the Saints, that whatever they undertake they soon accomplished."[35]

So it was that a four-day special conference convened in the new tabernacle at Miller's Hollow (later Kanesville) from 24 through 27 December, for instruction, song, inspiration, and dance. There were talks on the pending 1848 migrations and appointments of new captains; the need for missionaries; where those from Winter Quarters would settle on the east side; the Nauvoo Covenant; temple work; the importance of gathering to the valley; and the need to stay clear of Strang, Lyman Wight, and other detractors.

But it was the final Sunday session that everyone was impatient to attend. Over 1,000 people crammed into their new quarters, filling every corner; many spread out on buffalo robes on the floor, pushing up against the band and the choir. After John Kay, with violin accompaniment, had sung William Clayton's already beloved prairie anthem, "Come, Come, Ye Saints," Orson Pratt took the stand.

"We have been able to overcome apostates and the powers of darkness," he began,

> with the highest quorum taken away out of our midst. How much more shall we be able to overcome them when we have all the quorums flourishing. . . . The time has come when the Twelve must have their hands liberated to go to the ends of the earth.[36]

George A. Smith followed, saying when Joseph and Hyrum were martyred, "the Twelve had a right to nominate a Presidency or go ahead without one." Amasa Lyman continued the theme by saying "the interests of the [church] can't be served any longer without a President. The work is faltering for want of the servants of the Lord being set free. He who furnishes the materials is the man. He is at the head already. He has been acknowledged for years."[37]

Then, on motion of Elisha H. Grover, seconded by W. W. Major, the name of Brigham Young was presented for a sustaining vote as President of the Church, with Heber C. Kimball and Willard Richards as first and second counselors. A thousand hands were raised, without a single dissenting vote.

"There is nothing more done this day than I knew at the death of Joseph," Brigham said in his acceptance remarks. "Joseph told the Twelve 'There is not one principle or key to enter in the celestial kingdom but I have given you. . . . The kingdom is set up and you have the perfect pattern and you can lead the Kingdom in at the gate. I am going to rest.'" The meeting concluded with the entire congregation singing "The Spirit of God Like a Fire is Burning," ending with the sacred hosanna chorus shout reserved for such sacred occasions.[38]

"The Brethren Enjoyed Themselves First Rate"

The new year found the Latter-day Saints enjoying a sense of confidence they had not known since the early days of Nauvoo. A year before they were in a crisis, suffering and dying in epidemic numbers at Winter Quarters and all along their Iowa trail. Most had lost almost everything in Nauvoo. Their wanderings across Iowa had exacted the harshest toll. The call for the Battalion had drained them of sorely needed manpower at the most inconvenient of times. And through it all they had waited and wondered whether or not the mountain west really did hold promise and redemption.

Now so much had changed. Their fall harvests proved marvelously abundant. Their health was vastly improved. The mountain west was now a beckoning reality. The Battalion had completed its march to the Pacific and some—at least 47 of them—had already returned, despite the worst of conditions.[39] A new First Presidency had been reestablished and the Church was on firm footing once again. The long, dark night of persecution and hardship was at last giving way to renewed hope.

William Appleby, returning to the Bluffs in early December 1847 after an extended absence as presiding elder over the eastern U.S. branches, captured well the new upbeat tone:

> Ever since we entered Iowa [from Missouri] we have beheld, scattered along, the log houses of the brethren who were driven from Nauvoo by a cruel mob about 18 months ago. And indeed the country shows the industry of the Saints that their enemies cannot gainsay. Farms, fenced off in nearly every direction, some fields containing a hundred acres or more. . . . Corn, wheat, buckwheat, potatoes, cabbage, turnips, pumpkins, squashes, etc., have been raised, and they have cut and secured plenty of hay. Their cattle look well and everything else throughout the camps, considering the situation and circumstances they were placed in when they arrived here, looks comfortable and the prospect cheering.[40]

Optimism was in the winter air—an eager anticipation of the coming spring migrations—and a budding conviction that all might yet turn out. In short, it was a time to celebrate.

What happened at Miller's Hollow in the dead of winter is another example of pioneer optimism and the need to express it. Lasting five days from 16–20 January, the Seventies Jubilee held in the new log tabernacle caught the attention of Mormon and non-Mormon alike. Military officers came all the way from Fort Kearny to participate. Announced the last day of the succession conference, the Jubilee was touted as a time for all the Latter-day Saints, from Winter Quarters all the way back to Garden Grove, to assemble for instruction and exhortation, song and dance, celebration and congratulation.

Their largest gathering since the last days of Nauvoo, the Jubilee also provided leaders the ideal opportunity to promote the valley, organize the 1848 migration companies, call missionaries, and gather together enough signatures on a petition to establish their own post office and organize a new county—Pottawattamie—in western Iowa. Having lost most of their properties in Nauvoo and, to a lesser extent, in Winter Quarters, it would be best to ensure legal protection for their Iowa settlements and future improvements. To this end, Andrew Perkins and Henry W. Miller were appointed delegates to present the petition to organize a county, recently signed by 1,805 male members, to the Iowa legislature.[41]

Everyone agreed to call it a jubilee—everyone, that is, except their new President. "I attended meetings held on the 16th, 17th, 18th, 19th, and 20th in the Log Tabernacle, Miller's Hollow," Brigham recorded, "convened by the Seventies, which they called a Jubilee; but I told them it could not be considered a Jubilee spoken of in the revelation, for all bands were not broken, and I called it a jubilo." He went on to say, "The Saints enjoyed themselves first rate."[42]

His objections notwithstanding, the Jubilee (except for the first day of Sabbath preaching) consisted each day of speaking and instruction until mid-afternoon, followed by a sumptuous feast provided by the various branches from all over the settlements and concluded each night with concerts and dances. William Pitt's brass band provided most of the music. John M. Kay, the favorite singer of the camps, sang several times during these festivities, as did other singers and choirs. Since not all could fit into their tabernacle, now being used as a festival hall, most of the 5,000 to 6,000 who attended came at preassigned intervals and stayed for one or two days.

Strict rules were made on who could participate and on standards of behavior. For instance, the local high council ordered that "the marshall shall take any person who shall be found intoxicated or having liquor around this house during the meetings of the Jubilee and shall detain them until he or she shall pay one dollar."[43]

None were more pleased to hear about the Jubilee than the young people. To their way of thinking, it was way past time to have some fun and to get together to meet that pretty young lady or that fair-haired young man seen back along the trail. To the consternation of many a parent, some had already been going elsewhere for the privilege, attending "Gentile" dances down at Trader's Point, a few miles south of Miller's Hollow. And it was obvious that the arrival of so many young, beautiful Mormon women was attracting the attention of nearby soldiers and traders.

"We had a grand ball given me on my return from Grand Island," A. W. Sublette, a non-Mormon soldier, recorded on his return to Fort Kearny in December 1847.

> We have plenty of pretty girls on the opposite side of the river and 20 or 30 miles above this at the Mormon Town there is cords of them. They are moving down and settling round us hunting work such as have no other scenes of support. There is one at Boonville which takes them all. As I passed through there last summer she presented me with a handsome bouquet and a handsome little article since then. There is others near your home whom I have not nor will not forget.[44]

Dancing proved problematic for many of the older generation, particularly those of stern, Puritan-like New England background. And if their new president had not approved, there likely would not have been any. The serious-minded Woodruff, for instance, could hardly take it in:

> While there is so much depending upon us and our prayers, should we be satisfied with the record of this city of the Saints in the eternal world kept by the angels of heaven if we should hear read before an assembled world that the inhabitants of Winter Quarters, who were the Lord's anointed, . . . spent nine days of their time fiddling and dancing where they did one in prayer and praise to Almighty God?[45]

But Brigham would hear none of it. "It is perfectly right to dance," he said just days before the happy gathering, "but it is very wicked to sin. I council the people not to go to the dance tomorrow at the Point [Trader's Point] that is getting up by the soldiers there . . . if you want to dance, dance on this floor. . . . I would not go there and dance, God forbid, but I would come and dance with you."[46] "Everything that is calculated to fill the soul with joy is ordained of God and is proper for the Saints," he said at the opening of the Jubilee, "if they acknowledge God in all things and do not sin. But don't mingle with the wicked world and sin but serve the Lord with it. . . . You will never see any music or dancing in hell."[47]

Describing their good times, the ever-positive Irene Hascall wrote that

the Mormons . . . do not have any guess work in their exercises. They have a rule and the order of God for all their movements. They open their school with prayer and so they always do at their dancing parties or feasts. They have all the good and fat things they can procure for supper. I never saw a larger supply at any place. . . . There is some of the smartest and best men and women here there is in the world.[48]

And so it was that they made merry in the wilderness or, as their leader put it, "We had a blessed meeting—all hearts were comforted and lifted up above our trials and persecutions."[49]

Their good times did not end with the Jubilee. Several parties were held in February, including one hosted by those who had fought in the Battle of Nauvoo in September 1846. A special "figure was got up called the Battle of Nauvoo which was danced" by all who came and, as they had done in the several skirmishes, those who had worn red badges to distinguish themselves from their enemies did so again on the dance floor.[50] Later another dance, a Mormon Battalion Ball, was also held in the log tabernacle to celebrate the accomplishments and safe return of so many soldiers.[51]

The general conference of the Church convened at the log tabernacle in April 1848 for three days; final preparations were then put in place for the pending migration. Early in June, Brigham once again left for the valley, never again to return east, this time at the head of a combined camp of some 1,891 people for the valley. For at least the next four years, Kanesville served as the jumping off place for several thousand Latter-day Saints.

NOTES

1. Brigham Young to Alexander Badlam, 18 Nov. 1847, Brigham Young Papers.
2. Throughout October, others of the original pioneer camp arrived back, includ-

ing John Smith and Tunis Rappleye on 21 October and John Pack on 24 October (Historical Department Journals, 3–30 Oct. 1847).

3. Brigham Young to Parley P. Pratt, John Taylor, and the President of the Stake of Zion and High Council of the Great Salt Lake, 17 July 1847, Brigham Young Papers.

4. Historical Department Journals, 30 Oct. 1847.

5. General Church Minutes, 31 Oct. 1847, 3 P.M.

6. Journal of Wilford Woodruff, 31 Oct. 1847. See also Journal History, 31 Oct. 1847.

7. See chapter 2. See also Bennett, *Mormons at the Missouri*, 166–67.

8. Meeting of the Twelve and others, 8 and 9 Nov. 1847, Brigham Young Papers.

9. Ibid.

10. Meeting of the Twelve, 9 Nov. 1847, Brigham Young Papers. This proved to be a most sanguine expectation, because the discovery of California gold was only weeks away, and by 1849 the Gold Rush was in full throttle. Many argonauts eventually flooded the territory, enriching the local economies as no one in 1847 could have possibly anticipated (see Unruh, *The Plains Across*, 68, also 302–32).

11. Journal of William I. Appleby, 9 Dec. 1847, LDS Church Archives.

12. Journal History, 8 Apr. 1848. At the April conference of the Church in Iowa Territory, Orson Hyde motioned that "the place hitherto known as Miller's Hollow [be] named Kanesville in honor of Col. Thomas L. Kane who had ever been a true friend of the saints."

For more on these settlements, see Bennett, *Mormons at the Missouri*, 215–28. See also Gail George Holmes, "The LDS Legacy in Southwestern Iowa," *Ensign*, Aug. 1988, 54–57.

13. Manuscript History of Winter Quarters, 20 Oct. 1848, LDS Church Archives.

14. Minutes of an outdoor Sunday morning meeting at Winter Quarters, 14 Nov. 1847.

15. Ibid.

16. Ibid.

17. Journal of Joseph G. Hovey, 28 Oct. 1847, 47, LDS Church Archives.

18. "General Epistle from the Council of the Twelve Apostles to The Church of Jesus Christ of Latter-day Saints Abroad," 23 Dec. 1847, LDS Church Archives. See also *Comprehensive History of the Church*, 3:308–15. The original manuscript version of this document is in the Brigham Young Papers.

19. Brigham Young to "the rich saints in the United States," Journal History, 6 Dec. 1847.

20. General Church Minutes, 13 Nov. 1847.

21. Meeting of the Twelve, 15 Nov. 1847, Brigham Young Papers.

22. Meeting of the Twelve, 20 Nov. 1847.

23. Manuscript History of Winter Quarters, 23 Nov. 1847.

24. Sermon given by Amasa Lyman, 24 December, General Church History Minutes, 23–27 December 1847.

25. Minutes of a meeting of the Twelve at Orson Hyde's home, Miller's Hollow, Iowa Territory, 5 Dec. 1847, Brigham Young Papers.

26. Journal of Wilford Woodruff, 12 Oct. 1847.

27. See Bennett, *Mormons at the Missouri*, 199–214. See also Esplin and Arrington, "The Role of the Council of the Twelve."

28. "General Epistle from the Council of the Twelve Apostles to The Church of Jesus Christ of Latter-day Saints Abroad," 23 Dec. 1847, LDS Church Archives.

29. Miscellaneous Trustees Minutes, 15 Nov. 1847.

30. Miscellaneous Trustees Minutes, 15–16 Nov. 1847.

31. Meeting of the Twelve, 5 Dec. 1847, Brigham Young Papers.

32. Minutes of a meeting with the Twelve, 5 Dec. 1847, Brigham Young Papers.

33. Journal of Wilford Woodruff, 4 Dec. 1847; see also the Journal of Warren Foote, 3 Dec. 1847; and Meeting of the Twelve and other leaders, 23 Dec. 1847, Brigham Young Papers.

34. Journal of Wilford Woodruff, 4 Dec. 1847. A splendid reconstruction of the log tabernacle was completed in 1996 in Council Bluffs, Iowa, a tribute to the faith, industry, and generosity of the Latter-day Saints in the region.

35. Journal of William I. Appleby, 23 Dec 1847. The Mormon log tabernacle was certainly one of the largest buildings in all of Iowa Territory, certainly in the western regions and, outside of the Kirtland and Nauvoo temples, one of the largest meeting places the Latter-day Saints had yet erected. It was almost certainly the inspiration for the later construction of the famous tabernacle on Temple Square in Salt Lake City, which was completed 20 years later.

One Forty-niner later "visited the inside of the Mormon council house. It looks very large inside with a fire place 20 feet long, columns like tree trunks" (Journal of William B. Lorton, 22 May 1849). It was not called the "Kanesville" log tabernacle until at least April 1848.

36. Minutes of meeting, 24–27 Dec. 1847, Brigham Young Papers. John Smith was also sustained as Church Patriarch, succeeding Hyrum Smith.

37. Ibid.

38. Ibid.

39. Philemon C. Merrill, along with 15 others, had left the valley on 15 October on horseback and arrived in Winter Quarters 11 December. Six days later, after suffering from severe exposure and malnutrition, 32 other soldiers limped into town. They had traveled almost 4,000 miles since their departure from the Bluffs 17 months before, and were anxious to be with wife and family once more (Journal History, 11 and 17 Dec. 1847).

The story of their travels home is worthy of note, at least in passing. On the morning of 18 December, rumor had it that a group of Battalion soldiers had arrived in Winter Quarters the evening before. Emily Bunker, wife of Edward Bunker, prepared to go and inquire. "Just before she was to leave the house," the record tells "a knock was heard at the door. It proved to be Edward himself. He thought they were still in Garden Grove where he left them, but someone told him they had moved since he left. He was almost frozen and starved. It was necessary for him to remain in bed for several weeks and he was fed gruel every few hours just a few spoonfuls at a time at first. He had endured terrible privation on the return journey and had completed one of the most difficult marches on record" (Lois E. Jones, "George Abbot and His Descendants," unpublished, Missouri Historical Society, 6).

40. Journal of William I. Appleby, as quoted in Journal History, 2 Dec. 1847.

41. Journal History, 16 Jan. 1848.

Perkins and Miller traveled to Iowa City soon afterward, returning 6 March with news that the creation of Pottawattamie County had already been approved "precisely according to the terms of petition" (Brigham Young to Parley P. Pratt and John Taylor, 17 July 1848).

Pottawattamie County was officially organized 24 September 1848 with William Pickett organizing sheriff (William Snow to Brigham Young, 8 Oct. 1848, Brigham Young Papers).

The first representative to the Iowa Assembly from the new Pottawattamie County was Henry W. Miller; the second was Archibald Bryant. The first clerk was James Sloan; the first commissioners was R. H. Perkins, David D. Yearley, and George Coulson. The first county judge was T. Burdick.

Despite efforts by both Whig and Democrat to court the sizeable Mormon vote, the Mormon leaders encouraged a nonpartisan stand. Their objective was to leave, not settle. As Brigham said on one occasion: "Our policy is to slide between wind and water and get away as fast as possible" (Journal History, 24 Mar. 1848).

After the 1852 exodus, the Mormon presence steadily declined as waves of new settlers brought out farms and improvements at very respectable prices never known at Nauvoo. Miller's Hollow was renamed Kanesville in April 1848 at the general conference of the Church, but it, too, was eventually changed to Council Bluffs. For some years it became a favored jumping off spot for the Oregon and California trails.

42. Journal History, 20 Jan. 1848. See also Brigham Young to Parley P. Pratt and John Taylor, 17 July 1848, Brigham Young Papers.

43. Minutes of the Pottawattamie High Council, 8 Jan. 1848.

44. A[ndrew] Sublette to a friend named "Francis," 4 Dec. 1847, Ft. Kearny, William L. Sublette Papers, Missouri Historical Society.

45. Journal of Wilford Woodruff, 13 Feb. 1848.

46. Meeting of the Twelve, 23 Dec. 1847.

47. Journal of Wilford Woodruff, 17 Jan. 1848. Another reason they would not be denied was Hiram Gate's popular Winter Quarters dancing school that, at its peak, enrolled 440 pupils, all eager to try out their new steps and enjoy the round dances of the day (see Journal History, 14 Mar. 1848).

48. Irene Hascall to Col. Wilson Andrews of New Salem, Massachusetts, April 1847, Hascall Collection, Missouri Historical Society and LDS Church Archives.

49. Brigham Young to Orson Spencer, 23 Jan. 1847, Brigham Young Papers.

50. Journal of Wilford Woodruff, 3 Feb. 1848.

51. Journal History, 1 Feb. 1848.

II

"THE OPERATIONS OF THE CHURCH ARE PARALYSED WITH POVERTY"

The Salvation Missions of 1847–48

> We probably shall remain in this place [Winter Quarters] until
> next May, if we should live so long and then start for the
> mountains. . . . I am also destitute of clothing. My old coat
> that I am now wearing is an old broad cloth . . . as to our
> cooking utensils we have one pot that we used up on our store,
> when we had one, one black kettle without a lid, . . . four or
> five old knives, [and] three old broken forks to eat with. As to
> earthen dishes we have none. We have four 3-pint tin basins
> which we brought with us from Massachusetts nearly rusted out
> so as to have holes in them, 3 or 4 tin pans, 2 or 3 tin plates,
> 3 britannia cups, one tin cup, one old tin coffee pot and [an] old
> tea pot. . . . I wish you would write me soon informing me
> what the prospect is of raising money for me. . . . We fell to the
> hands of the bishops and are still living on the means of others.[1]

So wrote a desperate Lyman Hinnman in the summer of 1847. And his condition was representative of hundreds of other families then living in Winter Quarters. Those who had gone ahead in the emigration camp were generally the better prepared and provisioned. For those waiting to follow, their uppermost question was simple: "Where will the money come from?" Even Brigham Young was forced to admit the painfully obvious: "The operations of the Church are paralysed with poverty."[2]

Little wonder, then, that the primary reason for the call for missionaries in November 1847, just after the return of the Twelve from the Salt Lake Valley, was to raise money—from anyone, anywhere.

"I wish that Andrew would send me all the money that he has collected of mine," wrote an anxious John A. Wolfe to his mother in New York in February 1847, "as I am going a long journey and I know not how much expense I may be to before I may again be settled upon a farm."[3]

Even the First Presidency was reduced to begging for help. "I am confined to my bed by sickness, and in debt," Willard Richards wrote David Hollister in the spring of 1848. "And I know of no one who has the means. I therefore send to [you], in the name of the Lord, for help, and this the more freely as I know you have the heart to do good . . . so that you can send me one thousand dollars, which will relieve me from my present encumbrances."[4]

The poverty alluded to by Hinnman was everywhere. "Our camp is almost universally destitute of sugar and all the comforts of life vested in groceries of any kind," admitted Brigham in a letter to Kane near the end of 1847.

> Almost the entire sustenance of this great people consists in corn and garden vegetables, for our cattle have become few in number and our money expended, so that we cannot purchase pork. . . . We have had no raw material to manufacture; consequently, our clothing is worn and useless or threadbare and cold.
>
> While then, looking round us and seeing this people here in the wilderness, destitute of meat and clothing, the comforts of health and necessaries, of sickness, teams and wagons to move forward, or money to procure them. . . . We feel that it is a fit subject for an appeal to the American people.[5]

Unable to negotiate any further contracts with the United States for assistance in carrying mail or erecting forts along the Oregon Trail, it was Kane himself who had suggested the propriety of begging missions to the East. Why not make a direct appeal to the sympathies and humanitarian instincts of the American public? If large sums of money could be raised for Irish famine relief ("Black '47" or "the Great Hunger" killed a million Irish and drove a million and a half to America) and for victims of other tragedies, would not the plight of their fellow Americans in the wilderness touch an equally responsive chord?

Thus was the genesis of the begging missions of the winter of 1847–48, a little known but colorful attempt to rally public sympathy for the plight of the Latter-day Saints. From New Orleans to Charleston, from Cincinnati to Boston, the word had to get out. And in the process, if this small missionary force of some 100 to 150 men, sent literally without purse or scrip, could preach the gospel of gathering, reclaim friends and family members to the faith, deflect Strang and his missionary efforts, and in other ways set the "wheel awhirling," then so much the better.[6]

"THE BEST TEA PARTY EVER GOT UP IN WASHINGTON CITY"

The idea may not have entirely originated with Kane. At the request of Lorenzo Snow, a local leader at Mt. Pisgah, Charles R. Dana and Robert Campbell had earlier embarked on a five-month mission to the east coast, where together they raised a substantial sum of money for the Pisgah settlement. Their journey in the summer and fall of 1847, from the dusty plains of Iowa to the rose gardens of Washington, if not an overwhelming success, proved nonetheless to be an inspiration for the scores to follow them.[7]

They left Mt. Pisgah on their foray east in mid-July 1847, retracing their steps to Nauvoo. In Quincy, they called on Jane Brown, a member, who requested of her husband "to loan us some money. He refused to do so, but Sister Brown came . . . and slipped $2.50 into my hand as a donation to assist us on our journey."[8]

Soon afterward, while on a Mississippi steamboat southbound for St. Louis, Dana made known their mission to the captain, a Mr. Charles Dean, in hopes of both a discount in the fare and a chance to preach. He was scorned on both counts. "He absolutely refused to give me any privilege of lecturing to the passengers or to take us to St. Louis [for] less than full price," Dana recorded. "He said he knew enough about Mormonism and did not feel disposed to contribute anything to that people. May the Lord reward him according to his works."[9]

Once in St. Louis, Dana was presented with "a very good second hand hat" by a David Cundling, who had previously given him two shirts, two handkerchiefs, a white cravat, one collar, and one handkerchief. "Sister

Levee at St. Louis, *drawing by A. C. Warren, engraving by R. Hinshelwood*

Farnham also gave me a very good undergarment in exchange for a poorer one. May the Lord bless her and all that have administered to our wants and comforts."[10] And so the curses and blessings followed up and down the river lanes of America.

Onboard another steamboat, northbound on the Ohio River for Cincinnati, this intrepid companionship had better luck than before, winning permission "to lecture to the passengers which numbered some 150 persons." They must have sounded convincing enough, because afterward Dana "took up a collection [and] got $8.52 for the church. A young woman gave me 25 cents for the children."

It was on such riverboats that many first heard of the Mormon cause. "After a good deal of talk we retired to the deck," Dana continued,

> and was called upon by a man by the name of Charles Friedman, a Polander and a Jew. He told me had given 50 cents in the cabin, but he would give 50 cents more to be contributed to my own use if I pleased. He also told me it was the first time he had ever heard of Mormonism [and] was much displeased with the manner that we had been treated. Said he came here for freedom but seemed to feel a little uneasy lest he and his people should share the same fate.[11]

303

Making the rounds of editors, bankers, and law firms in Cincinnati, Dana "asked one man to relieve the Mormons. Said he: 'I thought the Mormons had all gone to Hell.' I told him that [the] Father had made no such requisition."[12]

With Campbell heading south to Fredericksburg, Virginia, to connect up with his companion later in Washington, Dana proceeded north on his own. At Kirtland, Ohio, he met with several "old Mormon families" who had long since abandoned their faith because of one disagreement or another. Staying with relatives of Lorenzo Snow, Dana reported that they "asked how many spiritual wives Lorenzo had. . . . Said if Lorenzo would come back they would be willing to help him. I expect it would be to a coat of tar and feathers, if anything."[13]

Eastbound on the Erie Canal, Dana's preaching caught the ear of Joshua R. Giddings, a Congressman from Ohio, who "very readily passed his hat and spoke in our behalf and, I believe, gave one dollar." Hoping to spend the night with his brother's family in Rochester, New York, Dana noticed very quickly that "they did not seem to want me to tarry long with them. Neither did they like my doctrine." Remaining only three hours and just long enough for a short dinner, he was soon on his way again.[14]

Once in Philadelphia, Dana met with Thomas L. Kane in order to get the necessary letters of introduction and recommendation to meet with high-ranking government officials. Dana was quick to notice the contrasts between the icy cold receptions so many had shown him and the warmth of Kane. "There we met Col. Kane and counselled with him concerning our mission. He takes the responsibility of laying our claims before the public. Also making his office a place of deposit and of appealing to his personal friends. [He] also intends to carry on the work of gathering means for us during the fall and winter."[15]

While awaiting Kane's paperwork, Dana took to visiting the rich and famous in Wilmington, Delaware, and in Baltimore, Maryland. But it is obvious Dana's patience was beginning to wear thin. "Lost most all my religion that I got last evening [at church]," his entry for 27 September began,

> but I attribute it to the fact that in soliciting aid from door-to-door I address myself to many persons that had rather give me kicks than coppers and say that the sooner we are out of existence the better for us. But as I feel disposed to pray for them, I ask the good Lord

to open the bowels of the Earth, or cause his servants to do it in due time, that such might be soon swallowed up.

The very next day, while canvasing various Baltimore law firms, the visitor was told by one attorney "that lawyers are hard cases. 'Yes' says I, 'my Master complained of them in his day, but I was in hopes that they would redeem themselves in this dispensation.'"[16]

In Washington Dana joined up with Campbell again and the pair from Pisgah fearlessly continued their rounds, explaining their mission to such officials as John T. Morgan, Secretary of the Navy; William Marcy, Secretary of War; William Medill, Secretary of the Office of Indian Affairs; and the Secretary of State, James Buchanan, who "gave me ten dollars." Finally, after several canceled appointments, Dana gained an audience with President James K. Polk, who listened politely to their message and sympathized with the sorry state of the Latter-day Saints. After their interview, "he referred me to K. Knox Walker, his private secretary, [who] gave me $10 in behalf of the President."[17]

At the suggestion of the mayor of Washington, Dana made the rounds of several leading clergymen and, with the support of a Madam Lefevre, struck on the idea of hosting a "Ladies Tea Party" in order to "carry out more effectually the object of raising means to alleviate our present suffering circumstances." Over 600 tickets were printed and newspapers in Washington, Baltimore, and Philadelphia carried notice of the coming event.

The big night finally arrived on 28 October. Scores of female guests representing Washington's aristocracy began arriving at "Mrs. Reed's" at 7 P.M. "I stood at the entry and sold tickets to the amount of $50," an excited Dana wrote. "Stayed all night in the saloon to keep watch of their silver plate." By the time the evening was over, he counted a contribution of $82.50 and noted that "a colored woman . . . wished to contribute her mite. Accordingly she gave me 12 1/2 cents."[18] He concluded his summary of the day's successes on an upbeat tone: "The best tea party ever got up in Washington City."[19]

Dana and Campbell left the capital immediately thereafter by traveling much the same way they had come, arriving back at Mt. Pisgah on 5 December. During their mission, they raised over $300, a good portion of which, however, had been used to meet their expenses. With admirable courage and obvious devotion, they set a standard for many others to follow.

"LITTLE ELSE BUT INSULTS"

Whether inspired by the boldness and success of the farm missionaries or concerned that too many voices were representing the Church unofficially in high places, the Council of the Twelve dispatched several of its members to the East and South. Furnished with official papers and assigned to specific missions, the first to leave Winter Quarters was Orson Hyde. His assignment was to return immediately to Philadelphia in Dana's wake and "to make a representation to get another government contract [in addition to the Mormon Battalion] to build forts through the help of [Col.] Kane" who by this time was acting as "our attorney in fact or, if you choose, our special agent."[20]

Leaving Miller's Hollow on the east side of the Missouri the second week of December, Hyde arrived in St. Louis after 12 days of hard riding. "But, Oh! To ride on horseback on the prairies, facing a cold wind always, for 450 miles I will not comment on," he wrote. "Neither how badly I was chapped from the calf of the leg to the highest seat of honor on the saddle."[21]

Once in St. Louis, in addition to raising $705.84 "from the saints in St. Louis to assist the presidency of the Church to remove to Great Salt Lake Valley," he "also secured a press and type . . . to be sent up by the first boat, with paper, ink, etc., and men to carry it on, also sash, doors, and glass for the house or office." Urging members to contribute liberally, Hyde warned them that if they attempted to hold back unnecessarily, "they would either go out of the Church or lose their money, and perhaps both."[22]

The money Hyde raised was immediately deposited with the dry goods firm of Beach and Eddy in St. Louis, as were most other funds raised by other Latter-day Saints elsewhere in America through bank deposit.[23] With the credit established at Beach and Eddy, every conceivable tool, utensil, conveyance, or other piece of hardware could be purchased and shipped upriver for future migrations.

Though unsuccessful in persuading Washington to contract out any other projects, Hyde remained in the East for almost two months fulfilling other requests. "I hope you will find the time to visit the best book stores in Boston and New York," Willard Richards asked of his traveling colleague,

City of St. Louis

to procure a sample of every useful treatise on juvenile education. Primers, pictorial cards, letters, modern maps, charts, diagrams, easy readings, choice stories, etc.—and any general salesman will be glad to furnish you a specimen for the purpose of making sale to our camp, if he knows his own interest.[24]

Three weeks later, Apostles Ezra T. Benson, Amasa Lyman, and Erastus Snow, in company with John Scott, Daniel Davis, William I. Appleby, Preston Thomas, and Thomas Flanigan took leave of Winter Quarters on their eventually separate missions. Their official purpose: "to solicit from the rich Saints and the benevolent of all classes donations for the relief of our poor and to assist the Camp of Israel to move forward to the places of their destination."[25]

After reaching Savanna, Missouri, some 130 miles south, they were faced with long delays because of ice flows on the Missouri. There the group divided: Benson, Lyman, Appleby, and Snow engaged a lighter, faster carriage to cut across Missouri to Hannibal on the Mississippi side of the state in time to catch a steam packet for St. Louis. Such a decision—to travel directly through the heartland of their Missouri enemies, who had driven out the Mormons just nine years before—demanded a certain amount of caution and imagination. While in Liberty, for instance, they put up at a "Mr. Higgins Hotel" who, as Appleby recorded, was "one of the

307

keepers of the jail in Liberty when Joseph Smith, Hyrum Smith and Lyman Wight were incarcerated in there by mobs. . . . Therefore we thought it prudent to keep who we were a secret." He then provided even more details.

> Knowing that bitter enmity still existed towards all that were called 'Mormons,' we deemed it prudent to travel 'incog' while in Missouri. Accordingly we passed as gentlemen, travelling for our pleasure and convenience under the assumed titles of Col. Benson of Massachusetts, Esqr. Mason of New Hampshire, (Mason being the middle name of Br. Lyman), Dr. Snow of Boston, and Judge Appleby of New Jersey—each one corresponding with our native state. Under the above appellation we travelled and fared well, and good attention and care was our reception at the different hotels and private houses where we put up.[26]

Once safely in St. Louis, the new arrivals called two meetings of all the local membership and raised $100, which was used to pay their pending travel costs and to print 3,500 copies of the "General Epistle of the Twelve" at a total cost of $30. Lyman and Appleby attended to the business of proof-reading, punctuation, and printing, all of which was done at the office of the *St. Louis Republican*.[27] The printing of the general epistle, and this on donated funds, represented the first printing by the Church in America in some two years; it would signal to believers and detractors alike that Mormonism, as it were, was back in business. Only after the printing was completed did the several missionaries leave St. Louis for their respective destinations, each carrying several hundred copies of the freshly printed epistle.

Lyman, Flanigan, and Preston Thomas pursued their mission by steamboat into the southern states, reaching Aberdeen, Mississippi, ("the central point of our mission") early in February. Along the way they preached in Memphis, Holly Springs, and Pantotoc. In addition to preaching, however, they had two other purposes. The first was to persuade as many friends and family members of William Crosby (who had earlier led a company of Mississippi Saints to Fort Laramie; see chapter 6) as possible to move to Winter Quarters. The second was to raise as much money as possible. If he expected persecution and prejudice, Lyman came away surprised: he returned in April with over $1500 ($1368 from Crosby himself) and also with an immigration company led by Crosby and John Brown, "which consisted of some 70 or 80 persons, about half blacks [servants] and 11 wagons."[28]

Lyman could speak only superlatively of antebellum southern hospitality. "In all our journeying in the Southern Country," he reported, "we found a general spirit of enquiring after Mormonism. The field is open for a rich harvest."[29] Lyman and his followers arrived back at Winter Quarters "at dusk" on 9 May 1848.

Meanwhile, with abundant energy and commitment, Appleby, Snow, and Benson spent their time in Ohio, Pennsylvania, New York, and several New England states, "exhorting and encouraging [the membership] to good works and circulating among them the Epistle of the Twelve." In New York City, they "spent a few days together in visiting the leading men of the city, the rich and the honorable and high minded. From some we received kind treatment, good wishes and free and liberal donations." But from most others: "little else but insults to our persons and contempt of our missions."[30]

While in Boston Erastus Snow collected almost $1,000, part of which ($100) came from Josiah Quincy, the mayor of Boston who had long held a very favorable impression of Joseph Smith and the Latter-day Saints.[31]

By the time they returned to St. Louis in early April, Snow and Benson had received in cash "about $2,000 besides some hundreds in goods and clothing"—enough money for Beach and Eddy to charter the steamboat *Mandan* from St. Louis to Winter Quarters for over 100 people and "about 50 tons of goods."[32]

And so the begging missions continued through hundreds of different communities and with hundreds of different stories. Thomas McKenzie, for instance, who left early in the spring, preached all over Ohio in towns like Portsmouth, Circleville, and Columbus but with little success.

In Cincinnati he, like Dana before him, met stern opposition. Finding it too expensive to rent a hall for preaching, he

> went from house to house calling on them for books or means to establish schools in the valley. Some that I called on were very abusive and told me to leave quick. They were very bitter to our people. . . . [Some] seem to have the disposition to drive out and destroy us as a people. They asked my how I dared to go round decent people. . . . I told them that they had driven us out from

their midst for no other reason than that we maintain that God had the prophet to speak from the Heavens again.[33]

And in Columbus, McKenzie tried the same approach with even less success. "I then went around the city from house to house and met with a deal of opposition," he continued.

> I went into the office of Doctor Skinner and found in this office six or eight men and among them a Baptist preacher. . . . The Doctor wanted me to take 4 oz. of poison and the preacher wanted me to perform a miracle. I told the preacher he was following in the footsteps of his master the Devil as he also was a sign seeker. The preacher, finding he could do nothing stirred the others against me but the Lord enabled me to speak to all of them and make the truth manifest. Yet in the whole city of Columbus I could not name one cent and the only person that offered to give me anything to eat was Mr. Lloyd who was very kind to me. He asked me to dinner and said he believed if any were right it was the Mormons.[34]

Moving on to Kirtland, he described it as "a den of wild spirits." While in the former Mormon headquarters, he attended in the temple a prayer meeting put on by Martin Harris and William E. McLellin, both of whom were still bitter towards the Church.[35]

William Clayton, meanwhile, received permission to revise and correct his emigration guide and prepare it for publication. With the growing number of emigrants heading west (and gold waiting to be found at Sutter's Mill that same season), a ready market might be willing to purchase an accurate and detailed guide to the west. Asked on several occasions to let out handwritten copies of the guide for his personal profit, Clayton declined. "I have had application for several copies," he admitted in a letter to Brigham, "but have not attempted to let one go without your permission."[36]

He and Lucius Scovil set out for St. Louis early that winter. By March 1848, Clayton could report that he had succeeded in publishing 5,000 copies of his guide, a work that soon won the attention and approval of overlanders everywhere as one of the finest works of its kind.[37]

The success of these missions, if measured only in dollars and cents, was not spectacular. As Snow put it, after subtracting their expenses, they netted "a very paltry sum to be sure when the necessities of our people are compared with the wealth of the South and East from which this title was received."[38]

However, they raised an estimated $10,000, no small feat considering a disbelieving and distrustful public and a hit-and-miss, one-time-only approach to fund-raising. It was money needed at a most critical hour that provided encouragement and hope to the waiting parties of emigrants. Perhaps these emissaries succeeded in less measurable ways, because "the most important feature of these missions," concluded Erastus Snow, "was in the fact that our application to the rich and the municipal authorities of the East afforded us an opportunity to prove before God and man the extent of their pretended sympathy for the exiled Saints."[39]

"WE HAVE NOW WHIPPED ALL OF OUR ENEMIES WITH ONE HAND TIED BEHIND US"

Of no less strategic importance to the welfare of the Church than the begging missions was the decision to revive their once sagging fortunes in the British Isles and to promulgate the gathering overseas. Since the evacuation of Nauvoo, British emigration had been at bay, stymied by the uncertain course of the exodus and the crisis of confidence in leadership (see chapter 1). Although John Taylor and Parley P. Pratt had cleaned house and remedied the situation the winter before, lingering problems remained.

An anxious Orson Spencer, assigned to remain in England to supervise Church affairs, could only see the positives and the limitless possibilities. During 1847 he liquidated almost half the debts run up by Reuben and Hedlock's joint stock scheme and restored a new sense of confidence. "The Saints in this land are united, peaceful and increasing in faith," he wrote. "The spirit of apostasy is as still as the grave. No one dares to move his tongue. . . . The increase of the Church during this year will probably not be less than 6,000, some say 8,000." Spencer was obviously buoyed at the reaccelerating rate of conversion.

The problem, however, was one of money, not desire.

> The Saints are poor and constantly urgent to emigrate. I am teased continually. They say, "Our means are lessening all the time and soon we shall have none to help ourselves to emigrate." If the times do not improve, many are bent on going to some parts of America for work, at all events. Now in case they cannot emigrate

to the proper destination, have you any special counsel to give them?[40]

Spencer, himself, made a special plea to return to America and rejoin his now motherless family. "I am willing to stay or go," he said in a letter to Brigham.

At the same time I love my young and tender family, and would love to guide the dear orphans with a father's care. . . . They are anxious to have me return to them. They have suffered not a little since I left them. Their oxen and cows and horse have all died save one and they have lived some of the time without flour, meal or meat, floor, door or window.[41]

Spencer's pleadings must have struck a responsive chord, because in December, Orson Pratt was called to go to England on a short mission, replace Spencer, and take charge of the British Mission. Pratt did not finally get away until the following May, when he and Levi Richards departed on their new assignment in company with five others.[42] Assigned to serve as emigration agent in New Orleans was Lucius N. Scovil, whose duties would be to supervise the arrival of the imminent British contingents and their forward migration by steamboat, via St. Louis, to the Bluffs. In the meantime, Wilford Woodruff was assigned to visit New England and the Maritime provinces of British North America.

Furnished with ample quantities of the general epistle, the British emissaries also carried with them instructions to collect and bring back as much tithing as possible. "Exert yourself to gather up tithing," wrote Brigham in his letter of release to Spencer,

and bring it with you in order to prepare for glass, nails, paints and such other articles as will be needed to bring from the States to assist in building up the Temple of the Lord in the Valley of the Great Salt Lake. And I earnestly desire Elders Orson Pratt and Levi Richards will use all their energies on this subject and assist you in gathering in the tithing until the time of your departure.[43]

The first manifestation of the resumption of British emigration came on 18 January 1848 when a small handful of Latter-day Saints left Liverpool on board the *Ringfield*, arriving in New Orleans 16 March 1848.[44] A month later, on 21 February, 120 Latter-day Saints sailed down the Mersey River, also bound for New Orleans, most of them paying their own way. And on 9 March, another 80 came on board the ship *Sailor Prince*. By the end of 1848, 650 British converts had made the long and dangerous voyage to New Orleans, where Scovil awaited them. What resumed as a mere trickle rose to a substantial stream of new faces in the years to come. Between 1849 and 1852, 26 schooners carried another 6,130 British Saints to their new home in America.[45]

Ironically, one reason for the reinvigoration of the British missionary efforts had been the rumored arrival of some of James Strang's more notable missionaries. That Strang was still a thorn in the Mormon side is evident in the wording of the general epistle itself where, in the very same paragraph declaring the reorganization of the First Presidency, there appeared this warning: "Since the murder of President Joseph Smith, many false prophets and false teachers have arisen, and tried to deceive many, during which time we have mostly tarried with the body of the Church, or been seeking a new location, leaving these prophets and teachers to run their race undisturbed, who have died natural deaths, or committed suicides."[46]

Strang, who had made significant gains in Illinois and Wisconsin and among the eastern branches of the Church, particularly in New York and Pennsylvania, dispatched to England such new and well-known conscripts as Martin Harris, one of the Three Witnesses to the Book of Mormon. In company with Lester Brooks, "old Bump" (as he was called) preached among several British Mormon congregations in late 1846. But their message fell largely on deaf ears. "They are determined to maintain their ground in that country at all costs," scribbled Brooks in a letter to George Adams.[47] Harris hurt his own cause by his rambling, self-condemning style of preaching and his lukewarm support of the Voree prophet. More an embarrassment and a hindrance than an advantage to the Strangite cause, Harris was discharged and returned to Ohio.

The failure of Martin Harris notwithstanding, Strang redoubled his overseas missionary efforts, convinced that the British Saints, whom he perceived as poor, restless, and discouraged, surely promised a fertile field. In the spring of 1847, another delegation, this time led by John E. Page, returned to England to resume where Harris had left off. However, due to the widespread circulation of the *Millennial Star* and its effective criticisms of Strang and his message, the disorganized and intermittent nature of his proselyting attempts, and the quick action of the Twelve to restore confidence and to revive immigration, Strang's message never gained a British following.

Consequently he concentrated his major efforts among Latter-day Saint branches in Illinois, Wisconsin, New York, and Pennsylvania. In fact, rarely did his missionaries proselyte outside the Mormon communities. Despite Strang's limited focus and every effort to downplay or even disregard his rearguard action, his success was a concern.[48] Far more than the pretensions of Sidney Rigdon to start his own church (whose following was already in decline) or any other, Strang must be regarded as a contributing factor in the mission calls of 1847–48. Jonathan C. Wright, Thomas McKenzie, James H. Glines, and several others were instructed to return to Illinois, eastern Iowa, and Wisconsin "to gather up the saints," "to hunt up saints that had been driven out of Nauvoo," and to stem the tide of defections. Even those missionaries who went to the east coast were instructed to contend with the Strang issue.

As early as February 1847, the Strangites (as they became popularly known) "had assumed the jurisdiction of the conference in western New York and were misguiding many."[49] Throughout 1847 they were canvassing throughout the eastern branches with some notable success in New York.[50] Reuben Miller, an eloquent Mormon preacher sent back earlier to reclaim Strang's believers, had previously converted to Strangism long enough to take many with him and, in his own eyes, make a fool of himself. "You know that this imp of Satan his injured me much and deceived me," he lamented in early 1847, "and led me into error, so that I denied the true authority and by that means lost blessings that may never be conferred on me. Now, while I have my foot on his neck, I feel like giving him what he so richly deserves."[51] With the vengeful zeal of one once betrayed, Miller went on to become one of Strang's most bitter enemies, publishing waybills, pamphlets, and broadsides critical of the Wisconsin prophet.

Strang's influence peaked in early 1848. The schism promoted by the earlier departure of Aaron Smith as a counselor in the First Presidency was but a minor deflection. Although William Smith converted over for a time, he was regarded, even by Strang's followers, as an opportunist, unstable emotionally, morally, and financially.[52] More disappointing was their failure to attract Emma Smith and Lucy Smith to the fold.[53] By late 1848, because of economic constraints and the inability to buy sufficient lands for a temple, Strang decided to relocate his Zion to Beaver Island, in northern

Lake Michigan, in the spring of 1849. Eventually over 2,600 of his follow-ers settled on Beaver Island, much to the consternation of local residents and fishermen, who viewed these "Mormon" newcomers with thinly-veiled contempt. In 1850 Strang printed his *Book of the Law of the Lord* and was crowned king of the Kingdom of God on earth. One of his most famous recruits while on Beaver Island was George Miller who had severed his con-nections with Brigham Young back at Winter Quarters in early 1847.

The downturn in Strang's fortunes can be traced to the reversal of his stand on the practice of plural marriage. Most damaging was the method of compromise. Many of those who had come with him in the first instance had done so because of their opposition to polygamy. To many of them, it came as a hard blow to learn that after meeting Elvira Field, a young Michigan schoolteacher, Strang had not only secretly married her but had also disguised her as a clerk, taking her with him all over the eastern branches in 1849 under the name of Charles C. Douglas. Once the suspi-cions of many were confirmed, Strang announced a new revelation con-doning the practice. But for many, the damage was irrevocable. If they found the doctrine detestable, then the deception was despicable. Despite these setbacks, Strang and his declining colony continued on Beaver Island until his assassination in the summer of 1856, after which mobs drove more than 2,000 of his followers from the Island.[54]

Very few of Strang's disenchanted followers ever came west. Along with others who believed in the Book of Mormon but could not follow Brigham Young, many eventually gravitated into the Reorganized Church of Jesus Christ of Latter Day Saints, which young Joseph Smith III was persuaded to organize and lead in 1860. A demographic profile of the earliest RLDS membership shows a disproportionately large percentage of the total cen-tered in eastern Iowa, Illinois, Michigan, Wisconsin, and Missouri—"stay backs" from the exodus.

Jonathan C. Wright, while back in Illinois in the winter of 1847–48 on his mission, used every stratagem in his power to revive the faithful. "Go immediately west," he warned his listeners, "for your salvation depended on it."[55] But in Alton, Springfield, and elsewhere he found bitter opposition to plural marriage. "Cold and dead and some twice dead and plucked up by the roots," he wrote. Others were "cold as a frozen potato."[56]

Whatever the real or perceived threat from Strang, by the spring of 1848 Mormon leaders were sounding confident, if for no other reason than that the Latter-day Saints had weathered a wilderness exile and located a new mountain home. It was all enough for Brigham to say, "We have now whipped all of our enemies with one hand tied behind us."[57]

The exodus may have lost more to indifference than to doctrinal discord. Many could ill afford the move west and, without local support or Church leadership, drifted away. Some were too sick to travel, while several decided not to leave their families. Others became rich while waiting in St. Louis or thriving on rich Iowa farmland and were hesitant to surrender what they had worked so hard to achieve. Such resented the constant call to sacrifice and "are fearful that they will be tithed too much. A number," wrote Orson Hyde in the spring of 1848, "are about ready to declare their independence, pay no more tithing and take no counsel but their own."[58] And as Noah Packard said of many still in Iowa: "There is a number of people in this region of country [Grant County] that are or have been Latter-day Saints, but as the saying is, they most of them lie low and keep dark, some for the sake of popularity join other denominations."[59]

And for some, there may have been one too many real or imagined personal offenses—a wagon borrowed and never returned, a disproportionate share of the promised goods, a bishop who may have played favorites, or any one of the very human reasons that have always tested the soul of allegiance. Some had overestimated their leaders and allowed the resultant disappointment to derail their faith. Brigham constantly warned against the gullibility and naivete of his people. "Let them be good Saints in whom you have reason to repose confidence," he warned by letter and by sermon.

> Many have come into this Church with a large amount of means and property, and they have bestowed it on Tom, Dick, and Harry, who have afterwards treated them scandalously, and it not only stumbles and shakes their faith in those persons, but they lose confidence in all their brethren and lose the good spirit; this leads to apostasy. Therefore, I would say, be judicious and wise with your means. . . . I would thus caution you against the rocks and precipices and danger on which others have stumbled, and some have become wrecked, driven to and fro till totally engulfed in the great deep of unbelief.[60]

And on another occasion:

If you have the good, charitable, mild, energetic Spirit of the Lord you will look over your brother's imperfections and look at your own, and you will find enough to do to wet your own garden, at least I have found it so with me. And if I had feeling to[ward] my Brethren and they wronged me, I would go according to the laws of Christ and be reconciled, and have satisfaction.[61]

Charles Dana and Jonathan Wright's missionary efforts in Nauvoo's outlying communities may indicate that defection and stay back rates were higher outside of Nauvoo. A higher percentage of those in outlying communities than those in Nauvoo did not emigrate to the west. In addition to those who went with Strang, an estimated 2,000 to 3,000 never made it across the Mississippi River.[62]

"HAS THE LORD TURNED BANKRUPT?" — THE NAUVOO TRUSTEES

While others were out filling short-term begging missions, there were three still in Nauvoo begging to be released from an extended special mission of their own. Appointed Nauvoo Trustees by the Twelve back on 4 January 1846, just one month before the first departures from Nauvoo, Joseph L. Heywood, John S. Fullmer, and Almon W. Babbitt had been empowered to represent the Church as well as many of its Nauvoo citizens. Their instructions had been to remain in the city and to supervise the many matters of unfinished business inevitably left behind in the wake of a forced evacuation. "I appointed the Trustees myself," Brigham noted, "Babbitt for lawyer, Fullmer for bulldog and growl, and Heywood to settle debts."[63] What they had anticipated would take no more than a year to complete dragged on for over three. Living through the darkest days of a city in fast decline, the Nauvoo Trustees' work is an unheralded story.

The three men were as well suited for their assignments as they were different in temperament, background, and training. Joseph Leland Heywood, 31 years of age, was from Massachusetts. He moved to Quincy, Illinois, in 1838; there he entered into the mercantile business with his brother-in-law. Four years later, he converted to Mormonism but did not move to Nauvoo until 1845. For a short period of time he ran a store on Main Street. Heywood, who knew as many of the anti-Mormons as the Mormons, was the diplomat—an intelligent, well-educated man, tall and slim in stature, with a kind and affable disposition. He was also good with figures. He had the knack of defusing potentially explosive situations.

John S. Fullmer, 39 years of age in 1846 and the oldest of the three, was from Pennsylvania. He became quite a wealthy landowner in Nauvoo and fought in the Battle of Nauvoo. He was apparently a man of detail and assertion, one who could hold his own in any argument and give as much as he took.

Almon W. Babbitt, the least likeable of the three, was a caustic, 32-year-old, ambitious lawyer. Babbitt had converted back in 1830, had been a member of Zion's Camp in 1834, and had assisted in the earlier closing up of Church affairs in Kirtland, Ohio. A cross of the brashness of a Sam Brannan and the ego of a George Miller, Babbitt was not fully trusted, even by his fellow trustees, and was suspected of advancing his own interests before those of the Church. Nevertheless he owned the legal skills necessary to settle in and out of court a host of complex issues.[64]

Their task proved overwhelming. Allowed to remain in the city with their families long enough to complete their assignment, their lives were in constant danger. Their first responsibility had been to confer with the Quincy and Carthage Committees, as representatives of the Twelve, and postpone the inevitable capture of the city. They needed to buy time for the departure of the poor and the sick and also to sell off properties to interested buyers at still-decent prices. Once the Battle of Nauvoo ended in September 1846, with its consequent destruction and devastation of property values, the task of disposing of Church and private real estate became even more difficult.

In addition to selling Church properties, including the temple (see chapter 1), they were responsible for paying outstanding Church debts, contesting legal actions, helping the poor and destitute still languishing behind, and keeping a watchful and caring eye on Emma Smith, widow of the Prophet, and her immediate family as well her mother-in-law, Lucy Mack Smith.

They also represented the private business concerns of many former citizens. Properties were to be sold at the best price possible and the proceeds credited either against past debts or toward future purchases. Individual tithing accounts often needed settling; those who had been advanced Church teams and wagons on credit had no other form of repayment. Several men who had worked as laborers on the construction of the temple were still unpaid. And when time permitted, the trustees were also to push the cause of gathering, counter opposition, and allay discontent—and all this as a Church calling without remuneration.

Misunderstood and unappreciated by their own people, whose property values plummeted as the city emptied, and distrusted by the anti-Mormons, who viewed them contemptuously as the last vestiges of an evil empire, the trustees inherited a lose-lose situation. Almost everyone with Nauvoo property and improvements got far less than they needed or deserved—no more than one-eighth the value and often far less than that at sale.[65] Ill feelings inevitably developed.

"The perplexity of business we can stand tolerably well," lamented Fullmer in a June 1846 letter,

> but when we do all that God gives us wisdom and liberty to do, and then to be reported, every now and then to [your] camp, for mal treatment, mal practice or some other mal, is going . . . rather too steep. But we know that we have a conscience void of offence and I believe that our President will do us justice.[66]

After Nauvoo's surrender, Heywood and Fullmer did all in their power to raise money to find food and supplies for the sick and dying. With Babbitt back east on other business, Fullmer remained home to deal with emergency matters while Heywood scoured up and down the Mississippi, in search of funds for the poor camps. Writing from St. Louis in October, Heywood painted a sad picture. "I am here for the purpose of soliciting aid for our destitute brethren and sisters embracing a great portion of the lame, halt and blind of the Church whose situation is totally deplorable scattered along the bank of the river opposite to Nauvoo."[67]

Concerned that Strang was maneuvering for possession of the temple, all three trustees travelled to Voree in early January 1847 to visit a repentant Reuben Miller and other friends and to listen to Strang preach. Their purpose was to try to ascertain his real intentions and to discover Emma's. Emma, a close friend to William Marks, former Nauvoo stake president and a convert to Strang, had left Nauvoo at peril of her life and family during the Battle of Nauvoo to settle upstream temporarily in Fulton, Illinois. In Voree that January, Emma refused invitations to hear Strang preach and rejected every persuasion to join his cause.[68] Always suspicious of Strang's pretentiousness and claims to leadership, Emma returned home to Nauvoo in the spring of 1847 with her three sons—Joseph, Alexander, and David—to take up residence once again in the charred and desecrated remnants of the City Beautiful.

Meanwhile, Babbitt, seeing their inability to find western buyers for the temple, made a trip east to Kirtland and New York in an attempt to sell both the Kirtland and the Nauvoo Temples to eastern interests. More than anything else, a temple sale would signify a successful end to their assignment.[69]

Babbitt returned with mixed results at best. The good news, at least from his perspective, was that he had been able to sell some Kirtland properties while blocking the sale of the Kirtland Temple by opponents of the Church. The bad news was recognition of "some forty suits of different kinds commenced against the Trustees," some for moneys lost as far back as the Kirtland bank collapse in 1837.[70]

The worst news, at least in the eyes of his colleagues, was Babbitt's perceived bungling of a very real sale opportunity. "We both feel quite dissatisfied with the mission of Bro. Babbitt east," a tired Heywood wrote in April 1847. To their way of thinking, Babbitt had kept them uninformed of his real intentions and worse, had backed away from a chance to sell the Nauvoo temple for $100,000 for inexplicable reasons. "You can judge of our feelings when it seemed as if there was a reasonable prospect of sale," complained Heywood, "and those prospects were blighted by the inattention and darkness of mind of one in whom we had a right to confide."[71]

Whatever the origin and outcome of Babbitt's mission, Brigham chose not to chastise his unruly, independent-minded subordinate, at least not at this time, but on hearing of the failed sale, he turned defiant:

> Has the Lord turned bankrupt? Or are his children so needy that they are obliged to sell their father's house for a morsel of bread? And if they should sell, how much bread would they get, after they had paid some millions of unjust debts, mortgages, cancelled claims, demands, attachments, fines, forfeitures, stripes, imprisonments, massacres, lawsuits, judgments, and the whole etceteras that united mobocracy could bring against you, before you could get one dollar removed from the vault to a place of safety. We leave you to answer this question.

Brigham concluded his letter with instructions to rent the temple and then "repair forthwith to this place with all your surplus funds and the . . .

Emma Smith,
portrait by Lee Greene Richards

books, records, papers, and moveable effects belonging to the Church."[72] And by vote of the Twelve, "it was resolved unanimously that we have the utmost confidence in the faithful discharge of their duties as Trustees-in-Trust in Nauvoo . . . and we tender to them our thanks and pray our Father in Heaven . . . to bless and prosper them."[73]

Heywood, unfortunately, took ill in May of 1847 and was unable to move west. Instead, he went to Quincy for care and recuperation. Fullmer and Babbitt were also detained, largely because of the late arrival of Church-owned lumber (via the Mississippi River) from the Wisconsin pineries, the sale of which was to pay off several pressing debts. "Some of our creditors have been to visit us and although disappointed at our delinquencies, they still manifest every confidence in our integrity."[74]

The anxious, restless trio would almost certainly have left Nauvoo in the fall of 1847 and "let the owls and bats revel in the habitation of the saints" had it not been for another major obstacle. On 23 December 1847, the Reverend William Hany, a Methodist preacher, performed the marriage of Joseph's widow, Emma, then 43 years of age, to Lewis C. Bidamon in the Carthage courthouse.[75] Their marriage sent immediate shock waves throughout the scattered Mormon communities, especially at Winter Quarters.

Brigham Young and Emma had long been in conflict over the sale of properties and the issue of plural marriage, which Emma would not believe her husband had ever practiced. Brigham and the Twelve and scores of other men and women believed otherwise. Both looked at the sale of properties in Joseph's name as trustee for the Church as belonging to themselves. Such disagreement festered until the two were hardly on speaking terms, each one feeling betrayed by the other. John M. Bernhisel remained the last, best connection between Emma and the fleeing Latter-day Saints, but when he left in the summer of 1847 only the trustees were left to take his place.

And while they tried to keep in contact, Babbitt, in particular, was an offence to Emma. He only exacerbated an already strained relationship when, on hearing of her marriage to Bidamon, he allegedly charged over to her home in an outrage and accused her of forsaking the faith.[76]

The overriding sentiment among most Latter-day Saints on hearing of Emma's remarriage was one of disappointment, if not disbelief, mixed with pity and anger. She was still loved and respected and many sympathized with her at the tragic loss of her husband. But Emma's actions were indeed a mystery, even to her many defenders. In the darkest days of Nauvoo's decline and fall, when all were leaving everything and at peril of their lives and families, many wondered and some took offence at her inaction and ultimate desire to stay back. For all her hurts, were her sorrows any greater than theirs? Were her personal and doctrinal differences so irreconcilable as to sever years of friendship and association? Why, when so many were sick and dying, did she not lend her love and help as in the past? Her stubborn aloofness raised a cluster of questions and inflicted many wounds.

And her marriage to Bidamon only deepened the collective disappointment. Though Bidamon was known by all alike as a friend to the Saints and a defender of Nauvoo, he had a less than sterling reputation and could not in any way be construed as a religious man. While some wondered how she could ever marry again, let alone to a nonbeliever, others were chagrined and crestfallen at what her marriage signified—a divorce with Mormonism, if not a repudiation of what her husband had lived and died for, a certain signal that she would never come west or bring her three sons. It was an irreconcilable parting of the ways.

Within days of their marriage, the Bidamons launched legal action to block any further sales of properties in Nauvoo—including the temple— that were in the name of Joseph as trustee. Their argument was that such transfer was illegal according to an obscure Illinois law that prohibited any religious corporation from holding more than ten acres of property. Acting under counsel of their own, the Bidamons argued that Joseph was not entitled to transfer such properties to the Church and that since many of the properties had been deeded to Joseph and Emma, she had prior claim to them. "This places [us] in the extremest difficulties as to title," Babbitt reported, "while it destroys the confidence of everyone and prevents those who would have purchased from doing so . . . a complete estoppel of our selling lands in the city."[77] No doubt Emma's purpose in bringing such action was to reclaim properties she felt belonged to the family and to repay some of the $70,000 in personal debts left by her husband. The truth is that neither the Church nor Emma realized much from the Nauvoo sales.[78]

Recognizing the impediment this action placed against all further sales, Fullmer expressed resignation, dejection, and a mounting compulsion to get away. "I do hope that it may not be my lot to have to remain here till such decision is had," he pleaded. "My heart is in the west with the Brethren, and I hope that I shall, in some way, be able to remove my family thither. . . . God is the helmsman of our bark, and he will run her into port yet, and in a way that perhaps we cannot see."[79]

Fullmer and Heywood finally received the much wanted go-ahead to quit Nauvoo in the spring of 1848. Their official release followed on 1 August, when they were formally replaced by David Cowen and John Snider.[80] Both men hurried to Winter Quarters in time to catch the last emigration train of the year, under the command of Willard Richards, and reached the valley 19 October 1848. Heywood became postmaster of the Great Salt Lake City the following spring and later served several other missions. Fullmer later moved to Davis County and eventually to Springville.

Babbitt remained behind, attending to various Church matters and promoting his own political interests. Later he became secretary of the Territory of Utah. Babbitt was killed in an Indian attack while traveling on the plains in 1856.[81]

The mission of the Nauvoo Trustees was difficult and demanding. Clearly they realized only a small fraction of the true value of most of the lands they were able to sell. Neither did they capitalize on any real chance of selling the temple. Nevertheless, they appeared to have done much, perhaps the best they could under such strained conditions. They certainly enabled many to come west who might not otherwise have been able to do so, and they mitigated circumstances that might have ended in tragedy for many others. And the trustees were responsible for sending west various supplies, equipment, libraries, and countless personal effects.[82]

"COME AND RETURN TO OUR FATHER'S HOUSE"

Of all the Winter Quarters missions of 1847–48, none was more successful or gratifying than that assigned to Phineas Young. On returning from the Valley with the company of the Twelve, it was apparent that the

time was ripe for him to make one last
effort to reclaim his brother-in-law,
Joseph Smith's scribe in translating the
Book of Mormon and one of the Three
Witnesses—Oliver Cowdery. Cowdery
had made it known for some time that
he was seriously considering returning
to the fold after a separation of almost
10 years. After leaving the Church in
Far West, Missouri, in 1838, Cowdery
practiced law in Ohio from 1840 until
1847 and then moved to Wisconsin to
join his brother. Only modestly successful in the law, Cowdery had kept in
close and friendly contact with the
Church through Phineas Young. At
one point, late in the summer of 1843,
he had even considered moving to
Nauvoo.[83]

Oliver Cowdery

After the death of Joseph Smith, an event that likely had a profound
effect on him, Cowdery offered his services to the Twelve as an "agent to
see President Polk on the subject of removal westward, if the council
desired."[84] Further evidence indicates that he seriously considered moving
west to join the migrations.[85] But plagued by increasingly poor health and
financial setbacks, Cowdery chose not to come.

Whatever his circumstance, by the time the Twelve returned to Winter
Quarters, Brigham obviously felt that Cowdery would be receptive to a personal invitation. "As we have frequently heard you through our mutual
brother, Phinehas H. Young," Brigham wrote in November 1847,

> we improve the present moment . . . of expressing to you our
> unbounded confidence and joy in those principles and doctrines of
> the Church . . . which we have so long taught and practiced amid
> scenes of persecutions and blood, and many of which, in former
> days, we have listened to with delight from your lips, and to the
> truth of which, we have heard you testify with unshaken confidence
> and to say to you in the spirit of Jesus, and by the calling where-
> unto we have been called, "Come, for all things are now ready, and

the Spirit and the Bride say Come and return to our Father's House, from whence thou hast wandered, and partake of the fatted calf, and sup and be filled."[86]

Cowdery responded directly in February, stating that he would visit the Mormon settlements early in the spring, "say as soon as the 6th of April, if possible." He likewise indicated he looked forward to "seeing many valuable old friends" and "of conversing on interesting subjects."[87]

Because of rapidly declining health and lack of means, Cowdery and his wife were unable to make it to the Bluffs that spring. Phineas himself went to Wisconsin in May to "bring him up" in the fall. The two men obviously discussed his return and many of the original differences which had led him out of the Church. Although it has been argued that Cowdery's real intent in returning was neither an endorsement of Brigham Young as President nor an acceptance of the direction of the Church but rather an attempt to regain leadership position and right many wrongs, the evidence suggests otherwise.[88]

The truth of the matter is that he had no other intention than to rejoin the Church as a humble member, despite past differences and hurts. He was too sick to do otherwise and may have recognized that his time was short. "His only ambition seemed to be to give himself and the remainder of his life to the Church," said Samuel W. Richards of Cowdery in 1848.[89]

Cowdery arrived in Kanesville some time in the middle of October and spoke to a large audience in the Kanesville tabernacle on 24 October. Wrote one eyewitness: "He bore a strong testimony to the authenticity of the Book of Mormon, and declared that an angel conferred the Priesthood on Joseph Smith and himself."[90]

George A. Smith, another witness of Cowdery's remarks, said that some time later, he and Orson Hyde spent an entire evening with Cowdery. "He told us he had come to listen to our counsel and would do as we told him. . . . He said that Joseph Smith had fulfilled his mission faithfully before God. . . . He was determined to rise with the church, and if it went down he was willing to go down with it."[91]

Cowdery's further comments during readmission hearings on his behalf some two weeks later are particularly helpful in understanding his true intentions. After speaking relative to his feelings, his long absence from the Church, and his reasons for leaving, he concluded:

I feel that I can [now] honorably return. I have sustained an honorable character before the world during my absence from you. . . . I have ever had the honor of the kingdom in view and men are to be judged by the testimony given. I feel to sanction what has been said today. I am out of the church. I know the door into the church, and I wish to become a member through the door. I wish to be a humble, private member. I did not come here to seek honor.

After his remarks and a great many questions from those in attendance, which queries Cowdery answered to the satisfaction of the entire Pottawattamie High Council, George W. Harris moved and E. M. Green seconded that "he be permitted to come in at the door he is so well acquainted with." About 2 P.M., 12 November 1848, in company with Reuben Miller who had also sought readmission of the same council, Cowdery was baptized under the hands of Orson Hyde.[92]

In retrospect, Cowdery's return, as important as it stands in the history of the Church, probably was as much the result of the personal ministry and unending interest of one man, Phineas Young, as any doctrinal or personal reconciliation. Phineas never gave up and repeatedly went far out of his way to persuade and inform. His was a mission of enduring importance. Unable to make the desired trek to the west, Cowdery wintered with his wife's relatives in Richmond, Missouri, some 250 miles southeast. Continued ill health forced him to stay in Richmond throughout 1849. He died 3 March 1850.[93]

The winter of 1847–48 was as busy a season as yet seen, despite the cold, and is important to this study for many reasons. Every effort possible was made to raise badly needed funds, reclaim doubters, put down contenders, sell off properties, and spur on the cause of gathering. With the various missions completed and Winter Quarters in the process of crossing east to the Iowa side, a general conference convened in April in the log tabernacle. Uppermost in their various sermons were plans and preparations for the 1848 migrations. The actual departure of the wagon trains waited for the arrival of several wagons from the Crosby settlements in the south and various shiploads of equipment from St. Louis. It would appear that the 1848 migrations were even larger than those of a year before— almost 2,000 souls in 623 wagons.[94] And they all went west according to "The Word and Will of the Lord." Brigham Young left the Missouri for the last time on 26 May 1848, never to return from the valley he and so many others had come to call home.

NOTES

1. Lyman Hinnman to "Brother and Sister Taylor," Winter Quarters, 27 June 1847, Lyman Hinnman Collection, LDS Church Archives.

2. Journal History, 7 Dec. 1847.

3. John A. Wolfe to Phebe Wolfe, 10 Feb. 1847, LDS Church Archives.

4. Willard Richards to David Hollister, 5 June 1848, Willard Richards Papers, LDS Church Archives.

5. Brigham Young to Thomas L. Kane, 6 Dec. 1847, Brigham Young Papers.

6. Certainly they had plenty of precedent to call such missionaries. Back in 1832, Joseph Smith had dictated a revelation at Kirtland, Ohio, to send several missionaries "into the south countries" and "into the eastern countries" (Doctrine and Covenants 75:8, 14).

7. Dana and Campbell were not the only "farm" missionaries. The poverty in both Mt. Pisgah and Garden Grove was so grinding that others were out "begging from the Gentiles." At least three others—Brothers Derby, Hunt, and Shirtliff—were out canvasing for the Garden Grove settlement in the winter of 1846–47, their destinations unknown. Together they "gleaned several hundred dollars" (Thomas Kington to Brigham Young, 18 Oct. 1847, Brigham Young Papers).

Apostle Orson Hyde, ecclesiastical leader over the Council Bluffs and Iowa settlements, on hearing of these early money missions, felt the cart was way ahead of the horse—"an imposition," he called it, without authority; he was displeased with Lorenzo Snow for sending them. "Mt. Pisgah and Garden Grove are celebrated for these kinds of missions and perhaps selfishness has prompted them," he said in a letter to Brigham (Orson Hyde to Brigham Young, 12 Nov. 1847, Brigham Young Papers).

Brigham, however, was disinclined to censure the grit and tenacity of his people, especially when at the time he himself had been a thousand miles away in the mountains. He considered it better to commend initiative than to stifle it. Nevertheless, he did instruct them to turn over "all such money and goods or effects as you have collected" to Hyde at the appropriate moment (Brigham Young to Robert Campbell and Charles R. Dana, 6 Dec. 1847, Brigham Young Papers).

8. Journal of Charles R. Dana, 26 July 1847, LDS Church Archives.

9. Journal of Charles R. Dana, 28 July 1847.

10. Journal of Charles R. Dana, 2 Aug. 1847.

11. Journal of Charles R. Dana, 4 Aug. 1847.

12. Journal of Charles R. Dana, 10 Aug. 1847.

13. Journal of Charles R. Dana, "Late August," 1847.

14. Journal of Charles R. Dana, 22 Aug. 1847.

15. Journal of Charles R. Dana, 1 Sept. 1847.

16. Journal of Charles R. Dana, 28 Sept. 1847.

17. Journal of Charles R. Dana, 18 Oct. 1847. It does not appear that Campbell was with Dana in his meetings with Polk and other members of his administration.

18. Journal of Charles R. Dana, 27 Oct. 1847.

19. "The Autobiography of Charles R. Dana," LDS Church Archives.

20. Brigham Young to Thomas L. Kane, 9 Feb. 1848, Brigham Young Papers. See also Journal History, 6 Dec. 1847.

21. Orson Hyde to Brigham Young, 28 Dec. 1847, Brigham Young Papers. Brigham and the rest of the Twelve were not about to sympathize with their partner who had not gone west to the mountains while on assignment to supervise the Church at the Bluffs. Most thought Hyde got the better end of the deal.

22. Orson Hyde to Brigham Young, 28 Dec. 1847, Brigham Young Papers. See also Journal History, 28 Dec. 1847. Hyde commented that "the public mind is very heavy" against the interests of the Latter-day Saints. And as for the rich members, he urged them to give handsomely and in the mean time "to remain here another year or two and send their money to the camp."

23. St. Louis was, of course, home to a large number of mercantile operations engaged in the emigration business. One of the primary reasons the Latter-day Saints chose the particular firm of Beach and Eddy was Mr. Beach's earlier visit to Winter Quarters to sell wares at decent prices. Brigham said that Beach "secured the affection of our people by his liberality, charity, and benevolence to the poor" (Council of the Twelve to Nathaniel Felt, 24 Nov. 1847, Brigham Young Papers).

The Beach and Eddy firm lasted only a couple of years afterward, apparently destroyed in the great St. Louis fire of 1850.

24. Willard Richards to Orson Hyde, 22 Dec. 1847, Willard Richards Papers. Washington was no longer in need of military regiments because the war with Mexico was won. Neither was Congress in favor of funding the construction of a string of forts across the plains, which would fan Indian hostilities unnecessarily. And it was too early to consider long post office runs.

25. "Journal of Erastus Snow," 27 Dec. 1847.

26. Journal of William I. Appleby, 4 Jan. 1848. See also Journal of Erastus Snow, Dec. 1847–Sept. 1850.

27. Journal of William I. Appleby, 14–20 Jan. 1848. See also Journal History, 17 Jan. 1848, and Journal of Amasa Lyman, 13–14 Jan. 1848, LDS Church Archives.

That so important a document in Latter-day Saint history as the "General Epistle" of the Twelve had to be printed with "begging" funds is telling evidence of the very real poverty that gripped the Church at this critical time.

28. Journal of Amasa Lyman, 19 Mar. 1848.

29. Journal of Amasa Lyman, 29 Feb. 1848. See also Journal of Preston Thomas, typescript, Utah State Historical Society.

Preston Thomas returned to the South later in 1848 to visit Lyman Wight at his settlement at Zodiac, Texas. Wight, once a trusted friend and confidant of Joseph Smith and an Apostle until his excommunication in 1848, had turned bitter against Brigham Young's plan of exodus. Once convinced that the presidency of the Church belonged to Joseph's son Joseph Smith III by right of blood line succession, Wight gave up that idea and came to see himself as the rightful heir. "If they wanted anything of him they must come and see him for he would not go to see them and that he considered them all apostates" (Journal of Preston Thomas).

For several months in late 1848, Lyman dispatched several missionaries of his own to the Kanesville area in a largely futile attempt to dissuade migration to the west and to increase acceptance of him as the new Mormon prophet. George Miller, on quitting the Mormon camps, visited with Wight and evaluated his claims closely before leaving him to follow Strang. "Lymanism," as his brand of Mormonism came to be called, eventually fell on hard times, and most of his followers eventually deserted him. Wight died in relative obscurity in 1858.

For a more comprehensive study of Wight's Texas settlement and defection, see Bitton, "Mormons in Texas," *Arizona and the West* 2 (Spring 1969): 5–26. See also Bennett, "Lamanism, Lymanism and Cornfields," *Journal of Mormon History* 13 (1986–87): 45–59 for a look at Wight's proselyting efforts in the Kanesville area in 1848 and 1849.

30. "Journal of Erastus Snow," Dec. 1847–Sept. 1850.

31. Journal History, 13 Mar. 1848. See also *Comprehensive History of the Church*, 2:349–51. Quincy, who visited Nauvoo in May 1844 and left with a very favorable impression of Joseph Smith, was mayor of Boston from 1845 to 1849.

32. Journal of Erastus Snow, Dec. 1847–Sept. 1850.

33. Journal of Thomas McKenzie, 26 May 1848, LDS Church Archives.

34. Journal of Thomas McKenzie, 1 Aug. 1848.

35. Journal of Thomas McKenzie, 30 Sept.1848.

36. William Clayton to Brigham Young, 15 Nov. 1847, Brigham Young Papers.

37. Journal History, 28 Mar. 1848. The guide was published by the *Missouri Republican* as *The Latter-day Saints' Emigrants' Guide: Being a Table of Distances, Showing all the Springs, Creeks, Rivers, Hills, Mountains, Camping Places, and All Other Notable Places, from Council Bluffs, to the Valley of the Great Salt Lake.* For an excellent reproduction and analysis of Clayton's guide, see *The Latter-day Saints' Emigrants' Guide*, ed. Stanley B. Kimball (1983).

That later travelers used Clayton's work is abundantly proven. For one of scores of examples, see Journal of Silas Newcombe, 4 June 1850. Because of Clayton's painstaking detail and accuracy, his guide was used even more than were Fremont's earlier works and became a standard text for overland trail migration for many years.

38. "Journal of Erastus Snow," Dec. 1847–Sept. 1850.

39. Ibid.

An unofficial and partial listing of those who served missions in the winter of 1847–48, in addition to those already mentioned, is as follows:

M. Atwart	J. K. Baldwin	J. Barrels
Gilbert Belnap	George Bradley	P. W. Cook
James W. Cummings	W. Cutler	John Dalton
L. Dayton	Elisha Edwards	Caleb Edwards
L. J. Etley	Lorin Farr	Joseph France
Jacob Frazier	George B. Gardner	Ian Glasgow
James H. Glines	George R. Grant	Elias Harmer
William Hewitt	Chandler Holbrook	Artemus Johnson
William A. King	David S. Laughlin	William Marks
John McKean	Peter Mesheck	Gilbert Morris
John Pack	Joseph Phippen	Peter Rank
John Rushen	John Scott	P. Shirts
John J. Tanner	Nathen Tanner	Samuel B. Thornton
E. Vincent	Chauncey G. Webb	Jonathan Wright
Phineas Young		

(General Church Minutes, 23 Nov. 1847).

40. Orson Spencer to Brigham Young, 1 Nov. 1847, Brigham Young Papers.

41. Ibid.

42. The others were Peter Clinton, James W. Cummings, Harrison Burgess, Eli B. Kelsey, and Hyrum H. Blackwell (Journal History, 23 Jan. 1848). See also Manuscript History of Winter Quarters, 11 May 1848.

43. Brigham Young to Orson Spencer, 13 July 1848, Brigham Young Papers.

44. Lucius M. Scovil to Willard Richards, 17 Mar. 1848, Willard Richards Papers, LDS Church Archives.

45. From the "Office Record" in LDS Church Archives. See also Journal History, 9 Mar. 1848. According to P. A. M. Taylor, church membership in the British Mission almost quadrupled between 1847 and 1851, reaching a peak of nearly 33,000, with perhaps as many more as 8,000 to 10,000 emigrating after 1852, thanks in large part to the Perpetual Emigration Fund (*Expectations Westward*, 20 and 47; see also Arrington, *Great Basin Kingdom*, 77–79; and *Deseret News 1997–98 Church Almanac*, 160).

46. "General Epistle from the Council of the Twelve."

47. Lester Brooks to George W. Adams, 12 Jan. 1847, Strang Papers.

48. As Willard Richards said of Strang's contentions in the fall of 1847: "If it does not blow in my eyes, [it] does me no harm; and if a kernel of wheat is blown away in the chaff, it may be gathered up by the fowls of Heaven. . . . So with those who have been blown away with Strangism. They are mostly like the chaff. There may [be] a few saints among them, but they are weak, very weak. And if they continue on the barren heaths of the Gentiles, they will wither and die" (Willard Richards to Reuben Miller, Journal History, 17 Sept. 1847).

49. Almon W. Babbitt to John S. Fullmer and Joseph L. Heywood, 3 Feb. 1847, Brigham Young Papers. See also Journal History, 3 Feb. 1847.

50. Nephibasheth Sirrine to Orson Hyde, 13 Nov. 1847, Brigham Young Papers.

51. Reuben Miller to Brigham Young, 5 Feb. 1847, Brigham Young Papers.

52. More concerned that William Smith, brother of the Prophet, might convert to Strang than he was anxious to see him come west, Brigham had little patience and lost all respect for him. He once confided that "it is surprising that a natural brother of Joseph should be such a fool" (Meeting of the Twelve, 4 Nov. 1847, Brigham Young Papers). Smith had been excommunicated from the Church in October 1845.

See also the reminiscence of W. W. Blair, 14 Feb. 1878, RLDS Church Archives, for an understanding of the general disrespect even those who stayed back had for William Smith.

53. Emma Smith apparently visited Voree on at least one occasion but made no effort to hear Strang preach (A. W. Babbitt, J. L. Heywood, and J. S. Fullmer to Brigham Young, 19 Feb. 1847, Brigham Young Papers).

54. Quaife, *The Kingdom of Saint James*, 174. Strang's followers settled mainly in Michigan, Wisconsin, and Minnesota. A few congregations remain to the present day. For a more thorough review of Strang's rise and fall, see the sources cited in Introduction, note 28.

55. Journal of Jonathan C. Wright, 31 Jan. 1848, LDS Church Archives.

56. Journal of Jonathan C. Wright, 23 and 25 Feb. 1848. Samuel Thornton, another missionary who traveled back to Illinois, gave a more optimistic report than his counterpart, reporting that "the Saints generally remained in great anxiety to hear

what to do, and rejoiced in the . . . spirit of the gathering." But even he admitted to baptizing "only one" in all his travels (Journal History, 12 Mar. 1848).

57. Journal of Wilford Woodruff, 6 Apr. 1848, a talk given at the Kanesville log tabernacle.

58. Orson Hyde to Brigham Young, 22 Apr. 1848, Brigham Young Papers.

59. Noah Packard to Brigham Young, 6 Feb. 1848, Brigham Young Papers.

60. Brigham Young to Brother Leonard, 5 Apr. 1848, Journal History.

61. Brigham Young to Brother Kesler, 14 Mar. 1848, Brigham Young Papers.

62. For a differing view on the numbers who stayed back, see Robert B. Flanders, *The Mormons Who Did Not Go West: A Study of the Emergence of the Reorganized Church of Jesus Christ of Latter Day Saints* (Madison: University of Wisconsin, 1954), 18–19.

63. Minutes of a Trustees Meeting, 22 Jan. 1847, Brigham Young Papers. They replaced Presiding Bishop Newel K. Whitney and Associate Presiding Bishop George Miller. Although John M. Bernhisel stayed back as a Church agent to help with some of the business, he was not one of the trustees.

64. For more on Babbitt, see an unpublished manuscript by Omer Whitman of Corona, California, in possession of the author. See also "To Nauvoo," in *Our Pioneer Heritage*, 11:518–21; Newell and Avery, *Mormon Enigma*, 229–30. Babbitt had earned a law degree in Cincinnati and had qualified for licences to practice in six states.

65. Joseph L. Heywood and John S. Fullmer to Brigham Young, 30 Nov. 1847, Brigham Young Papers.

66. John S. Fullmer to Brigham Young, 26 June 1846, Brigham Young Papers.

67. Joseph L. Heywood to Brigham Young, 2 Oct. 1846, Brigham Young Papers. Not all were happy, however, with the trustees despite their efforts. Henry Young, for instance, complained at how long they had had to wait at Montrose for rescue teams. Brigham shot back in defense of his appointees: "There need be no complaints," he warned, "for there were teams enough to take all away. . . . We think we can help better than you would be able to do under existing circumstances" (Henry Young to Brigham Young, 27 Oct. 1846; Brigham Young to Henry Young, 6 Nov. 1846, Brigham Young Papers).

68. Trustees to Brigham Young, 19 Feb. 1847, Brigham Young Papers.

69. Joseph L. Heywood to Heber C. Kimball, 21 Mar. 1847, Brigham Young Papers. If Babbitt returned with assured sales, "we may get through our mission here and soon be able to join our brethren in the west."

70. A. W. Babbitt to Brigham Young, 5 Apr. 1847, Brigham Young Papers. Of his work in Kirtland, Babbitt reported on the recent efforts of William E. McLellin and Martin Harris to reestablish "The Church of Christ" as the Church had once been called in Kirtland and to rebuild the city. Opposed to Brigham's claim to leadership and to Babbitt's land sale efforts, McLellin and Harris and scores of other disillusioned Latter-day Saints were trying to wrest legal control over several properties, including the Kirtland Temple.

Indications are that Babbitt was acting under secret commission of the Twelve, at least while he was in Kirtland. Unlike the Nauvoo Temple, which had been deeded to Joseph Smith Jr. as "Trustee-in-Trust for the Church and his successor as trustee for the Church of Jesus Christ of Latter-day Saints," a matter then still unresolved—the Kirtland Temple deed read for disposal only by the "President of the Church or his successor, to the use of the members of *the Church of Christ*" (italics added). In other words, their organization of a new Kirtland church was little more than a legal maneuver to gain possession of the temple (see Minutes of the Twelve, 22 Jan. 1848, Brigham Young Papers; see also Reuben McBride to Brigham Young, 1 Nov. 1848, Brigham Young Papers.) According to McBride, Harris and McLellin would also try to persuade David Whitmer to join their cause.

71. Joseph L. Heywood to Brigham Young, 20 Apr. 1847, Journal History. The potential buyers included a Mr. Hotchkiss and a Mr. Tuttle.

72. Brigham Young and Council to the Trustees, 13 Apr. 1847, Journal History. Brigham instructed them to do everything possible to rent the temple and "leave the lease and charge of the Temple with Judge Owens." It would appear that it was indeed rented out for a short period of time until later destroyed (see Brigham Young to the Trustees, 4 Nov. 1847, and Heywood to Young, 12 Jan. 1848, Brigham Young Papers).

73. Journal History, 22 Jan. 1848.

74. Joseph L. Heywood to Brigham Young, 13 Oct. 1847. Heywood praised the assistance of "saint-like" Hiram Kimball. A wealthy Commerce landowner before the Mormons ever came to Illinois, Kimball at one time owned more land in and around Nauvoo than perhaps any other person. He converted in 1842. Kimball's good name and standing helped to pay off several Church and private debts.

75. For more on Bidamon, see Newell and Avery, *Mormon Enigma*, chapter 18, 242–54.

76. Omer Whitman manuscript.

77. Almon W. Babbitt to Brigham Young, 21 Jan. 1848, Brigham Young Papers.

78. The matter was tied up in court for three and one-half years before a ruling was finally made in favor of the ten-acre law. Unfortunately, most of the proceeds from the state-directed auctions of property went to pay court costs, legal fees, and outstanding debts. Emma did manage to retain the Mansion House, the Homestead, the Nauvoo House, and their farm, but little else (see Newell and Avery, *Mormon Enigma*, 258–60 and 357–58). For more on the topic, see Dallin H. Oaks and Joseph I. Bentley, "Joseph Smith and Legal Process: In the Wake of the Steamship Nauvoo," *Brigham Young University Law Review* 3 (1976): 735–82.

79. John S. Fullmer to Brigham Young, 27 Jan. 1848, Brigham Young Papers. See also Journal History, 26 Jan. 1848.

80. From an "Affidavit of election for trustees held 1 August 1848, signed by A. W. Babbitt," on file at the RLDS Church Archives.

81. Omer Whitman manuscript. See also "To Nauvoo," in *Our Pioneer Heritage*, 11:518–21.

82. One property sale that occurred after the release of the trustees was that of the temple lot in Independence, Missouri. On 26 April 1848, the First Presidency admonished the heirs of the late Bishop Edward Partridge who still owned a deed to the property to sell it for $300 for them "to obtain means to emigrate to the Valley" (Journal History, 26 Apr. 1848).

83. In a letter to Phineas in August 1843, Oliver made the following inquiry: "You say there is a good opening in Hancock County for a good lawyer, and also holds out other flattering inducements for a poor man. . . . How many inhabitants are there in Nauvoo. . . . How many of the Church in Hancock County, in Iowa, etc.? How many lawyers? How do you go, by land or water?" (Oliver Cowdery to Phineas Young, 24 Aug. 1843, in Stanley R. Gunn, *Oliver Cowdery: Second Elder and Scribe* [1962], 182).

84. Journal History, 17 Oct. 1845.

85. Gunn, *Oliver Cowdery*, 184.

86. Brigham Young in behalf of the Council to Oliver Cowdery, 22 Nov. 1847, Willard Richards clerk, Brigham Young Papers.

87. Oliver Cowdery to Brigham Young, 27 Feb. 1848; Journal History, 27 Feb. 1848. See also Gunn, 193–94. Cowdery went on to say that he had long thought, as one of the Three Witnesses who had selected the original Twelve Apostles, that Phineas Young should long before have been appointed to that body, certainly in preference to William Smith. He also said that he had information to convey that might dissuade Brigham from going into the valley that summer. What news that was, precisely, is not known but it may have pertained to information on the West, perhaps Indian or emigrant movements or related matters.

88. Phillip R. Legg, *Oliver Cowdery: The Elusive Second Elder of the Restoration* (1989), 157–59.

89. As quoted in Gunn, *Oliver Cowdery*, 208.

90. Journal of Warren Foote, 21 Oct. 1848, LDS Church Archives.

91. Journal History, 20 Oct. 1848. See also Gunn, *Oliver Cowdery*, 205.

92. Pottawattamie High Council Minutes, 4 Nov. 1848. Many questions were asked of Cowdery relative to his course of past actions and present feelings, especially toward Joseph Smith and other Church leaders. Cowdery felt that some of those who had contributed to his leaving had "gone to the dust or left the church." He also appealed to those that knew the true circumstances of his going off to speak on his behalf. After even more remarks, the question was called up and all voted in the affirmative that he be rebaptized. "Many expressed their gratified feelings on the occasion" (Pottawattamie High Council Minutes, 4 Nov. 1848). There is no evidence to show that he was baptized in the Missouri River. It may have been a nearby stream.

93. For a review of the life of Oliver Cowdery, see Richard Lloyd Anderson, *Investigating the Book of Mormon Witnesses* (1981); see also Anderson, "Oliver Cowdery's Non-Mormon Reputation," *Improvement Era*, Aug. 1968, 18–26.

94. Brigham Young to George A. Smith, 13 July 1848, Brigham Young Papers.

12

"WE HAVE NOW LAID THE fOUNDATION fOR OUR COMING DAY"

The sun has risen beautiful. Nature smiles and Heaven whispers
"all is well," far beyond the graves of our fathers, the land of
nativity and the church bells of those who would oppress us in
this blest land . . . for we are all here in a land not polluted by the
Gentiles. It is the garden of the whole earth. . . . Come on, all of
you. I will not tell you anything about the road but this I will say
that the ox team salvation is a hard one. The road you will know
when you see it for it is so much worse than you [have] ever seen
that you could not believe me if I told you the truth.[1]

So wrote an exhausted and relieved Susanna Sheets to family and
friends back in Winter Quarters in mid-October, shortly after her
arrival in the Salt Lake Valley with the emigrant camp. "It was the
promised land of peace and rest," another remarked. "Yes, indeed it was
beautiful to us weary pioneers who had come, at the tiring pace of the oxen,
that slow and dreary thousand miles from Winter Quarters. . . . To me it
was not the desert that so many have called it."[2]

"HOW CHARMING TO WALK INTO A HOUSE"
What had once been mere dream and vision, the domain of the cricket
and the rattlesnake, was quietly becoming a destination, a home in the

making. Unlike their pioneer camp predecessors, the newly arrived emigrant companies could already see improvements. "Here we found a fort commenced and partly built by the pioneers, consisting of an enclosure of a block of ten acres with a wall, or in part of buildings of adobes or logs. We also found a city laid out and public square dedicated for a Temple of God. We found also much ground planted in late crops."[3]

The first emigration company to reach the valley was that of Captain Horace Eldridge who, with his 20 creaking wagons, was loudly cheered as they maneuvered the last couple miles down from the canyon out onto the valley floor, reaching the tiny settlement at 5 P.M. on 19 September 1847.[4] Within three weeks, every other company in Pratt and Taylor's camp had arrived, swelling the little city's population from approximately 150 to almost 1,650 souls. It was a time of rejoicing, tearful reunion, and profound relief. As Mary Kimball put it: "We had been cooking by sage brush fires and setting our table out doors for 14 weeks. . . . How charming to walk into a house and sit down to a table once more."[5]

Yet the sight of the tiny settlement did not instill an overbrimming confidence. Notwithstanding all the declarations, prophecies, and confirmations, every thinking person knew that it was an uncertain proposition, that the coming year would prove everything. Still very much a mountaintop experiment, they were unsure whether the settlement would last and their dream become reality. Would the early crops thrive? Could they make it through a high mountain winter? Would the spring planting prove successful? In short, would they survive? The final chapter in their exodus drama had yet to be written.

Brigham's parting instructions, as he left for Winter Quarters, were calculated to ensure their very survival. "Cultivate the soil" was a recurring admonition; he knew that many in the advancing companies would arrive with depleted provisions. Regarding the coming season, he said, "we recommend that you begin to plant and sow such seeds as soon as the snow is gone in the spring, or even before spring so that we may know, by experiments, whether it is possible to ripen grain in the valley before the summer's drought." Irrigate wherever possible. Beware of prairie or valley fires. Refrain from trading with the native populations, at least within the fort. Send back wagons to help on the poor "thus fulfilling the covenant which we made in the temple at Nauvoo." And last but not least, "defile not your inheritances . . . for the Lord God will have a holy people and they shall build up a holy city unto Him."[6]

The decision by the Twelve to create a Salt Lake "Stake of Zion" was of more than passing consequence or symbolic importance. To John Smith, president, Charles C. Rich, first counselor, and John Young, second counselor, were assigned the responsibility for spiritual direction over the settlement and for overseeing the operations of the Municipal Salt Lake High Council (with its jurisdiction over nonreligious matters in the absence of any other government).

Unlike either the Winter Quarters or the Pottawatamie settlements, where there were only high councils, the Salt Lake settlement was immediately formed into—or at least provision made for—a stake. Although the membership did not get to sustain the new presidency of the stake until the following October (and by that time an ailing John Smith was replaced by Charles C. Rich as president), the decision was of real ecclesiastical importance. It was a clear indication that their little settlement marked "the end of the road," their budding new City of Zion, and that they were finally in charge.[7]

The modern historian also owes much to Brigham's parting instructions. Although not one to spend time reading history, he was anxious to preserve an archive of their accomplishments. "As soon as the emigrating camps arrive at their destination," he directed, "let their several clerks return all their papers duly certified and signed by themselves and their captains to Brother Staines, their historian, who will receive and file all such papers and from them write a brief and explicit history of the movements of the whole camp."[8]

The city the arriving emigrants discovered was but a small fort enclosing 10 acres and some 30 log and adobe houses with a four-foot adobe wall almost completed around the perimeter. In addition, 84 acres of newly planted corn, potatoes, beans, buckwheat, and turnips had been cultivated; inheritance properties had been laid out in survey fashion stemming out from the temple block. Unfortunately, most of the late garden crops had not matured, except for "a few small potatoes from the size of a pea upward to that of half an inch in diameter."[9]

Not everyone welcomed the new arrivals with open arms. All the crops were doing well, wrote one disgruntled settler, "until the first companies came in, who turned their cattle loose and devoured our crops that would have been fit to harvest in a few days and of course devoured our means of subsistence."[10]

How much of the blame for a stunted harvest can be laid at the hoof of stray cattle or on early frost is hard to prove, but certainly the arrival of so many new faces, although expected, played havoc with the original settlement plans—the existing accommodations were entirely inadequate. The initial expectation of, if not direction to, the stake presidency was to have sufficient building material on hand to accommodate the needs of the new arrivals. Furthermore, the newcomers were to have been settled along divisional lines, that is, by first and second divisions with 350 men and their families in the first and 200 other families in the second division.[11]

The press of erecting suitable accommodations in time for the coming winter, however, led to an abandonment of the original scheme. "The Divisions have not been located so much in a body as we intended," President Smith admitted.

> The first companies that came in were in a hurry to secure houses for the winter, bought buildings more or less furnished, and shares in the wall in the old fort, without any thought of their position when the Divisions should be righted up; others, as they came in, were in the hurry and anxiety and urged [us] to allot them their building places. Accordingly two more blocks on the south were surrounded and nearly taken up before the rear companies came in.[12]

The divisions were not housed as instructed for the same reason that the emigration camp had not been organized as counseled: the camp had not come by division or in adopted family order. Consequently, as everyone scrambled for a temporary roof over their head, the original plan of housing, more or less by adopted family, could not be put in effect and had to be postponed, at least until more permanent settlements could take place in the "lands of their inheritance." Although not a major disruption, it may have been a contributing factor to the ultimate disuse of the adopted family order.[13]

Construction was well underway on a second and larger fort, on the south side and adjacent to the original fort, by the time of the first snowfall in early November. The South Fort was the same width but twice as long as the North Fort. "Our houses were built on the outside line [of the fort] . . . ," wrote Taylor, "with the highest wall outside, the roof sloping towards the interior. The windows and doors were placed on the side facing the enclosure, the outside being left solid, excepting loopholes—for protection. Our corrals, hay-stacks and stables were some distance behind and outside the fort."[14]

As in Winter Quarters, their new accommodations varied in size, comfort, and attractiveness. Some opted for the adobe house, and others chose to put up small log cabins, chinked with mud and straw. "We have a log house made of hewed logs, sixteen by eighteen and covered with planks and slabs," wrote one fortunate sister, better off than most.

> Our fireplace is made of clay pounded into one corner and the fireplace cut out just such shape as you please. The rest is sticks plastered outside and which makes it quite nice. We have quite a nice door made of fir boards which were sawed since we arrived. We have nothing but the boards of our wagon for floor yet. We have a window with five squares of ten by twelve glass and one of cloth pasted on. There is two beds at the east end of the room and curtains drawn across the room in front of the beds and a little chamber floor over the beds where we keep our provisions. . . . We expect to have a garden in front of our house. Our farming land is five or six miles from here. The houses are built adjoining each other in the form of squared enclosing ten acres each.[15]

Others had no choice but to live in their tents or wagons.

Because of the flat-roof construction, by far the biggest complaint of most wives and mothers was not the cold, because there was enough kindling wood to keep the fireplaces crackling all winter, but water dripping from above. "It storms and the house leaks bad," Patty Sessions recorded. "We had a wet bad time one night. We sat up most all night. It rained down through the house so I dipped up much water in the house and carried it out. We had no floor and it was very muddy and our things wet. . . . I was up nearly all night to keep Mary and the babe and things dry."[16]

As the women improved tents and cabins, many of the men were busy in the fields. With little time to spare, by late fall they had planted another 2,000 acres of wheat. "Great numbers of plows are incessantly going," Taylor reported, "and [we] are only prevented by the inclemency of the weather which occasionally is too severe. . . . We expect to put in the spring about 3,000 acres of corn and other grain."[17]

These little improvements and hurried attempts at settlement represented the down payment on their future and their thin line of survival. As Ezra T. Benson put it: "We have now laid the foundation for our coming day."[18] With winter fast approaching, the little colony looked to settle in, with provisions safely stored, nestled in the deep and unfamiliar shadows of the towering Wasatch Mountains. In the profound stillness and enveloping darkness of their mountain home, the Latter-day Saints waited and watched for the coming cold.

"There Is Some Here That Has the Heartache"

While most looked on in faith, a few others were not quite so sure. Where were the promised crops? What if the winter killed off their cattle and milch cows? Where would they go if provisions ran out? For some, the valley was a disappointment, and others remained in a restless fear.

The discontent that first winter can be traced to three factors: the lure of California, isolated soldier dissatisfaction, and ruined spring crops. Some thought Sam Brannan had been right when he mentioned under his breath before heading back to the coast that if this was not a God-forsaken country, it surely was a God-forgotten one! Why stay in the valley to freeze and starve when there was life and abundant opportunity further west?

Brannan was not alone in singing the merits of California. Many in the Battalion, after reaching the coast, were loud in its praises. "I can look over the city [Los Angeles] and see the beautiful orchards," one soldier had written,

> The vines are hanging with grapes. The trees are loaded with fruit . . . peaches, pears, apricots, pomegranates, oranges, lemons, figs and many other fruits which we have not been used to. The country is, in my opinion, first rate for the Saints . . . plenty of everything seems to grace the land . . . and the cows look well. They are much better than in the States.[19]

The contrast between where they were and where they might have been could not have been more dramatic.

After leaving the valley on 9 August to return to California, Brannan met several returning members of the Battalion at Donner Lake. Convincing several to return with him, Brannan told them that Brigham had erred in settling in the Salt Lake Valley and predicted that sooner or later Brigham would have to lead the Saints over to California the coming year.[20]

The decision of four families to quit the little settlement in October can probably be traced to this "California Fever." Too late in the season to venture over the forbidding high Sierra, they decided to move north 40 miles and camp in the vicinity of Miles Goodyear's farm (Fort Buenaventura) at the mouth of Ogden Canyon (the present site of Ogden, Utah). Alarmed at this sudden action, and anxious to prevent further defection, the Salt Lake High Council, the only government in the valley, sent a posse after the disgruntled party "requesting them to return as soon as possible. . . . Their minds are somewhat embittered and we shall do all we can to stop them."[21]

While some sought the use of force to bring them back, worried no doubt about the potential for stirring up trouble with the Indian tribes, others wisely tried a saner course of action. From the beginning, several leaders had worried about the Goodyear farm as a potential competing settlement, an alternative to the Salt Lake location. Now, with some of the $5,000 in Battalion discharge pay recently brought back by Captain James Brown available, a solution presented itself. At a cost of $1,950, Goodyear, a master in the bargaining process, was happily persuaded to sell off his land (to which he held no clear title) and modest improvements and pursue his horse-trading business on a much wider scale than he had ever before imagined. Uncertain of the Mormon intentions and of their military muscle, Goodyear was as pleased to sell as his new neighbors were anxious to buy. Unfortunately, he had little time to enjoy his fortune, dying a year later.[22]

With nowhere else to go, the disgruntled caravan slowly returned to Salt Lake. Although a relief party was dispatched to California late in November for provisions (led by A. Lathrop, Orrin Porter Rockwell, and E. C. Fuller) none of those desperate to leave was allowed to accompany them. As one eyewitness put it: "There is some here that has the heartache. They say they will go to California, but the Council will not let them go until the Twelve comes out."[23] Finally, in early March, long before the Twelve ever reached the valley, the unhappy settlers were allowed to move out.[24]

The California Fever of 1847 soon transformed itself into the Gold Fever of 1848, an infinitely greater draw because of the discovery of placer gold by Battalion soldiers at Sutter's Fort in Sacramento Valley in February 1848. Square in the center of America's most famous gold rush, Brannan was in the right place at the right time and made a fortune. In the process, he became California's first millionaire.

But even before his lucky day, Brannan had made up his mind never to return to the Wasatch and to take as many with him as possible. Never having openly promoted the Mormon cause after the arrival of the *Brooklyn*, Brannan was rapidly outgrowing his religion and everyone in it. And for those who had once stayed with him in the faith, it was a disappointing slide. "We live now in the midst of a heartless people," William Coray of the Battalion wrote in the spring of 1848, shortly after the initial tumult and excitement of John Sutter's discovery. "Our neighbors are made up of Missourians and runaway sailors, robbers and horse thieves. The basest gamblers constitute the aristocracy of the place. The Brethren who came out in the *Brooklyn*, with a few exceptions, mingle with them, and the Mormon girls, some of them, are married to drunken sailors and vagabonds."[25]

Coray then turned a critical pen on his former file leader.

> Mr. Brannan has taught this to them, by example and precept. I do not state this expecting that it will amount to a charge . . . but the facts you ought to know. He had collected $2,000 of the Company [Battalion pay] stating that he was owing the Church the same amount of tithing funds to bring off the ship. He has swindled them out of everything they had or could earn. . . . He has counselled his brethren to stay here, to lay out their money in the purchase of lots, ten or fifteen feet under water. This he advised me to do, a while ago. He undertook to build a meeting house worth $2 or $3,000 and wanted the Battalion to subscribe, as well as the others, but they went against it and it was no go. I have frequently heard him say, in preaching to the public, that the whole Kingdom of God was depending upon their or his movements in this place and I thought to myself, 'it stands upon a tottering foundation' for it is a fact he has influence over but two or three of his own company.[26]

Brannan never returned to the valley or to the Church. His colorful career and faith-to-fortune story later turned sour through mismanagement and wild speculation. Eventually he lost his fortune, fame, and family and died in poverty and neglect in 1889. Coray, reluctant in his criticism, was nonetheless accurate in his closing comment: "Speculation is his only study."[27]

The other related cause of unrest among some of the valley settlers, unlike Brannan and the California sun, was one more of their own making. For reasons already shown (see chapter 9), Pratt and Taylor had left Winter Quarters without bringing on as many of the Battalion families as instructed. The inevitable result was keen disappointment among a small number of the recently discharged soldiers who had just crossed the Sierra, expecting to greet their families again after a separation of 15 months and a march of over 2,000 miles. To wait another year was more than some could take. "Many of the Brethren that went in the Army have returned," wrote one settler. "Some have stayed in California, and some . . . that came here have apostatized, some going back to the States and some to California."[28]

A few of the more crestfallen secretly left camp on an almost suicidal midwinter march back to Winter Quarters, miraculously survived their trek, and reached their families at the Missouri half-starved and almost frozen to death (see chapter 10). Expressing the disappointment of some, one soldier put it this way: "If it were not that we know the gospel true there would be such a scattering as never was seen. Those boys who stood as saviors would have left the wealth of the church to their fate."[29]

In defense of their camp leaders, however, many Battalion families had refused to come west in the emigration camp and others had been unprepared for the rigors of the march. And once again, as in Winter Quarters, the need to care for the Battalion families, who in many ways paid the highest price for the success of the entire westward episode, prompted the calling of the first bishops in the Salt Lake valley—five of them at first—to watch over and provide for the needs of the members in both forts but more especially the wives and children of soldier fathers and husbands.[30]

Little wonder Brigham Young waxed eloquent in his praise of the Battalion and the sacrifices made by each man and his family.

> The enlistment of the Mormon Battalion in the service of the United States, though looked upon by many with astonishment and some with fear, has proved a great blessing to this community. It was indeed the temporal salvation of our camp; and although it has been attended with perils and privation, still this has more or less been the lots of us all and it has proved a weapon of our defense, a blockade in the way of our worst enemies under which the widows,

the poor, and the destitute and in fact all of this people have been sheltered. The unseen hand of Jehovah is over this people for good and in this thing we were enabled to outlast our enemies and the snare they laid for our feet became our anchor of safety for a season.[31]

While not all were happy with the prospects of staying on in the isolation of their new mountain home, for most it was relief and promise. "We are here in a land of peace and a land of plenty in every appearance [and] I wish you were all here," one woman wrote by candlelight on a cold January night.[32] "I am happy to say that all things are getting on tolerable well," declared Bishop Hunter, despite the obvious lack of various staples. "I believe it to be a good grain country, and I know it to be a better grass country than I ever was in before."[33] And in comparison to the death counts at Winter Quarters, "the health of the people is and has been generally good."[34]

Most settlers very willingly accepted Pratt's invitation to be rebaptized, as the pioneer camp had done five months earlier, to symbolize their loyalty and commitment.[35] Sunday services were held outdoors, weather permitting, with several members holding small worship meetings of their own. On Thursday night, 14 October, "the choir met to sing for the first time in the valley," as James Smithies reported. "I opened the meeting with prayer and we had a good time. The Lord blessed us while we were together. After singing was over Bro. Hanson played us one or two tunes on the violin."[36]

Among the sisters, many of whom were plural wives of absent husbands, the same spirit of welfare, relief, spiritual instruction, and female bonding that had characterized their lives in Winter Quarters and Nauvoo asserted itself again within the walls of the two forts. "Attended a meeting of the mothers in Israel" recorded Eliza R. Snow,

> at Ellen's, after the close of which Ellen spake in the gift of tongues. It was a rich treat. . . . Had a delightful meeting of the little girls. Susan and Martha received the gift of tongues, Sarah Kimball improved upon hers. . . . Sis. Chase spoke in tongues and blessed us. Praise the Lord, O my soul.[37]

Several day schools were conducted during the week in various homes for the children, and when they could celebrate, they surely did. Come Christmas morning, for example, their first in the valley, "They fired six guns, one to the east, one to the north, one to the west and three to the south. And they shaked the earth and broke several squares of glass in the windows. This afternoon we cast in our mites and had a good supper and we had a time of rejoicing afterwards." They even enjoyed a New Year's eve dance.[38]

"WE ATE UP THE LAST BREAD WE HAD IN OUR HOUSE"

And so the winter wore on. Although not as severe a winter as many had expected or as harsh as the year following, spring could not come too soon. By early January, provisions were running so dangerously low that by order of the high council the settlement was put on strict rations, limiting each person to about one-half pound of flour per day. Wild game and foodstuffs were so scarce by the end of February that several families were forced to rummage the countryside for whatever vegetation might be edible. They even tried eating crows, thistle tops, bark—anything that might offer nutrition and fill an empty stomach.[39]

Acting on the advice of visiting Indian parties who saw their plight, several went in search of the sego lily bulb, a wild plant, whose roots were said to be more nutritious than others. "I went out to dig roots for this is our principal living," wrote one settler. "Roots and milk with a little meal."[40] And if sego lilies ran short, any root would do. Remembered Priddy Meeks:

> We had to exert ourselves to get something to eat. I would take a grubbing-hoe and a sack and start by sunrise in the morning and go, I thought six miles before coming to where the thistle roots grew, and in time to get home I would have a bushel and sometimes more [of] thistle roots. And we would eat them raw. I would dig until I grew weak and faint and sit down and eat a root and then begin again. I continued this until the roots began to fail.[41]

One of the Battalion boys, an "adopted" son of Willard Richards, could only describe a bleak picture. "I am a soldier and the soldiers fare hard here this winter. There is some that has been three days without anything to eat save it be some roots."[42]

Verging on starvation, some ate they knew not what. "A neighboring child came to the door to get some medicine for Bro. Cheny," recorded Lorenzo Young and wife. "He was poisoned by eating roots. In about one hour after [he] had called to the door . . . Bro. Cheny was in a fit. We ran to him as soon as possible and he spoke twice. We carried him to the house and did all we could for him. He lived about half an hour then died. It was one of the most melancholy scenes I ever passed through."[43]

The long, late winter placed undue expectations on the promise of spring. When the first sign of milder weather came in mid-March, they were busy planting—prematurely as they soon discovered. "People have commenced plowing and planting," as early as the first week of March, "but it freezes a little [at] night."[44] Moderating late March weather prompted even more planting, but their eagerness was soon countered by April's fickleness and May's unseasonable cold. Isaac Haight recorded one disappointment after another:

> April 1: Weather cold and unpleasant. The ground covered with snow. Had a foot [of snow] this week. Our houses being flat-roofed they leaked very bad which makes it very unpleasant. The wheat that was sowed last fall looks very discouraging for a crop but we trust in the Lord that had brought us here will sustain us and not let us perish. . . .
>
> April 6: Ground froze some last night. The buckwheat is killed and many things in the garden. . . .
>
> April 28: Frost again this morning. Things killed in the gardens such as beans, cucumbers, melons, pumpkins and squashes. Corn hurt and some wheat killed.[45]

Then, as if the frost was not damaging and discouraging enough, on the morning of 27 May came the sound of an approaching army—from the direction of the mountains where no army should have been able to pass. Like a plague out of ancient Egypt let loose on a modern Israel, an overwhelming infestation of large, black crickets descended on the valley floor, devouring every living plant in its way.

> Wingless, dumpy, black, swollen-headed, with bulging eyes in cases like goggles, mounted upon legs of steel wire and clock-spring, and with a general personal appearance that justified the Mormons in comparing him to a cross of the spider and the buffalo, the Deseret cricket comes down from the mountains at a certain season of the year, in voracious and desolating myriads. . . . The assailants could not be repulsed. The Mormons, after their fashion, prayed and fought, fought and prayed, but to no purpose.

The "black Philistines" mowed their way even with the ground, leaving it as if touched with an acid or burnt by fire.[46]

The foregoing account was given two years after the fact by Thomas L. Kane. Although prone to popularizing the plight of the Latter-day Saints, in this case Kane was not exaggerating. "We had not anticipated any further trouble," wrote one observer,

> but today [27 May] to our utter astonishment the crickets came by millions sweeping everything before them. They first attacked a patch of beans and in twenty minutes there was not a vestige of them to be seen. They next swept our peas. Then came into our gardens [and] took everything clean. We went out with brush and undertook to drive them but they were too strong for us.
>
> 28 May: Last night we had a severe frost. Today crickets have commenced on our corn and small grain. They have eaten off 12 acres for Bro. Rosacrants, 7 for Charles and are now taking Edmunds.
>
> 29 May: Today they have destroyed 3/4 of an acre squash [in] our place, 2 acres of millet and our rye and are now to work on our wheat. What will be the result we know not.[47]

Every defensive tactic was employed to stem the voracious black tide, including the use of sticks, clubs, brooms, brushes, and willows. Even a five-year-old was given a wooden mallet to smash them to death, although with strict orders not to venture too far out.[48] Ditches were filled with water in an attempt to drown the pests. Fields were set afire in advance of the moving mass in an attempt to leave nothing for them to eat and confuse their movements. But all to no avail. If they moved on to the larger wheat fields with the same destructive effect, an already serious situation would turn ruinous.

The twin blows of their spring misfortune continued uninterrupted for days. By day the crickets devastated field after field while by night the late season frosts killed the remaining young seedlings. For many, it was too much to bear. "This morning's frost, in unison with the ravages of the crickets for a few days past," wrote Eliza R. Snow, "produces many sighs and occasions some long faces with those that for the moment forget that they are saints."[49] "Many of the saints began to think of leaving the valley, for fear of starvation," wrote another.[50]

Defeat of the Settlers/Arrival of the Gulls, *sculpture by Charles B. Hall*

Sensing the rising disappointment and waning allegiance, Charles C. Rich called for a special outdoor meeting early in June, in part to dissuade large numbers of settlers from abandoning the valley. "It was a beautiful day and a very solemn one too," Priddy Meeks recalled. While standing in an open wagon, Rich counseled the people to stay on. As if on a belated cue, what came next, from high overhead, was the shrill sound of sweet deliverance.

At that instant I heard the voice of fowls flying overhead that I was not acquainted with. I looked up and saw a flock of seven gulls.

347

In a few minutes there was another larger flock passed over. They came faster and more of them until the heavens were darkened with them and lit down in the valley till the earth was black with them; and they would eat crickets and throw them up again and fill themselves again and right away throw them up again. A little before sundown they left for Salt Lake, for they rested on a sandbar; a little after sunrise in the morning they came back and continued. I guess this circumstance changed our feeling considerable for the better.[51]

Wrote another eyewitness, "The first I knew of the gulls, I heard their sharp cry. Upon looking up I beheld what appeared like a vast flock of pigeons coming from the northwest. It was about three o'clock in the afternoon. . . . There must have been thousands of them. Their coming was like a great cloud; and when they passed between us and the sun, a shadow covered the field. I could see gulls settling for more than a mile around us."[52]

Some modern researchers have argued that the seagull salvation was discriminate, unseen by many and commented on by only a relatively small number of journal writers.[53] It does appear that "the colonists exhibited a thorough matter-of-factness about the miracle" at the time.[54]

Actually it was not at all unusual for seagulls to visit the fields, even in large numbers. No doubt they had been doing so since the arrival of the first settlers. What was different here was that the birds were preying on the crickets, not on the fields; and that they continued to do so day after day; and that they gorged themselves, regurgitated, and returned to gorge some more; and that they did so in different areas of the valley. "The crickets continue to eat our wheat," wrote Daniel Spencer, "but a large quantity of sea gulls came on to our corn land on Mill Creek and ate up all the crickets in the neighborhood. . . . The gulls left the ground in two weeks from the time they lit on the land."[55]

Another early settler, William Leany, returning to his small acreage on South Mill Creek,

noticed thousands of sea gulls dipping down to the earth as if turning summer saults [sic] and a Brother Jacob Secrist [sic] shouted "By heavens Bro. Leany, look how they are eating the crickets." And as soon as they were dead they seemed to light on the ditches and spew them up by double handfuls and go for more.[56]

348

If less dramatically than some earlier writers may have realized, the seagulls nevertheless began to turn the tide on the cricket hordes at the most critical time, enough to dent their progress and raise the hopes of the settlers. And timing proved to be everything. The crickets were destroyed. The grain crops were preserved and many once more looked forward in regained confidence, never to turn back.

Describing the episode almost a year to the day later, A. J. McCall, a gold-seeker on his way to California, credited it to "the great flocks of curlew, a fowl as large as a partridge, which soon gobbled up the crickets and saved the crops. . . . It is no marvel that these misguided people should believe they were the special favorites of the Almighty."[57]

"We Feel the Trying Time Has Passed"

By mid-July, everything was looking brighter. The weather turned bright and warm. The entire settlement was busy plowing new fields, replanting old ones, improving housing, retrieving lumber from the valleys, constructing mills, and sending back spare teams and wagons to assist the oncoming emigrant trains. By the end of July, 450 buildings, including cabins, makeshift blacksmith shops, tanneries, shoemaker and tailor shops, and more dotted the valley floor. They also counted three saw mills, two grist mills for grinding wheat, and a thrashing machine "propelled by water [that] will thrash and clean in good order 200 bushels per day."[58] The crop matured faster than expected; the first wheat was ground on 14 July. "It is very short for want of being irrigated in season yet some is very fine," wrote Haight. "The prospects for crops begin to brighten . . . enough to sustain the people here."[59]

All was so much on the mend that by early August Parley P. Pratt could write only good news to his oncoming file leaders.

> There were some 5,000 acres plowed, planted and sowed but owing to the destruction by grasshoppers, crickets and other insects we are not able to state how many acres will finally mature their crops. Our [spring] wheat harvest is over; the grain is splendid and clean but being mostly in shock and stack we cannot state the number of bushels; however . . . the wheat crop has done wonderfully well.
>
> . . . Our main fence is twelve miles long, not quite finished owing to the press of other matters . . . green peas have been so

plenty for a long time that we are becoming tired of them; cucumbers, squashes, beets, carrots, parsnips and greens are upon our tables as harbingers of abundance . . . and no one has starved. . . . We feel the trying time has passed . . . quiet union and peace prevail.[60]

It was all enough to celebrate! But rather than commemorate their arrival in the valley the year before (most had come at different times), they found abundant cause to celebrate their new harvests.[61]

To mark the occasion, the 10th of August was selected as a day of thanksgiving, a day "to celebrate the first harvest raised in the valley with songs of praise and thanksgiving." The entire population convened at the bowery on the temple block at 9 A.M., where a new Liberty Pole had been erected especially for the occasion. First to be hoisted to the top, against a backdrop of cannon fire and shouts of "Hosanna to God and the Lamb forever and ever, Amen," was a white flag, "our flag," as Levi Jackman put it, "not stained with any national device but pure and white [which] proudly floated in the pure, clean healthy northern breeze."[62] Next, below their standard, amid further shouts of acclamation, were raised a sheaf of wheat, a bundle of barley, another of oats, and lastly one of corn. They then assembled within and all around the bowery to listen to remarks from Pratt and Taylor. "All went off in good order and feelings," remembered Haight, and "a splendid dinner was spread under the bowery for the occasion."[63] After dinner, which lasted from noon till 2 P.M., the rest of the day was given over to dancing, instrumental music, "prayers and preaching."[64]

Sometime during their festivities, they sang Parley P. Pratt's new composition entitled "The Harvest Song," written specifically for the occasion and sung to the more familiar tune "How Firm a Foundation." His lyrics captured well the spirit of their gladness and freedom.[65]

> Let us join in the dance, let us join in the song,
> To the Jehovah the praises belong;
> All honor all glory we render to thee
> Thy cause is triumphant, thy people are free.
>
> The gentiles oppressed us the heathens with rage,
> Combined all their forces and hosts to engage;
> They plundered and scattered and drove us away,
> They killed their shepherd, the sheep went astray

Full long in the desert and mountains to roam,
Without any harvest without any home;
They're hungry and thirsty and weary and worn,
They seemed quite forsaken and left for to roam.

But lo in the mountains new sheep folds appear,
And a harvest of plenty our spirits to cheer;
This beautiful vale is a refuge from woe,
A retreat for the Saints when the scourges o'erflow.

The States of Columbia to [pieces] may rend,
And mobs all triumphant bring peace to an end;
The star spangled banner forever be furled,
And the chains of a tyrant encircle the world.

The storms of commotion distress every realm,
And dire revolutions the nations o'erwhelm;
Tho Babylon trembles and thrones cast down be,
Yet here in the mountains the righteous are free.

The fact that no American flag was hoisted that day to the top of their Liberty Pole, itself an expression of their new freedom from outside rule, along with Pratt's lyrics, are both further evidence that they felt joy and enormous relief at being free from their persecutors and believed that the hand of the Lord would yet surely visit their oppressors.

Irene Hascall worded it this way:

This is our place of residence. It is in the midst of the rocky mountains surrounded on every side by impassable mountains and just one passage in and another on the west side which will not take much labor to stop an army of ten thousand. Now let the mobbers rage. The Lord has provided this place for us and if we are faithful the trouble and calamities of the Gentile nation will not harm. When all is past we will step forth from our hiding place, the secret chamber spoken of in the Bible. I wish you would come and stay with us. You would if you could see the future. But live in darkness, we know this is true, what you call Mormonism.[66]

None of the above should be construed as an attempt by the Latter-day Saints to remain forever apart or to ever secede from the United States. Most well knew that the Manifest Destiny of American expansion was on the way west and that they, unwittingly perhaps, were part of it. Many of the returning soldiers were certain that their territory was about to become part of America. In fact, news of the war-ending Treaty of Guadalupe Hidalgo in which Upper California had been ceded by Mexico to the United States would reach them early in the fall, if it had not already.[67]

The point is that for now they were safe and secluded and free to live and worship as they pleased. And if and when America must catch up to them, they would be in a position of political power as the first settlers, an advantage which they had never enjoyed before. In fact, Brigham and other leaders were at that very moment preparing a petition to Congress for a Mormon territorial government. Although their dream of popular rule would be marked with conflict and disappointment over the next half-century, they would now ensure every advantage possible.[68]

While preparing for the new arrivals, few were expecting the return of one man who had been away serving a mission to the Society Islands. Leaving his family, then in Nauvoo, on 1 June 1843, Addison Pratt had spent the past five years proclaiming the Book of Mormon in the Sandwich Islands (Hawaii), Tahiti, and a dozen other islands all over the South Pacific. His return, via California, to his new transplanted home in the mountains not only says much about the settlement but even more about the emotion of reunion as missionaries and soldiers returned to their families. "As we drew near the forts," he recalled,

> we began to meet our friends coming out to meet us. Bro. Haight told me he knew the house my family lived in and he would conduct me there. We found them in the South Fort, in a house with Sister Rogers . . . she had been confined the night before with a young child, and my wife who had been up with her had come into her travelling wagon that stood near the door and was still used to sleep in, to take a nap, as every house was crowded to overflowing.
>
> My oldest daughter Ellen was down on her knees, scrubbing the floor. Bro. Haight stepped in and said, "Ellen, here is your father." She jumped up, as I stepped in after him, and caught hold of my hand, with an expression that was as wild as a hawk, and exclaimed, "Why, Pa Pratt!! have you come?" The next two, Frances and Lois, were soon on hand and looked equally surprised. The youngest, Ann, was out to play. She was soon called, and when she came in, she stood and eyed me a while with a very suspicious

look, when one of her sisters tried to force her up to me, to shake hands, saying, "That is pa" when she jerked her hand away and said, "It is not" and left the room.

Their mother soon came in. She looked quite natural and quite as young as when I left home, being more fleshy now, than then. At Winter Quarters she, with the rest of the family, all but the youngest, suffered under severe fits of sickness, and the scurvy deprived her of her upper front teeth, and when she spoke, her voice was unnatural. Except that, I could discover no change in her. . . . It was some like the meeting of strangers than the meeting of a family circle. I shall never forget it![69]

Anxious to convince his youngest child of who he was, Pratt took her out to his wagon and opened a large chest filled with "a variety of curiosities, such as she had never seen before," including "the grandest selection of sea shells that had ever been seen by anybody." "'Don't you think I was a very kind Father to remember you when so far away, and make such choice selections and bring them to you?' She readily answered in the affirmative. I then added, 'You believe now that I am your father do you not?' She readily answered, 'Yes!!' Then said I, 'Step forward and give me a kiss, and these things are yours.'"[70]

Meanwhile Brigham arrived in the valley with his division on Wednesday, 20 September, and was immediately escorted about the settlement by Bishop Hunter and some others. Heber C. Kimball and his division arrived four days later, on a Sunday. After adjourning the scheduled worship meetings in the bowery in order to give him and his company an opportunity to attend, another hymn, this one composed by Eliza R. Snow, was sung "by the whole choir" welcoming the two leaders and their respective companies into the valley. By the time Willard Richards and his division arrived three weeks later (11 October) 2,417 new faces were looking for a home. To meet the needs of the new arrivals, an addition to the city's east side was surveyed and a decision made to lay off two other cities, one 10 miles to the north and the other 10 miles to the south of the original settlement.

The final spike in this transcontinental story, the culmination of their new beginning, occurred at the semiannual conference of the Church which opened in the bowery on Friday, 6 October. Dedicated almost exclusively to such pressing temporal matters as housing, lands and inheritances, crops, continued explorations and much more, there was nevertheless more at stake than crickets and cucumbers. One unfinished matter of ecclesiastical business of enormous consequence to them and this study had yet to be addressed.

This marked the first time for many in the audience to welcome Brigham Young not just as President of the Quorum of the Twelve but as President of the Church. Neither had Pratt and Taylor, as members of the Quorum of the Twelve, yet had the chance to sustain the concept of a reestablished First Presidency, let alone the specific men to fill it. Along with all the others in the emigration camp, they had been absent from the special conference at Council Bluffs the previous December where a new First Presidency had been sustained.

The two had missed the extensive discussions back at Winter Quarters on the topic. How much they had discussed the matter while at the Sweetwater, as the two camps met, is not clear. It would appear, however, that up until two months before, the matter was still unsettled in Pratt's mind, at least. "We were somewhat startled to find the Twelve dispersed in a great measure," Pratt had written Brigham early in 1848 after hearing of the many begging missions east, "some to one and some to another point on the globe insomuch that a quorum of them will hardly be together very soon."[69]

The nature and content of the important discussions between Brigham and Kimball and Pratt and Taylor are not available. What is clear, however, is that whatever questions might have remained over the matter of succession in the Presidency, as well as the matter of valley inheritances, was reconciled. Consequently, after adjourning Saturday to allow the Battalion use of the bowery for a day of rest and recreation (which had been earlier postponed because of bad weather), the conference reconvened on Sunday, 8 October, at 11 A.M. in the bowery on the temple block. After singing and an opening prayer by John Taylor, Parley P. Pratt stepped forward and nominated Brigham Young as the President of the Church, with Heber C. Kimball and Willard Richards counselors. All "carried without a dissenting voice."[72] Pratt concluded: "We must say that it is as it should be."[73]

NOTES

1. Susanna Sheets and husband, Elijah, to her mother and friends in Winter Quarters, 15 Oct. 1847, Amos Milton Musser Family Collection, LDS Church Archives.

2. "God and Gold—1847," in *Our Pioneer Heritage*, Carter, 16:494.

3. *Autobiography of Parley P. Pratt*, 360.

4. Journal History, 19 Sept. 1847. Actually, three others—William Staines, Thomas Bingham, and Joseph W. Young—had already reached the Salt Lake settlement, sent ahead as special messengers. Joseph Young had arrived as early as 31 August (Journal History, 31 Aug. and 19 Sept.).

5. Mary Ellen Able Kimball, "A Sketch of Pioneer History," 16 Sept. 1847, LDS Church Archives.

6. "An Epistle to the Saints in Great Salt Lake Valley," by Brigham Young, written 20 miles east of South Pass, 9 Sept. 1847, Journal History; see also General Church Minutes, 1 Aug. 1847.

7. Much has been written about the continuing role of the Council of Fifty in the early government of these settlements (see Arrington, *Great Basin Kingdom*, 50; see also Hansen, *Quest for Empire*).

The Council of Fifty was composed essentially of the same men that made up the Twelve Apostles and the various municipal high councils. It was a debating society, a discussion forum for political considerations. It was the political arm for ecclesiastical discussion. But it wielded no authority at Winter Quarters, at Council Bluffs, or at Salt Lake. It convened at the wish of Church leaders. The Salt Lake Stake and high council answered to the new First Presidency and the Quorum of the Twelve.

8. "An Epistle to the Saints in Great Salt Lake Valley," by Brigham Young, written 20 miles east of South Pass, 9 Sept. 1847, Journal History.

9. "Journal of Erastus Snow," 26 Aug. 1847. Special care was given to the potato crop and its resilience to early frost because it was a perfect jump-start on the next season. See also Neff, *History of Utah*, 104.

10. Reminiscences and Journal of John Steele, 1848–1898, 2 Nov. 1847, LDS Church Archives.

11. The desire to settle by division may have been an attempt to settle along adopted family lines, with those belonging to the Brigham Young and other families in one division and those under Heber C. Kimball and other Apostles in the other division.

12. John Smith, Charles C. Rich, and John Young to Brigham Young, 14 Oct. 1847, Brigham Young Papers.

13. For more on the dissolution of the adopted family order, see Irving, "The Law of Adoption," *BYU Studies* 14 (Spring 1974): 291–314. See also Bennett, *Mormons at the Missouri*, 163–64.

14. As quoted in Roberts, *The Life of John Taylor*, 193.

15. Irene Hascall to Ophelia M. Andrews, 5 Mar. 1848, Hascall Papers.

16. Journal of Patty Sessions, 28 and 31 Mar. and 4 May 1848.

17. From a letter of John Taylor, as quoted in Campbell, *Establishing Zion*, 10.

18. General Church Minutes, 14 Nov. 1847.

19. William Muir to Brigham Young, 16 May 1847, Brigham Young Papers.

20. Sam Brannan to Brigham Young and the Council, 17 Oct. 1847, Brigham Young Papers. See also Campbell, "The Apostasy of Samuel Brannan," *Utah Historical Quarterly* 27 (1959): 156–67. Although Brannan was not out to destroy the valley settlement, he was certainly convinced that California "continues to grow stronger and stronger in our favor."

21. John Smith to Brigham Young, 4 Oct. 1847, Brigham Young Papers; Journal of Eliza R. Snow, 7–10 Oct. 1847. See also the Journal of James Smithies, 6 Oct. 1847, LDS Church Archives.

22. Goodyear died 12 November 1849, at the age of 32 (Campbell, "Miles Morris Goodyear," in Hafen, *The Mountain Men*, 2:188).

23. Susanna Sheets to her family, 11 June 1848, Amos Milton Musser Family Collection.

24. John Smith and Counselors to Brigham Young, 6 Mar. 1848, Brigham Young Papers. The decision to prohibit their departure sooner may not have been as heavy-handed as it looks. Battalion soldiers had been over the passes earlier and had witnessed firsthand the difficulty—and the tragedies—of going over in the wrong season. It should also be pointed out that a few others in 1848 had chosen to quit their westward trek even before arriving at the valley. Although efforts were made to change their minds, no physical force was ever used to stop them.

25. William Coray to Willard Richards, [pre-July] 1848, Willard Richards Papers. Other soldiers had also written of the dark side to the California glow, which in part may explain why so few of them stayed back. "There is in this country three evils which have ruined the country," wrote William Muir. "The first is drinking so much wine and whisky. The next is gambling, betting at Monterey horse racing on Sunday. The last and worst in my opinion is whoring with the Indian women" (William Muir to Brigham Young, 6 May 1847, Brigham Young Papers).

26. Ibid.

27. For more on Brannan, see the sources listed in chapter 6, note 82. For all that has been written on Brannan, more should now be written, with so many new sources available. Brannan quit his church and did live the roller coaster ride of rags to riches; however, he did much good for what became the city of San Francisco and attracted much early settlement to California.

28. Journal of Isaac Chauncey Haight, 1 Jan. 1848.

29. Journal of John Steele, 20 Dec. 1848, in "Extracts from the Journal of John Steele," *Utah Historical Quarterly* 6, no. 1 (Jan. 1933): 20.

30. The original five bishops were J. B. Nobles, Tarleton Lewis, John S. Higbee, Jacob Foutz, and Edward Hunter. Foutz died later that winter (see Salt Lake High Council Minutes, 7 Mar. 1847, LDS Church Archives).

31. Brigham Young to Noah Packard, 4 Apr. 1848, Brigham Young Papers.

32. Susanna Sheets to her family, 18 Jan. 1848, Amos Milton Musser Family Collection.

33. Edward Hunter to Brigham Young, 4 Mar. 1848, Brigham Young Papers.

34. John Smith and Counselors to Brigham Young, 6 Mar. 1848. During the winter, only 12 people died, compared to the several hundreds back at the Missouri in the previous two winters.

35. Journal of James Smithies, 28 Nov. 1847. "He wished them to remember their covenants to keep them and to put a stop to all their lying and taking the name of God in vain and their stealing and to put away their evil doings from before the eyes of the Lord."

36. Journal of James Smithies, 17 Oct. 1847.

37. Journal of Eliza R. Snow, 2–7 Nov. 1847.

38. Journal of James Smithies, 25 and 31 Dec. 1847.

39. Arrington, *Great Basin Kingdom*, 49.

40. Journal of James Smithies, 17 May 1848. The sego lily remains the state flower of Utah.

41. "Journal of Priddy Meeks," *Utah Historical Quarterly* 10 (1942): 163.

42. S. M. St. John to Willard Richards, 9 Jan. 1848, Willard Richards Papers.

43. Journal of Lorenzo Young, 21 Feb. 1848, LDS Church Archives.

44. Irene Hascall to her family, 5 Mar. 1848, Hascall Papers.

45. Journal of Isaac Chauncey Haight, 1–6 Apr. 1848.

46. Kane, *The Mormons*, 66.

The so-called Mormon Cricket, technically identified as *Anabrus simplex*, is 1.25 inches long. Traveling in hordes as big as a city block or more, they moved up to two miles per day. They not only consumed vegetation but other insect and animal life as well, including rattlesnakes, evergreen trees, and sagebrush (see Frank T. Cowan, *Life Habits, History and Control of the Mormon Cricket*, U.S. Dept. of Agriculture Technical Bulletin No. 161 [1929], 26–27). Such infestations are rare today because most crickets have been destroyed in the maze of irrigation ditches throughout the valley.

47. Journal of Lorenzo Young and wife, 27–29 May 1848.

48. Manomas Andrus, "Biography of Manomas Lavina Gibson Andrus: 1842–1922," typescript, 2, Harold B. Lee Library, Brigham Young University; quoted in William G. Hartley, "Mormons, Crickets, and Gulls: A New Look at an Old Story," *Utah Historical Quarterly* 38 (Summer 1970): 224–39. Hartley's article is an excellent revised study of the cricket and the seagull.

49. Journal of Eliza R. Snow, 28 May 1848.

50. Journal of Isaac Chauncey Haight, 4 June 1848.

51. "Journal of Priddy Meeks," 164. See also Arrington, *Charles C. Rich*, 128.

52. Journal History, 9 June 1848.

53. Hartley, "Mormons, Crickets, and Gulls," 233–35.

54. Morgan, *The Great Salt Lake*, 215.

55. Journal of Daniel Spencer, 3 July 1848, LDS Church Archives.

Modern research has shown that this was probably not the first, nor would it be the last, incident of seagull-insect confrontation. As Hartley has shown, thousands of seagulls invaded grasshopper-infested fields near Mandan, North Dakota, in 1921, in Montana in 1924, in Saskatchewan in 1933, in Oregon in 1937 and 1947, and in Utah again in 1952 ("Mormons, Crickets, and Gulls," 237). What cannot be minimized, however, is that the miracle of the gulls came when it did, where it did. For this reason, the seagull remains the state bird of Utah.

56. Autobiography of William Leany (spring, 1849), 14, LDS Church Archives.

57. Journal of A. J. McCall, 21 July 1849, in "The Great California Trail in 1849: Wayside Notes of an Argonaut," 57, manuscript, Oregon Historical Society.

58. The most admired grist mill was that erected by John Neff, who had also been responsible for erecting the successful mill at Winter Quarters.

59. Journal of Isaac Chauncey Haight, 16 July 1848.

60. Parley P. Pratt and Council to Brigham Young, 9 Aug. 1848, Brigham Young Papers.

61. The first account of celebrating on 24 July did not come until the following summer, in recognition of the date Brigham Young and his party entered the valley.

62. Journal of Levi Jackman, 10 Aug. 1848.

63. Journal of Isaac Chauncey Haight, 10 Aug. 1848.

64. Journal of Patty Sessions, 10 Aug. 1848.

65. Journal of Levi Jackman, 10 Aug. 1848.

66. Irene Hascall to Ophelia Andrews, 5 Mar. 1848, Hascall Papers.

67. Morgan, *The Great Salt Lake*, 220. The Treaty of Guadulupe Hidalgo was signed 2 February 1848. According to the terms, Mexico ceded Texas with the Rio Grande boundary, New Mexico (including Arizona), and Upper California (including San Diego) to the United States.

68. Leonard Arrington, *Great Basin Kingdom*, 42. See also H. H. Bancroft, *History of Utah* (1889), 444.

69. *Journals of Addison Pratt*, 358–59.

70. Ibid.

71. Parley P. Pratt to Brigham Young, 8 Aug. 1848, Brigham Young Papers.

72. "Epistle to Orson Hyde, George A. Smith, and Ezra T. Benson," from Brigham Young, 9 Oct. 1848, in James R. Clark, ed., *Messages of the First Presidency of The Church of Jesus Christ of Latter-day Saints*, 6 vols. (1965–75), 1:344.

73. Pratt to Young, 8 Aug. 1848, Brigham Young Papers.

ЄPILOGUЄ

We'll find the place which God for us prepared,
Far away in the West,
Where none shall come to hurt or make afraid;
There the Saints will be blessed.[1]

This book deliberately ends in the predawn of Utah history and at the threshold of the great Mormon migrations that would see approximately 60,000 people come to Deseret, their new mountain Zion, between 1849 and the completion of the transcontinental railroad 20 years later. Like a tiny, swinging pedestrian bridge spanning the deep river gorge below, the Mormon Exodus of 1846–1848 was the tenuous, essential connecting link between a turbulent past in the East and a brighter future in the West. And it was a pathway laid at considerable sacrifice and breathtaking risk.

An essential fact to remember is that there was no practical certainty that their journey would be successful and that their new settlement would prosper. The stakes were enormous! Had they failed in their march, had they failed to discover in time a new place and a new Zion—and convinced the membership to follow suit—it is entirely possible that The Church of Jesus Christ of Latter-day Saints would have broken up. As their leader put it:

> If the Church is blown to the four winds and never gathered again, remember I have told you, how, when, and where to gather,

and if you do not go now, remember and bear me witness in the day of judgment. When God tells a man what to do, he admits of no argument, and I want no arguments.[2]

The underlying theme of this entire study has been that the exodus of the Latter-day Saints was for the survival of the Church—Joseph Smith's grand enterprise, the message of Cumorah. Though patently obvious from a retrospective viewpoint, this imperative created drama, suspense, and a great deal of anxiety and trepidation. There was no survival, no future in their beloved "City of Joseph," and anyone anywhere close to the situation knew it. Mormonism was a despised, hunted, misunderstood, and maligned American religion, and America would have nothing to do with it. They had to either get out of Nauvoo or face extermination. Thus was born one of the great forced migrations in American history.

Surely there can be no doubt that this was an exodus in every sense of the word—a "going out," a "mass departure," a "going forth of many persons," a forced migration of an entire people, a church on the move. There is no parallel to it in all of American history. And although the migrations continued for years after the last date covered in this book, by August 1848 the essentials of their exodus had all been put into place—a mass following, a successful trek across the desert of America, and a new settlement.

At the outset of this study, it was argued that for the salvation of the Church at least seven things would have to happen. Obviously the first was to flee. And get out they did! Under the bold and daring leadership of Brigham Young, as adroit politically as he was careful spiritually, 12,000 Latter-day Saints made their way across Iowa and reached the Missouri River by the fall of 1846. And by the fall of 1848, some 4,200 of these had resettled in the Rocky Mountains; many more thousands were waiting their time to come. The dimension, coherency, and discipline of the migration, the going out as one, and the overall commitment of the people to make it succeed are a tribute to their faith and determination and a lasting salute to the leadership of Brigham Young and those others who assisted him. It was an exodus of necessity.

Once committed and on the way west, their urgent need was to find a place "to stick the stake," a new home large enough to accommodate their present and future needs, far enough away to ensure their space and freedom, and healthy enough to sustain their crops and support their living.

While some of their number sought for California or Texas or the Tongue River, most followed their leaders to the valley of the Great Salt Lake, a spot they more or less had determined before crossing the Mississippi. Although some tried to dissuade them and others found it a disappointment, most made peace with the choice and waded into the desert experiment with abundant hope and energy.

Much has been written about the triumph of discovery and of finding "the right place." And well it should be. Yet it may be that one of the more enduring characteristics of their long, dusty quest was not the finding of place but something less tangible—the discovery of mission and a rising awareness of fulfilling prophecy. To Orson Pratt and others, it meant hope, confirmation, and acceptance that their sufferings and persecutions, their wanderings in the wilderness, and everything they had stood for and believed was redeemed in this long tedious march to the valley. Such a sense of a modern Israel fulfilling ancient prophecy became a wonderful motivation, an inspiration, a timely glue that helped keep them together. This matter of evolving self-perception, their own interpretation of their expanding role, their unfolding errand into the wilderness, cannot be minimized as a vital factor in their success in finding and keeping their place. It was an exodus of redemption and of prophecy fulfilled.

A third essential to their survival as a religious body was the restructuring of their government, the reestablishment of a new First Presidency, and more to the point the reconviction among the majority of the people that God had called a new prophet. The murder of Joseph Smith and the dissolution of the original presidency had wrought devastation in the hearts of many of his followers. Some could not be reconciled to leadership by the Twelve and sought solace elsewhere. Indeed, one argument of this study has been to show that although James Strang, Sidney Rigdon, and a handful of others laid claim to the leadership and future of the Church, it was Strang in particular who showed initial, surprising strength and worrisome appeal. And for a time, as the membership of the Church lay strewn and uprooted across the plains, the uncertainty of it all, the fear of the unknown, the cost in money and health and loved ones, and the absence of a prophet leader— all these contributed to a certain real hesitation and withholding of support.

Yet one very real heritage or result of the exodus was that it made a prophet of Brigham Young in a way perhaps no other circumstance could have. Surely it is not coincidental that he left Nauvoo as president of a depleted Quorum of the Twelve, a leader among equals, but came back to the Missouri as President of the Church with a strong and revitalized quorum. And as "The Word and Will of the Lord" had indicated, there would be no other quorum, no other authority greater than the Twelve, save the First Presidency. The trials and uncertainties of their westward march made of him an even greater leader than before. By the time they settled at the Great Salt Lake, for the vast majority there was no longer any doubt who should lead the Church. Much attention has been devoted to the several discussions and disagreements among many of Brigham's colleagues, in part to show that there was, at first, some uncertainty on the matter of a new First Presidency. This may have come as somewhat of a surprise to those who have long assumed that the reestablishment of this quorum was a foregone conclusion. Such active deliberations in tents, in wagons, and by the fire of the willow patch confirm the fact that this was no careless power grab.

Some have argued that Brigham Young was a power seeker, anxious to take advantage and fill a vacuum of authority through the overbearing strength of his own personality. The historical evidence shows, however, that such was not the case, that his fellow leaders, men of strong mind and independent character, were not given to intimidation or browbeating, despite his chastisements and rebukes. When finally they concluded that Brigham should be the next President of the Church, they did so more or less willingly and accepted new mission assignments near and far under his direction. They may not have always liked his style, but they revered and respected him for what he had accomplished and, in the process, came to believe that God had invested the future of the Church in his hands.

Likewise, the unanimous support of the people, at least of those who were in the process of going west, of his leadership and of his Presidency was by no means a routine matter. The fact that most refused to follow George Miller or James Emmett at the Missouri, or Sam Brannan to California, or James Strang to Beaver Island is all-compelling evidence that they sensed in Brigham a man in whom they could put their trust and faith. While it is true that there were thousands who stayed back—many of whom in Illinois, Missouri, and Iowa eventually coalesced around the person of Joseph Smith III and the Reorganized Church of Jesus Christ of Latter Day Saints—most of the members were satisfied with Brigham's leadership. It was, then, an exodus of leadership—prophetic leadership—a willingness to accept a new First Presidency. And with it was laid the principle of apostolic succession and its corollary, apostolic supremacy over any and all other quorums or parties in the Church.

The fourth fact of the exodus is that they came to see it as a refiner's fire, a biblical-type chastening of God's people. Early Latter-day Saint doctrine called for a tried and a tested people. But at no other time in their short history were they called on to receive such refining. Their belief explains the fact that while so many died at Winter Quarters and along the Iowa trail, there was never a hint of rebellion or of mass defection. In fact, their trials only deepened their determination. "We mean to conquer or die trying,"[3] was Brigham's challenge to the foe. Or as William Clayton put it in his anthem to their modern pilgrimage: "And should we die before our journey's through, Happy day! All is well!"[4]

If they were God's people, they would accept God's will. They had already learned this lesson a dozen years before in Zion's Camp. If they would not live and die for that which they so dearly believed, and take God's rebukes and redemptions, no amount of wagon trails would ever bring them success. Their many sermons and writings abundantly attest that either they would go as God's people or they would not go at all! It became an exodus of reformation.

The corollary to this divine schooling on the high plains of America must surely be that if God would chasten them, a modern Israel, he would surely prove their oppressors and discomfort their enemies. Running through their many writings, as clear and as deep as their new irrigation streams in the valley, was their conviction that God would surely and eventually visit America in justice. The recurring renunciations of their past allegiances and the early celebrations of their newfound freedom are all abundant proof of an attitude of collective hurt and expectant retribution. Their several Liberty Poles, white flags of purity, Jubilees, harvest songs and poems and letters all point to a profound disappointment in civil authority and man-made governments—especially of the America they once knew and loved. It was an attitude that would soften only with the passage of time and the inevitable accommodation with the nation's expanding borders.

One of the enduring ironies of the exodus is that at the moment of their maximum distrust and open disdain of the United States, the Latter-day Saints were persuaded, once again by the artful negotiation of their leader, to join in the Army of the West in an extended and memorable march to California, a march of trial and sacrifice. Although it underscored their devotion more to their leader than to their country, this critical decision resulted in a desperately-needed infusion of cash and supplies, deterred political enemies bent on their discomfort, if not destruction, and did much to ensure the overall success of the enterprise.

They would also go as a covenant people. Another central theme has been the fact that they saw their Nauvoo temple covenants and ordinances as an essential part of their success. Certainly the Nauvoo Covenant of October 1845, in which they promised to do all in their power to bring on the sick and the poor, was an enduring call to sacrifice that each one was reminded of repeatedly. In return, Brigham saw to it that certain temple blessings, particularly temple marriages for those about to go off to war, were quietly granted on an exigency basis. A practical leader, Brigham was never tied by tradition; he interpreted and applied doctrines to the solutions of immediate, practical problems.

He also understood the motivating force and the defining power of covenants and of the place of temple worship when, on 26 July in the valley, he proclaimed with a wave of his cane the site of the new Salt Lake Temple—the covenant heritage of Nauvoo transplanted to the mountain-tops. To have done otherwise would have betrayed the trust of his people, many of whom had spent months laboring on the construction of the Nauvoo Temple. Though the Salt Lake Temple would not be completed for almost half a century, the place of covenants and of the temple endowment was a unifying, motivating force, a central defining element to their faith. It was, then, an exodus of covenant.

Neither can one ignore the all-important economic considerations. Having examined everything from temple sales to tithing, from battalions to begging missions, it is now clear how they paid for it all. Besieged and bankrupt, the Church was carried on the backs of its believers. Ultimately it was the incredible sacrifice of means and properties, time and talent, pleasures and comforts, and lives and liberties that made it all possible. Whether the soldier's wife foregoing her husband's discharge pay for the help of others, the father surrendering Church wagons in the mudflats of Mt. Pisgah, or the loss of friends and of entire families in the mud huts of Winter Quarters, this was and will forever be an exodus of endurance and sacrifice.

Of no less importance to the success of their cause was the rediscovery of the printing press. To thwart the early and impressive gains of Strang, if nothing else, and certainly to reestablish the doctrine of gathering and the resumption of the great British migrations, the ability to print was essential to their missionary and gathering success. The declaration and dissemination of printed epistles provoked the spirit of gathering on an international scale and signalled to many anxious, watching eyes that their westward experiment had succeeded. With donated funds from a handful of St. Louis members, they were finally able to break their silence and send out the word by missionary, poster, mail, and express. It became an exodus of "publishing peace."

Finally, through it all there was the faith and hope of a deeply religious people. Their task was less to preserve a culture than it was to save a religion—not a routine migration of excited and courageous individuals to the west but a going forth to Zion of an entire faith. Because their people were of several lands, it was not an ethnic exercise as much as it was a spiritual one. And although Brigham became their prophet-leader and proved his qualities, the truth remains that this was a people who were wont to be led. These were men and women who believed deeply in their cause and in their faith and who would largely remain committed and together despite the deaths of Winter Quarters or the crickets of Salt Lake. It was, in the end, their exodus of faith.

Fifty years ago, during the centennial celebrations of the arrival of the pioneers in the Salt Lake Valley, J. Reuben Clark, then of the First Presidency, penned the following lines, which are as appropriate now as they were then. It is only fitting that he should again have the final word.

> So through dust and dirt, dirt and dust, during the long hours, the longer days—that grew into weeks and then into months, they crept along till, passing down through its portals, the valley welcomed them to rest and home. The cattle dropped to their sides, wearied almost to death; nor moved they without goading, for they too sensed they had come to the journey's end.
>
> That evening was the last of the great trek, the mightiest trek that history records since Israel's flight from Egypt, and as the sun sank below the mountain peaks of the west and the eastern crags were bathed in an amethyst glow that was a living light, . . . they of the last wagon, and of the wagon before them, and of the one before that, and so to the very front wagon of the train, these all sank to their knees in the joy of their souls, thanking God that at last they were in Zion—"Zion, city of our God."[5]

NOTES

1. William Clayton, "Come, Come Ye Saints," *Hymns of The Church of Jesus Christ of Latter-day Saints* (1985), no. 30.

2. Journal History, 28 June 1846.

3. Journal History, 16 Apr. 1847.

4. "Come, Come, Ye Saints."

5. J. Reuben Clark, "To Them of the Last Wagon," in Conference Report, Oct. 1947, 158; reprinted in *Ensign*, July 1997, 38.

APPENDIX

The Pioneer Camp of 1847

1. ADAMS, BARNABAS L.
   Born in 1812 near Perth, Upper Canada
   Died in 1869 near Salt Lake City, Utah

2. ALLEN, RUFUS
   Born in 1814 in Litchfield County, Connecticut
   Died in 1887 in Ogden, Utah

3. ANGELL, TRUMAN OSBORN
   Born in 1810 in North Providence, Rhode Island
   Died in 1887 in Salt Lake City, Utah

4. ATWOOD, MILLEN
   Born in 1817 in Wellington, Connecticut
   Died in 1890 in Salt Lake City, Utah

5. BADGER, RODNEY
   Born in 1823 in Waterford, Vermont
   Died in 1853 in Salt Lake County, Utah

6. BAIRD, ROBERT ERWING
   Born in 1817 in Londonderry, Ireland
   Died in 1875 in Ogden, Utah

7. BARNEY, LEWIS
   Born in 1808 in Hollen Purchase, New York
   Died in 1894 in Mancos, Colorado

8. BARNUM, CHARLES D.
   Born in 1800 near Brockville, Leeds County, Canada
   Died in 1894 in Salt Lake City, Utah

9. BENSON, EZRA T.
   Born in 1811 in Mendon, Massachusetts
   Died in 1869 in Ogden, Utah

10. BILLINGS, GEORGE PIERCE
    Born in 1827 in Kirtland, Ohio
    Died in 1896 in Manti, Utah

11. BOGGS, FRANCIS
    Born in 1807 in Belmont County, Ohio
    Died in 1889 in Washington, Utah

12. BROWN, GEORGE WASHINGTON
    Born in 1827 in Newbury, Ohio
    Died in 1906 in Charleston, Utah

13. BROWN, JOHN
    Born in 1820 in Sumner County, Tennessee
    Died in 1897 in Pleasant Grove, Utah

14. BROWN, NATHANIEL THOMAS
    Born (date and location unknown)
    Died in 1848 in Council Bluffs, Iowa

15. BULLOCK, THOMAS
    Born in 1816 in Leek, Staffordshire, England
    Died in 1855 in Coalville, Utah

16. BURKE, CHARLES ALLEN
    Born in 1823 in Kirtland, Ohio
    Died in 1888 in Minersville, Utah

17. BURNHAM, JACOB D.
    Born in 1820 in New York
    Died in 1850 in Greenwood Valley, California

18. CARRINGTON, ALBERT
    Born in 1813 in Royalton, Vermont
    Died in 1889 in Salt Lake City, Utah

19. CARTER, WILLIAM
    Born in 1821 in Ledbury, England
    Died in 1896 in St. George, Utah

20. CASE, JAMES
    Born in 1794 in Litchfield, Connecticut
    Died in 1858 in Sanpete County, Utah

21. CHAMBERLAIN, SOLOMON
    Born in 1788 in Old Canaan, Connecticut
    Died in 1862 in Washington, Utah

22. CHESLEY, ALEXANDER PHILIP
    Born in 1814 in Bowling Green, Virginia
    Died in 1884 in Orange, Australia

23. CLAYTON, WILLIAM
    Born in 1814 in Penwortham, Lancashire, England
    Died in 1879 in Salt Lake City, Utah

24. CLOWARD, THOMAS POULSON
    Born in 1823 in Chester County, Pennsylvania
    Died in 1909 in Payson, Utah

25. COLTRIN, ZEBEDEE
    Born in 1804 in Ovid, New York
    Died in 1887 in Spanish Fork, Utah

26. CRAIG, JAMES
    Born in 1821 in Ireland
    Died in 1868 in Santa Clara, Utah

27. CROSBY, OSCAR
    Born about 1815 in Virginia
    Died in 1870 in Los Angeles, California

28. CURTIS, LYMAN
    Born in 1812 in New Salem, Massachusetts
    Died in 1898 in Salem, Utah

29. CUSHING, HOSEA
   Born in 1826 in Boston, Massachusetts
   Died in 1854 in Salt Lake City, Utah

30. DAVENPORT, JAMES
   Born in 1802 in Danville, Vermont
   Died in 1885 in Richmond, Utah

31. DECKER, ISAAC PERRY
   Born in 1840 in Winchester, Illinois
   Died in 1916 in Provo, Utah

32. DEWEY, BENJAMIN FRANKLIN
   Born in 1829 in Westfield, Massachusetts
   Died in 1904 in Chloride, near Kingman, Arizona

33. DIXON, JOHN
   Born in 1818 in Cumberland, England
   Died in 1853 near Parley's Park, Salt Lake City

34. DRIGGS, STARLING GRAVES
   Born in 1822 in Pennsylvania
   Died in 1860 in Parowan, Utah

35. DYKES, WILLIAM
   Born in 1815 in Philadelphia, Pennsylvania
   Died in 1879 in Nebraska

36. EARL, SYLVESTER H.
   Born in 1815 in Ohio
   Died in 1873 in Middleton, Utah

37. EASTMAN, OZRO FRENCH
   Born in 1828 in Windham County, Vermont
   Died in 1916 in Idaho Falls, Idaho

38. EGAN, HOWARD
   Born in 1815 in Tullamore, King County, Ireland
   Died in 1878 in Salt Lake City, Utah

39. EGBERT, JOSEPH TEASDALE
   Born in 1818 in Vincennes, Indiana
   Died in 1898 in Ogden, Utah

40. ELDREDGE, JOHN SUTHERLAND
    Born in 1831 in Canaan, New York
    Died in 1873 in Charleston, Utah

41. ELLSWORTH, EDMUND
    Born in 1819 in Paris, New York
    Died in 1893 in Show Low, Arizona

42. EMPEY, WILLIAM A.
    Born in 1808 in Osnabrook Township, Stormont County,
       in eastern Canada
    Died in 1890 in St. George, Utah

43. ENSIGN, HORACE DATUS
    Born in 1826 in Westfield, Massachusetts
    Died in 1866 in Ogden, Utah

44. EVERETT, ADDISON
    Born in 1805 in Wallkill, New York
    Died in 1885 in St. George, Utah

45. FAIRBANKS, NATHANIEL
    Born in 1823 in Queensbury, New York
    Died in 1853 near Sacramento, California

46. FARR, AARON FREEMAN
    Born in 1818 in Waterford, Vermont
    Died in 1903 in Logan, Utah

47. FITZGERALD, PERRY
    Born in 1814 in Fayette County, Pennsylvania
    Died in 1889 in Draper, Utah

48. FLAKE, GREEN
    Born in 1828 in Anson County, North Carolina
    Died in 1903 in Idaho Falls, Idaho

49. FOWLER, JOHN SHERMAN
    Born in 1819 in New York City, New York
    Died in 1860 in Sacramento, California

50. FOX, SAMUEL BRADFORD
    Born in 1829 in Adams, New York
    Died (date and location unknown)

51. FREEMAN, JOHN MONROE
    Born in 1823 in Chatham, Connecticut
    Died in 1850 in Carson Valley, Nev.

52. FRINK, HORACE MONROE
    Born in 1832 in Livingston County, New York
    Died in 1874 in San Bernardino, California

53. FROST, BURR
    Born in 1816 in Waterbury, Connecticut
    Died in 1878 in Salt Lake City, Utah

54. GIBBONS, ANDREW S.
    Born in 1825 in Union, Ohio
    Died in 1886 in St. Johns, Arizona

55. GLEASON, JOHN STREATER
    Born in 1819 in Livonia, New York
    Died in 1904 in Pleasant Grove, Utah

56. GLINES, ERIC
    Born in 1822 in New Hampshire
    Died in 1881 in Santa Rosa, California

57. GODDARD, STEPHEN H.
    Born in 1810 in Clinton County, New York
    Died in 1898 in San Bernardino, California

58. GRANT, DAVID
    Born in 1816 in Arbroath, Scotland
    Died in 1868 in Mill Creek, Utah

59. GRANT, GEORGE R.
    Born in 1820 in New York
    Died in 1889 in California

60. GREENE, JOHN YOUNG
    Born in 1826 in New York
    Died in 1880 in Salt Lake City, Utah

61. GROVER, THOMAS
    Born in 1807 in Whitehall, New York
    Died in 1886 in Farmington, Utah

62. HANCOCK, JOSEPH
    Born in 1800 in Springfield, Massachusetts
    Died in 1893 in Payson, Utah

63. HANKS, SIDNEY ALVARUS
    Born in 1820 in Madison, Ohio
    Died in 1870 near Parley's Park, Utah

64. HANSEN, HANS CHRISTIAN
    Born in 1806 in Copenhagen, Denmark
    Died in 1890 in Salina, Utah

65. HARMON, APPLETON MILO
    Born in 1820 in Conneaut, Pennsylvania
    Died in 1877 in Holden, Utah

66. HARPER, CHARLES ALFRED
    Born in 1816 in Upper Providence, Pennsylvania
    Died in 1900 in Holladay, Utah

67. HENRIE, WILLIAM
    Born in 1799 in Pennsylvania
    Died in 1883 in Bountiful, Utah

68. HIGBEE, JOHN S.
    Born in 1804 in Tate Township, Ohio
    Died in 1877 in Toquerville, Utah

69. HOLMAN, JOHN GREENLEAF
    Born in 1828 in Byron Center, New York
    Died in 1888 in Rexburg, Idaho

70. HOWD, SIMEON
    Born in 1823 in Camden, New York
    Died in 1862 in Beaver, Utah

71. IVORY, MATHEW
    Born in 1800 in Philadelphia, Pennsylvania
    Died in 1885 in Beaver, Utah

72. JACKMAN, LEVI
    Born in 1797 in Orange County, Vermont
    Died in 1876 in Salem, Utah

73. JACOB, NORTON
    Born in 1804 in Sheffield, Massachusetts
    Died in 1879 in Glendale, Utah

74. JOHNSON, ARTEMAS
    Born in 1809 in Remson, New York
    Died (date and location unknown)

75. JOHNSON, LUKE S.
    Born in 1807 in Pomfret, Vermont
    Died in 1861 in Salt Lake City, Utah

76. JOHNSON, PHILO
    Born in 1814 in Newton, Connecticut
    Died in 1896 in Payson, Utah

77. KELSEY, STEPHEN
    Born in 1830 in Montville, Ohio
    Died in 1900 in Paris, Idaho

78. KENDALL, LEVI NEWELL
    Born in 1822 in Lockport, New York
    Died in 1903 in Springville, Utah

79. KIMBALL, ELLEN SANDERS
    Born in 1825 in Ten, Thelemarken, Norway
    Died in 1871 in Salt Lake City, Utah

80. KIMBALL, HEBER C.
    Born in 1801 in Sheldon, Vermont
    Died in 1868 in Salt Lake City, Utah

81. KING, WILLIAM A.
    Born in 1821 (location unknown)
    Died in 1862 in Boston, Massachusetts

82. KLEINMAN, CONRAD
    Born in 1815 in Bergweiler, Lauday, Bavaria
    Died in 1907 in St. George, Utah

83. LAY, HARK
Born in 1825 in Monroe County, Mississippi
Died in 1890 in Union, Utah

84. LEWIS, TARLETON
Born in 1805 in Pendleton District, South Carolina
Died in 1890 near Teasdale, Utah

85. LITTLE, JESSE CARTER
Born in 1815 in Belmont, Maine
Died in 1893 in Salt Lake City, Utah

86. LOSEE, FRANKLIN G.
Born in 1815 in Belmont, Maine
Died in Lehi, Utah (date unknown)

87. LOVELAND, CHAUNCEY
Born in 1797 in Glasgow, Connecticut
Died in 1876 in Bountiful, Utah

88. LYMAN, AMASA MASON
Born in 1813 in Lyman Township, New Hampshire
Died in 1877 in Fillmore, Utah

89. MARBLE, SAMUEL HARVEY
Born in 1822 in Phelps, New York
Died in 1914 in Round Valley, Arizona

90. MARKHAM, STEPHEN
Born in 1800 in Avon, New York
Died in 1878 in Spanish Fork, Utah

91. MATHEWS, JOSEPH LAZARUS
Born in 1809 in Johnson County, North Carolina
Died in 1886 in Pima, Arizona

92. MILLS, GEORGE
Born in 1778 in England
Died in 1854 in Salt Lake City, Utah

93. MURRAY, CARLOS
Born in 1829 in Ontario County, New York
Died in 1855 near the Humboldt River, Nevada

94. NEWMAN, ELIJAH
Born in 1793 in Hampshire County, Virginia
Died in 1872 in Parowan, Utah

95. NORTON, JOHN WESLEY
Born in 1820 in Lisbon, Indiana
Died in 1901 in Panguitch, Utah

96. OWEN, SEELEY
Born in 1805 in Milton, Vermont
Died in 1881 near Flagstaff, Arizona

97. PACK, JOHN
Born in 1809 in New Brunswick, Canada
Died in 1885 in Salt Lake City, Utah

98. PEIRCE, ELI HARVEY
Born in 1827 in Uwchland, Pennsylvania
Died in 1858 in Salt Lake City, Utah

99. POMEROY, FRANCIS M.
Born in 1822 in Somers, Connecticut
Died in 1883 in Mesa, Arizona

100. POWELL, DAVID
Born in 1822 in Edgefield District, South Carolina
Died in 1883 in Santa Rosa, California

101. PRATT, ORSON
Born in 1811 in Hartford, New York
Died in 1881 in Salt Lake City, Utah

102. RAPPLEYE, AMMON TUNIS
Born in 1807 in Ovid, New York
Died in 1883 in Kanosh, Utah

103. REDDEN, RETURN JACKSON
Born in 1817 in Hiram, Ohio
Died in 1891 in Hoytsville, Utah

104. RICHARDS, WILLARD
Born in 1804 in Hopkinton, Massachusetts
Died in 1854 in Salt Lake City, Utah

105. ROCKWELL, ORRIN PORTER
Born in 1815 in Manchester, New York
Died in 1878 in Salt Lake City, Utah

106. ROCKWOOD, ALBERT PERRY
Born in 1805 in Holliston, Massachusetts
Died in 1879 in Salt Lake City, Utah

107. ROLFE, BENJAMIN WILLIAM
Born in 1822 in Romford, Maine
Died in 1892 in Salt Lake City, Utah

108. ROOKER, JOSEPH
Born in 1818 (location unknown)
Died in 1895 in Oceanside, California

109. ROUNDY, SHADRACH
Born in 1789 in Rockingham, Vermont
Died in 1872 in Salt Lake City, Utah

110. SCHOFIELD, JOSEPH SMITH
Born in 1809 in Winchester County, New York
Died in 1875 in Bellevue, Utah

111. SCHOLES, GEORGE
Born in 1812 in Chadderton, Lancashire, England
Died in 1857 in Cottonwood, Utah

112. SHERWOOD, HENRY G.
Born in 1785 in Kingsbury, New York
Died in 1857 in San Bernardino, California

113. SHUMWAY, ANDREW PURLEY
Born in 1833 in Millbury, Massachusetts
Died in 1909 in Franklin, Idaho

114. SHUMWAY, CHARLES
Born in 1808 in Oxford, Massachusetts
Died in 1898 in Johnson, Utah

115. SMITH, GEORGE ALBERT
Born in 1817 in Potsdam, New York
Died in 1875 in St. George, Utah

116. SMOOT, WILLIAM COCKHORN ADKINSON
Born in 1828 in Tennessee
Died in 1920 (location unknown)

117. SNOW, ERASTUS
Born in 1818 in St. Johnsbury, Vermont
Died in 1888 in Salt Lake City, Utah

118. STEVENS, ROSWELL
Born in 1808 in Grand River, Upper Canada
Died in 1880 in Bluff, Utah

119. STEWART, BENJAMIN FRANKLIN
Born in 1817 in Jackson, Ohio
Died in 1886 north of Payson, Utah

120. STEWART, JAMES WESLEY
Born in 1825 in Fayette County, Alabama
Died in 1913 in Cokeville, Wyoming

121. STRINGHAM, BRIANT
Born in 1825 in Windsor, New York
Died in 1871 in Salt Lake City, Utah

122. SUMME, GILBARD
Born in 1802 in Randolph County, North Carolina
Died in 1867 in Harrisburg, Utah

123. TAFT, SETH
Born in 1796 in Mendon, Massachusetts
Died in 1863 in Salt Lake City, Utah

124. TANNER, THOMAS
Born in 1804 in Bristol, Gloucestershire, England
Died in 1855 in Salt Lake City, Utah

125. TAYLOR, NORMAN
Born in 1828 in Grafton, Ohio
Died in 1899 in Moab, Utah

126. THOMAS, ROBERT T.
Born in 1820 in Richmond County, North Carolina
Died in 1892 in Provo, Utah

127. THORNTON, HORACE
    Born in 1822 in Hinsdale, New York
    Died in 1914 in Manti, Utah

128. THORPE, MARCUS BALL
    Born in 1822 in New Haven, Connecticut
    Died in 1849 while sailing off Cape Horn

129. TIPPETS, JOHN HARVEY
    Born in 1810 in Wittingham, New Hampshire
    Died in 1890 in Farmington, Utah

130. VANCE, WILLIAM PERKINS
    Born in 1822 in Jackson County, Tennessee
    Died in 1914 in Lund, Nevada

131. WALKER, HENSON
    Born in 1820 in Manchester, New York
    Died in 1894 in Pleasant Grove, Utah

132. WARDLE, GEORGE
    Born in 1820 in Cheddleton, England
    Died in 1901 in Vernal, Utah

133. WARDSWORTH (OR WORDSWORTH), WILLIAM SHIN
    Born in 1810 in Salem County, New Jersey
    Died in 1888 in Springville, Utah

134. WEILER, JACOB
    Born in 1808 near Churchtown, Pennsylvania
    Died in 1896 in Salt Lake City, Utah

135. WHEELER, JOHN
    Born in 1802 in Kean County, South Carolina
    Died (date and location unknown)

136. WHIPPLE, EDSON
    Born in 1805 in Dummerston, Vermont
    Died in 1894 in Colonia Juarez, Chihuahua, Mexico

137. WHITNEY, HORACE KIMBALL
    Born in 1823 in Kirtland, Ohio
    Died in 1884 in Salt Lake City, Utah

138. WHITNEY, ORSON K.
Born in 1830 in Kirtland, Ohio
Died in 1884 in Salt Lake City, Utah

139. WILLIAMS, ALMON M.
Born in 1807 in New York
Died in 1884 on the Pottawattamie lands

140. WOODRUFF, WILFORD
Born in 1807 in Farmington, Connecticut
Died in 1898 in San Francisco, California

141. WOODWARD, GEORGE
Born in 1817 in Monmouth County, New Jersey
Died in 1903 in St. George, Utah

142. WOOLSEY, THOMAS
Born in 1806 in Pulaski County, Kentucky
Died in 1897 in Wales, Utah

143. YOUNG, BRIGHAM
Born in 1801 in Whitingham, Vermont
Died in 1877 in Salt Lake City, Utah

144. YOUNG, CLARISSA DECKER
Born in 1828 in Freedom, New York
Died in 1889 in Salt Lake City, Utah

145. YOUNG, HARRIET PAGE WHEELER
Born in 1803 in Hillsboro, New Hampshire
Died in 1871 in Salt Lake City, Utah

146. YOUNG, LORENZO DOW
Born in 1807 in Smyrna, New York
Died in 1895 in Salt Lake City, Utah

147. YOUNG, LORENZO SOBIESKI
Born in 1841 in Winchester, Illinois
Died in 1904 in Shelley, Idaho

148. YOUNG, PHINEHAS HOWE
Born in 1799 in Hopkinton, Massachusetts
Died in 1879 in Salt Lake City, Utah

HISTORIOGRAPHICAL ESSAY

Rather than provide a definitive historiographical essay to so large a body of writings on the Mormon exodus, the purpose of this short review is to highlight those works, published and otherwise, that were most helpful in the writing of the present study.

PRIMARY SOURCES

As the reader has by now discovered, this work is founded on primary documentation and archival materials, many of which have not been published previously. Of all such manuscript material, by far the most beneficial were the papers and correspondence of Brigham Young, housed in the Church Historical Department of The Church of Jesus Christ of Latter-day Saints in Salt Lake City, Utah. This remarkable archive consists primarily of his incoming and outgoing letters, sermons, minutes of quorum meetings, hearings, financial records, and related items. No accurate account of this period in Church history is possible without utilizing this resource.

An extension of the Brigham Young papers are the General Church Minutes, a collection of minutes of meetings of senior quorums within the Church and of other discussions, sermons, and presentations during the period between the death of Joseph Smith in June 1844 and the reorganization of the First Presidency in December 1847. A remarkable resource, these detailed accounts give clarity and understanding of a difficult formative period.

The individual writings and journals of several other prominent leaders have likewise been highly useful. Although some of these have been published in one form or another, I have relied on my study of the originals wherever possible. Especially helpful and noteworthy are such model journals as those written by William Clayton, Wilford Woodruff, Thomas Bullock, Horace K. Whitney, Erastus Snow, Willard Richards, Howard Egan, Patty Sessions, Eliza R. Snow, and Hosea Stout. The diaries and journals of other, lower-level leaders also proved of worth, including those of Charles R. Dana, William Appleby, and Norton Jacob. The letters of Irene Hascall are a proven resource.

Other unpublished Church sources used in the work include the minutes of the Winter Quarters High Council from 1846 to 1848, of the Pottawattamie High Council from 1847 to 1852, and of the Salt Lake High Council from 1847 to 1848. Likewise, the records of clerks of various traveling companies were a valuable resource.

Surprisingly beneficial was the vast scrapbook-like vertical file of diary entries, minutes, excerpts from correspondence, articles, editorials, and more that make up the Journal History, likewise found in the LDS Church Historical Department. Compiled by Andrew Jenson and his staff many years ago, this resource is unequalled for its breadth of coverage and scope of content. Though lacking in the letters of senior Church leaders, it is nonetheless an indisputable resource, an essential first stop on the road to serious study of nineteenth-century Mormon history.

In addition to Mormon sources, a great many other archival records of contemporaries have been utilized to give balance and perspective. Among those most heavily relied upon were the journals and diaries of such other overlanders as Joseph W. Wood, Isaac Pettijohn, Joel Palmer, Charles Peabody, Silas Newcombe, William A. Hockett, Lansfield B. Hastings, and James Clyman. The locations of these journals are identified in the bibliography.

Besides the above journal collections, two particularly fruitful archival collections of letters and related materials were the James Jesse Strang Papers and the writings of Lilburn W. Boggs and his son, William Boggs. The study of the Strang papers at Yale and at Independence provided a deeper understanding and appreciation of the effort he made to create an alternative to Brigham Young's westward initiative.

SECONDARY SOURCES

The literature of the Mormon migration is its own large and growing library, as are the even more voluminous writings on the Oregon and California Trails. No accurate understanding of the Mormon movement, in context of the westward migrations of the time, is possible without the study of such essential works as John D. Unruh Jr.'s *The Plains Across* (1982), Merrill J. Mattes's *The Great Platte River Road* (1969), Andrew Child's *Overland Route to California* (1946), and Ray Allen Billington's and Martin Ridge's *Westward Expansion* (1982).

Among those works providing a rich, comprehensive perspective, few yet rival the detail, color, and passion of B. H. Roberts's *Comprehensive History of the Church of Jesus Christ of Latter-day Saints* (6 volumes). Though somewhat dated, Roberts is still full of insight and scholarly observation, the essential introduction to the serious study of all of nineteenth-century Mormon history.

Among the earliest works on the topic are Jules Remy's *A Journey to Great Salt Lake* (1861), Hubert H. Bancroft's *The History of Utah* (1889), and Henry Inman's and William F. Cody's *The Great Salt Lake Trail* (1898).

Some of the better known studies in this century have been Cecil E. McGavin's *The Mormon Pioneers* (1947), *Exodus to Greatness* by Preston Nibley (1947), Wallace Stegner's well-known *The Gathering of Zion* (1964), and Joseph E. Brown's heavily illustrated *The Mormon Trek West* (1980). What Nibley lacked in critical writing he made up in detail and the inclusion of unpublished accounts, surprising in scope for a work written a half century ago.

Stegner, not a Latter-day Saint, has written what is arguably the best, most readable study of the Exodus. Like Bernard DeVoto before him, Stegner found inspiration in the remarkable sacrifice of the pioneers. While saluting their courage and devotion, Stegner remained ever critical of their faith. A master at capturing the human drama, Stegner misunderstood the essential motivation, the spiritual underpinnings, even the ecclesiastical politics involved.

Other modern writers have included elements of the story in broader studies or biographies. Most noteworthy are Leonard J. Arrington in his classic work, *Great Basin Kingdom* (1958), and two of his biographical stud-ies—*Charles C. Rich* (1974) and, more recently, *Brigham Young: American Moses* (1985). Stanley B. Kimball, *the* scholar of the trail itself, must also be mentioned not only for his editing of William Clayton's *The Latter-day Saints' Emigrants Guide* (1983) but also for his biography, *Heber C. Kimball: Mormon Patriarch and Pioneer* (1981). For trail aficionados, Kimball's maps, trail guides, and studies are unsurpassed for precision, insight, and exact-ness. Likewise, the scholarship of Dale L. Morgan—as evidenced in his *The Great Salt Lake* (1947), *Overland in 1846: Diaries and Letters of the California-Oregon Trail* (1963), and his numerous articles on related topics—has been highly beneficial. Morgan anticipated the findings from even the most recently discovered manuscript collections as perhaps no other writer.

These represent just some of the works found to be most useful in the present study. All others are referenced in the bibliography itself.

SELECTED BIBLIOGRAPHY

Printed Sources

BOOKS

Aikawa, Jerry K. *Rocky Mountain Spotted Fever.* Springfield, Ill.: Charles C. Thomas, 1966.

Allen, James B. *Trials of Discipleship: The Story of William Clayton, a Mormon.* Urbana: University of Illinois Press, 1987.

Allen, James B., and Glen M. Leonard. *The Story of the Latter-day Saints.* Salt Lake City: Deseret Book, 1992.

Anderson, Richard Lloyd. *Investigating the Book of Mormon Witnesses.* Salt Lake City: Deseret Book, 1981.

Arrington, Leonard J. *Brigham Young: American Moses.* Urbana: University of Illinois Press, 1985.

———. *Charles C. Rich: Mormon General and Western Frontiersman.* Provo, Utah: Brigham Young University Press, 1974.

———. *Great Basin Kingdom: An Economic History of the Latter-day Saints 1830–1900.* Cambridge: Harvard University Press, 1958.

Arrington, Leonard J., and Davis Bitton. *The Mormon Experience: A History of the Latter-day Saints.* New York: Vintage Books, 1980.

Bailey, Paul. *Sam Brannan and the California Mormons.* Los Angeles: Westernlore Press, 1943.

Bancroft, Hubert H. *History of Utah.* San Francisco: History Company, 1889.

Bennett, Richard E. *Mormons at the Missouri, 1846–1852: "And Should We Die."* Norman: University of Oklahoma Press, 1987.

Billington, Ray Allen, and Martin Ridge. *Westward Expansion: A History of the American Frontier.* 5th ed. New York: Macmillan, 1982.

Bitton, Davis. *The Redoubtable John Pack: Pioneer, Proselyter, Patriarch.* Salt Lake City: Eden Hill, 1982.

Black, Susan Easton, and William G. Hartley, eds. *The Iowa Mormon Trail: Legacy of Faith and Courage.* Orem, Utah: Helix Publishing, 1997.

Bonney, Edward. *The Banditti of the Prairies.* Norman: University of Oklahoma Press, 1963.

Bradley, James L. *Zion's Camp 1834: Prelude to the Civil War.* Logan, Utah: James L. Bradley, 1990.

Bringhurst, Newell G. *Saints, Slaves, and Blacks: The Changing Place of Black People within Mormonism.* Westport, Connecticut: Greenwood, 1981.

Britt, A. *An America That Was: What Life Was Like on an Illinois Farm Seventy Years Ago.* Barre, Mass.: Barre Pub., 1964.

Brooks, Juanita. *Mountain Meadows Massacre.* Norman: University of Oklahoma Press, 1962.

Brown, John. *Autobiography of Pioneer John Brown, 1820–1896.* Arr. John Zimmerman Brown. Salt Lake City: John Z. Brown, 1941.

Bryant, Edwin. *What I Saw in California: Being the Journal of a Tour . . . in the Years 1846, 1847.* New York: D. Appleton and Co., 1848.

Bush, Lester E. Jr. *Health and Medicine among the Latter-day Saints: Science, Sense, and Scripture.* New York: Crossroad Publishing, 1993.

Campbell, Eugene E. *Establishing Zion: The Mormon Church in the American West, 1847–1869.* Salt Lake City: Signature Books, 1988.

Carter, Kate B., comp. *Heart Throbs of the West.* 12 vols. Salt Lake City: Daughters of Utah Pioneers, 1939–51.

———. *Our Pioneer Heritage.* 20 vols. Salt Lake City: Daughters of Utah Pioneers, 1958–77.

Catlin, George. *North American Indians.* 2 vols. Edinburgh: John Grant, 1926.

Child, Andrew. *Overland Route to California.* Los Angeles: N. A. Kovach, 1946.

Chittenden, Hiram Martin. *The American Fur Trade of the Far West.* 2 vols. 1901. Reprint, Stanford: Academic Reprints, 1954.

Chittenden, Hiram Martin, and Alfred Talbot Richardson. *Life, Letters and*

Travels of Father Pierre-Jean De Smet, S. J., 1801–1873. 4 vols. New York: Francis P. Harper, 1905.

Christensen, Clare B. *Before and After Mount Pisgah.* Salt Lake City: Clare B. Christensen, 1979.

The Church of Jesus Christ of Latter-day Saints. *A Collection of Sacred Hymns for the Use of the Latter-day Saints.* Selected and published by J. C. Little and G. B. Gardner. Bellows Falls, Ill.: Blake and Bailey, 1844.

————. *The Doctrine and Covenants of The Church of Jesus Christ of Latter-day Saints.* Salt Lake City: Deseret Book, 1981.

Clark, James R., comp. *Messages of the First Presidency of The Church of Jesus Christ of Latter-day Saints.* 6 vols. Salt Lake City: Bookcraft, 1965–75.

Clarke, Dwight L. *Stephen Watts Kearney: Soldier of the West.* Norman: University of Oklahoma Press, 1961.

Clayton, William. *The Latter-day Saints' Emigrants Guide: Being a Table of Distances, Showing All the Springs, Creeks, Rivers, Hills, Mountains, Camping Places, and All Other Notable Places, from Council Bluffs, to the Valley of the Great Salt Lake.* St. Louis: Missouri Republican, 1848. Reprint, ed. Stanley B. Kimball. Gerald, Missouri: Patrice Press, 1983.

————. *William Clayton's Journal: A Daily Record of the Journey of the Original Company of "Mormon" Pioneers from Nauvoo, Illinois, to the Valley of the Great Salt Lake.* Salt Lake City: Deseret News, 1921.

Connor, Seymour V. *North America Divided: The Mexican War, 1846–1848.* New York: Oxford University Press, 1971.

Cook, Lyndon W. *The Revelations of the Prophet Joseph Smith: A Historical and Biographical Commentary of the Doctrine and Covenants.* Provo, Utah: Seventy's Mission Bookstore, 1981.

Dana, E. *Geographical Sketches on the Western Country, Designed for Emigrants and Settlers.* Cincinnati: Looker, Reynolds, 1819.

Daughters of Utah Pioneers. *An Enduring Legacy.* 10 vols. Salt Lake City: 1978–1987.

Delano, Alonzo. *Across the Plains and Among the Diggings.* New York: Wilson-Erickson, 1936.

Deseret News 1993–1994 Church Almanac. Salt Lake City: Deseret News, 1992.

Deseret News 1997–1998 Church Almanac. Salt Lake City: Deseret News, 1996.

de Smet, Pierre-Jean. "Letters and Sketches: With a Narrative of a Year's Residence Among the Indian Tribes of the Rocky Mountains." In *Early Western Travels 1748–1846*, vol. 7. Cleveland: 1906.

DeVoto, Bernard. *Across the Wide Missouri*. Boston: Houghton Mifflin, 1947.

———. *Year of Decision, 1846*. Boston: Little, Brown and Co., 1943.

Dodge, Richard Irving. *The Plains of North America and Their Inhabitants*. Ed. Wayne R. Kime. Newark: University of Delaware Press, 1989.

Dufour, Charles L. *The Mexican War: A Compact History 1846–1848*. New York: Hawthorn Books, 1968.

Egan, Howard. *Pioneering the West 1846 to 1878: Major Howard Egan's Diary*. Ed., comp. William M. Egan. Richmond, Utah: Howard R. Egan Estate, 1917.

Eggenhofer, Nick. *Wagons, Mules and Men: How the Frontier Moved West*. New York: Hastings House Publishers, 1961.

Evans, Beatrice Cannon and Janath Russell Cannon, eds. *Cannon Family Historical Treasury*. Salt Lake City: George Cannon Family Association, 1967.

Evans, John Henry. *One Hundred Years of Mormonism: A History of The Church of Jesus Christ of Latter-day Saints from 1805 to 1905*. Salt Lake City: Deseret Sunday School Union, 1909.

Farnham, Thomas J. *Travels in the Great Western-Prairies, the Anahuac and Rocky Mountains, and in the Oregon Territory*. New York: Da Capo Press, 1973.

Ferris, Benjamin G. *Utah and the Mormons: The History, Government, Doctrines, Customs and Prospects of the Latter-day Saints*. New York: Harper and Brothers, 1854.

Fitzpatrick, Doyle C. *The King Strang Story: A Vindication of James J. Strang, the Beaver Island Mormon King*. Lansing, Mich.: National Heritage, 1970.

Flanders, Robert Bruce. *Nauvoo: Kingdom on the Mississippi*. Urbana: University of Illinois Press, 1965.

———. *The Mormons Who Did Not Go West: A Study of the Emergence of the Reorganized Church of Jesus Christ of Latter Day Saints*. Madison: University of Wisconsin, 1954.

Fletcher, Robert J., and Daisy Whiting Fletcher. *Alpheus Cutler and The Church of Jesus Christ*. Independence, Mo.: The Church of Jesus Christ, 1974.

Fremont, John C. *The Expeditions of John Charles Frémont.* Ed. Donald Jackson and Mary Lee Spence. 2 vols. Urbana: University of Illinois Press, 1973.

Glover, William. *The Mormons in California.* Ed. Paul Bailey. Los Angeles: Glen Dawson, 1954.

Golder, Frank Alfred. *The March of the Mormon Battalion from Council Bluffs to California.* New York: Century Co., 1928.

Gowans, Fred R., and Eugene E. Campbell. *Fort Bridger: Island in the Wilderness.* Provo, Utah: Brigham Young University Press, 1975.

Gray, Charles Glass. *Off at Sunrise: The Overland Journal of Charles Glass Gray.* Ed. Thomas D. Clark. San Marino, California: Huntington Library, 1976.

Gunn, John C. *Gunn's Domestic Medicine.* 1830. Reprint, Knoxville: University of Tennessee Press, 1986.

Gunn, Stanley R. *Oliver Cowdery: Second Elder and Scribe.* Salt Lake City: Bookcraft, 1962.

Gunnison, J. W. *The Mormons, or Latter-Day Saints, in the Valley of the Great Salt Lake.* Philadelphia: Lippincott, Grambo and Company, 1852.

Hafen, LeRoy R. *Broken Hand—The Life of Thomas Fitzpatrick: Mountain Man, Guide and Indian Agent.* Denver: Old West Publishing, 1931.

Hall, William. *The Abominations of Mormonism Exposed. Containing Many Facts and Doctrines Concerning that Singular People During Seven Years' Membership with Them from 1840 to 1847.* Cincinnati: I. Hart and Company, 1851.

Hallwas, John E., and Roger D. Launius, eds. *Cultures in Conflict: A Documentary History of the Mormon War in Illinois.* Logan, Utah: Utah State University Press, 1995.

Hammond, George P., ed. *The Larkin Papers: Personal, Business, and Official Correspondence of Thomas Oliver Larkin, Merchant and United States Consul in California.* Berkeley: University of California Press, 1953.

Hansen, Klaus J. *Quest for Empire: The Political Kingdom of God and the Council of Fifty in Mormon History.* Lansing: Michigan State University Press, 1967.

Harden, Victoria A. *Rocky Mountain Spotted Fever: A History of a 20th-Century Disease.* Baltimore: Johns Hopkins University Press, 1990.

Hargrave, Catherine Perry. *A History of Playing Cards and a Bibliography of Cards and Gaming.* Boston: Houghton and Mifflin, 1930.

Harmon, Appleton Milo. *Appleton Milo Harmon Goes West*. Ed. Maybelle Harmon Anderson. Berkeley: Gillick Press, 1946.

Hartley, William G. *My Best for the Kingdom: History and Autobiography of John Lowe Butler, A Mormon Frontiersman*. Salt Lake City: Aspen Books, 1993.

Hastings, Lansford W. *The Emigrant's Guide to Oregon and California*. Cincinnati: George Conclin, 1845.

Hill, Edward E. *The Office of Indian Affairs, 1824–1880: Historical Sketches*. New York: Clearwater Publishing, 1974.

Hughes, Delila Gardner. *The Life of Archibald Gardner*. West Jordan, Utah: Gardner Family Association, 1939.

Hultkrantz, Ake, and Carling Malouf. *The Shoshone Indians*. New York and London: Garland Publishing, 1974.

Hyde, George E. *Indians of the High Plains: From the Prehistoric Period to the Coming of Europeans*. Norman: University of Oklahoma Press, 1959.

———. *Red Cloud's Folk: A History of the Oglala Sioux Indians*. Norman: University of Oklahoma Press, 1937.

———. *A Sioux Chronicle*. Norman: University of Oklahoma Press, 1956.

Inman, Henry, and William F. Cody. *The Great Salt Lake Trail*. New York: Macmillan, 1898.

Irving, John Treat, Jr. *Indian Sketches Taken During an Expedition to the Pawnee Tribes [1833]*. Norman: University of Oklahoma Press, 1955.

Jackson, Richard H., ed. *The Mormon Role in the Settlement of the West*. Provo, Utah: Brigham Young University Press, 1978.

Johnsgard, Paul A. *The Platte: Channels in Time*. Lincoln: University of Nebraska Press, 1984.

Josselyn, Amos Platt. *The Overland Journal of Amos Platt Josselyn*. Ed. J. William Berrett. Baltimore: Gateway Press, 1978.

Journal of Discourses. Reported by G. D. Watt. 26 vols. 1854–86. Reprint, Salt Lake City: Lithographic Reprints, 1966.

Kane, Thomas L. *The Private Papers and Diary of Thomas Leiper Kane, A Friend of the Mormons*. Ed. Oscar Osburn Winther. San Francisco: Gelber-Lilienthal, 1937.

Kimball, Stanley B. *Heber C. Kimball: Mormon Patriarch and Pioneer*. Urbana: University of Illinois Press, 1981.

Kurz, Rudolph Friederich. *Journal of Rudolph Friederich Kurz: An Account of His Experiences Among Fur Traders and American Indians on the Upper*

Mississippi and Missouri Rivers During the Years 1846 to 1852. Trans. Myrtis Jarrell. Ed. J. N. B. Hewitt. Washington, D.C.: Government Printing Office, 1937.

Larpenteur, Charles. *Forty Years a Fur Trader on the Upper Missouri: The Personal Narrative of Charles Larpenteur 1833–1872.* Ed. Elliott Coues. 2 vols. New York: Francis P. Harper, 1898.

Launius, Roger D. *Zion's Camp: Expeditions to Missouri, 1834.* Independence, Mo.: Herald Publishing House, 1984.

Launius, Roger D., and Linda Thatcher, eds. *Differing Visions: Dissenters in Mormon History.* Urbana: University of Illinois Press, 1994.

Lee, John D. *A Mormon Chronicle: The Diaries of John D. Lee 1848–1876.* Ed. Robert Glass Cleland and Juanita Brooks. 2 vols. San Marino, California: The Huntington Library, 1955.

Lee, John D. *Journals of John D. Lee 1846–47 and 1859.* Ed. Charles Kelly. San Francisco: Rolla Bishop Watt, 1938.

Legg, Phillip R. *Oliver Cowdery: The Elusive Second Elder of the Restoration.* Independence, Mo.: Herald Publishing House, 1989.

Le Sueur, Stephen C. *The 1838 Mormon War in Missouri.* Columbia: University of Missouri Press, 1987.

Lienhard, Heinrich. *From St. Louis to Sutter's Fort, 1846.* Trans., ed. Erwin G. and Elisabeth H. Gudde. Norman: University of Oklahoma Press, 1961.

Little, James A. *From Kirtland to Salt Lake City.* Salt Lake City: Juvenile Instructor Office, 1890.

Loomis, Leander V. *A Journal of the Birmingham Emigrating Company: The Record of a Trip from Birmingham, Iowa, to Sacramento, California, in 1850.* Ed. Edgar M. Ledyard. Salt Lake City: Legal Printing Company, 1928.

Madsen, Brigham D. *The Shoshoni Frontier and the Bear River Massacre.* Salt Lake City: University of Utah Press, 1985.

Malouf, Carling, and Ake Hultkrantz. *Shoshone Indians.* New York: Garland Publishing, 1974.

Marcy, Randolph B. *The Prairie Traveler: A Handbook for Overland Expeditions.* Ed. Richard F. Burton. London: Trubner and Co., 1863.

Mattes, Merrill J. *The Great Platte River Road: The Covered Wagon Mainline Via Fort Kearny to Fort Laramie.* Lincoln: Nebraska State Historical Society, 1969.

Mayhew, Henry, and Samuel M. Smucker. *The Religious, Social, and Political History of the Mormons or Latter-day Saints.* New York City: C. M. Saxton, 1858.

McCall, A. J. *The Great California Trail in 1849.* New York: Steuben Courier Print, 1882.

McGavin, E. Cecil. *The Mormon Pioneers.* Salt Lake City: Stevens and Wallis, 1947.

McKiernan, F. Mark. *The Voice of One Crying in the Wilderness: Sidney Rigdon, Religious Reformer 1793–1876.* Denver: Colorado Press, 1971.

McMurtrie, Douglas C. *The Beginnings of Printing in Utah.* Chicago: John Calhoun Club, 1931.

Miller, David E., and Della S. Miller. *Nauvoo: The City of Joseph.* Santa Barbara and Salt Lake City: Peregrine Smith, 1974.

Miller, David Harry, and Jerome O. Steffen, eds. *The Frontier: Comparative Studies.* Norman: University of Oklahoma Press, 1977.

Mitchell, Augustus. *Accompaniment to Mitchell's New Map of Texas, Oregon, and California.* Philadelphia: Augustus Mitchell, 1846.

———. *Texas, Oregon and California.* Oakland: Biobooks, 1948.

Morgan, Dale L. *Dale Morgan on Early Mormonism: Correspondence and a New History.* Ed. John Phillip Walker. Salt Lake City: Signature Books, 1986.

———. *The Great Salt Lake.* Indianapolis: Bobbs-Merrill, 1947.

———, ed. *Overland in 1846: Diaries and Letters of the California-Oregon Trail.* 2 vols. Georgetown, California: Talisman Press, 1963.

Myres, Sandra L. *Westering Women and the Frontier Experience 1800–1915.* Albuquerque: University of New Mexico Press, 1982.

Nadeau, Remi. *Fort Laramie and the Sioux Indians.* Englewood Cliffs, New Jersey: Prentice Hall, 1967.

Neff, Andrew L. *History of Utah 1847 to 1869.* Salt Lake City: Deseret News, 1940.

Nelson, John Young. *Fifty Years on the Trail: A True Story of Western Life.* As described to Harrington O'Reilly. Norman: University of Oklahoma Press, 1963.

Newell, Linda King, and Valeen Tippetts Avery. *Mormon Enigma: Emma Hale Smith.* Garden City, N.Y.: Doubleday and Co., 1984.

Nibley, Preston. *Exodus to Greatness: The Story of the Mormon Migration.* Salt Lake City: Deseret News Press, 1947.

Oaks, Dallin H., and Marvin S. Hill. *Carthage Conspiracy: The Trial of the Accused Assassins of Joseph Smith*. Urbana: University of Illinois Press, 1979.

Osmond, Alfred. *The Exiles: A True and Tragic Story of Heroic Struggles and Masterful Achievements*. Salt Lake City: The Deseret News Press, 1926.

Packard, Wellman. *Early Emigration to California, 1849–1850*. Bloomington, Ill.: M. Custer, 1928.

Palmer, Joel. *Journal of Travels Over the Rocky Mountains to the Mouth of the Columbia River*. Cincinnati: J. A. and U. P. James, 1847.

Pancoast, Charles Edward. *A Quaker Forty-Niner*. Philadelphia: University of Pennsylvania Press, 1930.

Park, Clara Horne. *Joseph Horne: Pioneer of 1847*. Salt Lake City: Family Organization of Joseph Horne, 1961.

Parker, Ramuel. *Journal of an Exploring Tour Beyond the Rocky Mountains . . . in the Years 1835, '36, and '37*. Reprint, Minneapolis: Ross & Haines, 1967.

Parkman, Francis. *The Oregon Trail*. New York: Macmillan, 1930.

Patton, Annaleone D. *California Mormons by Sail and Trail*. Salt Lake City: Deseret Book, 1961.

Pearson, G. C. *Overland in 1849 from Missouri to California by the Platte River and the Salt Lake Trail*. Ed. Jessie H. Goodman. Los Angeles: 1961.

Phillips, P. Lee. *A List of Maps of America in the Library of Congress*. Washington, D.C.: Government Printing Office, 1901.

Pike, Zebulon M., *An Account of Expeditions to the Sources of the Mississippi. . . .* Philadelphia: C. and A. Conrad and Co., 1810.

Pletcher, David M. *The Diplomacy of Annexation: Texas, Oregon, and the Mexican War*. Columbia, Missouri: University of Missouri Press, 1973.

Pratt, Addison. *The Journals of Addison Pratt*. Ed. S. George Ellsworth. Salt Lake City: University of Utah Press, 1990.

Pratt, Orson. *The Orson Pratt Journals*. Comp., arr. Elden J. Watson. Salt Lake City: Elden J. Watson, 1975.

Pratt, Parley P. *Autobiography of Parley P. Pratt*. Salt Lake City: Deseret Book, 1938.

Pritchard, James Avery. *The Overland Diary of James Avery Pritchard, 1849*. Ed. Dale L. Morgan. Denver: F. A. Rosenstock, 1959.

Quaife, Milo. *The Kingdom of Saint James: A Narrative of the Mormons*. Newham, Connecticut: Yale University Press, 1930.

Read, George Willis. *A Pioneer of 1850: George Willis Read.* Ed. Georgia Willis Read. Boston: Little, Brown, and Co., 1927.

Remy, Jules. *A Journey to Great Salt Lake City.* 2 vols. London: W. Jeffs, 1861.

Reynolds, John. *My Own Times, Embracing also the History of My Life.* Belleville, Ill.: B. H. Perryman and H. L. Davison, 1855.

Ricketts, Norma Baldwin. *The Mormon Battalion: U.S. Army of the West, 1846–1848.* Logan: Utah State University Press, 1996.

Ricks, Joel Edward. *Forms and Methods of Early Mormon Settlement in Utah and the Surrounding Region, 1847 to 1877.* Logan: Utah State University Press, 1964.

Riegel, O. W. *Crown of Glory: The Life of James J. Strang, Moses of the Mormons.* New Haven: Yale University Press, 1935.

Roberts, Brigham H. *A Comprehensive History of The Church of Jesus Christ of Latter-day Saints.* 6 vols. Salt Lake City: Deseret Book, 1930.

———. *The Life of John Taylor.* Salt Lake City: George Q. Cannon and Sons, 1892.

Roe, Frank Gilbert. *The North American Buffalo: A Critical Study of the Species in its Wild State.* 2nd ed. Toronto: University of Toronto Press, 1951.

Russell, Carl P. *Guns on the Early Frontiers: A History of Firearms from Colonial Times through the Years of the Western Fur Trade.* New York: Bonanza Books, 1957.

Schindler, Harold. *Orrin Porter Rockwell: Man of God, Son of Thunder.* Salt Lake City: University of Utah Press, 1983.

Schlissel, Lillian. *Women's Diaries of the Westward Journey.* New York: Schocken Books, 1982.

Scott, Reva L. *Samuel Brannan and the Golden Fleece: A Biography.* New York: Macmillan, 1944.

Shipps, Jan. *Mormonism: The Story of a New Religious Tradition.* Urbana: University of Illinois Press, 1985.

Shumway, George, Edward Durell, and Howard C. Frey. *Conestoga Wagon 1750–1850: Freight Carrier for 100 Years of America's Westward Expansion.* Williamsburg, Va.: Early American Industries Association and George Shumway, 1964.

Smith, Andrew F. *The Saintly Scoundrel: The Life and Times of Dr. John Cook Bennett.* Urbana: University of Illinois Press, 1997.

Smith, Joseph, Jr. *History of The Church of Jesus Christ of Latter-day Saints.* Ed. Brigham H. Roberts. 7 vols. Salt Lake City: Deseret Book, 1973.

Stanley, Reva. *The Archer of Paradise: A Biography of Parley P. Pratt.* Caldwell, Idaho: Caxton Printers Ltd., 1937.

Stegner, Wallace. *The Gathering of Zion: The Story of the Mormon Trail.* Salt Lake City: Westwater Press, 1964.

Stewart, George R. *The California Trail: An Epic with Many Heroes.* New York: McGraw-Hill Book Co., 1962.

Stout, Hosea. *On the Mormon Frontier: The Diary of Hosea Stout 1844–1861.* 2 vols. Ed. Juanita Brooks. Salt Lake City: University of Utah Press, 1964.

Strang, James J. *The Diary of James J. Strang.* Ed. Mark A. Strang. East Lansing: Michigan State University Press, 1961.

Taylor, P. A. M. *Expectations Westward: The Mormons and the Emigration of Their British Converts in the Nineteenth Century.* Edinburgh and London: Oliver and Boyd, 1965.

Taylor, Samuel W. *The Kingdom or Nothing: The Life of John Taylor, Militant Mormon.* New York: Macmillan, 1976.

Transactions of the Annual Reunions of the Oregon Pioneer Association. Portland, Oregon.

Tullidge, Edward W. *History of Salt Lake City.* Salt Lake City: Star Printing, 1886.

———. *The Women of Mormondom.* New York: Tullidge and Crandall, 1877.

Tyler, Daniel. *A Concise History of the Mormon Battalion to the Mexican War 1846–1847.* Glorieta, New Mexico: Rio Grande Press, 1969.

Unruh, John D., Jr. *The Plains Across: The Overland Emigrants and the Trans-Mississippi West, 1840–1860.* Urbana: University of Illinois Press, 1982.

Van Noord, Roger. *King of Beaver Island: The Life and Assassination of James Jesse Strang.* Urbana: University of Illinois Press, 1988.

Van Wagoner, Richard S. *Sidney Rigdon: A Portrait of Religious Excess.* Salt Lake City: Signature Books, 1994.

Walker, Henry Pickering. *The Wagonmasters: High Plains Freighting from the Earliest Days of the Santa Fe Trail to 1880.* Norman: University of Oklahoma Press, 1966.

Webber, Bert. *Indians along the Oregon Trail.* Medford, Ore.: Webb Research Group, 1989.

Weltfish, Gene. *The Lost Universe: Pawnee Life and Culture.* Lincoln: University of Nebraska Press, 1965.

Westbrook, G. W. *The Mormons in Illinois; With an Account of the Late Disturbances Which Resulted in the Assassination of Joseph and Hyrum Smith.* St. Louis: Ustich and Davies, 1844.

Wheat, Carl I. *Mapping the Transmississippi West, 1540–1860.* 6 vols. San Francisco: Institute of Historical Cartography, 1957–1963.

Whitney, Orson F. *History of Utah.* 4 vols. Salt Lake City: George Q. Cannon and Sons, 1892–1904.

———. *Life of Heber C. Kimball: An Apostle.* Salt Lake City: Juvenile Instructor, 1888.

Williams, Elizabeth Whitney. *A Child of the Sea, and Life Among the Mormons.* Harbor Springs, Michigan: Elizabeth W. Williams, 1905.

Woodruff, Wilford. *Journal of Wilford Woodruff 1833–1898.* 7 vols. Ed. Scott G. Kenney. Salt Lake City: Signature Press, 1983.

Young, Brigham. *Manuscript History of Brigham Young, 1846–1847.* Comp. Elden Jay Watson. Salt Lake City: Elden J. Watson, 1971.

ARTICLES

Aldous, Jay A. "Mountain Fever in the 1847 Mormon Pioneer Companies." A paper delivered at the Mormon History Association Conference, 24 May 1997, Omaha, Nebraska. Publication pending.

Aldous, Jay A., and Paul S. Nicholes. "What Is Mountain Fever?" *Overland Journal* 15, no. 1 (Spring 1997): 18–23.

Alford, Terry L. "The West as a Desert in American Thought Prior to Long's 1819–1820 Expedition." *Journal of the West* 8, no. 4 (1969): 515–25.

Allin, Lawrence C. "'A Mile Wide and an Inch Deep': Attempts to Navigate the Platte River." *Nebraska History* 63 (Spring 1982): 1–15.

Alter, J. Cecil. "Bibliographers' Choice of Books on Utah and the Mormons." *Utah Historical Quarterly* 24 (1956): 215–31.

Anderson, Emma L. "History of the Cutlerite Faction of the Latter-day Saints." *Journal of History* 13, no. 40 (October 1920).

Anderson, Richard Lloyd. "Oliver Cowdery's Non-Mormon Reputation." *Improvement Era*, Aug. 1968, 18–26.

Andrews, Thomas F. "The Controversial Hastings Overland Guide: A Reassessment." *Pacific Historical Review* 37, no. 1 (1968): 21–34.

———. "Lansford W. Hastings and the Promotion of the Salt Lake Desert Cutoff: A Reappraisal." *Western Historical Quarterly* 4 (Apr. 1973): 133–50.

Andrus, Hyrum L. "Joseph Smith and the West." *BYU Studies* 2, no. 2 (1960): 129–47.

Aquila, Richard. "Plains Indian War Medicine." *Journal of the West* 13, no. 2 (1974): 19–43.

Arrington, Chris Rigby. "Pioneer Midwives." In *Mormon Sisters: Women in Early Utah*, ed. Claudia Bushman. Cambridge, Mass.: Emmeline Press, 1976.

Arrington, Leonard J. "Mississippi Mormons." *Ensign*, June 1977, 46–51.

Arrington, Leonard J., and Dean May. "'A Different Mode of Life': Irrigation and Society in Nineteenth-Century Utah." *Agricultural History* 49, no. 1 (1975): 3–20.

Beecher, Maureen Ursenbach. "Women's Work on the Mormon Frontier." *Utah Historical Quarterly* 49 (Summer 1981): 276–90.

Bengston, B. E. "An Ancient Village of the Grand Pawnee." *Nebraska History* 14, no. 2 (1933): 124–29.

Bennett, Richard E. "'Dadda, I Wish We Were Out of This Country': The Nauvoo Poor Camps in Iowa, Fall 1846." In *The Iowa Mormon Trail: Legacy of Faith and Courage*, ed. Susan Easton Black and William G. Hartley. Orem, Utah: Helix Publishing, 1997.

———. "Eastward to Eden: The Nauvoo Rescue Missions." *Dialogue: A Journal of Mormon Thought* 19 (Winter 1986): 100–108.

———. "Finalizing Plans for the Trek West: Deliberations at Winter Quarters, 1846–1847." *BYU Studies* 24 (Summer 1984): 301–20.

———. "Lamanism, Lymanism, and Cornfields." *Journal of Mormon History* 13 (1986–87): 45–59.

———. "Mormon Renegade: James Emmett at the Vermillion, 1846." *South Dakota History* 15, no. 3 (Fall 1985): 217–33.

———. "Mormons and Missourians: The Uneasy Truce." *The Midwest Review*, second series, 9 (Spring 1992): 12–21.

———. "'A Samaritan Had Passed By': George Miller—Mormon Bishop, Trailblazer, and Brigham Young Antagonist." *Illinois Historical Journal* 82, no. 1 (Spring 1989): 2–16.

Bitton, Davis. "Mormons in Texas: The Ill-Fated Lyman Wight Colony 1844–1858." *Arizona and the West* 2 (1969): 5–26.

Black, Susan Easton. "Nauvoo on the Eve of Exodus." In *The Iowa Mormon Trail: Legacy of Faith and Courage*, ed. Susan Easton Black and William G. Hartley. Orem, Utah: Helix Publishing, 1997.

Boggs, Lilburn W. "Route to the Pacific." *St. Louis Weekly Reveille*, 22 May 1848. Missouri Historical Society. St. Louis, Missouri.

Boyack, Hazel Noble. "Historic Fort Laramie: The Hub of Early Western History, 1834–1849." *Annals of Wyoming* 21, nos. 2, 3 (1949): 170–80.

Bringhurst, Newell G. "The Mormons and Slavery: A Closer Look." *Pacific Historical Review* 50 (Feb. 1981): 329–38.

Burgess, William. "Indian Office Documents on Sioux-Pawnee Battle." *Nebraska History* 16, no. 3 (1935): 148.

Burns, Ric. "'Never Take No Cutoffs': On the Oregon Trail." *American Heritage* 44, no. 3 (1993): 60–76.

Campbell, Eugene E. "The Apostasy of Samuel Brannan." *Utah Historical Quarterly* 27 (1959): 157–67.

———. "Authority Conflicts in the Mormon Battalion." *BYU Studies* 8 (Winter 1968): 127–42.

———. "Miles Morris Goodyear." In *The Mountain Men and the Fur Trade*, ed. LeRoy Hafen, 2:179–88. Glendale, Calif.: Arthur H. Clark, 1965–72.

Cannon, George Q. "Topics of the Times." *Juvenile Instructor*, 15 Dec. 1883, 377–78.

Carter, Harvey L. "Tim Goodale." In *The Mountain Men and the Fur Trade*, ed. LeRoy Hafen, 7:147–53. Glendale, Calif.: Arthur H. Clark, 1965–72.

Christy, Howard A. "Open Hand and Mailed Fist: Mormon-Indian Relations in Utah, 1847–52." *Utah Historical Quarterly* 46 (Summer 1978): 216–35.

Clark, J. Reuben. "To Them of the Last Wagon." Conference Report, October 1947, 154–60. (Reprinted in *Ensign*, July 1997, 34–39.)

Crawley, Peter, and Richard L. Anderson. "The Political and Social Realities of Zion's Camp." *BYU Studies* 14 (Summer 1974): 406–20.

Crosby, Jesse W. "The History and Journal of the Life and Travels of Jesse W. Crosby." *Annals of Wyoming* 11 (July 1939): 169–87.

Cutright, Paul Russell. "'I Gave Him Barks and Saltpeter.'" *American Heritage* 15 (Dec. 1963): 58–60, 94–101.

De Villiers, Baron Marc. "Massacre of the Spanish Expedition of the

Missouri (Aug. 11, 1720)." Trans. Addison E. Sheldon. *Nebraska History* 4, no. 1 (1921): 2–29.

Dodge, Grenville M. "Biographical Sketch of James Bridger." *Annals of Wyoming* 33 (Oct. 1961): 159–77. (A reprint of a 1924 article in the same journal.)

Dunbar, John. "The Presbyterian Mission Among the Pawnee Indians in Nebraska, 1834–1836." *Collections of the Kansas State Historical Society* 11 (1909–1910): 323–32.

Edwards, Paul M. "William B. Smith: 'A Wart on the Ecclesiastical Tree.'" In *Differing Visions: Dissenters in Mormon History*, 140–57. Ed. Roger D. Launius and Linda Thatcher. Urbana: University of Illinois Press, 1984.

Ellis, Everett L. "To Take a Scalp." *Annals of Wyoming* 31 (Oct. 1959): 140–43.

Esplin, Ronald K. "'A Place Prepared': Joseph, Brigham and the Quest for Promised Refuge in the West." *Journal of Mormon History* 9 (1982): 85–111.

Ewers, John C. "Intertribal Warfare as the Precursor of Indian-White Warfare on the Northern Great Plains." *Western Historical Quarterly* 6, no. 4 (1975): 398–410.

"First Wagons to Reach the Rocky Mountains. Extract from a letter from Messrs. Smith, Jackson and Sublette to the Secretary of War, in October 1829 . . ." *Annals of Wyoming* 11 (Apr. 1939): 116.

Flores, Dan. "Bison Ecology and Bison Diplomacy: The Southern Plains from 1800 to 1850." *Journal of American History* 78 (Sept. 1991): 465–85.

Forrest, James Taylor. "What a Sight it Was!" *American Heritage* 12, no. 2 (1961): 46–55.

Geer, Ralph C. "Occasional Address." *Transactions of the 4th Annual Reunion of the Oregon Pioneer Association for 1876*. Salem: Oregon Pioneer Association, 1877, 33–36.

Gibson, Harry W. "Frontier Arms of the Mormons." *Utah Historical Quarterly* 42 (Winter 1974): 4–26.

Gillespie, A. S. "Bud." "Saddles." *Annals of Wyoming* 34 (Oct. 1962): 212–17.

Goetzmann, William H. "Death Stalked the Grand Reconnaissance." *American Heritage* 23, no. 6 (1972): 44–48, 92–95.

Gowans, Fred R. "Fort Bridger and the Mormons." *Utah Historical Quarterly* 42 (Winter 1974): 49–67.

Graham, Stanley S. "Routine at Western Cavalry Posts, 1833–1861." *Journal of the West* 15, no. 3 (1976): 49–59.

Grant, Ellsworth S. "Gunmaker to the World." *American Heritage* 19, no. 4 (1968): 5–11, 86–91.

Green, T. L. "'Scotts Bluffs, Fort John.'" *Nebraska History* 19, no. 3 (1938): 175–88.

Greenburg, Dan W. "How Fort William, Now Fort Laramie, Was Named." *Annals of Wyoming* 12 (Jan. 1940): 56–63.

Groh, George. "Doctors of the Frontier." *American Heritage* 14, no. 3 (1963): 10–11, 87–91.

Hafen, LeRoy R. "Mountain Men before the Mormons." *Utah Historical Quarterly* 26 (1958): 305–16.

———. "Thomas Fitzpatrick and the First Indian Agency of the Upper Platte and Arkansas." *Mississippi Valley Historical Review* 15 (1928): 374–79.

Hanson, Charles E., Jr. "Fur Trade Activities in the Fort Laramie Region: 1834–1849." *Journal of the West* 26, no. 4 (1987): 8–13.

Hanson, Charles E., Jr., and Veronica Sue Walters. "The Early Fur Trade in Northwestern Nebraska." *Nebraska History* 57 (Fall 1976): 291–314.

Harrington, Leonard E. "Journal of Leonard E. Harrington." *Utah Historical Quarterly* 8 (Jan. 1940): 13–19.

Harris, Earl R. "Courthouse and Jail Rocks: Landmarks on the Oregon Trail." *Nebraska History* 43 (Mar. 1962): 29–50.

Hartley, William G. "Mormons, Crickets, and Gulls: A New Look at an Old Story." *Utah Historical Quarterly* 38 (Summer 1970): 224–39.

Hastings, Loren B. "Diary of Loren B. Hastings." *Transactions of the 51st Annual Reunion of the Oregon Pioneer Association [1923]*.

Hefner, Loretta L. "Amasa Mason Lyman, the Spiritualist." *Journal of Mormon History* 6 (1979): 75–87.

Hoffert, Sylvia D. "Childbearing on the Trans-Mississippi Frontier, 1830–1900." *Western Historical Quarterly* 22 (Aug. 1991): 272–88.

Hogan, Edward R. "Orson Pratt as a Mathematician." *Utah Historical Quarterly* 41 (Winter 1973): 59–68.

Holmes, Gail George. "The LDS Legacy in Southwestern Iowa." *Ensign*, Aug. 1988, 54–57.

Horne, M. Isabella. "Pioneer Reminiscences." *Young Women's Journal,* July 1902, 292–95.

Hultkrantz, Ake. "The Shoshones in the Rocky Mountain Area." *Annals of Wyoming* 33 (1961): 19–41.

"Indian Office Documents of Sioux-Pawnee Battle." *Nebraska History* 16, no. 3 (1935): 147–55.

Irving, Gordon, "The Law of Adoption: One Phase of the Development of the Mormon Concept of Salvation, 1830–1900." *BYU Studies* 14 (Spring 1974): 291–314.

Jackson, Richard H. "The Mormon Village: Genesis and Antecedents of the City of Zion Plan." *BYU Studies* 17 (Winter 1977): 223–40.

———. "The Use of Adobe in the Mormon Cultural Region." *Journal of Cultural Geography* 1 (1980): 82–95.

Jackson, Richard H., and Robert L. Layton. "The Mormon Village: Analysis of a Settlement Type." *Professional Geographer* 28, no. 2 (1976): 136–41.

Japp, Phyllis M. "Pioneer Medicines: Doctors, Nostrums, and Folk Cures." *Journal of the West* 21, no. 3 (1982): 15–22.

Jensen, Richard L. "Transplanted to Zion: The Impact of British Latter-day Saint Immigration upon Nauvoo." *BYU Studies* 31 (Winter 1991): 77–87.

Jessee, Dean C. "Brigham Young's Family: The Wilderness Years." In *The Exodus and Beyond: Essays in Mormon History,* ed. Lyndon W. Cook and Donald Q. Cannon, 24–48. Salt Lake City: Hawkes Publishing Co., 1980.

Kelly, Charles. "The Hastings Cutoff." *Utah Historical Quarterly* 3 (July 1930): 67–82.

Kimball, Stanley B. "The Saints and St. Louis, 1831–1857: An Oasis of Tolerance and Security." *BYU Studies* 13 (Summer 1973): 489–519.

King, Charles R. "The Woman's Experience of Childbirth on the Western Frontier." *Journal of the West* 29, no. 1 (1990): 76–84.

Langum, David J. "Pioneer Justice on the Overland Trails." *Western Historical Quarterly* 5 (Oct. 1974): 421–39.

Larson, T. A. "Dolls, Vassals, and Drudges: Pioneer Women in the West." *Western Historical Quarterly* 3 (Jan. 1972): 5–16.

Leavitt, Judith Walzer. "'Science' Enters the Birthing Room: Obstetrics in

America since the Eighteenth Century." *Journal of American History* 70 (Sept. 1983): 281–304.

Lee, John D. "Diary of the Mormon Battalion Mission: John D. Lee." Ed. Juanita Brooks. *New Mexico Historical Review* 42 (July 1967): 165–209.

Lewis, G. Malcolm. "Three Centuries of Desert Concepts in the Cis-Rocky Mountain West." *Journal of the West* 4, no. 3 (1965): 457–68.

Long, Stephen H. "Major Long's Account of the Republican Pawnee and the Kansas Villages." *Nebraska History* 10, no. 3 (1927): 204–25.

Lupton, David W. "Fort Platte, Wyoming, 1841-1845: Rival of Fort Laramie." *Annals of Wyoming* 49, no. 1 (1977): 83–92.

Lyon, T. Edgar. "Orson Pratt: Pioneer and Proselyter." *Utah Historical Quarterly* 24 (1956): 261–73.

———. "This is the Place." *Utah Historical Quarterly* 27 (1959): 203–7.

Mantor, Lyle E. "Fort Kearny and the Westward Movement." *Nebraska History* 29 (Sept. 1948): 175–79.

Mattes, Merrill J. "Chimney Rock on the Oregon Trail." *Nebraska History* 36 (Mar. 1955): 1–26.

———. "The Council Bluffs Road: A New Perspective on the Northern Branch of the Great Platte River Road." *Nebraska History* 65 (Summer 1984): 179–94.

———. "The Council Bluffs Road: Northern Branch of the Great Platte River Road." *Overland Journal* 3 (Fall 1985): 30–42.

———. "Hiram Scott, Fur Trader." *Nebraska History* 26, no. 3 (1945): 127–61.

———. "New Horizons on the Old Oregon Trail." *Nebraska History* 56, no. 4 (1975): 555–67.

Mattison, Ray H. "The Indian Frontier on the Upper Missouri to 1865." *Nebraska History* 39, no. 3 (1958): 241–66.

———. "Indian Missions and Missionaries on the Upper Missouri to 1900." *Nebraska History* 38, no. 2 (1957): 127–54.

———. "The Military Frontier on the Upper Frontier." *Nebraska History* 37, no. 3 (1956): 159–82.

———. "The Upper Missouri Fur Trade: Its Methods of Operations." *Nebraska History* 42, no. 1 (1961): 1–28.

McDermott, John D. "James Bordeaux." In *The Mountain Men and the Fur Trade*, ed. LeRoy Hafen, 5:65–80. Glendale, California: Arthur H. Clark, 1965–72.

Meeks, Priddy. "Journal of Priddy Meeks." *Utah Historical Quarterly* 10 (1942): 144–223.

Miller, David E. "The Donner Road through the Great Salt Lake Desert." *Pacific Historical Review* 27 (Feb. 1958): 39–44.

———. "The First Wagon Train to Cross Utah, 1841." *Utah Historical Quarterly* 30 (1962): 40–51.

Mills, H. W. "De Tal Palo Tal Astilla." *Historical Society of Southern California Annual Publications* 10 (1917): 86–173.

Morgan, Dale L. "The Changing Face of Salt Lake City." *Utah Historical Quarterly* 27 (1959): 209–32.

———. "The Church of Jesus Christ of Latter-day Saints." *Western Humanities Review* 5 (Winter 1950–51): 1–33.

———. "Miles Goodyear and the Founding of Ogden." *Utah Historical Quarterly* 21 (1953): 195–218, 307–29.

———. "The Mormon Ferry on the North Platte." *Annals of Wyoming* 21, nos. 2, 3 (1949): 111–23, 124–33.

———. "The State of Deseret." *Utah Historical Quarterly* 8 (April, July, Oct. 1940): 65–83.

Morrell, Joseph R. "Medicine of the Pioneer Period in Utah." *Utah Historical Quarterly* 23 (1955): 127–44.

Morris, Ralph C. "The Notion of a Great American Desert East of the Rockies." *Mississippi Valley Historical Review* 13, no. 2 (1926): 190–200.

Mortensen, A. R. "Mormons, Nebraska and the Way West." *Nebraska History* 46, no. 4 (1965): 259–71.

Moynihan, Ruth Barnes. "Children and Young People on the Overland Trail." *Western Historical Quarterly* 6 (July 1975): 279–94.

Munkres, Robert L. "Ash Hollow: Gateway to the High Plains." *Annals of Wyoming* 42 (Apr. 1970): 5–43.

———. "Independence Rock and Devil's Gate." *Annals of Wyoming* 40 (Apr. 1968): 23–40.

———. "The Plains Indian Threat on the Oregon Trail before 1860." *Annals of Wyoming* 40 (Oct. 1968): 193–221.

———. "Wives, Mothers, Daughters: Women's Life on the Road West." *Annals of Wyoming* 42 (Oct. 1970): 191–224.

Munro, J. B. "Mormon Colonization Scheme for Vancouver Island." *Washington Historical Quarterly* 25 (July 1934): 278–85.

Nichols, Roger L. "Stephen Long and Scientific Exploration on the Plains." *Nebraska History* 52 (Spring 1971): 51–63.

Oaks, Dallin H., and Joseph I. Bentley. "Joseph Smith and Legal Process: In the Wake of the Steamboat *Nauvoo*." *Brigham Young University Law Review* 3 (1976): 735–82.

Parrish, William E. "The Mississippi Saints." *The Historian* 50 (Aug. 1988): 489–506.

Partoll, Albert J. "Anderson's Narrative of a Ride to the Rocky Mountains in 1834." *Frontier and Midland* 19, no. 1 (1938). (Reprinted in *Sources of Northwest History* 27:1–12.)

Peltier, Jerome. "Moses 'Black' Harris." In *The Mountain Men and the Fur Trade*, ed. LeRoy Hafen, 4:103-17. Glendale, California: Arthur H. Clark, 1965–72.

Pratt, Ann Agatha Walker. "The Pratt Story." In *Our Pioneer Heritage*, comp. Kate B. Carter, 17:225–26. Salt Lake City: Daughters of Utah Pioneers, 1958–77.

Quayle, Thomas. "God and Gold—1847." In *Our Pioneer Heritage*, comp. Kate B. Carter, 16:487–504. Salt Lake City: Daughters of Utah Pioneers, 1958–77.

Quinn, D. Michael. "The Practice of Rebaptism at Nauvoo." *BYU Studies* 18 (Winter 1978): 226–32.

Quist, John. "John E. Page: An Apostle of Uncertainty." *Journal of Mormon History* 12 (1985): 53–68.

Reid, John Phillip. "Replenishing the Elephant." *Oregon Historical Quarterly* 79 (1978): 64–90.

Rich, Mary A. "Incidents of the Rich Company." In *Heart Throbs of the West*, comp. Kate B. Carter, 4:348–50. Salt Lake City: Daughters of Utah Pioneers, 1939–51.

Richmond, Robert W. "Developments Along the Overland Trail from the Missouri River to Fort Laramie, Before 1854." *Nebraska History* 33 (Sept. 1952): 154–79.

Riley, Glenda. "The Spectre of a Savage: Rumors and Alarmism on the Overland Trail." *Western Historical Quarterly* 15 (Oct. 1984): 427–44.

Rose, Blanche E. "Early Utah Medical Practice." *Utah Historical Quarterly* 10 (1942): 14–33, 44–48, 84–104.

Russell, William D. "King James Strang: Joseph Smith's Successor in the Restoration Movement." In *The Restoration Movement: Essays in Mormon*

History, ed. F. Mark McKiernan, Alma P. Blair, and Paul M. Edwards, 231–56. Lawrence, Kansas: Coronado Press, 1973.

Scrimsher, Lila Gravatt. "The Medicinal Herbs of Our Forefathers." *Nebraska History* 50 (Fall 1969): 309–21.

Sheldon, Addison E. "The North Brothers and the Pawnee Nation." *Nebraska History* 15, no. 4 (1934): 297–304.

Smaby, Beverly P. "The Mormons and the Indians: Conflicting Ecological Systems in the Great Basin." *American Studies* 16 (Spring 1975): 35–48.

Smith, Joseph F. "The Repetition of Sacred Ordinances." *Juvenile Instructor*, 1 Jan. 1903, 18–20.

Snow, Erastus. "Journal of Erastus Snow." *Utah Humanities Review* 2 (Apr. 1948).

Steele, John. "Extracts from the Journal of John Steele." *Utah Historical Quarterly* 6 (Jan. 1933): 3–28.

Stewart, George R. "The Prairie Schooner Got Them There." *American Heritage* 13, no. 2 (1962): 4–17, 98–102.

Stewart, Omer C. "Ute Indians: Before and After White Contact." *Utah Historical Quarterly* 34 (Winter 1966): 50–52.

Stringham, Guy E. "The Pioneer Roadometer." *Utah Historical Quarterly* 42 (Winter 1974): 258–72.

Taine, Hyppolite. "Taine's Essay on the Mormons." Trans. Austin E. Fife. *Pacific Historical Review* 31 (Feb. 1962): 49–65.

Taylor, P. A. M. "The Mormon Crossing of the United States, 1840–1870." *Utah Historical Quarterly* 25 (1957): 319–37.

Thompson, M. J. "Early Church Recollections." *Juvenile Instructor*, 15 July 1897, 431.

Trennert, Robert A. "The Mormons and the Office of Indian Affairs: The Conflict Over Winter Quarters, 1846–1848." *Nebraska History* 53 (Fall 1972): 381–400.

Van Wagoner, Richard S. "The Making of a Mormon Myth: The 1844 Transfiguration of Brigham Young." *Dialogue: A Journal of Mormon Thought* 28 (Winter 1995): 1–24.

Warren, Gouverneur K. "Bonneville's Expedition to Rocky Mountains 1832–'33, –'34, –'35, –'36." *Annals of Wyoming* 15 (July 1943): 220–28.

Watson, Douglas S. "Herald of the Gold Rush: Sam Brannan." *California Historical Society Quarterly* 10 (1931): 298–301.

West, Elliott. "The Youngest Pioneers." *American Heritage* 37, no. 1 (1985): 90–96.

White, Richard. "The Winning of the West: The Expansion of the Western Sioux in the Eighteenth and Nineteenth Centuries." *Journal of American History* 65, no. 2 (1978): 319–43.

Whitney, Helen Mar Kimball. "Our Travels Beyond the Mississippi." *Woman's Exponent* 12 (1883–84): 102–86 passim and 13 (1884–85): 2–91 passim.

Wyman, Walker D. "Council Bluffs and the Westward Movement." *Iowa Journal of History* 47, no. 2 (1949): 99–118.

Young, Clara Decker. "A Woman's Experiences with the Pioneer Band." *Utah Historical Quarterly* 14 (1946): 173–76.

PAMPHLETS/BOOKLETS/NEWSPAPERS/ GOVERNMENT REPORTS

Berkebile, Don H. "Conestoga Wagons in Braddock's Campaign, 1755." U.S. National Museum Bulletin #218. Contributions from the Museum of History and Technology. Washington: Smithsonian Institute, 1959.

Black, Susan Easton. "The Mormon Temple Square: The Story behind the Scenery." Las Vegas: KC Publications, 1993.

Convers, Josiah B. "A Brief History of the Hancock Mob in the Year 1846." St. Louis: Cathcart and Prescott, 1846.

Cowan, Frank T. "Life Habits, History, and Control of the Mormon Cricket." U.S. Dept. of Agriculture Technical Bulletin no. 161. Washington, D.C.: Government Printing Office, 1929.

Ellison, Robert. "Fort Bridger, Wyoming: A Brief History." Casper, Wyo.: The Historical Landmark Commission of Wyoming, 1931.

———. "Independence Rock: The Great Record of the Desert." Casper, Wyo.: Natrona County Historical Society, 1930.

"General Epistle from the Council of the Twelve Apostles to the Church of Jesus Christ of Latter-day Saints, Abroad, Dispersed Throughout the Earth." 23 December 1847. LDS Church Archives, LDS Church Historical Department. Salt Lake City, Utah.

"In Honor of the Pioneers: A Monument Unveiled at Pioneer View, July 25th, 1921." Salt Lake City: Bureau of Information, 1921.

Jenson, Andrew. "Day-by-Day with the Utah Pioneers. A Chronological Record of the Trek Across the Plains. A Revision of the Accounts

Published April 5, 1897 to July 24, 1897 in *The Salt Lake Tribune.*" (Reprinted 6 April 1947 to 24 July 1947 in *Deseret News.*)

Kane, Thomas L. "The Mormons." A discourse delivered before the Historical Society of Pennsylvania, 26 March 1850. Philadelphia: King and Baird, Printers, 1850.

Lewis, Catherine. "Narrative of Some of the Proceedings of the Mormons." Lynn, Mass., 1848.

Millennial Star 8 (1846), 9 (1847), and 12 (1850).

Oakly, Obadiah. "The Oregon Expedition of Obadiah Oakly." A pamphlet reprinted from the *Peoria (New York) Register,* 1914. Mss #1508. Oregon Historical Society.

Pratt, Orson. "New Jerusalem; or The Fulfilment of Modern Prophecy." Liverpool: R. James, Printer, 1849.

"Report of the Committee Appointed by the Chamber of Commerce upon the Trade, Commerce and Manufacturers of St. Louis." St. Louis: Missouri Republican Office, 1852.

St. Louis Daily Union. 12 June 1847.

U.S. Congress. Senate. *Report of the Office of Indian Affairs.* 27th Cong., 3d sess., 1842.

———. *Report of the Commission of Indian Affairs.* 28th Cong., 1st sess., 1843.

———. *Report of the Office of Indian Affairs.* 29th Cong., 1st sess., 1845.

———. *Report of the Office of Indian Affairs.* 29th Cong., 2d sess., 1846.

———. *Annual Report of the Commission of Indian Affairs.* 30th Cong., 1st sess., 1847.

Van Dusen, Increase McGee. "'Sketch of the Rise, Progress and Disposition of the Mormons' by John Thomas . . . To Which Is Added an Account of the Nauvoo Temple Mysteries and Other Abominations Practised by the Mormons Previous to Their Emigration for California." London: Arthur Hall, 1847.

Voree (Wisconsin) Herald. 1846–1847.

Westbrook, G. W. "The Mormons in Illinois: with an Account of the Late Disturbances which resulted in the Assassination of Joseph and Hyrum Smith." St. Louis: Ustick and Davies, 1844.

Young Women's Journal 13–15 (1902–1904).

Manuscripts

Journals and Diaries
(as studied in their unpublished format)

Allen, Andrew Jackson. Journal. Joel Ricks Collection. LDS Church Archives, LDS Church Historical Department. Salt Lake City, Utah.

Allen, Frank. Journal. LDS Church Archives.

Andrus, Milo. Journal. LDS Church Archives.

Appleby, William I. Journal. LDS Church Archives.

Ashley, Algeline Jackson. Journal. The William Huntington Library. San Marino, California.

Black, John Smith. Journal. Harold B. Lee Library. Brigham Young University. Provo, Utah.

Bowering, George K. Journal. LDS Church Archives.

Brown, Lorenzo. Journal. Huntington Library.

Bruff, J. G. Journal. Huntington Library.

Bullock, Thomas. Journal. LDS Church Archives.

Calkins, Jonathan. Journal. LDS Church Archives.

Cannon, Leonora. Journal. LDS Church Archives.

Clark, John William. Journal. LDS Church Archives.

Clayton, William. Journal. LDS Church Archives.

Clyman, James. Journal. Bancroft Library. Berkeley, California.

Crane, Addison M. Journal. Huntington Library.

Crosby, Jesse W. Journal. LDS Church Archives.

Dana, Charles Root. Journal. LDS Church Archives.

Edmands, Thomas. Journal. The Huntington Library.

Egan, Howard. Journal. Huntington Library.

Egbert, Eliza Ann. Journal. University of California at Los Angeles. Special Collections.

Empey, William Adam. Journal. Huntington Library.

Evans, James W. Journal. Bancroft Library.

Everett, Addison. Journal. LDS Church Archives.

Field, James. Journal. Mss #520. Oregon Historical Society. Portland, Oregon.

Fielding, Joseph. Journal. LDS Church Archives.

Flanigan, James H. Journal. LDS Church Archives.

Foote, Warren. Journal. LDS Church Archives.

Gardner, Robert. Journal. LDS Church Archives.

Gates, Jacob. Journal. LDS Church Archives.

Geer, Elizabeth (Dixon) Smith. Journal. Oregon Historical Society.

Glines, James Harvey. Journal. LDS Church Archives.

Gorgas, Solomon A. Journal. Huntington Library.

Gray, Charles G. Journal. Huntington Library.

Haight, Isaac Chauncey. Journal. LDS Church Archives.

Harden, Absalom B. Journal. Mss #77. Oregon Historical Society.

Harmon, Appleton Miles. Journal. LDS Church Archives.

Harper, Charles Alfred. Journal. LDS Church Archives.

Hastings, Lansford W. Journal. Mss #660. Oregon Historical Society.

Higbee, John S. Journal. LDS Church Archives.

Historical Department Journals. Of the LDS Church Historical Department. LDS Church Archives.

Hockett, William A. Journal. Mss #1036. Oregon Historical Society.

Hoover, Vincent A. Diary. Huntington Library.

Hovey, Joseph G. Journal. LDS Church Archives.

Howells, J. E. Journal. Mss #659. Oregon Historical Society.

Hundsaker, Samuel. Diary. Huntington Library.

Huntington, William. Journal. LDS Church Archives.

Jackman, Levi. Journal. LDS Church Archives.

Jacob, Norton. Journal. LDS Church Archives.

Johnson, Joseph H. Journal. Huntington Library.

Johnson, Levi S. Journal. LDS Church Archives.

Johnson, Luke S. Journal. LDS Church Archives.

Kilfoyle, James. Diary. Special Collections. Utah State University, Logan, Utah.

Kimball, Heber C. Journal. LDS Church Archives.

Kingsbury, Joseph Corodon. Special Collections. Utah State University.

Leany, William. Journal. LDS Church Archives.

Lee, John D. Journal. LDS Church Archives.

Lord, Israel Shipman Pelton. Journal. Huntington Library.

Lorton, William B. Journal. Bancroft Library.

Lyman, Amasa. Journal. LDS Church Archives and Huntington Library.

Lyman, Eliza Maria Partridge. Journal. LDS Church Archives.

Martindale, William. Journal. LDS Church Archives.

McCall, A. J. Journal. As recorded in "The Great California Trail in 1849: Wayside Notes of an Argonaut." Oregon Historical Society.

McKenzie, Thomas. Journal. LDS Church Archives.

Meeks, Priddy. Journal. LDS Church Archives.

Mendenhall, William. Journal. LDS Church Archives.

Mooreman, Madison Berryman. Journal. Huntington Library.

Murdock, Gideon Allen. Journal. LDS Church Archives.

Newcombe, Silas. Journal. Huntington Library.

Oakley, John. Journal of the 5th 50 of the 1st Camp of the Church of Latter-day Saints journeying to California. (Found in front of the William C. Staines Journal.) LDS Church Archives.

Parke, Charles R. Journal. Huntington Library.

Peabody, Charles. Journal. Missouri Historical Society. St. Louis, Missouri.

Peace, David Egbert and Hannah Pegg. Diary. Mss #60. Oregon Historical Society.

Pettijohn, Isaac. Journal. Bancroft Library.

Pratt, Orson. Journal. LDS Church Archives.

Pulsipher, John. Journal. Utah State Historical Society. Salt Lake City, Utah.

Raynor, James. Diary. Mss #1508. Oregon Historical Society.

Rich, Charles C. Journal. LDS Church Archives.

Richards, Mary Haskin Parker. Journal. LDS Church Archives.

Richards, Willard. Journal. LDS Church Archives.

Rockwood, Albert P. Journal. LDS Church Archives.

Rogers, Samuel H. Journal. Special Collections. Brigham Young University.

Scott, James Allen. Journal. LDS Church Archives.

Sessions, Patty. Journal. LDS Church Archives.

Sessions, Perrigrine. Journal. LDS Church Archives.

Sheets, Elijah Funk. Journal. LDS Church Archives.

Shepherd, Cyrus. Diary. Mss #1219. Oregon Historical Society.

Smith, John, Dr. Diary. Huntington Library.

Smith, John Lyman. Journal. LDS Church Archives.

Smithies, James. Journal. LDS Church Archives.

Snow, Eliza R. Journal. LDS Church Archives.

Snow, Erastus. Journal. LDS Church Archives.

Snow, Lorenzo. Journal. LDS Church Archives.

Spencer, Daniel. Journal. LDS Church Archives.

Staines, William C. Journal. LDS Church Archives.

Steele, John. Journal. LDS Church Archives.

Talbot, Theodore. Journal. Mss #773. Oregon Historical Society.

Taylor, Leonora Cannon. Journal. LDS Church Archives.

Terry, Thomas S. Journal. LDS Church Archives.

Thomas, Preston. Journal. Utah State Historical Society, Salt Lake City, Utah.

Tippets, John Harvey. Journal. LDS Church Archives.

Watson, Gilbert. Journal. Archives of the Reorganized Church of Jesus Christ of Latter Day Saints. Independence, Missouri.

Whipple, Nelson Wheeler. Journal. LDS Church Archives.

Whitaker, Jacob. Journal. LDS Church Archives.

Whitney, Horace K. Journal. LDS Church Archives.

Wilkins, James F. Journal. Huntington Library.

Wood, Joseph W. Journal. Huntington Library.

Woodruff, Wilford. Journal. LDS Church Archives.

Wright, Jonathan C. Journal. LDS Church Archives.

Young, Lorenzo Dow [and Harriett D. Young]. Journal. LDS Church Archives.

AUTOBIOGRAPHIES AND REMINISCENCES,
ACCOUNTS, CORRESPONDENCE FILES, AND
OTHER UNPUBLISHED ARCHIVAL COLLECTIONS

Abbot, George. "George Abbot and His Descendants." Ed. Lois E. Jones. Missouri Historical Society. St. Louis, Missouri.

Adams, William. "History of William Adams." LDS Church Archives.

Anderson, William Marshall. "Anderson's Narrative of a Ride to the Rocky Mountains in 1834." Mss #1508. Oregon Historical Society.

Andrus, Manomas Lavina Gibson. "Biography of Manomas Lavina Gibson Andrus: 1842–1922." Harold B. Lee Library. Brigham Young University. Provo, Utah.

———. "Pioneer Personal History Interview with Manomas Lavina Gibson Andrus, St. George, Utah, Wife of Captain James Andrus." Manuscript Division. Library of Congress. Washington, D.C.

Babbitt, Almon W. "Affidavit of election for trustees held 1 August 1848, signed by A. W. Babbitt." Archives of The Reorganized Church of Jesus Christ of Latter Day Saints. Independence, Missouri.

Baker, Charlotte Leavitt. "Sketch of Charlotte Leavitt Baker's life given by sister Mary Jensen, April 25, 1919." Manuscript Division. Library of Congress. Washington, D.C.

Barnes, Thomas L. "Recollections of the Mormons." Huntington Library.

"The Bennion Family of Utah." Manuscript. LDS Church Archives.

Benton, Thomas Hart. "A List of References on Thomas Hart Benton." Comp. Florence S. Hellman. Missouri Historical Society.

Bidwell, John. "California, 1841–48. An Immigrant's Recollections of a Trip Across the Plains and of Men and Events in Early Days Including the Bear Flag Revolution." Bancroft Library.

Bishops Ledger. Tithing Record Book, 1846–1852. LDS Church Archives.

Blain, William. Letters. Mss #1035. Oregon Historical Society.

Blakeslee, James. Papers. LDS Church Archives.

Boggs, William Montgomery. "Life of Gov. Lilburn W. Boggs, by his son." Bancroft Library.

———. "A Short Biographical Sketch of Lilburn W. Boggs by his son, William M. Boggs." Missouri Historical Society.

———. "Statement of William Montgomery Boggs." 27 January 1886. Bancroft Library.

Bossinger, F. Papers. Huntington Library.

Brannan, Samuel. Fragmentary remarks of his expedition to California with the Mormons. Huntington Library.

Brown, James. Collection. LDS Church Archives.

Brown, James Stephens. Papers. Utah State Historical Society.

Brown, J. Henry. "Autobiography of J. Henry Brown (1878)." Mss #1002. Oregon Historical Society.

Bullock, Thomas. Papers and letters. LDS Church Archives.

Bunker, Edward. "Autobiography of Edward Bunker." Manuscript Division. Library of Congress. Washington, D.C.

Campbell, Robert. "A Narrative of Colonel Robert Campbell's Experiences in the Rocky Mountains Fur Trade from 1825 to 1835." Missouri Historical Society. 1825.

Coleman, Arthur D. "Pratt Pioneers of Utah." LDS Church Archives.

Council Point [Iowa] Branch. Minutes. LDS Church Archives.

Cowdery, Oliver. Letters. Huntington Library.

Crawford, P. W. "Narrative of the Overland Journey to Oregon." Bancroft Library.

Crosby, Jesse W. "The History and Journal of the Life and Travels of Jesse W. Crosby." LDS Church Archives.

Cummings, Benjamin Franklin. Papers. LDS Church Archives.

Cummins, Sarah. J. Autobiography and Reminiscences. Mss #1508. Oregon Historical Society.

Dana, Charles R. "The Autobiography of Charles R. Dana." LDS Church Archives.

Denig, Edwin T. "History of the Indian Tribes." Colbertson Family Collection, 1855. Missouri Historical Society.

Dilworth, John Taylor. Letters. LDS Church Archives.

Drips, Andrew. Collection. Missouri Historical Society.

Easton (Black), Susan Ward. "Pioneers of 1847: A Sesquicentennial Remembrance." LDS Church Archives.

Espenschied, Lloyd. "An Early Wagon Builder of St. Louis, Missouri: Louis Espenschied, 1821–1887 and His Family." Missouri Historical Society.

"The Foster Family. California Pioneers." Huntington Library.

Gardner, Archibald. Autobiography and Account Book. LDS Church Archives.

Gardner, Jane. Autobiography. LDS Church Archives.

Garner, K. R. "Salt Lake Endowment House, 1855–1889." LDS Church Archives.

Garrison, Martha Ellen Rogers. Reminiscences. Mss #607. Oregon Historical Society.

General Church Minutes. A collection generally of minutes of the Quorum of the Twelve Apostles, written mainly by Thomas Bullock, clerk. LDS Church Archives.

Glines, James Henry. Autobiography. LDS Church Archives.

Goddard, G. M. Letters. Photostat. Missouri Historical Society. (Original at the Minnesota Historical Society.)

Greenwood, William. Papers. Archives and Special Collections. Harold B. Lee Library. Brigham Young University. Provo, Utah.

Hansen, Peter Olsen. Autobiography. LDS Church Archives.

Harrington, Leonard E. Reminiscences. LDS Church Archives.

Hascall, Irene. Papers. LDS Church Archives.

———. Collection. Missouri Historical Society.

Haun, Catherine Margaret. "A Woman's Trip Across the Plains in 1849." Reminiscence. Huntington Library.

Henderson, John H. Autobiography. LDS Church Archives.

Hill, George Washington. Incidents. LDS Church Archives.

Hinnman, Lyman. Collection. LDS Church Archives.

Historical Department Journals. LDS Church Archives.

Hockett, William A. Reminiscences. Oregon Historical Society.

Holbrook, Joseph. Autobiography. LDS Church Archives.

Holmes, G. "Reflections on Winter Quarters." LDS Church Archives.

Horne, M. I. "Pioneer Reminiscences." LDS Church Archives.

Hundsaker, Samuel. Autobiography. Oregon Historical Society.

Huntington, William. "A History of William Huntington." William Huntington Collection. LDS Church Archives.

Jackman, Levi. Letters. LDS Church Archives.

Journal History of The Church of Jesus Christ of Latter-day Saints. Comp. Andrew Jenson. LDS Church Archives.

Kane, Thomas L. Collection. Special Collections. Brigham Young University.

Kimball, Abraham A. Reminiscences. LDS Church Archives.

Kimball, Christeen G. Correspondence. LDS Church Archives.

Kimball, Heber C. Papers. LDS Church Archives.

Kimball, Mary Ellen Able. "A Sketch of Pioneer History." LDS Church Archives.

Kraut, Ogden. "A Short History of Re-Baptism." LDS Church Archives.

Lyman, Amasa. Collection. LDS Church Archives.

Maffitt, Pierre Chouteau. Collection. Missouri Historical Society.

McBride, John Rogers. "Narrative of a Trip Across the Plains in 1846." Mss #458. Oregon Historical Society.

———. "The Route by Which the Mormons entered Salt Lake Valley in 1847." Mss #P-F29. Bancroft Library.

McCall, A. J. "The Great California Trail in 1849: Wayside Notes of an Argonaut." Mss #1508. Oregon Historical Society.

McMurtrie, Douglas. "The Date of the First Printing in Nebraska." LDS Church Archives.

Miles, Samuel. "Biography of Samuel Miles, the son of Samuel and Prudence Miles." Manuscript Division. Library of Congress.

Moesser, Joseph Hyrum. Autobiography. LDS Church Archives.

Morgan, Dale. Newspaper Collection. "Mormons and the American Far West." Huntington Library.

Murphy, Joseph. Day Book. Joseph Murphy Papers. Missouri Historical Society.

Murray, Fanny. Letter of Fanny Murray. Division of Special Collections and Archives. Merrill Library. Utah State University Library. Logan, Utah.

Musser, Amos Milton. Family Correspondence. LDS Church Archives.

Nauvoo Trustees. Miscellaneous (Nauvoo) Trustees Minutes. LDS Church Archives.

Nibley, Charles W. "Account Concerning Erastus Snow and the Mormon Pioneers, 1920." LDS Church Archives.

Office of Indian Affairs. Papers. National Archives and Records Service. Washington, D.C.

"Office Record." A record kept by the most prominent clerks and early historians of the Church. LDS Church Archives.

Ogden, Kent. "A Short History of Re-Baptism." LDS Church Archives.

Park, John. Papers. LDS Church Archives.

Phelps, Mary Ann Rich. Autobiography. LDS Church Archives.

Porter, Nathan Tanner. Reminiscences. LDS Church Archives.

Pottawattamie High Council. Minutes. 1846–1852. LDS Church Archives.

Pratt, Parley P. Papers and Autobiography. LDS Church Archives.

Putnam, James. Letters. LDS Church Archives.

Putnam, Jonas. Letters. LDS Church Archives.

Rich, Charles C. Papers. LDS Church Archives.

Rich, Sarah D. Pea Rich. Autobiography. LDS Church Archives.

Richards, Willard. Papers. LDS Church Archives.

———. Family Letters 1840–1849. LDS Church Archives.

Ricks, Joel E. Collection. "Incidents in the Life of George Washington Hill" in "Cache Valley Historical Material." LDS Church Archives.

Riter, Levi Evans. Collection. LDS Church Archives.

Robbison, A. B. "Growth of Towns: Olympia, Fernswater, Portland and San Francisco." 1878. Bancroft Library.

Rogers, Isaac. Letters. LDS Church Archives.

Ross, John E. "Narrative of an Indian Fighter." Mss #P-A 63. Bancroft Library.

Salt Lake High Council. Minutes. 1847. LDS Church Archives.

Schmoelder, Captain B. "Schmoelder: Guide for Emigrants to North America." Huntington Library.

Smith, Bathsheba W. Record Book. Special Collections. Brigham Young University.

Smith, Darling. "The Story of Darling Smith, Pioneer of 1847." Mss #901. Oregon Historical Society.

Smith, George A. Memoirs. The Huntington Library.

Smith, H. H. "The Lyman Wight Colony in Texas 1846–58." Utah State Historical Society. (Original at the University of Texas, Austin, Texas.)

Snider, Cecil. Newspaper Collection. New York City Public Library.

Snow, Eliza R. "Sketch of My Life." LDS Church Archives and Bancroft Library.

Spencer, Daniel. Letters. LDS Church Archives.

Stanton Family. Collection. Mss #475. Oregon Historical Society.

Steele, John. Reminiscences and Journal, 1848–1888. LDS Church Archives.

Strang, Elvira E., and Charles J. Strang. "Biographical Sketch of J. J. Strang." James J. Strang Papers. Beinecke Rare Book and Manuscript Library. Yale University. New Haven, Connecticut.

Strang, James J. Papers. Beinicke Rare Book and Manuscript Library. Yale University. New Haven Connecticut.

———. Papers. Reorganized Church of Jesus Christ of Latter Day Saints Archives.

Sublette, A. Papers. Missouri Historical Society.

Tanner, Mary Jane. Memoirs. LDS Church Archives.

Tanner, Sidney. Letters. Archives and Special Collections. Harold B. Lee Library. Brigham Young University. Provo, Utah.

Taylor, James. Papers and letters. Mss #1006. Oregon Historical Society.

Wallace, George Benjamin. "Daily History of the George Benjamin Wallace Emigration Company," as recorded by J. C. Kingsbury 1847. LDS Church Archives.

West, George Miller. Autobiography. Mss #1508. Oregon Historical Society.

Whitaker, George. "Life of George Whitaker: A Utah Pioneer." Utah State Historical Society.

Whitman, Marcus. Letters. Mss #1203. Oregon Historical Society.

———. "Marcus Whitman, Missionary of Oregon." Missouri Historical Society.

Whitman, Omer. "Almon Whiting Babbitt." Unpublished. In author's possession.

Whitney, Helen Mar Kimball. Autobiography. LDS Church Archives.

———. Family Papers. Division of Special Collections and Archives. Merrill Library. Utah State University. Logan, Utah.

Wight, Lyman. Correspondence and "An Address by Way of An Abridged Account and Journal of My Life from February 1844 to April 1848. With an Appeal to the Latter-day Saints." LDS Church Archives.

Winter Quarters. Manuscript History of Winter Quarters. LDS Church Archives.

Winter Quarters High Council. Minutes. 1846–1848. LDS Church Archives.

Wolfe, John A. Letters. LDS Church Archives.

Young, Brigham. Papers. An extensive collection of voluminous correspondence, sermons, and other writings including some minutes of meetings of the Twelve. LDS Church Archives.

THESES, DISSERTATIONS, AND SPECIAL STUDIES

Arrington, Leonard J., and Esplin, Ronald K. "The Role of the Council of the Twelve During Brigham Young's Presidency of the Church of Jesus Christ of Latter-day Saints." *Task Papers in LDS History*, no. 31, 1979. LDS Church History Department.

Chase, Daryl. "Sidney Rigdon: Early Mormon." Master's thesis, University of Chicago, 1931.

Christian, Lewis Clark. "A Study of Mormon Knowledge of the American Far West Prior to the Exodus (1830–February 1846)." Master's thesis, Brigham Young University, 1972.

———. "A Study of the Mormon Westward Migration Between February 1846 and July 1847 . . ." Ph.D. diss., Brigham Young University, 1976.

Ehat, Andrew F. "Joseph Smith's Introduction of Temple Ordinances and the 1844 Mormon Succession Question." Master's thesis, Brigham Young University, 1982.

Esplin, Ronald K. "The Emergence of Brigham Young and the Twelve to Mormon Leadership, 1830–1841." Ph.D. diss., Brigham Young University, 1981.

Hanson, Margaret E. "Removal of the Indians from Nebraska." Master's thesis, Colorado State College of Education, 1949.

Jensen, Therald N. "Mormon Theory of Church and State." Ph.D. diss., University of Chicago, 1938.

O'Neil, Emily Ann. "Joseph Murphy's Contribution to the Development of the Great American West." Master's thesis, St. Louis University, 1947.

Peterson, Paul H. "An Historical Analysis of the Word of Wisdom." Master's thesis, Brigham Young University, 1972.

———. "The Mormon Reformation." Ph.D. diss., Brigham Young University, 1981.

Yurtinus, John F. "A Ram in the Thicket: The Mormon Battalion in the Mexican War." Ph.D. diss., Brigham Young University, 1975.

INDEX

Adams, Augusta (Young), 90n
Adams, George J., 12, 17, 28n
Adams, George W., 313
Adobe homes, 235–36
Adoption, law of, 81–83, 92n, 237–39, 337
Allen, James, 40, 43, 62, 282
Allen, Orville M., 46
Allis, Samuel, 143n
Allred, James, 62n
American Fur Company, 98–99, 171
Anderson, William, 130
Angell, Truman O., 74
Apostasy. *See* Defection
Appleby, William I., 293, 307–9
Armament, 122–24, 142–43n
Ashley, Henry, 98–99
Ashworth, Captain, 185
Astor, Jacob, 98
Atchison, David R., 4

Babbitt, Almon W., 317–23, 331n
Barney, Thomas, 74
Barnum, Charles D., 74
Bartleson-Bidwell Trail, 228
Battalion, Mormon. *See* Mormon Battalion
Battle of Nauvoo. *See* Nauvoo, Battle of

Beach and Eddy, dry goods firm of, 306, 309, 328n
Beaumont, Charles, 134, 144–45n
Beaver Island, 314–15
Bennett, John C., 12, 17, 28n
Bennion, Ann, 264–65
Bennion, John, 264
Benson, Ezra T.: in pioneer company, 73, 142n, 214, 237; returns to Winter Quarters, 267, 283–84; supports Brigham Young, 289–90; goes on fundraising mission, 307–9; returns to Valley, 339
Benton, Thomas, 10, 42
Bernhisel, John M., 321, 331n
Bidamon, Lewis C., 321–22
Bidwell, John, 150
Big Mountain, 208, 213–15
Billings, George, 180
Billington, Ray, 96
Bingham, Thomas, 355n
Bissonette, Joseph, 120–21
Black Hills country, 178–79
Blackburn, John, 247n
Blackwell, Hyrum H., 330n
Boggs, Francis, 223n
Boggs, Lilburn W., 4, 64n, 75, 176–77, 195
Boggs, William Montgomery, 177

Bonneville, Benjamin L. E., 133
Bordeaux, James, 174–78, 191, 197n
Bouvoir, James, 181, 191
Bowman, William, 185, 200n
Brannan, Sam: establishes Saints in
    California, 48, 192, 202–3n; promotes
    California settlement, 194–96, 206,
    231, 339–42, 356n
Bridger, Fort, 178–79, 196, 204–7, 221n
Bridger, James, 99, 171, 192–94, 202n,
    224n, 233
British Isles, converts from, 49, 63n,
    311–12, 330n
Brooklyn, 48, 192, 194, 202n
Brooks, Lester, 313
Brown, Elias, 222n
Brown, George, 74, 120
Brown, James, 231, 247n, 250n, 340
Brown, Jane, 302
Brown, Jesse S., 247n
Brown, John H., 188
Brown, John: in pioneer company, 76–77,
    142n, 214–15, 217, 223n; in
    Mississippi company, 173, 196–97n;
    scouts road in Salt Lake Valley, 228;
    leads another emigrant group, 309
Brown, Thomas, 75, 90n, 126–27, 130,
    184, 206
Bryant, Archibald, 299n
Bryant, Edwin, 105, 207
Buchanan, James, 305
Buenaventura, Fort, 209
Buffalo, 101, 108, 130–35, 144n
Bullock, Thomas: records Iowa trek,
    46–47, 59; keeps records for pioneer
    company, 74, 117–18, 138–39, 153,
    206; comments on trek west, 120, 156,
    184–86, 191, 206, 209–10, 217
Bunker, Edward and Emily, 298n
Burdick, T., 299n
Burgess, Harrison, 330n
Burke, Charles, 223n
Burnham, J. D., 223n
Burr, Aaron, 185

California Fever, 339–40
California Star, 192, 202n
Camp of Israel, 32, 36–37
Campbell, Robert, 99, 111n, 171, 302–5

Cannon, George Q., 266–67
Carrington, Albert, 74–75, 227, 236
Carthage Convention, 6, 26n, 45, 318
Case, James, 77, 122, 124, 126
Catholic Church, 54–56
Chamberlain, Nancy, 275n
Chamberlain, Solomon, 119–20, 275n
Chapman, Benjamin, 16
Cheffolan, Chief, 125
Cheny, Bro., 344–45
Chesley, A. P., 223n
Chesney, Alex., 223n
Chesney, James, 197n, 223n
Chicago Company, 103
Chimney Rock, 147–48
City Creek, 218, 226
Clark, William, 98
Clayton, William: is part of pioneer
    company, 74, 116; describes trek west,
    130, 133, 148, 151, 166–67, 180,
    184–85; tracks mileage and trail route,
    137–39, 145n; arrives at Fort Laramie,
    173; remembers Joseph Smith, 190;
    comments on Salt Lake Valley, 192,
    210, 217–18, 226–27; publishes
    guidebook, 310, 329n
Clinton, Peter, 330n
Clyman, James, 74, 127–28, 180, 207
Colorado Tick Fever, 211, 222n
Communication, 136–39
Consecration funds, 49
Cook, Harriet (Young), 90n
Cooke, Philip St. George, 173
Coray, William, 341–42
Coulson, George, 299n
Council Bluffs, Iowa, 45, 58, 252, 299n
Council of Captains, 122
Council of the Fifty, 71–72, 355n
Cowdery, Oliver, 286, 324–26, 333n
Cowen, David, 323
Cox, Thomas, 103
Craig, John, 209–10, 222n
Crickets, 345–48, 357n
Crosby, Jesse, 256
Crosby, Oscar, 77, 91n, 223n
Crosby, William, 173, 308–9
Crow, Benjamin B., 197n, 223n
Crow, Elizabeth Jane, 197n
Crow, Elizabeth, 197n

Crow, Harriet, 197n
Crow, Ida Vinda Exene, 197n
Crow, Ira Minda Almarene, 197n
Crow, John McHenry, 197n, 223n
Crow, Robert, 172–73, 178, 197n, 223n
Crow, Walter H., 197n, 223n
Crow, William Parker, 173, 197n, 223n
Cummings, James W., 330n
Cundling, David, 302
Curtis, Asa, 13
Curtis, Lyman, 74, 223n
Cutler, Alpheus, 108, 113n, 280

Dalton, Edward, 247n
Dana, Charles R., 302–5
Dana, E., 102
Davenport, James, 198n
Davis, Daniel, 307
Dean, Charles, 302
Decker, Isaac Perry, 76, 90n, 216
Decker, Lucy Ann (Young), 90n
Defection: from within, 3–4; to Strang, 11–16, 59, 61n, 313–15; causes problems with emigrants, 106–7; without harm from Saints, 170n. See also Miller, George; Strang, James; Wight, Lyman
Desert, problems of, 95, 102
Devil's Gate, 187
Disease, 58–59, 210–12, 222n
Doniphan, Alexander W., 4, 173
Donner Mountain, 216
Donner party, 103, 177, 192, 194–95, 202n, 208
Douglas, Ralph, 236
Drum, James, 236
Dunbar, John, 126, 143n
Dust, 128–29

Eames, Ellis, 120, 141n
Earl, Sylvester H., 236
East Canyon, 213, 215
Echo Canyon (Red Fork), 210, 212–14
Edwards, Jonathan, 156
Egan, Howard: in pioneer company, 74, 142n, 145n, 182–83, 184, 188; in Salt Lake Valley, 217, 220, 229
Egbert, Joseph, 223n
Eldridge, Alanson, 119

Eldridge, Horace S., 69, 335
Eldridge, John, 126–27, 223n
Elkhorn River, 118, 121–22, 253
Ellsworth, Edmund, 199n
Emigrants, other: go to Oregon, 99–102, 135–36; are suspicious of Mormons, 103–6; have trouble with Indians, 120–22; organization of, 142n; at Fort Laramie, 176; are behind the pioneer company, 178–79, 183–86
Emigration Camp, 169n, 253–56, 270, 276n
Emigration Canyon, 208, 215–16, 218
Emmett, James, 44, 69–70, 72
Empey, William, 133–34, 199n
Ensign Peak, 228–30
Everett, Addison, 74, 125, 143n, 242
Ewing, Esther, 263

Fairbanks, Nathaniel, 163, 223n
Farming, communal, 227
Farnham, Sister, 303
Farr, Aaron, 131
Farr, Winslow, 286
Field, Elvira, 315
Field, James, 148
Fielding, Joseph, 72
Finances, of Church, 47–57, 62n. See also Fundraising missions, Nauvoo Trustees, Tithing
Fires, 133, 135
First Presidency, 86, 272–73, 289–90, 292, 354, 361–62
Fitzpatrick, Thomas, 99, 102, 110–11, 115n, 171
Flag, 190–91, 201n
Flake, Green, 77, 91n, 223n
Flanigan, Thomas, 307–9
Fort Bridger, 178–79, 196, 204–7, 221n
Fort Buenaventura, 209
Fort Hall, 209
Fort John, 171
Fort Laramie, 99, 171–74, 196n
Fort Pierre, 99
Fort Platte, 196n
Fort Pueblo, 173
Fort William, 99, 171
Fourth of July, 188–90, 201n
Foutz, Bishop, 274

Fowler, John S., 153
Freedom, Gabriel, 179, 182
Freeman, John M., 223n
Fremont, John C., maps and descriptions by, 71, 83, 93n, 99–100, 102, 188, 207
Friedman, Charles, 303
Frost, Burr, 74, 175, 236
Fuller, E. C., 340
Fullmer, John S., 317–23
Fundraising missions, 302–11
Fur trading, 96–99

Garden Grove, Iowa, 36–37
Gardner, Archibald, 264
Gardner, Robert, 264–65
Geer, Elizabeth, 221n
Geer, Ralph C., 103–4, 222n
General Epistle, 284–86, 308, 328n
Gibbons, Andrew S., 182
Giddings, Joshua R., 304
Gleason, John S., 223n
Glines, Eric, 199n
Glines, James H., 314
Goddard, G. M., 104
Goddard, Stephen H., 74, 142n, 242
Gold Rush, 340–41
Goodyear, Miles, 209–10, 221–22n, 340
Gorgas, Solomon, 154
Gould, Samuel, 236
Grand Island, 44, 280
Grant, David, 223n
Grant, Jedediah, 65n, 69, 190–91, 201n, 253, 263
Gray, Charles G., 155
Great American Desert. See Desert
Great Basin, 9–10, 99. See also Salt Lake Valley
Great Salt Lake, The, 225–26
Green, E. M., 326
Gribble, William, 247n
Grieve, James H., 181, 191
Grosclaude, Justin, 70
Grover, Elisha H., 292
Grover, Thomas, 62n, 184, 198n

Haight, Isaac, 25, 345, 350, 352
Hale, Jonathan H., 62n
Hall, Fort, 209
Hamilton, Reverend W., 55

Hancock, Joseph, 131, 236
Hanks, Ebenezer, 247n
Hansen, Hans, 223n
Hany, William, 321
Harlan-Young party, 207
Harmon, Appleton M., 74, 138, 142n, 145n, 180, 199n
Harper, Charles, 74
Harris, George W., 62n, 286, 326
Harris, Martin, 310, 313, 331n
Harris, Moses (Black), 192–93, 201–2n
Hascall, Irene, 23, 296, 351
Hascalls, Ursuline, 257–58
Haskell, Thales, 266
Hastings Cutoff, 103, 177, 206–7
Hastings, Lansford W., 177, 184–85, 202n, 206–8, 221n
Haun, Catherine Margaret, 121, 154
Haws, Peter, 71
Hedlock, Reuben, 50
Heywood, Joseph Leland, 53, 317–23
Higbee, John S., 142n, 153, 198n
Hill, George W., 252
Hinnman, Lyman, 300
Hockett, William, 121
Holbrook, Joseph, 70
Hollister, David, 301
Horn, Moses, 48
Horne, Isabella, 276n
Horne, Orson, 267
Howells, J. E., 157
Hudson's Bay Company, 98
Hudspeth, James M., 207
Hunt, Gilbert, 247n
Hunter, Edward, 252, 274, 343, 353
Huntington, William, 35, 41, 52
Hyde, Heman, 62n
Hyde, Orson: goes to England, 49, 86; goes with the Mormon Battalion, 54; comments of, 55–56, 63n, 90n; describes Miller's Hollow, 282, 297n; goes on fundraising mission, 306, 316; baptizes Oliver Cowdery, 326; censures Pisgah fundraising, 327n

Independence Rock, 187, 200–201n
Independence, Missouri, temple lot, 332n
Indians, Great Basin. See Ute Indians, Shoshone Indians

Indians, Plains: Mormons arbitrate issues of, 57; trade furs, 96–98; relocation of, 100–101; emigrants have trouble with, 100–101, 108–9; Mormons suspected of liaison with, 104–8; population of, 113–14n; want Mormons off their land, 282. *See also* Pawnee Indians, Sioux Indians
Irrigation, 218, 226–28
Israel, Camp of, 32, 36–37
Israel, modern, v, xiii, 7, 81–83, 92n, 243–45, 361, 363

Jackman, Levi, 127–28, 216, 223n, 350
Jacob, Norton: in pioneer company, 74, 119, 142n; comments of, 152, 184, 186, 190, 193, 195; returns to Winter Quarters, 245
Jennings, Obadiah, 185, 200n
Jerking, 144n
John, Fort, 171
Johnson, Luke S.: in pioneer company, 74, 89n, 130–34, 142n, 183, 199n; practices medicine, 116, 177–78, 181, 223n
Johnson, Philo, 74
Joint Stock Society, 50
Jordan River, 228

Kane, Thomas L., 42–43, 283, 285, 301, 304, 346
Kanesville, Iowa, 283, 296, 297n, 299n
Kartchner, William D., 173
Kay, John, 292, 294
Kearny, Stephen W., 42, 101, 110
Kelsey, Eli B., 330n
Kelsey, Stephen, 75, 223n
Kendall, Levi N., 223n
Kimball, Ellen Sanders, 76, 90n
Kimball, Heber C.: is leader in pioneer company, 73, 76, 82–84, 88, 130–34, 138; comments on exodus-mission, 164, 166; arrives at Fort Laramie, 173–74; knows destination, 191; sends Orson Pratt ahead, 212, 214; arrives in Salt Lake Valley, 228, 234–35, 237–40; rebaptizes members, 242–43; returns to Winter Quarters, 245, 284; is

sustained in First Presidency, 290, 292; returns to Salt Lake City, 353
Kimball, Hiram, 332n
Kimball, Mary, 335
Kinyon, boy, 264
Kirtland Temple, 54–56, 65, 320, 331n
Kurz, Rudolph, 168

La Ramie, Jacques, 196n
Ladies Tea Party, 305
Land distribution, 237, 249n
Laramie, Fort, 99, 171–74, 196n
Lathrop, A., 340
Lay, Hark, 77, 91n, 223n
Leany, William, 348–49
Lee, John D., 53, 92n
Lewis, Meriwether, 98
Lewis, Tarleton, 122, 181, 242
Liberty Pole, 253, 275n, 280, 350–51
Lienhard, Heinrich, 207, 226
Lisa, Manuel, 98
Little Mountain, 208, 215
Little, Archibald, 197n
Little, Jesse C., 42, 53–54, 65, 74, 126, 153, 217
Log tabernacle, 291–92, 294–96, 298n
Long, Stephen H., 95, 102
Louisiana Purchase, 96–98
Loup Fork, 108, 118–19
Lyman, Amasa: in pioneer company, 73, 164, 174, 197n; in Salt Lake City, 237; returns to Winter Quarters, 284, 287; supports Brigham Young, 292; goes on fundraising mission, 307–9
Lyman, Eliza Maria Partridge, 259–60
Lyman, Louisa M., 149–50

Major, W. W., 286, 292
Marcy, William, 305
Markham, Stephen, 119, 122, 142, 166, 223n, 227
Marks, William, 12, 319
Mathews, Joseph, 126–27, 142n, 217, 223n, 228
Mattes, Merrill J., 101–2
McBride, Abigail, 255
McCall, A. J., 349
McKenzie, Thomas, 309–10, 314
McLaughlin, John, 98, 100

McLellin, William E., 12, 310, 331n
Medical practices, 212, 223n
Medicine Arrow fight, 109
Medill, William, 305
Meeks, Priddy, 255, 344, 347–48
Merrill, Moses, Reverend, 143n
Merrill, Philomon C., 298
Mexican War, 61n, 100–101
Millennial Star, 23, 313
Miller, George, 44, 69–72, 88n, 124, 315, 328n, 331n
Miller, Henry W., 62n, 291, 294, 299n
Miller, Reuben, 162, 314, 326
Miller's Hollow, 282, 291, 294, 297n, 299n
Miracle, of the quail, 46–47
Mission house, Pawnee, 126, 143n
Missions, fundraising, 302–11
Mississippi Saints, 172–74, 230, 247n
Missouri Fur Company, 98
Mitchell, Augustine, 84, 93n, 102
Mitchell, R. B., 40–41
Montrose, Iowa, 45–46
Morgan, John T., 305
Morgan, Rachel, 200n
Morgan, William, 185, 200n
Morley, Isaac, 62n, 86, 252, 275n
Mormon Battalion: call of, 40–43, 53; news of, 77; suspicions about, 107; sick members of, 173–74, 206; arrives in California, 194; feelings of, for Salt Lake Valley, 202n; arrives in Salt Lake Valley, 230–31, 247n; builds homes, 235; families of, 252–53, 275n; meets Emigration Camp, 277n; celebration of, 296; returns to Winter Quarters, 298n, 342; some of, get California Fever, 339–41, 356n
Mormon Ferry, 183–85, 199n
Mountain Dell Canyon, 215
Mountain Meadows Massacre, 200n
Mountain men, 96–99
Mt. Pisgah, 36–37, 59, 302–3
Mud, 33–35
Murdock, James, 46
Murdock, John, 62n
Murphy, Joseph, 51, 64n
Music, 168

Myers, Lewis B., 179, 181, 197–98n, 223n

Nauvoo Bell, 254
Nauvoo Covenant, 21, 29–30n, 253, 364
Nauvoo Temple, 54–57, 65n, 318–20, 322
Nauvoo Trustees, 32, 52, 55–57, 317–23
Nauvoo, Battle of, 24, 45–46, 296, 318
Nauvoo, Illinois, 4–6, 20–25
Neff, John, 357n
Newcomb, Silas, 136, 247–48n
Newman, Elijah, 223n
Northwest Company, 98
Norton, John W., 74

Ogden, Peter Skene, 98
Old Fort, 248n
Ordinance work, temple, 20–21, 81–82, 93n
Oregon Trail, 135
Oregon, migration to, 99–100, 103, 112n, 121
Owashtecha, Chief, 152

Pack, John: in pioneer company, 122, 131, 142, 148, 191; arrives in Salt Lake Valley, 214, 217; returns to Winter Quarters, 297n
Packard, Noah, 316
Paden, Isaac, 29n
Page, John E., 12–13, 28, 86, 162, 288, 313
Palmer, Joel, 103, 222n, 276n
Pancoast, Charles Edward, 167–68n
Panic of 1837, 99
Parke, Charles, 188–89
Parker, Samuel, 143n
Parker, William, 12
Parkman, Francis, 105, 112n, 175–76, 197n
Partridge, Edward, 332n
Pawnee Indians, 108–10, 114n, 120–22, 124–27, 141n, 143n
Pawnee mission house, 126, 143n
Perkins, Andrew W., 62n, 294, 299n
Perkins, R. H., 299n
Perkins, William G., 62n
Persecution, of Saints, 3–4
Pettijohn, Isaac, 142n, 145n, 156, 185

Pickett, William, 52, 64n, 299n
Pierce, Margaret, 262
Pierce, Mrs., 262
Pierre, Fort, 99
Pike, William, 298
Pike, Zebulon M., 102
Pitt, William, band of, 43, 294
Platte River road, 70–71
Platte River Valley, 102–3, 135
Platte River, 128–29, 181–83
Platte, Fort, 196n
Plural marriage, 6, 15, 278n, 315
Poison Pond, 186
Polk, James K., 42, 110, 305
Polygamy. *See* Plural marriage
Pomeroy, Francis M., 74, 199n
Porter, Nathan Tanner, 143n
Post office, prairie, 136–37
Pottawattamie County, 294, 299n
Pottawattamie High Council, 45–46, 291, 326
Powell, David, 223n
Prairie constitution, 122–24, 142n
Prairie council meetings, 268–74, 278n
Prairie post office, 136–37
Pratt, Addison, 169–70n, 352–53
Pratt, Ann (daughter of Addison), 352–53
Pratt, Ann (wife of Parley), 261–62, 274
Pratt, Ellen, 352
Pratt, Frances, 352·
Pratt, Lois, 352
Pratt, Orson: makes list of provisions, 37; in pioneer company, 73, 84; makes travel observations, 118–19, 138, 145n, 139, 187; early life of, 141n; rebukes camp, 166; arrives in Fort Laramie, 174; crosses the Platte, 183–84; approves *Brooklyn* voyage, 202n; in Salt Lake Valley, 212–17, 226, 234, 237; sermonizes, 244–45, 250n; describes Valley, 269; returns to Winter Quarters, 282, 286; supports Brigham Young, 289, 292; goes to England, 312
Pratt, Parley P.: goes to England, 49, 84; describes pioneer company, 61n; arrives in Winter Quarters, 84–85; leads Emigration Camp, 253; reorganizes Camp, 254; is criticized

for Camp, 268, 270–72, 278n; comments on Valley, 349–50; sustains First Presidency, 354
Provost, Etienne, 100
Pueblo, Fort, 173
Pulsipher, John, 9, 107
Putnam, Jonas, 17

Quail, miracle of, 46–47
Quincy Convention, 6, 318
Quincy, Josiah, 309
Quorum of the Twelve: leads church, 11, 71; decides to sell temples, 55–56; needs to travel west, 86; chooses land in Salt Lake City, 237–39; meets together in prairie council, 268; chooses First Presidency, 288–90

Rappleye, Tunis, 245, 297n
Real estate, in Nauvoo, 21–22, 54–56. *See also* Nauvoo Trustees
Rebaptism, 242–43, 250n
Redden, Return Jackson, 75, 89–90n, 132, 184, 223n
Reed, James Frazier, 208
Reed's Route, 208, 213, 215
Reformation, 165–66, 170n
Relocation, Indian, 100–101
Rendezvous system, 98–99
Reorganized Church of Jesus Christ of Latter Day Saints, 315
Reshaw, John, 173
Rich, Charles C., 86, 137, 253, 266–67, 336, 347–48
Rich, Mary A., 261
Richards, Amelia, 252
Richards, Levi, 312
Richards, Mary, 79
Richards, Phineas, 62n
Richards, Samuel W., 325
Richards, Willard: in pioneer company, 74, 126, 137, 160, 174, 183, 190, 201n; in Winter Quarters, 82–83; early life of, 143n; treats Rocky Mountain fever victims, 212; arrives in Salt Lake Valley, 214, 216–17, 226, 237; medical training of, 223n; hosts Church leaders in Winter Quarters, 281; sustained in First Presidency,

290–92; begs for money and books, 301, 306–7; returns to Salt Lake City, 353

Rigdon, Sidney, 11, 27, 314
Riter, Levi Evans, 221–22n
River crossings, 118–19, 141n, 182, 198n
Road Tax Crew, 180
Roadometer, pioneer, 138, 145n
Robbison, A. B., 177
Rockwell, Orrin Porter: in pioneer company, 75, 126–27, 130–34, 148, 184–85; enters Salt Lake Valley, 217, 223n; goes to California, 340
Rockwood, Albert P.: in pioneer company, 118–19, 122, 127, 140, 179–80, 185; stricken with Rocky Mountain fever, 212–13
Rocky Mountain Company, 98
Rocky Mountain Fever, 210–12, 222n
Rogers, Isaac, 93n
Roundy, Shadrach, 75, 122, 223n, 245
Russell, William H., 207

Sabbath worship, 153–56
Saleratus, 187, 200n
Salt Lake City: laying out of, 230, 239, 246–47n; surveyed, 236–37; land distribution in, 237–40; described, 268–69; at time of Emigration Camp, 334–36
Salt Lake Endowment House, 249–50n
Salt Lake Temple, 241–42, 364
Salt Lake Valley, 215, 217, 226–27
Santa Fe Trail, 100
Sarpy, Peter B., 96, 111n, 124–25
Schofield, Joseph S., 74
Scott, Hiram, 157
Scott, John, 307–9
Scottsbluff, Nebraska, 147–49, 156–58
Scovil, Lucius, 71, 310, 312
Seagulls, 347–48, 357n
Sessions, Patty, 260, 263, 338
Sessions, Perrigrine, 268
Seventies Jubilee, 294–96
Sheets, Susanna, 334
Sherwood, Henry G., 74, 120, 236, 240
Shoshone Indians, 232, 234, 248n
Shumway, Andrew P., 75, 242
Shumway, Charles, 125, 142

Simpson, George, 98
Sioux Indians, 101, 108–10, 114n, 151–53
Slavery, 91n
Sloan, James, 299n
Smallpox, 101, 110
Smet, Pierre de, 233–34
Smith, Aaron, 314
Smith, Alexander, 320
Smith, David, 320
Smith, Emma: has financial problems, 48, 63; tries to stop sale of temple, 55, 322, 332n; takes care of Lucy Mack, 87; rebuffs Strang, 314, 319–20; is watched over by Nauvoo Trustees, 318; remarries, 321
Smith, George A.: on the sale of temples, 55; in pioneer company, 73, 118, 139–40, 163–64, 205; arrives in Salt Lake Valley, 214, 216–17, 237; describes deserted Winter Quarters, 283; goes on mission, 286; supports Brigham Young, 292; helps Oliver Cowdery, 325
Smith, Hyrum, 1, 190, 200n
Smith, Jedediah, 99
Smith, John, 201n, 245, 252, 272, 297n, 336–37
Smith, Joseph, III, 12, 315, 320
Smith, Joseph, Jr.: martyrdom of, 1–3; in Nauvoo, 4–6; had plans to move to the Rocky Mountains, 9; Strang claims, named him prophet, 12–18; left complicated financial issues, 47–48, 322–23, 331–32n; comparisons made to, 163, 169n; was assisted in escape from Liberty Jail, 185; is remembered, 190–91; 200n; set layout of City of Zion, 246–47n
Smith, Lucy Mack, 87, 314, 318
Smith, Moses, 16, 18, 29
Smith, William, 12, 56, 65, 69, 288, 314, 330n
Smithies, James, 343
Smoot, Abraham O., 253
Smoot, William C., 175
Snider, John, 323
Snow, Artimesia, 88
Snow, Eliza R., 190, 261–62, 264, 274, 343, 346, 353

Snow, Erastus: in pioneer company, 73, 88, 152, 158, 164, 184; stricken with Rocky Mountain fever, 211; arrives in Salt Lake Valley, 214–16, 226; rebaptizes members, 242; meets with Emigration Camp, 269–70; goes on fundraising mission, 307–9, 311

Snow, Lorenzo, 59, 302

South Pass, 188–89

Spalding, Eliza, 102

Spencer, Aurelia, 162

Spencer, Daniel, 62n, 253, 348

Spencer, Orson, 311–12

Sprague, Hezekiah, 255

Squires, William H., 247n

Staines, W. C., 254, 264, 336, 355n

Stampede, 167–68n, 261–62

Stanton, Charles T., 208

Stanton, Phebe, 105–6

Steele, John, 174, 247n

Stevens, M., 154

Stevens, Roswell, 174

Stewart, Benjamin, 198n

Stewart, James, 223n

Stout, Hosea, 37, 75, 254, 275–276n, 280

Strang, James J.: leads defection, 12–18, 28–29n, 72, 86, 288–89, 330n, 361; enjoys despair of Saints, 38–39, 59, 61; wants temple, 55–56, 65n, 319; renounces Brigham Young, 69; sends missionaries, 162, 313–14. *See also* Defection

Sublette, Milton, 99, 171

Sublette, William, 171

Sugar Creek, 32

Summe, Gilburd, 223n

Sweetwater River, 187

Taft, Seth, 142n, 218, 223n

Taine, Hyppolite, xiii

Tanner, Mary Ann Mount, 266

Tanner, Sidney, 59

Tanner, Thomas, 236

Taylor, John: goes to England, 49–50, 84; arrives in Winter Quarters, 85; leads Emigration Camp, 253, 267–68; is criticized for Camp, 268, 274, 278n; in Salt Lake Valley, 338

Taylor, Norman, 223n

Taylor, Samuel W., 278n

Temple block, 229, 236, 249n

Temples, 20–21, 54–57. *See also* Kirtland Temple; Nauvoo Temple; Ordinance Work

Terrill, Joel J., 236

Therlkill, George W., 173, 197n, 223n, 240

Therlkill, Harriet Anne, 241

Therlkill, James William, 197n

Therlkill, Martilla Jane, 197n, 240–41

Therlkill, Milton Howard, 197n, 240

Thomas, Preston, 307–9, 328n

Thomas, Robert, 223n

Thompson, Samuel, 223n

Thorpe, Marcus B., 223n

Thorton, Horace, 223n

Thorton, Samuel, 330–31n

Tippetts, John, 77, 91, 124, 131, 174

Tithing, 22, 48–49, 53

Treaty of Guadalupe Hidalgo, 352, 358n

Tucker, Reverend Mr., 55

Tucker, William, 181

United States government: 42, 53–54, 107, 282, 305–6. *See also* Kane, Thomas L.; Little, Jesse C.; Mormon Battalion

Unruh, John D., 103, 112n

Ute Indians, 231–34, 248n

Van Dusen, Increase McGee, 106–7

Vance, William, 156, 229

Vancouver Island, 50–51, 63n

Villasur, Pedro de, 108–9

Voree Herald, 14–16, 38, 61n

Wagons, 51, 60n, 64, 257–58

Walker, Henson, 74

Walker, K. Knox, 305

Wallace, George B., 267

War of 1812, 98

Ward, Thomas, 50

Wardle, George, 74

Weather problems, 33–35, 117–18, 150–51

Weatherby, Jacob, 254, 275n

Weber Canyon, 207–8, 213

Wells, Daniel H., 24n

Whitaker, George, 32–33
White, D. E., 101
Whitman, Marcus and Narcissa, 99,
  101–2, 143n
Whitney, Helen Mar Kimball, v, 33,
  35–36, 81, 92n, 258
Whitney, Horace K.: on trek through
  Iowa, 36, 92n; in pioneer company,
  134, 141n, 143n, 148–49, 152, 183;
  comments on destination, 191,
  193–95, 209; describes Echo Canyon,
  213; in Salt Lake Valley, 217, 239–40
Whitney, Newell K., 54, 280, 331n
Whitney, Orson F., 76
Wight, Lyman, 12, 27, 71, 86, 288,
  328–29n
William, Fort, 99, 171
Williams, Thomas, 206, 247
Winter Quarters, Nebraska, 45, 56–58,
  190, 252, 279–80, 282–83
Wolfe, John A., 301
Wood, J. M., 154
Wood, Joseph, 151, 155, 189
Woodbury, Ann, 265
Woodrie, James, 181, 191
Woodruff, Wilford: on safety in the
  Rocky Mountains, 7; at Council
  Bluffs, 39; goes to England, 50;
  authorizes sale of Nauvoo Temple, 56;
  in pioneer company, 73, 84, 122;
  spiritual comments of, 107, 122, 139,
  160, 163, 166; travel comments of,
  128, 132, 136, 173, 184–85, 198n;
  fishes at Fort Bridger, 205–6; on route
  to Salt Lake Valley, 210, 214; arrives
  in Salt Lake Valley, 218–20, 227,
  236–37; leaves the Valley, 245; meets
  with Emigration Camp, 270; arrives at
  Winter Quarters, 280; sustains
  Brigham Young, 290; comments on
  Seventies Jubilee, 295; goes on
  mission, 312
Woodward, George, 256–57
Woodworth, Lisander, 247n
Woolsey, Thomas, 77, 91n, 124, 131, 174
"Word and Will of the Lord, The,"
  69–72, 77–81, 88n, 159–60, 252,
  270–72, 326
Word of Wisdom, 165–66, 169–70n
Wright, Jonathan C., 286, 314–15

Yearley, David D., 299n
Young, Brigham: 2; prepares Saints for
  exodus, 3–4, 7, 10–15, 18, 27n; crosses
  Iowa, 31–32, 36–39; proclaims "word
  and will of the Lord," 67–72, 79–82,
  88n; organizes companies, 72–74,
  121–22; institutes law of adoption,
  82–83, 91–92n; leaves Winter
  Quarters, 84–86; deal with Indians,
  108, 125–27; praises and chastises,
  139, 155–66; arrives at Fort Laramie,
  173–74; helps build the ferry, 183;
  orders flag, 191; stricken with Rocky
  Mountain Fever, 211–13; sends
  planting party ahead, 214–17; arrives
  in Salt Lake Valley, 218–20, 228–29,
  234–35, 237; leaves Valley, 245;
  criticizes Pratt and Taylor, 268–72,
  274; seeks to reorganize First
  Presidency, 272–73, 288–90; arrives at
  Winter Quarters, 280; persuades
  Saints to go West, 284–85; is sustained
  as President of the Church, 288–90,
  292, 361–63; sends out missionaries,
  301, 306, 312, 316–17, 327n; contacts
  Oliver Cowdery, 324–25; returns to
  Salt Lake City, 353
Young, Clara Decker, 10, 76, 90n
Young, Harriet Page Wheeler Decker,
  75, 90n, 260
Young, Henry, 331n
Young, John, 253, 336
Young, Joseph W., 355
Young, Lorenzo Dow, 10, 75, 185, 216,
  260
Young, Lorenzo Subieski, 76, 90n, 216
Young, Phineas, 118, 142, 279, 286,
  323–26

Zion, concept of, 7–8, 244–45, 249–50n
Zion's Camp, 19–20, 163
Zion's March, 163